THE
FIXERS

■ ■ ■

THE
FIXERS

∎ ∎ ∎

The Bottom-Feeders, Crooked Lawyers,
Gossipmongers, and Porn Stars Who
Created the 45th President

Joe Palazzolo and
Michael Rothfeld

RANDOM HOUSE
NEW YORK

For my wife, Tara
—J.P.

For my daughters, Annabel and Georgia
—M.R.

Contents

■ ■ ■

PART II ▪ THE UNRAVELING

Prologue

■ ■ ■

DONALD TRUMP SAT in his office on the twenty-sixth floor of Trump Tower, facing David Pecker, the sixty-four-year-old publisher of the tabloid of record, the *National Enquirer*. The wall to Trump's left was tiled with awards and photos of the recently announced presidential candidate. Young Trump on framed covers of *Playboy, GQ,* and *Fortune*. Trump mugging with Ronald Reagan. Trump with John F. Kennedy Jr. His desk was covered in stacks of papers and more magazine covers with his face on them.

Two months before the August 2015 meeting, Trump had wafted down the escalator into the atrium of his midtown high-rise to announce his presidential candidacy. Pecker, a self-made millionaire from the Bronx, and Trump, the Queens-born scion of an outerborough developer, had been confidants for two decades, though neither man regarded the other as a close friend. Their relationship was a series of chits accrued and favors cashed in.

Pecker's celebrity gossip and personal lifestyle empire—his company, American Media Inc., also published *Globe* and *Star,* and several sports and fitness magazines—hadn't printed a bad word about Trump since 1999, the year he became chief executive. In more recent years, the publisher had assiduously promoted Trump's political rise. Trump, in return, fed American Media tips, offered Pecker business advice, and lent the mustached publisher entrée into Trump's world of wealth and celebrity.

Their conversation at Trump Tower had been arranged by Michael Cohen, Trump's special counsel at the Trump Organization, the family business. Cohen had styled himself as the loyal guardian of Trump's image and reputation. A former personal injury lawyer and taxi medallion owner who hailed from the suburbs of Long Island, Cohen had in recent years transformed himself into Trump's armed press attaché—he wore a gun in an ankle holster—who made liberal use of legal threats to keep bad headlines about his boss to a minimum.

Pecker and Cohen had collaborated on an ad hoc basis in 2011, the last time Trump made a show of contemplating a presidential run. With Cohen's encouragement, the *National Enquirer* had breathlessly promoted Trump's exploratory bid, while *Globe* had propelled the birther conspiracy theory that Trump used to attack President Barack Obama and raise his own political profile. Now that Trump was running for real, the collaboration needed to be more intentional.

When the Trump Tower meeting began, Pecker had taken the single seat opposite Trump at his desk, while Cohen remained standing. After a while, Cohen went looking for a chair and pulled it over.

What can Pecker do to help the campaign? Trump wanted to know as they sat in his office. Pecker had some ideas. He could use the *Enquirer* to slime Trump's political opponents, both Republican and Democrat, he said. Pecker warned Trump that opportunists might come forward trying to peddle dirt about him, including tales of his exploits with women. Pecker's tabloids, which paid for scoops, were a natural destination for tipsters with information to sell. Pecker told Trump he could intercept harmful stories and make sure they never surfaced.

Pecker already had a template to follow. In 2003, the *Enquirer* had vacuumed up damaging information about the sexual proclivities of Arnold Schwarzenegger, a soon-to-be business partner at Pecker's muscle magazines, when the action hero ran for governor of California. American Media paid potential purveyors of salacious information about the movie star, bottling them up with exclusive source contracts. A decade later, Pecker's company shelled out $20,000 for a photocopied image of Schwarzenegger as a young bodybuilder naked on a couch, taking it off the market.

Pecker's offer to Trump wasn't based on idle speculation. On the heels of his 2011 presidential flirtation, an adult movie star named Stormy Daniels and her manager had shopped her story of a one-night stand with Trump to celebrity publications. A legal threat from Cohen prevented the story from taking off, but it was a close call. Not long after that, reporters sniffed around rumors of an affair between Trump and Karen McDougal, the 1998 Playboy Playmate of the Year. McDougal had called Trump, who told her not to worry, and the rumors subsided.

Ever since the campaign launch, Pecker and Cohen had worked to stanch a possible problem. Trump's office had been contacted by a digital media outlet that had found old pictures of Trump in which he appeared to be leaning in to autograph a stripper's bare breasts. Cohen referred the company's founder to Pecker. Pecker already knew the man—the same one who'd sold him the naked photocopy of Schwarzenegger—and assured him the Trump pictures were worthless. Then Pecker stalled him with discussions of business they might do together.

At their meeting, Trump welcomed Pecker's willingness to assist. *Work with Michael,* he said. When an issue came up, Pecker would call Cohen, who would dutifully inform Trump.

Pecker left Trump's office that day with his mission assigned. Within three months, his purpose had become even clearer. A former doorman at a Trump building approached the *Enquirer* in November 2015. He said he had heard that Trump had fathered a daughter out of wedlock with a female employee. Was it true? The tabloid didn't know. Nonetheless, when the doorman threatened to take the information elsewhere, the *Enquirer,* with Pecker's blessing, paid off the doorman to keep the rumor a secret.

Trump valued the role that Pecker and Cohen were willing to play in his presidential campaign, fixing problems, mopping up his old messes so he could remain free of their stench. Others had done the same for Trump in the past. Roy Cohn, the disgraced counsel to Senator Joe McCarthy turned lawyer to the powerful, had shepherded the young Trump along in his rise in New York City four decades earlier. Cohn had manipulated the media and the legal system to secure business advantages for Trump and weave his myth as a fabulously successful developer who transformed his father's collection of middle-class apartment buildings in Brooklyn and Queens into a Manhattan-based empire of glittery luxury condominium towers. When gentler tactics failed, Cohn tried to scare Trump's opponents into submission. He was the fixer by which Trump judged all others.

PART I

. . .

THE DEALS

1.

THE FIRST FIXER

■ ■ ■

DONALD TRUMP KEPT a photo of Roy Cohn on his office desk. If a business meeting wasn't proceeding as planned, Trump might point to the photo and say, in so many words, *You don't want to mess with me. Just look at this mug. That's my lawyer.*

This affinity for the battle had bound the two men, forging one of the defining relationships of both of their lives. It began in the early 1970s, with Trump a few years shy of his thirtieth birthday. Cohn was a celebrity lawyer and celebrated villain who'd served as the right hand of Republican senator Joseph McCarthy in his anti-Communist crusade. Cohn, who hailed from a New York Democratic family and was the son of a state judge, had left McCarthy's employ after a series of nationally televised congressional hearings revealed the pressure tactics he used against the U.S. Army to obtain preferential treatment for his friend and fellow Communist hunter, a private named G. David Schine.

He'd returned to New York unbowed and built a private practice that pivoted on his ruthless intelligence—he had a photographic memory—and the public perception of his ethical and moral flexibility. Juries had acquitted him in three criminal trials, clearing him of charges including jury tampering, bribery, blackmail, and making false statements. These triumphs over the government he had once served only enhanced Cohn's reputation as a rogue who did whatever it took to win. So in 1973, when Trump spotted him at Le Club, an East Fifty-fifth Street restaurant frequented by New York's glitterati, he wandered over to Cohn's table for advice about a legal problem of his own.

Trump was the little-known son of a politically connected developer from a German immigrant family. Eager to build something grander than Fred Trump's monotonous red-brick, rent-regulated projects, the young developer had moved to Manhattan to explore his own ambitions in society, government, and business. He wanted to trade Forest Hills for Fifth Avenue.

At Cohn's table that day, Trump explained that his father's real estate company was under attack from the United States Department of Justice, which was accusing it of discriminating against minorities in its rental buildings. Trump told Cohn that he and his father had spent the afternoon talking to lawyers at a prestigious Wall Street firm. They had advised the Trumps to settle.

"What do you think we should do?" Trump asked.

"My view is tell them to go to hell and fight the thing in court and let them prove that you discriminated, which seems to me very difficult to do, in view of the fact that you have black tenants in the building," Cohn said. "I don't think you have any obligation to rent to tenants who would be undesirable, white or black, and the government doesn't have a right to run your business."

Trump hired Cohn to take on the Justice Department, launching a professional relationship that would evolve into a much more personal one. For years to come, they would socialize at parties and in clubs. Trump sought advice from Cohn on politics, business, and marriage. Cohn, whose homosexuality and promiscuity were an open secret, often surrounded himself with men like Trump—heterosexual, younger, fair-haired, and good-looking. With his charm, self-confidence, and ambition, Trump was a trophy client, the biggest he'd ever had.

IN THE YEARS Cohn represented Trump, from the early 1970s until the mid-1980s, he also tended to a colorful roster of clients who included mobsters like Carmine Galante, the brutal head of the Bonanno crime family, and "Fat Tony" Salerno, a boss of the Genovese family; wealthy women divorcing their husbands; New York Yankees owner George Steinbrenner; artist Andy Warhol; Cardinals Francis Spellman and Terence Cooke; and disgruntled stockholders who used Cohn's name and the fear it inspired to extract settlements from companies.

The attorneys who worked for him, and many who opposed him, considered Cohn a brilliant lawyer whose potential was almost limitless, if only he put in a bit more effort. And played fair. He often relegated case preparation to his limo rides to the courthouse, submitting the young associate attorneys riding with him to lightning-round interviews. "Who's the judge?" was usually his first question. Next was "What are the parties' names?" He was famously late for hearings and conferences, in effect letting the meter run while his opponents racked up ever larger bills from their lawyers.

The Roy Cohn playbook demanded a relentless show of strength. The tactics he deployed in a fight appealed to Trump, who had internalized some of them before he met Cohn: Attack—mercilessly. Never admit you're wrong. Declare complete victory, even when making concessions. Follow through only when pressed, and only as much as required.

Cohn's performance as defense lawyer for the Trumps in their battle with the federal government over alleged housing discrimination reflected his fight-over-flight essence perfectly. The 1973 lawsuit by the U.S Department of Justice's Civil Rights Division accused the Trumps' management company of violating the Fair Housing Act, a landmark 1968 civil rights law signed by President Lyndon B. Johnson a week after the assassination of Martin Luther King Jr.

The government's four-page lawsuit offered only the broad outlines of its case. The suit said the Trumps had violated the law by refusing to rent to blacks, which they did by telling them apartments weren't available when in fact they were, and by using a more onerous set of terms and conditions when the company did deign to rent to people of color.

Cohn's answer was to attack.

"This case represents an abuse of process," Cohn wrote in a December 11, 1973, affidavit to the court, calling the discrimination allegations "totally unfounded."

"The Civil Rights Division did not file a lawsuit. It slapped together a piece of paper for use as a press release, and only secondarily as a court document," he said.

The Justice Department's evidence included the account of a doorman at a Trump building in Brooklyn who told FBI agents that the superintendent had directed him to tell prospective black tenants that the rent was twice as high as it actually was. A Trump rental supervisor reported that Fred Trump had personally instructed the employee not to rent to blacks or people on welfare.

For his part, Donald Trump told the judge he was "shocked" by the allegations of racial bias. He'd learned of the case one morning while listening to the radio in his car. The government hadn't warned him it was coming, Trump complained. Television news picked it up, and the next day *The New York Times* carried a front-page story.

"To find our name blackened in the press before we had received formal notification and had an opportunity to have a trial or even answer is unfair and unjust," Trump said, calling the allegations "outrageous lies."

Cohn asked the judge to dismiss the case and countersued the government, alleging, with moxie but little else, that the Civil Rights Division and the U.S. attorney's office in Brooklyn had made "untrue and unfair" statements to newspapers in a news release announcing the case. No matter that the U.S. government was immune from defamation claims. Cohn asked for damages in the amount of $100 million, a number Judge Edward R. Neaher called a "tidy sum" before dismissing the countersuit.

The parties reached a settlement in principle by the end of January 1975, but Cohn dragged out the negotiations for five months, once skipping town for Bermuda instead of meeting with a government attorney who waited at his office to finalize the deal. Under the proposed agreement, the Trumps would admit no wrongdoing but would agree to rent to people of color. Trump Management's officers would have to familiarize themselves with state, federal, and local civil rights laws, adopt a compliance program, and take steps to train Trump employees on fair-housing requirements. It was the outcome the government had sought from the beginning.

Cohn didn't want the government to issue a news release announcing the settlement. He suggested a joint statement by the Trumps and the Justice Department, an idea rejected out of hand by the government. Cohn, on this occasion, gave in.

"They will say what they want, and we will say what we want," he said.

Both sides claimed victory.

• • •

TRUMP HATED LAWYERS who dithered and then mailed him huge legal bills. He looked down on those who preferred to settle without a fight. He liked and respected lawyers who could do battle. That was Cohn to a T. Even better, Trump wasn't charged full freight by Cohn, who enjoyed the cachet of counting him as a client. Quickly, Trump came to occupy a regular place in Cohn's social orbit, at the 21 Club and at Studio 54, the legendary nightclub run by his clients Steve Rubell and Ian Schrager. He regularly appeared at the lavish parties Cohn threw at his East Sixty-eighth Street townhouse on New Year's Eve, and on July 4 at his home in Greenwich, Connecticut.

Cohn's circle featured a young Warhol; a young Barbara Walters; the fashion icon C. Z. Guest; the oil heir Ricky di Portanova; the publisher Malcolm Forbes; Norris Church Mailer, the wife of novelist Norman Mailer; and many others. At Cohn's Greenwich parties, a visitor could glimpse Estée Lauder to one side, the young investor Ronald Perelman to another, and Carmine DeSapio, the dethroned head of Tammany Hall, sitting in a corner with dark sunglasses. The borough presidents of Manhattan, Brooklyn, the Bronx, and Queens milled about. Mingling with the bold-faced names were budding artists, B-list actors, judges, young lawyers, gay and straight, and their dates, watching the scene in amazement.

For the aspirational Trump, Cohn's scene seemed the perfect place to burnish his profile as an up-and-coming young playboy. And of course, to meet beautiful women. At the townhouse, where guests wandered up and down the floors inspecting Cohn's collection of oddities, including, at one point, a life-size ceramic zebra, the lawyer would hold court. But when Trump showed up midway through a party, Cohn would abandon whomever he'd been talking to and rush to fawn over him.

Along with granting Trump entrée into this nightlife scene, Cohn schooled him in the art of using the media. Cohn befriended many journalists, the more influential the better. Among them were radio commentator Walter Winchell and gossip mavens Leonard Lyons and Aileen Mehle, who wrote a column as Suzy. He appeared in public with Walters, a rising star in TV news, to whom he was once supposedly engaged.

Cohn understood before his time and taught Trump that all publicity, negative or not, was good if it raised your profile and showed the world you were in the game. He took journalists to lunch at Le Cirque, entertaining them with fantastic off-the-record stories, and called to feed them gossip items—not infrequently about himself, perhaps in connection with one of his clients in a celebrity divorce.

But he also used his reputation to try to intimidate reporters who were writing negative stories about Trump or to plant stories that would help his young client. David Rosenthal was a twenty-one-year-old reporter at the *New York Post* in 1974. Rosenthal had been picking through the contribution logbooks at the New York State Board of Elections when he discovered a stream of large donations to Democratic gubernatorial candidate Hugh Carey emanating from givers listing their addresses at low- and middle-income apartment buildings in the outer boroughs. Rosenthal looked up the addresses and found that those buildings were all owned or managed by Fred Trump. It seemed that Trump had skirted campaign-finance limits by making straw donations through his tenants. Rosenthal reported the Trump contributions in a story for the newspaper and got a call from Cohn after it published.

"You piece of shit! We are going to ruin you! You have a lot of fucking nerve!" Cohn yelled.

Rosenthal, unnerved, went to his editors after the call and relayed his conversation with Cohn. Paul Sann, the executive editor, told him he must have done something right to be on the receiving end of Cohn's threat, treating it as if it were a rite of passage. The editors knew from experience that Cohn liked to try to put the fear in reporters but rarely followed through.

Through Cohn, Trump met Cindy Adams, who in the 1970s started working for a local city newspaper, *Our Town*. Adams was married to comedian Joey Adams (real name: Joseph Abramowitz), a close friend of Cohn's who was the emcee of choice at parties for powerful figures in New York politics and the Roman Catholic Church.

At a small dinner party, Cindy Adams turned to the tall, blond man seated beside her and asked, "Who are you?"

"I'm Donald Trump," he said, to which Adams replied, "What's a Donald Trump?"

At that moment, she noticed Cohn standing behind her.

"One day, this kid is going to own New York," Cohn said.

Adams and Trump became fast friends.

As TRUMP PURSUED plans in the mid-1970s to buy and convert the run-down Commodore Hotel, on Forty-second Street, into a Grand Hyatt, Cohn facilitated his success by helping him obtain an unprecedented forty-year tax break. He nurtured connections for Trump in the administration of New York City mayor Abe Beame and, with a combination of intimidation and media manipulation, worked to sway the judges who would be ruling on the property condemnations Trump needed.

Trump also had to manage another important interest group: organized crime. Cohn served as a bridge between Trump and the mob-controlled construction companies and union officials the developer dealt with on his building projects—this was a time when the construction industry was dominated by organized crime families. One Trump contractor, S&A Concrete Inc., was secretly owned by Cohn's client Fat Tony Salerno and Gambino boss Paul Castellano, whom Cohn also knew. Biff Halloran, a mob-linked former Cohn client, supplied concrete for Trump's Hyatt project and for Trump Tower.

In the early 1980s, Cohn arranged the nearly $2 million purchase of two apartments on the fifty-ninth and sixtieth floors of Trump Tower by one of his clients, Robert Hopkins, a Lucchese family associate. At the closing, attended by Trump, Hopkins arrived with a briefcase full of cash. The money was delivered via a Trump limousine to a bank that did business with a Trump casino. Hopkins, six foot five and 250 pounds, used the Trump Tower apartments for managing more than a hundred betting parlors citywide that took in $500,000 a week in cash.

In 1988, an investigator working for Manhattan U.S. Attorney Rudy Giuliani interviewed Trump as part of a probe into the developer's role in possible money laundering during the apartment purchases. Shortly after the interview, Trump was quoted by reporters as saying that he could raise $2 million in half an hour if Giuliani ran for mayor in 1989. The probe was dropped without becoming a formal investigation. Trump ended up raising $41,000 as co-chairman of Giuliani's campaign.

● ● ●

AS THE TWENTY-SIX-YEAR-OLD political operative made his pitch, Cohn sat in a second-floor dining room, eyes bloodshot, in a silk robe with chest hair pressing out and a medal around his neck. Roger Stone, a fresh-faced acolyte of Richard Nixon, had come to see Cohn, who'd agreed to take a behind-the-scenes role in the nascent presidential campaign of Republican Ronald Reagan. After an hour's wait, Cohn's secretary ushered Stone in to see Cohn, who introduced the portly man sitting with him as Tony Salerno. With his fingers, Cohn ate three burnt strips of bacon off his plate and scooped cream cheese into his mouth. Then Salerno left.

Stone explained that he'd need office space, volunteers, union contacts, and money to try to make a dent against Reagan's more establishment opponents in the byzantine primary process in New York. Staring out the bay window, Cohn snapped his fingers. "You know what you need?" he said. "You need Donald Trump. Do you know Donald Trump?"

After paying a visit to the developer's father in Brooklyn, Stone found his way to Trump's office in Manhattan. Trump asked Stone question after question as he guzzled soda. *Is Reagan too old? Can he carry California? Show me how you get to 270 electoral votes. What about New Jersey? What about Florida? What about Texas?* Trump said he had supported Carter in 1976, calling it a mistake.

"I like your guy," Trump said. "And I think he's going to win, you know why? Because he's got a look. In the television age, you've got to have the look. If you don't have the look, you're going nowhere."

"Tell me what you need," Trump said.

Trump arranged for Stone to get cut-rate office space, first at a dumpy hotel patronized by prostitutes and next to a swingers' club, and then in an empty townhouse next to the 21 Club. And he got money: bundles of checks from Trump vendors that he picked up at Fred Trump's office. He fielded calls and had meetings with Donald Trump, who wanted updates on Reagan's progress.

That campaign cemented the friendship between Cohn and the young Stone, who stayed in a second-floor bedroom at the townhouse for a while and who was always game for a free meal whenever the lawyer came by around 6 P.M. looking for dinner and drinking companions. He'd listen to Cohn as he funneled items to gossip columnists for the next day's papers over cognac and a cigar.

Reagan's victory in the New York primary and the 1980 general election gave Cohn a direct line into the White House. At Cohn's request, Reagan sent a note to Stone when Cohn threw him a thirtieth birthday party at the 21 Club. Trump, who had done his part for Reagan, also was photographed with the president.

For his part, Stone opened a lobbying shop with two new partners, Paul Manafort and Charles Black. Within a few years, the firm began working for Donald Trump. Stone's firm helped Trump by lobbying the Army Corps of Engineers for permission to dredge the waters near Atlantic City to accommodate his yacht, the *Trump Princess*. Stone also helped him get a waiver to build a tower slightly taller than existing height limits in Chicago and got involved with everything from traffic patterns in Atlantic City to tax and casino issues.

The Reagan race also brought Stone a new client, Thomas Kean, who had previously lost a race for governor of New Jersey. Stone helped elect Kean governor in a close 1981 campaign. Two years later, Kean backed Trump's sister, Maryanne Trump Barry, a federal prosecutor eyeing a vacant seat on the U.S. District Court of New Jersey. Barry, a top aide to the U.S. attorney in Newark, had limited trial experience and wasn't seen by the local bar association as a top candidate for the post. But, as Donald Trump had relayed to Stone, she didn't want her brother's help. "She wants to do it on her own," Trump said.

"I think that would be a mistake—at a minimum, you should get Roy to make some calls," Stone told him.

Cohn later told Stone to let Trump know that Barry's appointment was all set. In September 1983, Reagan made Barry a federal judge. She and Trump both called Cohn to thank him. The new judge also thanked Cohn at her induction ceremony for federal court. And when Trump threw his sister a party to celebrate the appointment at the Grand Hyatt in Manhattan, Cohn—who had also been at her wedding—stood among the most honored guests.

TRUMP WAS ON the cusp of becoming a household name in the early 1980s. He sat down with NBC's Tom Brokaw to discuss New York real estate in August 1980 as Trump Tower, a monument to his rise, was under construction. Brokaw described Trump as a young man who "took his father's rather modest, by current standards, real estate empire in Brooklyn and expanded it considerably." The newsman marveled that one floor of the fifty-seven-story tower was going for a cool $11 million. At the same time, Trump's Grand Hyatt New York, for which he and Cohn had obtained a forty-year tax break from the city, was nearing its opening.

"Mr. Trump, what's left in your life? You're thirty-three years old, you're worth all this money," Brokaw said. Did Trump aspire to be a billionaire?

"No, I really don't. I just want to keep busy and keep active and be interested in what I do, and that's all there is to life as far as I'm concerned," Trump said. "I really am not looking to make tremendous amounts of money. I'm looking to enjoy my life, and if that happens to go with it, that's fabulous."

But Trump's preoccupation with his image, with making people believe he was the richest developer in the city, was evident, and Cohn lent his reputation to Trump's mythmaking.

In 1981, *Forbes* was preparing its inaugural Forbes 400, the magazine's ranking of America's richest people. Trump, who was now expanding into Atlantic City, spent an afternoon with reporter Jonathan Greenberg, exaggerating the size of the Trump empire and his claim to it.

Trump told Greenberg that his family owned 23,000 apartments in the outer boroughs—more than double the Trumps' actual stock, as journalists would later discover. The younger Trump said he alone held 80 percent of them. (In fact, Fred Trump retained legal ownership of his residential buildings and would until his death, in 1999. The elder Trump, however, played along.) According to Donald, his family was worth more than $900 million, a figure that assumed each apartment was valued at $40,000.

Greenberg thought the valuation was absurdly high.

"Okay, then $20,000 each," Trump allowed. That would mean the Trumps were worth $500 million, still enough to top the list of New York real estate tycoons.

Greenberg remained skeptical. Cohn later called the reporter at his desk.

"This is Roy. Roy Cohn! You can't quote me! But Donny tells me you're putting together this list of rich people. He says you've got him down for just $200 million! That's way too low, way too low!" Cohn told him. "Listen, I'm Donny's personal lawyer, but he said I could talk to you about this. I am sitting here looking at his current bank statement. It shows he's got more than $500 million in liquid assets, just cash. That's just Donald, nothing to do with Fred, and it's just cash."

Greenberg offered to have a courier drop by to pick up the bank statement.

"Just trust me," Cohn said.

Greenberg said he needed to see the paperwork.

"It's confidential!"

Forbes estimated Fred and Donald Trump were worth $200 million—about $100 million each—placing them in the bottom tier of major real estate developers listed by the magazine.

Cohn and Trump angled to improve the Trumps' position in the annual rankings the following year. Cohn called Greenberg again and told the reporter that Donald Trump was now worth more than $700 million. He said Trump had received $250 million from the sale of his interest in a casino project in Atlantic City, a part of which Trump used to "liquidate certain other things, which made his overall position very impregnable." That was about ten times what Trump had actually made on the project.

Cohn plowed on. "Trump Tower has been going like a house afire, and the profits on that are much higher than had been anticipated, and the same is true with Grand Hyatt," he told Greenberg. "On top of which he's been in a series of private transactions, and he files with banks for between $700 to $750 million."

Finally, Cohn took aim at a Trump rival. He suggested that the LeFrak family, which had built a huge development called LeFrak City in Queens, was worth less than the $500 million *Forbes* had estimated. Trump had previously badmouthed Richard LeFrak, who was also rising in his father's business, to Greenberg.

"He's taken such a bath at LeFrak City, he's taken a real bath there," Cohn said.

Despite the misinformation, *Forbes* inflated the net worth of Trump *père et fils* to $200 million each.

The mythology of Donald Trump was taking hold. *The New York Times* profiled Trump in 1983, describing him as a "brash Adonis from the outer boroughs bent on placing his imprint on the golden rock." The newspaper reported that the Trump empire comprised 25,000 units.

The humility Trump had shown three years earlier in his interview with Tom Brokaw was nowhere to be found. "Not many sons have been able to escape their fathers," Trump told the *Times*. "At 37, no one has done more than I in the last seven years."

By THE EARLY 1980s, Cohn's past began catching up with him. He was loyal to his friends, but not all his clients were his friends. He'd been profoundly unethical in some of his dealings with them. In the 1960s, he borrowed $100,000 from a wealthy client he'd represented in a divorce and refused to pay her back for a decade and a half. After the client, Iva Schlesinger, sued Cohn, he claimed it wasn't really a loan at all. He and Schlesinger had a loose agreement in which she paid him as an advance against future legal services, Cohn said, despite extensive documentary evidence to the contrary. Cohn's firm still hadn't fully repaid her in 1982, when he was accused by a New York disciplinary committee of professional misconduct in Schlesinger's case and three others.

One of the other allegations was that Cohn had manipulated his client Lewis S. Rosenstiel, founder of the Schenley Distillers empire, as the man lay dying in Mt. Sinai Hospital in Miami, nearly blind and suffering from Alzheimer's disease. In the 1975 episode, Cohn guided Rosenstiel's hand to sign a codicil that made the lawyer an executor of the millionaire's will. Cohn left behind another document at the hospital, an old divorce filing, in place of the codicil, to cover his tracks.

As Cohn's disciplinary case ground on, he took on his final assignment for Trump. The two, teacher and student, appeared on *Good Morning America* on October 18, 1984, the day after they filed a lawsuit against the National Football League, a gambit to make money on an upstart football league Trump had bought into the year before. Sitting side by side, Trump, wearing a charcoal suit and red patterned tie, and Cohn, in a brown suit and pink shirt, were introduced to viewers as, respectively, the owner of the New Jersey Generals, one of the teams in the young United States Football League, and the league's special counsel.

The USFL had coalesced as a rival league whose original twelve teams played their first season in the spring of 1983, during the NFL offseason. Trump quickly became the face of the league and its de facto leader when he purchased the Generals that year, his star power drawing much-needed press attention to the USFL. Trump agreed to pay $9 million for the team on the condition that the league was still in existence when the payments came due. Trump later said he paid $5 million in total.

He was the driving force behind the USFL's decision to move to a fall schedule and compete with the NFL helmet to helmet. ("If God had wanted football in the spring, he wouldn't have created baseball," Trump once said.)

But before the new league could take on the NFL, it needed to get television networks to carry and pay for its games. The NFL had contracts with ABC, CBS, and NBC. The USFL had contracts with ABC and the fledgling ESPN to air the spring games. But the major networks didn't want to cross the NFL by picking up USFL games in the fall.

Trump promised the other USFL owners that the lawsuit would force the NFL to make a deal. The case wouldn't go to trial, he assured them. The USFL lawsuit, filed in federal court in Manhattan, alleged that the NFL was a monopoly that hamstrung the USFL's ability to contract for television coverage. The new league sought more than $1 billion in damages from the NFL. Some USFL owners hoped the lawsuit would compel the NFL to admit more teams—namely theirs—though Trump denied it at the time.

"If we weren't discriminated against so badly, as the NFL has done, this league would be very, very successful," Trump said in his *Good Morning America* interview.

That same day, Cohn and Trump held a press conference. Cohn did his utmost to create the impression of his new opponent as a sinister force. He alleged, without providing evidence, that the NFL had appointed a secret committee of four prominent owners to strangle the USFL in the cradle. "We have reliable reason to believe we know who they are and what they are doing," Cohn said. Trump volunteered that the NFL was "petrified of the suit."

The NFL's lawyers promptly alerted the judge overseeing the case, Peter K. Leisure, to Trump and Cohn's media tour, accusing the duo of trying the case in the press. At a hearing days later, Leisure, showing his irritation, told the parties that he didn't want to see any more press conferences, issuing a gag order. A few weeks later, in late 1984, Trump received a letter from a New York lawyer, Harvey Myerson, who was as brash as Cohn and about a decade younger but still relatively unknown. In the letter, Myerson told Trump that the USFL's attorneys weren't serving him well. He touted his own ability to marshal a multipronged attack on the NFL, starting with a more aggressive press strategy.

Cohn had been a loyal friend, an unabashed booster of Trump's success. "Donald Trump is probably one of the most important names in America today," Cohn said in a television interview that same year. "He is, as I say, the closest thing to a genius that I've ever met in my life." But in Myerson, Trump had found someone younger and healthier to do the job he needed done. He insisted that the league commissioner replace Cohn with Myerson as lead counsel.

Friends of Cohn's began to see his decline in 1985, and soon the general public became aware of it, too. AIDS had dimmed Cohn's legendary intellect. He was often disoriented, his law partners noticed. The New York *Daily News* declared him "on the verge of death," while other publications reported that Cohn was receiving treatment for Kaposi's sarcoma, a cancer associated with AIDS. He used string-pulling to get in front of the line for treatment at the National Institutes of Health, where he received an experimental drug called AZT. Cohn received well wishes from Ronald Reagan as his three-week hospital stay was ending in November 1985.

"NANCY AND I ARE KEEPING YOU IN OUR THOUGHTS AND PRAYERS. MAY OUR LORD BLESS YOU WITH COURAGE AND STRENGTH. TAKE CARE AND KNOW THAT YOU HAVE OUR CONCERN," the president wrote in a telegram.

Cohn regained some of his strength after the treatment, but the "remission," as he called it, was short-lived.

Beyond the USFL case, Cohn could feel his onetime apprentice pulling away. Calls came less frequently. Legal business went elsewhere. "Some people are too busy to see me now," the weakened Cohn said when his cousin David Marcus visited him in Palm Beach. On another occasion, he was more blunt about Trump: "I can't believe he's doing this to me," Cohn said. "Donald pisses ice water."

• • •

ON OCTOBER 23, 1985, Trump arrived to testify on Cohn's behalf before the Departmental Disciplinary Committee of the New York Supreme Court, which was responsible for investigating complaints against attorneys in Manhattan and the Bronx. The panel, which met on the thirty-ninth floor of a black office building at Madison Avenue and Twenty-sixth Street, was weighing whether Cohn should be disbarred based on the four misconduct complaints lodged against him, including the one pertaining to Iva Schlesinger. The committee's recommendation, once made, would be sent to a panel of judges in the eighty-five-year-old courthouse next door to decide whether to strip Cohn of his license to practice law.

Trump sat at a small table inside a hearing room, facing a row of windows that looked out on Gramercy, a tony Manhattan neighborhood of brownstones and grand apartment buildings. To his right, seven men and women on the committee, most of them lawyers, regarded him from behind a dais.

Despite their growing distance, Trump, now thirty-nine years old, praised Cohn while avoiding any mention of his darker side, much like the parade of other prominent friends who had come to testify on his behalf.

"In the course of being represented by him and meeting him and other people, have you come to have an opinion of his honesty and integrity?" Michael Mukasey, Cohn's lawyer, asked Trump.

"Yes, I have."

"What is it?"

"I think Roy is perhaps, if I summed it up in one word, I think the primary word I'd use is his loyalty. He is a very loyal person, and I know he is a controversial character in a lot of respects, and I hear about it, but I can only speak from my experience and he has been extremely loyal and extremely honest as far as our dealings have been concerned."

Mukasey had no further questions, but a panelist wanted to know what Trump meant in calling Cohn controversial. What had he heard?

"Only in the sense that the press, you know, sort of portrays Roy as a little controversial," Trump said, again assuring the committee that the Cohn he knew was altogether different.

"He has been extremely straight and extremely loyal, and you can't ask for a lot more than that in terms of a lawyer," Trump said.

In early 1986, Trump invited Cohn for what seemed like a farewell dinner at Mar-a-Lago, his newly purchased Palm Beach resort. Trump hosted the dinner with his wife, Ivana, a Czech-born former skier he had married in 1977. Before their marriage, Cohn had negotiated a pre-nuptial agreement on terms that were highly favorable to the devel-oper, assigning a crony of his—a lawyer to whom he'd dispensed work—to represent Trump's fiancée. That episode, which had embit-tered Ivana Trump at the outset of their marriage, had long receded by the time of the Mar-a-Lago dinner. At the table, the place settings were ornate, and a gold candelabra rested on the table. Guests paid tribute to the dying lawyer.

Trump called Cohn to check in as his illness progressed, though they weren't working together anymore. With Cohn sidelined, the NFL called Trump's bluff. The trial that he had told USFL owners wouldn't happen was scheduled to begin in May 1986. By the spring of that year, Cohn was near death. He looked skeletal in a green cardigan as he sat for a March interview with *60 Minutes*. He continued to deny—categorically—that he was gay and that he had AIDS, though some of Cohn's friends knew the truth about his diagnosis and be-lieved he'd been quietly pushing to increase federal funding for re-search into the growing epidemic. CBS's Mike Wallace told Cohn the news show had learned from sources that Cohn's name was in an NIH database of AIDS patients.

"Well, I shouldn't be. I'm glad you told me that. I'll get that taken care of very fast," Cohn said, insisting that he had liver cancer and that it was in remission.

Cohn gave no quarter when asked about the attorney disciplinary committee of the state court in Manhattan, which had been eyeing him since at least 1982.

"These people come from the liberal legal establishment in New York, and they're the country club set and the martinis and the tennis matches on Saturday afternoon and all that," Cohn said. "Certain members of the panel do not conceal their intense dislike for me."

The disciplinary committee recommended that the Appellate Divi-sion of the New York Supreme Court, the ultimate arbiter of Cohn's professional fate, take away Cohn's license to practice law. On June 23,

1986, a panel of judges on the court ruled in an unsigned opinion—meaning the outcome was unanimous—that Cohn's misconduct was "inexcusable," and it disbarred him.

Trump and his new lawyer failed in their fight against the NFL the following month, though Myerson won the trial, in the strictest sense. On July 29, 1986, a jury in Manhattan found that the NFL enjoyed monopoly power, but the jurors saw fit to award the USFL a mere $3 in damages. In essence, the jury determined that the USFL had its own management failures to blame for its financial problems. Myerson still got paid: The NFL had to pony up $5.5 million to the USFL to cover its attorneys' fees. The young football league folded after the 1985 season, having lost nearly $200 million in its three years of existence.

Cohn died a week later.

Trump stood in the back at Cohn's memorial service that October, one of hundreds who had come to pay their respects. Tom Bolan, Cohn's law partner and close friend, blamed his disbarment on a "lust for revenge" by the liberal establishment for his service to McCarthy. While his friends lavished praise in eulogizing him, they also acknowledged the complicated nature of the man. Cohn could be loyal, warm, and generous, but also vicious, cold, and vain, Roger Stone said. The guests sang "God Bless America," and then they dispersed.

2.

GREATASSETS

■ ■ ■

FOR ALL DONALD Trump's perceived success in the 1980s, including a *New York Times* bestseller, *Trump: The Art of the Deal*, he began the next decade buried in debt and publicly feuding with his wife.

Trump, employing some of the lessons imparted to him by Roy Cohn, had aggressively courted publicity during his rise, making himself a household name, and now he was suffering for it. The New York tabloids were positively giddy about the combustion of Trump's marriage and his affair with Marla Maples, an aspiring actress who was nearly fifteen years younger than his wife, Ivana. Trump had begun seeing Maples in the late 1980s, stashing her in a suite in the Hotel St. Moritz, just down the street from his Plaza Hotel, which Ivana managed for him.

Ivana confronted Maples in Aspen on New Year's Eve in 1989, while vacationing in the ski town with the Trump kids. Maples and her friend Kim Knapp were also in town, staying in a condo on Trump's dime. On the day of the encounter, Ivana and Donald were eating lunch at Bonnie's Restaurant, an Aspen staple located halfway down the mountain, when Ivana noticed Maples at another table with Knapp. The Trumps started to argue, loudly enough that other diners noticed. Then Ivana got up and approached Knapp, mistaking her for Maples, and began to yell at her. Ivana returned to Trump, argued some more, and was soon back at Maples's table, asking her if her name was "Moolah." (Ivana had learned Maples's name earlier, when an Aspen realtor called her husband and referred to "Marla." Ivana, listening on a second handset, had heard the name as "Moolah.")

"It's out! It's out! It's finally out," Maples shouted.

"I have a happy marriage," Ivana said. "I'm very happy. Stay away from him! Stay away from us!"

At the *National Enquirer*, reporters learned of the episode and planned to report it in the issue that would close on Monday, February 12, 1990. On the previous Friday, Mike Boylan, vice chairman of the *Enquirer*'s parent company, American Media Inc., called Jack Nusbaum, a lawyer in New York who represented both the publisher and Trump, to give the mogul a heads-up that the story was coming.

At 1:30 A.M., Boylan's phone rang at home. On the other end, Trump was calling from Japan, where he'd traveled to watch Mike Tyson fight Buster Douglas. Trump denied the Aspen story and took a threatening tone. When that tactic didn't work, he tried cajoling, to no effect, and hung up.

It didn't matter. Ivana Trump's side had leaked the story to the New York *Daily News*'s Liz Smith, who was the first to report, on February 11, 1990, that Donald and Ivana Trump were splitting up. (The *Enquirer*, a few days later, published its version with an exclusive photo of Trump and his two women at Aspen.) The *Daily News* scoop touched off days of tabloid cover stories. Cindy Adams, to whom Roy Cohn had introduced Trump, was now a gossip columnist at the *New York Post*, and she was furious that the scoop had been fed to her competitor. Trump found her more accommodating than Smith, who was speaking with Ivana. The headlines made it clear who was allied with whom:

The *Post*, on February 13: "Ivana to Donald at secret sitdown: GIMME THE PLAZA! . . . the jet and $150 million, too."

The *Daily News*, on February 13: "'IVANA BETTER DEAL': Mrs. T brands Donald's $25M pre-nuptial pact a fraud." (This agreement was an updated version of the one negotiated by Cohn and Lawrence Levner, the lawyer he and Trump had arranged to represent Ivana.)

The *Post*, on February 14: "The Trump affair: DON JUAN! Secret visits to model Marla at Hotel St. Moritz."

Smith had yet another *Daily News* cover story on February 15 that described Ivana Trump as a woman scorned. Smith reported crowds cheering for her outside La Grenouille, a posh French restaurant in Midtown, while inside, Ivana's friends, including Smith, moved the poor woman to tears with their support.

The *Post* had another scoop in the works. Valerie Salembier, the president of the tabloid, got a call from a major *Post* advertiser, a friend of hers who owned a New York department store. He told her that his trainer was Maples's roommate. Maples had confided to the trainer that she was dating Donald Trump and having the best sex of her life. The trainer had blabbed to her client, Salembier's friend. Salembier immediately took the tip to *Post* editor Jerry Nachman, who was giddy. He assigned the story to reporter Bill Hoffman.

The front page of the next day's *Post* was a public relations coup for Trump. "Marla boasts to her pals about Donald: 'BEST SEX I'VE EVER HAD.'"

As Trump's marriage imploded, he had bigger problems than the tabloids. Real estate markets swooned as the country slipped into a recession. Trump could no longer keep up with his payments. He owed more than $3.4 billion and faced personal financial ruin: $830 million of Trump's business debts carried his personal guarantee. Trump's billion-dollar casino, the Trump Taj Mahal in Atlantic City, was barely breaking even, and it was siphoning money from his other two casinos. He fell off the Forbes 400 list of the wealthiest Americans, his net worth in 1990 dropping to an estimated $500 million—a generous estimate—from $1.3 billion the previous year.

Trump and Cohn, before he died in 1986, had made a practice of exaggerating his net worth to boost his ranking on *Forbes*'s list. Now he had been banished. Trump, refusing to admit his fortune had shrunk, blamed his removal on the magazine's recently deceased publisher, Malcolm Forbes. The magazine was exacting retribution, Trump alleged, because the real estate tycoon had once kicked Malcolm Forbes out of the bar at the Plaza Hotel for bringing in underage men.

In the middle of this free fall, Trump put out a second book, *Trump: Surviving at the Top*. Critics derided it as an ego trip, though the book still briefly landed on the bestseller list. Trump sat down with ABC News's Barbara Walters in August 1990, around the time of his book's release, for his first extended interview in months. Perhaps for the first time in his life, Trump had been avoiding the media, or most of it anyway. After Cohn introduced them, Walters had helped Trump build his legend in her first interview with the young developer in 1987, flying with him over Manhattan in a helicopter as they regarded the skyline. But three years later, Walters acted as if she'd been had.

At the start of the interview, Trump blamed his financial problems on the economy and lashed out at journalists for singling him out. "I hope the general public understands how inherently dishonest the press in this country is," he told Walters, who brushed away the comment and neatly summarized his year of financial woes.

Trump was on the verge of bankruptcy, she said. The Taj Mahal was in trouble. So was the Plaza. He had more debt than he could pay. His airline, Trump Shuttle, was running out of cash, squeezed by spiking jet fuel prices, a consequence of the Gulf War.

"What I am saying to you is, you did overextend yourself, okay?" Walters said. "How are you going to get out of this mess, surviving at the top, when everything is down and you owe a tremendous amount of money? Are you going to sell the Plaza? Are you going to sell the shuttle?"

"The answer is because I have great assets, and the assets are doing very well," Trump said. In fact, Trump soon would be forced to sell the shuttle and the Plaza and steer all three of his casinos through bankruptcy.

Trump refused to discuss his relationship with Maples, but Walters pressed on.

"Do you believe in fidelity in marriage?" she asked.

"Yes, absolutely I do. Absolutely," Trump said. "I think that there's nothing better than a good marriage. There's nothing worse than a bad marriage. I'm absolutely a believer in marriage. I'm an absolute believer in fidelity, but if a marriage isn't working, that's a different ball game."

The Trumps settled their divorce case the following year. Ivana had contested their prenuptial agreement in court, arguing that it was fraudulent, and had sought half of her husband's empire. But she ultimately took a deal that was nearly equal to the terms of the couple's prenup. She got $14 million, an apartment in the Upper East Side tower called Trump Plaza, a forty-five-room mansion in Greenwich, Connecticut, and the use of Mar-a-Lago for one month per year.

Their battles weren't quite over. Trump later litigated to uphold a "gag clause" on his ex-wife—a built-in nondisclosure agreement—that he'd inserted into one of their nuptial contracts as she made plans to publish a novel based on their marriage. After he won, Trump called Cindy Adams to declare "total fucking victory" in the *New York Post*. He sued Ivana, who'd gone ahead with *For Love Alone*, for $25 million, but they later settled their differences, stopped litigating, and made peace.

Trump, at the time of his divorce settlement, was on a monthly allowance of $450,000 from the banks that had agreed to loan him more money to pay his bills. He was forced to sell his super-yacht, *Trump Princess,* and his Boeing 727. But he convinced his creditors that he was worth more to them wealthy than dead broke. His brand could still sell. And they agreed, on several occasions, to tweak his restructuring agreement to make it easier for Trump to meet his financial obligations.

3.

PECKER'S PATH

■ ■ ■

BEFORE DAVID PECKER was the chairman of the tabloids, he was chief executive of Hachette Filipacchi Media U.S., the publisher of glossy passion and fashion publications like *Elle, Road & Track,* and *Woman's Day*.

Pecker traveled an unlikely path, beginning as an accountant in CBS's magazine division in 1979 and rising to one of the most powerful positions in magazine publishing. He had no editorial experience and had never worked in an advertising department.

By the time he grew close to Donald Trump in the mid-1990s, Pecker had become among the most controversial and innovative publishers in the magazine industry, a chauffeured renegade who accommodated advertisers and bottom-fished for sinking magazines, slashing costs and quickly making a profit while competitors turned up their noses and lost money.

Trump and Pecker solidified their not quite friendship in 1996. That winter, Pecker rented out Trump's Palm Beach resort, Mar-a-Lago, to host a party for advertisers. John F. Kennedy Jr., whose pop-culture-and-politics magazine *George* was published by Hachette, mingled with the guests. So did New York governor George Pataki, who was paid $30,000 by Hachette to speak at an annual convention for the beauty industry that was also taking place nearby in Florida. They were joined at Mar-a-Lago by executives like Fred Langhammer and Arie Kopelman, the heads of Estée Lauder and Chanel, respectively. It was a glitzy affair. Trump, with his now-wife Marla Maples by his side, tried to sell guests at Pecker's party on memberships at Mar-a-Lago.

Soon, Pecker would use Trump's private club again for a conference of Hachette executives from around the globe, and he and the celebrity developer would hatch a deal to publish *Trump Style,* a combination of Trump branding and advertising in a magazine to be handed out at Trump properties.

Both men weathered personal and professional crises during their courtship. Trump's second marriage collapsed in short order, an implosion documented scene by scene in the tabloids, the *National Enquirer* chief among them. Meanwhile, Pecker's efforts to please another business partner, the ultra-wealthy investor Ronald Perelman, exploded into a national news story. A staff outcry over Pecker's move to kill a magazine story unfavorable to a Perelman business venture led to his portrayal in the ensuing media coverage as a publisher-villain who would sacrifice editorial integrity to protect a friend.

Eventually, similar story lines would resurface and converge when Pecker, against the advice of his Hachette executives, left the chic magazine world to become part owner and chief executive of the country's top tabloid publisher.

THE *ENQUIRER* HAD a complicated relationship with Donald Trump in the 1980s and most of the 1990s. The tabloid invested itself in covering his love life, and Trump found that he had more to gain by providing the *Enquirer* with access than by cutting it off. He remained friendly with the tabloid's staff even after his encounter with Boylan over the Aspen confrontation between Maples and Ivana Trump. Even on negative stories, he could sometimes shape the coverage, calling reporters and editors directly. "Just make sure you say she's beautiful," he'd admonish *Enquirer* staff when they wrote about one of his dalliances. Sometimes Trump successfully bartered information.

Trump's relationship with Marla Maples held particular fascination for the *Enquirer.* The couple almost made it easy for the tabloid. For one thing, they broke up regularly, each jilt and reconciliation justifying a new round of stories. Maples and Trump provided the *Enquirer* with broad access, sometimes using the tabloid to telegraph threats and offers of reconciliation to each other, an intermediary role the publication was happy to fill.

When Trump and Maples leaked their plans to marry, the *Enquirer* ran photos of her posing in wedding dresses for a cover story in April

1993, and then gleefully reported the following month that the wedding was off. Trump had insisted that Maples, several months pregnant with their child, sign a prenup mirroring his $25 million pact with Ivana. "But when the time came to sign the agreement in late April, she found that Donald had reneged and was offering her far less," the tabloid reported. The agreement was metered so that Maples wouldn't get the full amount unless they stayed married for ten years. "He was trying to rent me," the *Enquirer* quoted Maples as telling a "pal."

Maples eventually returned to the table and signed an agreement, but now Trump was dragging his feet on the wedding. In the meantime, their daughter, Tiffany Trump, was born. The *Enquirer* landed a photo exclusive of the new baby girl in November 1993.

The tabloid's last issue of the year teased a "TRUMP WEDDING SPECIAL" on its cover and carried a story inside that explained Trump's reason for finally tying the knot. Trump, the *Enquirer* reported, had been watching a news report in his office about a mass shooting on the Long Island Rail Road. "I was shocked," the tabloid quoted Trump as telling a close friend. "I realized how something can come along and ruin your plans for no reason at all."

After this supposedly existential moment, he picked up the phone and called Maples, who was in West Palm Beach with their daughter. "When I saw what happened on the train, I figured life is short, and I want to do this now," the *Enquirer* quoted him as telling Maples.

They were married on December 20, 1993, in Trump's Plaza Hotel—the same hotel that Ivana had managed for Trump.

Three years later, a local police officer working a night shift in Florida found Maples and her bodyguard, Spencer Wagner, under a lifeguard station in Ocean Ridge, ten miles south of Mar-a-Lago.

The *Enquirer*, closely tied in with the police, learned of the incident from its sources. Larry Haley was the *Enquirer* editor who oversaw Trump coverage; he had often been invited to parties at Mar-a-Lago. He swallowed hard as he prepared to tell the mogul over the phone that his wife had been caught in a compromising situation with another man. Trump was silent at the news. Soon after, Trump called Haley back to say he had talked to Maples and that nothing had happened.

Desperate to stop the story, Trump got on the phone with Mike

Boylan, vice chairman of the publisher. He asked Boylan how much profit the publisher made on each issue, suggesting he would pay the *Enquirer* to forget about the story. *Millions,* Boylan told him. *Well, I'm not going to pay that,* Trump said.

The *Enquirer* broke the story in its May 7, 1996, edition, playing it big on the cover: "Shock for Trump! / MARLA CAUGHT WITH HUNK / Cops interrupt late night beach frolic."

Afterward, Trump denied that his wife had an affair and claimed that Maples was on the beach that night because she urgently had to pee. The tabloid knew, however, that the claim wasn't true: The police had seen her limousine near the beach, driven away, and come back an hour later to find the car still parked, before finding Maples and Wagner indisposed. Trump fired the bodyguard, and one of his representatives called the Ocean Ridge police chief, Ed Hillery.

"The Donald wants to have someone interview the officer," the caller said.

"Well, tell 'The Donald' that 'The Ed' says no," quipped Hillery.

Soon after the story, Trump called *Enquirer* editor in chief Steve Coz trying to save face. "I already told her I was dumping her, Steve," Trump said. He and Maples would soon break up for good.

It would be the last time Trump attempted to quash a big *Enquirer* scoop and failed. In the coming years, he wouldn't even have to try, but for now, his new friend David Pecker was still at Hachette.

The news wasn't all bad. Trump had regained some of his footing financially. He had washed away the last of his personal debt the previous year, and now, in 1996, he entered a deal to wind down his debt-restructuring agreement, with cash from asset sales. He would soon start working with a ghostwriter on a third book, *Trump: The Art of the Comeback.*

DAVID PECKER HAD grown up distant from wealth, celebrity, and power. He was born in the Bronx in 1951 to Jacob Pecker, a rough-hewn native New Yorker and Jewish bricklayer who went by "Jack" and spoke fluent Italian, and Mary Pecker, a homemaker who had emigrated from Russia with her family as a girl. Neither husband nor wife had schooling past the eighth grade. Still, Mary was refined and glamorous, with long blond hair. Her family disapproved of Jack—they called him a *bulvan,* Yiddish for "loudmouth" or "boor." David was the youngest of the couple's three children by far; he was born fifteen years after his sister, Elaine, and twelve years after his brother, Joel, whom the family called Yussie.

In 1955, the Peckers left a cramped apartment in a working-class neighborhood in the Bronx for a fast-growing New York suburb about a mile outside the city. Pecker's father, by this time, had his own construction company, working on projects with his brother Phil. He'd built the foundation for a single-family home in New Rochelle, part of a postwar housing development that had been farmland in the recent past. The contractor who hired him went bankrupt, offering Jack Pecker the house as payment for his work. Their new home had two kitchens, and Mary kept the furniture covered in plastic sheeting. Like his brother, Joel, David was moonfaced and overweight. He took a ribbing at school for the slang meaning of his last name. His cousins thought he came off as arrogant, on the rare occasions when they saw him, but he charmed adults like his aunts and uncles and grandparents.

Jack Pecker died of complications from diabetes in 1967, when David was sixteen years old. His father had no life insurance. Joel tried to step into Jack Pecker's shoes as head of the construction company, but business sagged. David got an after-school job as a delivery boy for a drugstore to help out with the family's bills. As a student at New Rochelle High School, he discovered he had a knack for numbers, and after graduating, in 1969, he kept the family afloat with small-time accounting jobs while taking business courses at Westchester Community College. His mother was ill, and his sister, in the midst of a breakdown, moved back in with the family after a nasty divorce that gave her ex-husband custody of their two children.

Pecker transferred to Pace University, a four-year college with a campus in White Plains, where he graduated in 1973 with a degree in business administration. He accepted a job as a junior accountant at Price Waterhouse, but Pecker started a tax business on the side to supplement his income, carrying a gun to protect himself when he had to walk around with payroll cash.

Pecker's entry into the media world came in 1979, when he became an accountant in CBS's magazine division, based in Greenwich, Connecticut. The best-known of the publisher's eighteen magazines was the housewife-oriented *Woman's Day.* The company also owned *Modern Bride, Car and Driver, Road & Track,* and *Field & Stream.*

Pecker had come to CBS Magazines with a reputation for competence and hard work. He had a rule: When asked to do something by a superior, never say no. He was no longer overweight. Lean from running, Pecker wore his black hair slicked back and had grown his mustache, adding years to his round face. He worked punishing hours. Excel spreadsheets didn't yet exist. He and his team tabulated numbers on mainframe computers, printing them on enormous reams of computer paper. Sometimes the calculations were done by hand.

Over eight years at the publisher, he climbed steadily up the rungs of the finance department. A spinoff of CBS Magazines in 1987 accelerated his rise. By that time, Art Sukel, the company's chief financial officer, had promoted Pecker to controller, elevating him over two other candidates. Sukel had reservations about the accountant, who was known to fly into rages and curse out subordinates when they disappointed him. He wasn't a born manager, but Pecker knew the company's books better than anyone.

That year, French publisher Hachette approached CBS Inc. and made an unsolicited $600 million offer for the magazine division. But the French were outbid by a group of CBS Magazines executives with backing from Prudential. The home team included CBS Magazines president Peter Diamandis and his top executives, Bob Spillane and Sukel.

Executives from CBS Inc. and CBS Magazines and their bankers negotiated the terms inside a midtown Manhattan boardroom. When CBS and the lenders had questions about the numbers, the CBS Magazine executives called in Pecker, who always had the answers. He became one of the architects of the leveraged buyout, the fourth man on the Diamandis team. The new company was named Diamandis Communications Inc., and Pecker was promoted to vice president after the sale.

Pecker soon married Karen Balan, the secretary of a former CBS Magazines executive named Jay Burzon. Pecker had met Balan at Burzon's going-away party. Balan's father, Martin, had run a printing press in Brooklyn whose clients included *Variety* and *Screw* magazine, a weekly pornographic tabloid that overcame obscenity laws and other legal obstacles, paving the way for a thriving porn industry.

Diamandis and his team expected to flip the magazines in three to five years, but to their surprise, a suitor arrived much sooner. Hachette, outbid by Diamandis eight months earlier, now returned, offering $712 million for the newly spun-off company, which had plenty of cash on hand already. The stock Diamandis had given out suddenly had value. More than twenty employees became millionaires almost instantly. David Pecker was one of them. His share was $10 million. Soon after the windfall, Pecker and his wife moved to a luxurious home in Greenwich and he bought a Rolls-Royce.

Hachette left Diamandis in control, at least initially, and moved them into new offices at 1633 Broadway, in what became known as the Hachette building, along with the company's flagship, *Elle*. The French referred to Diamandis, Spillane, Sukel, and Pecker as "the Gang of Four."

Unbeknownst to Pecker, he'd nearly lost his place in the gang. Diamandis and Spillane had to talk Sukel out of firing him. Sukel acknowledged Pecker's role in the CBS and Hachette deals—the French publisher relied on Pecker's savvy in the same way Prudential and CBS had—but Sukel said Pecker was a liability as a manager: "He treats his employees like shit." Spillane and Diamandis argued that Pecker's intimate knowledge of the company's finances was too valuable to jettison. They needed him, and so he stayed.

The company was looking for acquisitions in early 1989, a few months after the original owner of the *National Enquirer* died. In 1952, Generoso "Gene" Pope Jr. bought the *New York Enquirer*, a weekly paper best known, to that point, for facing charges of sedition after rabidly opposing U.S. intervention in World War II. Pope, a former CIA analyst and a childhood friend of Roy Cohn's, was the son of Generoso Pope Sr., a New York political power broker who owned the Italian American newspaper *Il Progresso*. Gene Pope transformed the *Enquirer* from a moribund New York broadsheet into a national tabloid, moving it to Lantana, Florida, in 1971. By the time of his death, it had a circulation of 4.3 million.

Along the way, the *Enquirer* had redefined the genre, investing heavily in celebrity news and scandals, gaining entrée into supermarkets across the country, and, given its popularity, inspiring copycats and forcing mainstream outlets to take notice and emulate it. Pope dictated in his will that the executors of his estate auction off the company to the highest bidder, placing no conditions on the sale. Pecker and Diamandis Communications executives Didier Guérin and Jean-Louis Ginibre flew to Lantana on a scouting mission. Pecker was smitten with the *Enquirer*'s huge circulation. Guérin was impressed with the business but skeptical. Hachette, starting with its flagship, *Elle*, was built on ad dollars. When they returned to New York and conferred with Paris, Hachette executives agreed with Guérin's view that the *Enquirer* was too risky and against type for the French company.

The sale of the *Enquirer*, a cash cow with millions of copies sold every week, had attracted the interest of publishers from around the world. Hachette advanced a lowball bid of $375 million. A joint venture of New York–based publisher Macfadden Holdings Inc. and media investment company Boston Ventures LP won the bidding for the *Enquirer* and its sister publication, *Weekly World News*, with an offer of $412.5 million. But Pecker kept his eye on the tabloid publisher, continuing to dig into its numbers in his spare time.

A RIFT OPENED up between the U.S. executives at Diamandis Communications and their French overseers within a couple of years. Diamandis resisted what he saw as Hachette's encroachment on his turf, while Hachette sought to wring more money from a company for which industry observers were now saying the French had overpaid. Hachette, which had borrowed $480 million to fund the Diamandis purchase, began missing the projections it had given its bankers.

Diamandis decided to leave the company after a turbulent board meeting on September 18, 1990. The next day, French executive Didier Guérin offered the top job to Diamandis's number two, Spillane, who declined. If Diamandis was leaving, he and Sukel were, too, they told Hachette. "That's okay. We have David," a French executive told them. Diamandis, Spillane, and Sukel had expected Pecker to walk out with them. But he wanted to stay. Pecker felt he still owed the French after they had put up hundreds of millions to buy the publishing company, making him and the other top executives rich. Diamandis, Spillane, and Sukel never forgave what they saw as Pecker's betrayal in the name of ambition.

At thirty-eight, Pecker's power and influence were growing within the company. The departure of Diamandis left a jumbled hierarchy atop the newly named Hachette Magazines Inc. Officially, French executive Daniel Filipacchi took over for Diamandis on an acting basis, but in practice, a troika of executives were in charge, all holding multiple lofty titles.

Within a year of deft infighting, Pecker convinced Filipacchi to give him a trial period as president of the company. Pecker would run Hachette's U.S. subsidiary the way he wanted for a year, and if Filipacchi wasn't satisfied by the end, Pecker would leave. Pecker had finally gained a foothold that he would not relinquish until the moment of his choosing.

4.

I'LL BUY IT

■ ■ ■

PECKER WAS AT his peak at the publisher in the mid-1990s. Annual revenue had increased under his management from $560 million in 1990 to $790 million in 1994. He had purchased several dying magazines from the bargain bin, dramatically cutting costs—i.e., staff—to make them profitable. Pecker's bottom-fishing made him the butt of jokes in the industry, but Hachette's healthy balance sheet put Pecker in good stead with the French.

Steve Florio, the chief executive of Condé Nast, approached Pecker at an event at the 21 Club in Manhattan after the binge of acquisitions by Hachette.

"David, I've got a '52 Buick with no engine in it; are you interested?" Florio said.

Pecker smiled. "Florio, I'll buy it," he said.

Publishing executives also mocked Pecker's advertising innovations as tacky. Hachette sanctioned a cover of *Elle* in 1994 that split down the middle and opened onto an ad for cosmetics company Elizabeth Arden. Hachette executives called it a "French door" cover. The next year, at an annual conference of publishers, Florio was asked about the propriety of housing ads on magazine covers. "Pecker is not here," he said, drawing chuckles from the crowd.

If other publishers found the ads distasteful at the time, they'd soon emulate Hachette. The company also experimented with ads that unfolded from the front or back cover of the magazine, like accordions. Pecker even tried publishing two magazines in one, with a cover on either side. A reader could flip over the magazine and read an entirely different publication, as if it were a reversible jacket.

Pecker's staff appreciated his willingness to defy conventions. He encouraged his employees to think creatively, and he wasn't afraid to fail. But he was a demanding and sometimes volatile boss. If a publisher failed to land an advertising contract or a finance employee didn't finish a report on time, they could expect him to explode, screaming obscenities and threatening to have their jobs. If he wasn't yelling at someone, he was yelling about someone, complaining to his executives. "What the fuck? Can you believe this person?" When one of his executives mildly objected to his criticisms, Pecker shot back, "Stop making excuses for these fucking people." Pecker's change in demeanor during his eruptions could seem almost cartoonish. His face would darken, his eyes would narrow, his nose would flare, and his mustache would curl as he yelled in a New York accent.

At the same time, Pecker was quick with praise for a job well done, and he paid well. On more than one occasion, he used his connection to cosmetics maker Estée Lauder to introduce employees to the breast cancer unit at Memorial Sloan Kettering Cancer Center, one of the nation's top cancer treatment and research institutions. Evelyn Lauder, Estée Lauder's daughter-in-law, had raised most of the money for the center's breast cancer unit, and Estée Lauder cosmetics counters raised millions of dollars for cancer research.

Those below him had to strive to remain in his good graces or risk his wrath. But Pecker courted men and women of higher rank and status, doing them little favors. He used his relationships with automakers, through *Road & Track* and *Car and Driver,* to get friends on the list for exclusive vehicles. He helped them get their hands on cutting-edge consumer electronics from companies whose gadgets and ads appeared in Hachette's passion publications. If you were a celebrity or person of power, he would bend over backward, his executives noticed.

Pecker tried to look the part of the high-powered publishing executive. He wore $300 Brioni shirts monogrammed with his initials—DJP—and chomped on Cohiba cigars. People around him wondered if he was overdoing it, his sense of style just a little off. Rival publishers snickered that he seemed like a used-car salesman, as much for his appearance as for his business practices.

Pecker's work ethic, prodigious as it was, meant his executives were always on call, though he kept odd office hours. He worked from home most mornings, conducting calls with the executives in France. Pecker often arrived at the office around 11 A.M., left after a couple of hours for a business lunch, and then returned to the office after 3 P.M. He usually worked until at least 8 P.M., before heading out to dinner, often another business meal.

Among his favorite spots was Rao's, an Italian restaurant in East Harlem that was one of the toughest reservations in New York. Rao's had four tables and six booths, and they were full five nights a week. If you didn't know where you were, the restaurant looked like any red-sauce joint in New York: walls decked out with pictures of Frank Sinatra and Christmas lights, white tablecloths, a jukebox along the wall. Tables mostly went to regulars anointed by Frankie Pellegrino, Rao's gatekeeper and co-owner, and his aunt before him.

Pecker hadn't heard of the restaurant in 1989, when a potential client at Procter & Gamble promised to close on a business deal if Pecker could get him into Rao's. Pellegrino turned Pecker away for six months, before finally calling the publisher one day and offering the executive a table that night. At dinner, Pecker and his Procter & Gamble guests spotted corporate raider Ronald Perelman, director Woody Allen, and record producer Clive Davis at other tables. Pellegrino asked Pecker if Hachette's *Woman's Day* would review a line of jarred pasta sauce Rao's was launching. Pecker landed the advertising contract with Procter & Gamble, and *Woman's Day* ran a piece on Rao's sauce. The following year, Pellegrino offered Pecker a regular six-seat table, on the third Thursday of every month.

Pecker later put Pellegrino on Hachette's payroll as a writing consultant on film projects involving the publisher. Some of Pecker's executives, seeing Pellegrino around the office, thought the job was an attempt to curry favor with the man who rejected would-be diners so often that his nickname was Frankie No.

PECKER FED THE perception that he was a bottom-line guy who thought little of the content—his word—of the magazines he oversaw, except in terms of its financial potential. He seemed aloof to the craft of journalism and failed to anticipate the resistance he got when he meddled in editorial decisions for business reasons.

In May 1996, the two top editors of *Premiere Magazine,* one of Hachette's properties, resigned after Pecker killed a planned column about action star Sylvester Stallone and Planet Hollywood. Corie Brown, *Premiere*'s West Coast editor, had been reporting on Stallone's falling-out and legal dispute with his former stepfather and manager, Anthony Filiti, over Stallone's investment in the theme restaurant chain.

The day after Brown interviewed executives at Planet Hollywood, Pecker's editorial director, Jean-Louis Ginibre, told *Premiere* editor Chris Connelly to spike the piece. Brown hadn't even written it yet. The *Premiere* staff knew why Ginibre wanted to make sure she never did: Pecker's relationship with Ron Perelman, half owner of *Premiere*. Perelman had entered into a deal with Planet Hollywood the previous year to open restaurants based on comic book characters owned by Perelman's Marvel Entertainment.

Premiere had built its reputation on covering the movie industry with independence, and its employees were proud of the respect the publication commanded in Hollywood. The first hint that life under Pecker would be different had come soon after Hachette and Perelman acquired the magazine. Pecker met the staff for lunch at Michael's in Santa Monica. He struck magazine employees as wide-eyed about Hollywood, bristling with excitement that he was about to be a player in the movie industry. But he was also painfully out of his element, wearing his expensive suit and cuff links in a town where real power dressed in jeans, T-shirts, and sport jackets. He volunteered to the group of film buffs that his favorite movie star was Jean-Claude Van Damme, a skilled martial artist but hardly a De Niro. Pecker soon made it clear that he envisioned *Premiere* less as a leader in hard-hitting industry news than a soft-focused chronicler of Hollywood talent.

When the order came down to quash the column, Connolly and his deputy, Nancy Griffin, tried to figure out how to maintain the magazine's integrity without falling on their swords, but their bosses in New York wouldn't budge. So they plotted an exit that would make as much noise as possible, thinking if they didn't, Pecker would cover his tracks. When Connolly and Griffin resigned in protest, Brown stayed behind to serve as an on-the-record source at *Premiere* who could attest to the effort to kill her column. She and other members of *Premiere*'s staff called every journalist they knew to tell them what had happened, sharing Connolly and Griffin's resignation letter—and Pecker's personal cellphone number.

"Because we feel that the editorial integrity and credibility of *Premiere* is the magazine's most precious asset, we will not kill Corie Brown's column for July as we have been ordered to do by ownership," the resignation letter said.

The PR strategy worked. National newspapers picked up the story, highlighting Pecker's interference and Perelman's business relationship with Planet Hollywood. As the bad press piled up, Pecker dispatched Ginibre to *Premiere*'s Santa Monica offices to confront Brown.

What will it take to make you go away? he wanted to know.

Brown asked for severance for the departing editors. Ginibre agreed. Then he asked her what it would cost for Hachette to buy her notes for the column to prevent her from publishing it elsewhere. Brown was taken aback. Two editors had just given up their jobs to avoid corrupting the magazine, and Brown was now about to leave hers. Ginibre and Pecker thought they could buy her silence? No way. Brown resigned and later took the column to *New York* magazine.

Pecker publicly explained his decision to stifle the column as a response to readers' desires.

"After the research we've done, it is clear the *Premiere* reader is not interested in investigative journalism," Pecker told *The Wall Street Journal*. "They are interested in movie stars and Hollywood talent."

It was not a good look, but Pecker was unapologetic.

"The last time I looked, I'm the CEO of the company," he said.

IN 1997, MONTHS after Donald Trump's separation from Marla Maples, he and Pecker reached a deal to publish a custom magazine, *Trump Style,* for guests at Trump's properties. With nearly thirty titles, Hachette's U.S. unit could leverage its buying power with printers and paper sellers to produce niche publications at a price that beat what Trump could get on his own.

When Pecker told his senior vice president for corporate sales, Nick Matarazzo, that they were publishing a magazine for Donald Trump, Matarazzo joked, "*Trump Style*? That's like the oxymoron of the century."

"Just go sell the shit, Matarazzo," Pecker said.

Steve McEvoy, the ad director for *Elle,* was tasked with attracting advertisers to *Trump Style*. Trump, of course, wanted the top luxury brands to appear in his magazine. McEvoy and his team frequently dealt with the Guccis and Cartiers of the world in their work for *Elle,* which was competing with *Vogue* for primacy among fashion magazines. Pecker thought McEvoy's team would have the best chance of fulfilling Trump's wishes. But *Elle's* ad staff, one of the best in the business, couldn't sell *Trump Style*. The most exclusive brands weren't interested.

McEvoy got a call on his cellphone one day while weaving through Manhattan foot traffic. It was Pecker's assistant. She had him on the line.

"Where are we at with Valentino?" Pecker wanted to know.

The Italian clothes company had rebuffed McEvoy's advances, but he hedged on the phone with his boss.

"Valentino isn't in yet," McEvoy told him.

Pecker exploded.

"I can't fucking believe you can't sell this!" Pecker shouted. "I will fucking fire you, and you go back and tell your boss"—the publisher of *Elle*—"that I'll fire him, too."

As Pecker upbraided him, McEvoy conveniently started having connection issues. "I'm sorry, David. I'm losing you," he said, before the call dropped.

Later that day, McEvoy went to see Matarazzo to figure out how concerned he should be about Pecker's tongue-lashing.

"Nick, this will blow over, right?"

Matarazzo said he wasn't so sure. Pecker was furious.

Weeks later, McEvoy got a call to come to Pecker's office. Waiting for him when he arrived was an envelope containing a five-figure bonus. That was Pecker. He could threaten your job one day and shower you with cash the next. John F. Kennedy Jr., whose *George* magazine Pecker helped create, once said of him, "David makes you sick, and then he makes you well."

Outside of work, Pecker's family had suffered two losses in short order. His sister Elaine, who had been suffering from mental illness for years, was hit by a bus and killed the same year he inked the deal for

Trump Style. Pecker had long taken care of his sister, renting her an apartment in Greenwich and providing a care assistant for her. He'd unknowingly been stuck in the traffic jam resulting from the bus accident. Her death came only a year after that of their brother Joel, who had suffered from kidney disease. Pecker hosted a meal at a Queens diner for mourners after his sister's funeral.

5.

BUSINESS FIRST

■ ■ ■

FROM HIS PERCH at Hachette, Pecker enjoyed prominence and prestige rivaling that of any U.S. magazine executive. But he had begun to chafe under the control of the French. Pecker wanted more. For several years, he had been a man possessed of a vision: He wanted to run his own company. In his spare time on the weekends, he and some of his executives would look at companies and compare notes. At one point in the mid-1990s, he made the rounds at private equity firms, seeking backing to make an offer for Playboy Enterprises Inc., the media empire founded by Hugh Hefner, which was battling declining circulation and whose flagship pinup magazine had grown stale.

In 1998, the *National Enquirer* came up for sale again. Its owners, Boston Ventures and Macfadden Holdings, which had bought it from Gene Pope a decade earlier, were eager to exit the business, which had been immensely profitable but now seemed like a melting ice cube. The outline of it was still there, but under the heat lamp of a digital revolution and changing demographics, it wouldn't be for long, they believed.

The company was still seeing substantial profits and revenues, exceeding $300 million a year, mainly from the *Enquirer* and *Star*. The tabloids' owners had agreed to purchase *Star* from the Australian-born media mogul Rupert Murdoch in 1990 for more than $400 million in cash and preferred stock, packaged it with the more outrageous, black-and-white *Weekly World News,* and taken it public in 1991 as Enquirer/Star Group Inc. Three years later, the company rebranded itself as American Media Inc.

But the readers were aging, and younger generations were reading less. Newsstand sales had been steadily declining. The *Enquirer's* circulation, which had been 4.3 million when they bought it, had slid dramatically, to 2.3 million, while *Star's* had suffered similarly steep declines. The *Enquirer's* top executives, Peter Callahan and Mike Boylan, had to respond by increasing the cover price from 75 cents per issue (where it had been since they bought it) to $1.49. It was a troubling trend they joked would eventually lead to them selling a single copy for $300 million. Even more worrisome, the 1990s had seen signature tabloid stories like the O. J. Simpson murder trial cross over to mainstream media, a seismic shift in the landscape that had eaten into the market for the sensationalism once dominated by the *Enquirer* and its peers.

When the *Enquirer* went on the block, demand was nothing like the mad rush Pope's heirs had seen when they auctioned the scandal sheet off a decade earlier. David Pecker was an obvious candidate. He connected with Evercore Partners, a boutique New York investment firm headed by Roger Altman, the former Clinton administration treasury secretary. The point man on the deal was Evercore's Austin Beutner, who had participated in the last and more competitive sell-off of the company as a young associate at Blackstone Group.

Pecker and his Evercore partners planned to take the company private again. They weren't daunted by the trends buffeting the tabloid industry. They saw Callahan and Boylan as relics of a bygone magazine era who had failed to innovate. They believed the hard-charging Pecker could overcome the company's structural problems with a new emphasis on advertising. They had plans to buy the competing tabloids owned by Globe Communications Inc.—*Globe,* the *National Examiner,* and *Sun*—bring them under the same roof as American Media's titles, and save money through economies of scale. Evercore bought the *Enquirer* and its sister publications for $773 million, paying $292 million in cash and assuming $481 million in debt. Pecker and Beutner told reporters they planned a $50 million marketing campaign and might launch teen and Spanish-language editions and television projects. When the deal was announced, in February 1999, Beutner called the *Enquirer* and *Star* "probably two of the largest under-marketed and under-promoted papers in the country." Pecker, who received an ownership stake in American Media under the deal, said he wanted to take the successful brands and "build a publishing company on top of that."

"This is a sensational opportunity," Pecker said. He thanked the French executives at Hachette for the opportunity they had given him. "Hachette knew what I wanted," he said. "At my stage in life, I'm 47 years old, I'm getting the material equity interest in a company I've wanted, I'll be a principal, and I'll get to take a company to the next level, the way I did at Hachette. And I'll have $50 million to do it with."

FIRST AMONG PECKER'S priorities was to make the *National Enquirer* more serious.

The company ran a help-wanted ad that read, "If you think we're reporting on two-headed babies and space aliens, don't bother applying." Pecker issued a challenge: If a reader found an alien, a UFO, or a picture of Elvis in the *Enquirer*, he'd give $50,000 to a charity of the reader's choice. "I want people to think of the *National Enquirer* as a credible newspaper and a credible news-gathering force," he said. Never mind that the *Enquirer* hadn't run UFO stories for many years. (That was the province of the wackier *Weekly World News*.) Pecker wanted to alter public perceptions and shake things up.

Shake them up he did, starting with a wave of firings. Tony Hoyt, the *Enquirer* publisher the previous owners had hired away from Hearst, had been warned by his old friend Peter Diamandis never to turn his back on Pecker. But Pecker had publicly said he looked forward to working with Hoyt, who had previously been publisher of *Cosmopolitan* and earned a hefty salary, and privately treated him warmly.

The moment Pecker closed on the deal in May 1999, his secretary summoned Hoyt to see the new boss immediately. Hoyt had a lunch scheduled at the Four Seasons with Helen Gurley Brown, the former *Cosmopolitan* editor, so he arrived at Pecker's office in the early afternoon. Hoyt referred to the *Enquirer* as a "rag" while discussing the brand. Pecker fired him. His investors had just paid hundreds of millions of dollars for that rag.

Other firings followed.

As he settled in, Pecker called an executive retreat for his top editors and advertising executives, who flew in from around the country to the gathering in Montauk, at the tip of Long Island's South Fork. Looking around, the editorial staff found themselves outnumbered by the employees from advertising. Pecker wanted to know how they could help him increase circulation and bring in advertising, in particular for cars and cosmetics.

Pecker set about glossing up the *Enquirer* and rendering it more upscale, like *People*. He increased the use of color and improved the quality of the paper, while saving money by reducing the tabloid's dimensions and page count. He launched a $50 million national television advertising campaign and hired a design guru from New York to refashion typefaces, fonts, and the logo.

Then, with guidance from his top business aides in New York, Pecker began to dictate what news the *Enquirer* played. Those who had worked there for years saw this new regime as the end of Generoso Pope's vision.

He launched weekly Page One meetings on Fridays, weighing three or four options for the cover that would be finalized late Monday night. Joining the meetings, his advertising and marketing chiefs whispered in Pecker's ear about whether they thought a particular story would sell, or how to position it. Pecker installed videoconferencing equipment in American Media's New York office, where Pecker sometimes worked, to beam himself into the Florida newsroom.

Soon he added a second Page One meeting on Wednesdays, barely a day after the previous week's edition had closed. Pecker's marketing aide, Kevin Hyson, thought online reader panels could provide even more information about which stories would sell, so *Enquirer* editors were told to create mock-ups of several potential covers after the Wednesday meetings and send potential cover stories electronically to a group of readers who were asked to express their preferences for the next big scoop of the week.

While reader surveys influenced the front page, *Enquirer* reporters and editors learned before long that the new chief executive had no qualms about using the tabloid in service of potentially lucrative relationships, whether protecting his allies or promoting them.

It was a business-first approach to the news.

SOME OF THE paparazzi who serviced the *Enquirer* fretted that Pecker's arrival would erode the value of pictures of one of their juiciest subjects: John Kennedy Jr.

Photographers had captured Kennedy and then-girlfriend Carolyn Bessette fighting while walking their dog in a New York City park in February 1996, and sold the pictures and a video to the *Enquirer*. The paper printed the photos below a headline blaring, "JFK's Ugly Rage at Lover." A short article chronicled them shoving each other and Kennedy ripping the engagement ring off Bessette's finger and sobbing, before they made up and he handed her back the ring. "Battle over— for now. JFK's under pressure: Carolyn wants to marry, but he's reluctant, and his magazine *George* isn't selling." Kennedy and Bessette married that fall.

But the paparazzi's fears were moot. Soon after Pecker's arrival, on July 16, 1999, Kennedy, his wife, and his sister-in-law died when the small Piper Saratoga he was piloting crashed into the Atlantic Ocean on a foggy night en route from New Jersey to a wedding on Martha's Vineyard.

At *Star*'s headquarters, in Tarrytown, north of New York City, the news came in early the next morning. Editor Phil Bunton was among the many American Media employees who had heard Pecker talk about his friendship with Kennedy. Bunton warily dialed his boss and broke the news. Pecker was devastated. "We've got to do the whole of next week's issue on this," Bunton told him. Pecker initially rejected the idea, thinking that sensationalizing it would be a betrayal of his friend, notwithstanding that the untimely death of President John F. Kennedy's heartthrob son was a story made for tabloids. By the end of the day, Pecker came around.

The *Enquirer*, too, devoted its entire issue to Kennedy. On the cover, under the banner "The New National Enquirer," the tabloid ran Kennedy's name in huge capital letters, a giant picture of him smiling, and an inset photo of him saluting his father as a small boy. "The life & death of America's favorite son," it read.

Inside, Pecker printed a letter from himself in a script font—as if it were handwritten—on a full page titled "My friend, John F. Kennedy Jr." Alongside a picture of him and Kennedy wearing tuxedos, he described their first lunch meeting, how he'd become excited at Kennedy's vision for *George* within minutes and sealed a handshake deal before their lunch had ended. Pecker recalled traveling across the country with Kennedy to sell the magazine to advertisers, and the younger man telling his sister Caroline that it resembled a political campaign.

"I will always be very grateful to John for some words he shared with me when I was coming under some fire from the press in 1996," Pecker wrote, referring to the criticism he'd taken for suppressing the *Premiere* article. "John said that one of the things his mother always told him when he was going through a rough period was that 'in time, this too shall pass.' And he was right."

In a slight that stung, Pecker wasn't among the 350 people invited to a memorial mass for Kennedy and his wife at the Church of St. Thomas More, on Manhattan's Upper East Side.

AS THE *ENQUIRER* and Pecker mourned Kennedy's death in the last week of July 1999, the tabloid planted a seed for the ambitions of another of the new boss's celebrated friends. "Get ready for President Trump? Poll shocker," screamed a short item on the *Enquirer*'s second page. With apologies to Al Gore, the *Enquirer* wrote, "the real battle is between George W. Bush and Donald Trump!"

The survey randomly polled a hundred people and found Bush at 39 percent and—stunningly, it said—Trump, the "New York billionaire tycoon," at 37 percent, without having bothered to campaign. Gore trailed with only 24 percent. The article quoted sixty-five-year-old retiree Carol Sue Chamberlain of Laguna Hills, California, singing Trump's virtues:

"I am so sick of politicians and Washington. Trump makes things happen and he is at home with the guy on the street.

"He's the only one I have faith in!"

In the ensuing months, Trump cited the *Enquirer*'s poll as evidence of his viability as a presidential candidate in a series of mainstream media interviews, sometimes exaggerating the results.

"*National Enquirer* did a poll that's unbelievable, that says I win," Trump told Larry King in a forty-minute interview in October on CNN, where he announced his decision to form an exploratory committee. "Now maybe when I start campaigning, I'll do worse. Perhaps I shouldn't campaign at all. I'll just, you know, I'll ride it right into the White House."

A registered Republican, Trump was pondering a bid for the nomination of the Reform Party, founded by billionaire Ross Perot. His exploration was guided by Roger Stone, the political adviser Roy Cohn had introduced to him during Reagan's first campaign. Trump had the support of the Reform Party's top elected official, Jesse Ventura, the Minnesota governor and former professional wrestler. Trump told King that he wanted to bring back the "spirit" he felt had been lost in the United States. He said Oprah would be his first choice as a running mate. As president, he'd be "a class act," like Reagan and Eisenhower—and unlike Bill Clinton, who could have been a great leader except "for the whole thing with Monica and Paula Jones," Trump said. "I would never lie," he promised. "I've been really a public figure for a long time. I think everything is known about me."

In November, Pecker handed his friend another platform, devoting a page of the *Enquirer* to an essay entitled "Why I Should Be President." The piece was excerpted from a forthcoming Trump book, *The America We Deserve.*

Trump made a few campaign trips, traveling in a Boeing 727 emblazoned with his name in gold. His platform included universal health care, fair trade deals, taxing the rich, and cutting the national debt. In polls not published by the *Enquirer,* voters scored Trump in the single digits. His new girlfriend, Slovenian model Melania Knauss, was quizzed by NBC's Matt Lauer about whether Trump would propose and what kind of first lady she'd be if he were elected. "I think I would be very traditional, like Jackie Kennedy," she said.

After Ventura quit the Reform Party over an internal power struggle, Trump backed out, saying the party was too dysfunctional a home for him. Pat Buchanan, the former Nixon adviser, won the party's nod instead.

The presidential flirtation was over, for now, and David Pecker had done his part. He didn't ask much of Trump, but Pecker did see some return. When he was staying at his home in Florida, Pecker made sure to find out if Trump was at Mar-a-Lago and when he'd be returning to New York. Pecker didn't like to fly commercial, so he'd hang around a few extra days until he could catch a ride back in Trump's jet.

Among the *Enquirer* staff, Trump acquired a moniker that would apply to a select group of celebrities who were off-limits for the tabloid's traditional sensational coverage. Like these others, Trump was unofficially branded an FOP—a Friend of Pecker.

PECKER DIDN'T EXACTLY ingratiate himself with his staff. He canceled the lavish Christmas party that his predecessors had held at the Breakers, a historic Palm Beach hotel, saying he was going to use the money he saved for bonuses. Editors were rewarded for hitting sales targets, prompting some of them to hoard the best stories and spread them out over several weeks.

After initially saying he had no plans to move the *Enquirer* and *Star* offices, he decided to house all of them at *Globe*'s facilities in Boca Raton, declaring it the "tabloid center of the world."

He had already saved money by making deep cuts to staff at the *Globe* papers, which American Media bought for $105 million in late 1999. Pecker reckoned that he could reduce costs significantly more by consolidating *Star*'s operations with those of the other papers in Boca. Most *Star* employees wouldn't move from the New York suburbs to Florida, saving him the trouble of laying them off. Pecker sensed the hostility. He'd earlier instructed employees to monitor the coffeepots at the Tarrytown office, fearful someone might spike them. He launched an investigation when someone keyed his black Corvette at the underground garage at the Boca office, and then limited garage access to the company's top brass.

He seemed hurt that an employee would dislike him enough to take it out on his Corvette. "I was really upset because I offered employees things they never had under previous ownership," Pecker told a reporter for the *Sun-Sentinel* in Fort Lauderdale in early 2000. "Next thing I know, someone scratches my car." Pecker had obtained a permit to carry a concealed firearm in Florida. But he assured the *Sun-Sentinel* reporter that he was never strapped while on the job.

He started another investigation when payroll records were discovered in a dumpster. He ordered a third investigation when he suspected that a staffer was leaking scoops to the British tabloids before they were published in the *Enquirer*. For this, he tapped celebrity private detective Bo Dietl. Pecker had met Dietl at Rao's and previously recommended him to *Star*'s editors, who sent him to Colorado to look into the unsolved JonBenét Ramsey murder case. Dietl wrote that he'd pinpointed "a surprise prime suspect," then never identified one by name. On the case of the leaks to the British, Dietl flew down to Florida, stayed at a luxury hotel, and investigated. He even interrogated Pecker's in-house security chief. But Dietl couldn't find a culprit. Pecker went ballistic when he received the PI's substantial bill.

"THE HOTTEST PUBLICATION in America right now is the *National Enquirer*—and no one in the establishment press is snickering," *Washington Post* media writer Howard Kurtz declared in a February 2001 column. His adulation, as a member of the Washington establishment, was warranted. The *Enquirer* began the year with two scoops that Kurtz's paper and other respectable news outlets had picked up, citing the tabloid's original reports.

First, the *Enquirer* revealed in January that Jesse Jackson had a love child with his girlfriend. The tabloid's headline enthused that the married civil rights leader and former presidential candidate "even took pregnant mistress to meet Clinton in the Oval Office." The next month, the *Enquirer* revealed that Hillary Clinton's brother Hugh Rodham had received $200,000 from an herbal supplement marketer who was pardoned by President Bill Clinton. The *Enquirer* published a photo of the wire transfer from A. Glenn Braswell, who had been convicted of fraud and perjury, to Rodham's firm in Jacksonville, Florida, and reported that Braswell had sought the pardon on January 12, a little more than a week before Bill Clinton left office. Rodham returned the money when it became public.

The tabloid had doled out checks to sources in both stories, unlike its mainstream counterparts, who confirmed the news. But no one disputed their accuracy. Kurtz wasn't the only media observer to note the tabloid's scoops. Others produced think pieces that hyped the fusion of celebrity culture and politics and the celebrity tabloid's potential gatekeeper role in this new landscape. It was lost on no one that the *Enquirer,* beginning with Gene Pope's vision, had been an architect of the celebrity culture that was now enfolding politics and business—or that the mainstream press had for some time now bought into that celebrity culture and advanced it, albeit in more sepia tones.

The Clinton story was no accident or stroke of luck. Pecker had given editor Steve Coz license to assign about a dozen reporters to pick through Clinton's eleventh-hour pardons, an incredible commitment of resources. Coz dismissed talk of the *Enquirer* taking on Washington. Clinton was a special case, "the Tom Cruise of politics," he told Kurtz. He was the first tabloid president, but he wouldn't be the last.

6.

FIRST CATCH

■ ■ ■

IN EARLY AUGUST of 2003, *National Enquirer* reporter David Wright placed an urgent call to Gigi Goyette, a former child actress living in Los Angeles. Wright told her that the *Enquirer* wanted to purchase her story of a long-running affair with Arnold Schwarzenegger, who had just jumped into the race to unseat the sitting governor of California in that fall's special election.

Goyette was confused. She and Wright had been through this dance before, working together on a blockbuster story two years earlier that had helped drive Schwarzenegger, the Austrian-born bodybuilding champion turned movie action hero, out of the 2002 governor's race. She had been paid for her information then. Why did the tabloid want to pay her again?

Goyette couldn't have known, but the reason had nothing to do with the *Enquirer*'s long history of investigating Schwarzenegger's womanizing ways and everything to do with an alliance he had since forged with David Pecker, who was trying to resuscitate American Media's flagging finances. Only a month before, the two men had met in secret to discuss a business partnership with the potential to be lucrative for both of them—especially with Schwarzenegger in the governor's office. That deal was still on the table when Wright called Goyette. This time the *Enquirer*—based on Pecker's orders—wanted to buy her story to silence her.

Wright had spent several weeks with Goyette in the spring of 2001, when Schwarzenegger first publicly mulled a campaign for governor as a Republican.

The *Enquirer* had paid Goyette $30,000 for her story. Before it ran,

Enquirer editor David Perel told Wright to get her out of town so other media wouldn't be able to find her. The paper flew Goyette, her son, her boyfriend, and Wright to Whistler, the Canadian ski resort town.

While they were there, the story hit newsstands and blew up: "AR-NOLD'S MISTRESS: HIS SHOCKING 7-YEAR AFFAIR." The *Enquirer* reported that the affair had begun when Goyette, an aspiring actress who had been an extra on *Little House on the Prairie* and *The Brady Bunch,* was only sixteen. The story also said they'd made love in a hotel where Schwarzenegger was staying with his wife, Maria Shriver, the television journalist and member of the Kennedy clan.

It was a tipping point for Schwarzenegger, who, as a Republican moderate, didn't think he had a great shot at winning a state primary for governor that year anyway. In recent months *Premiere,* in a piece called "Arnold the Barbarian," had reported on other alleged extramarital affairs, his steroid use, and his heart surgery. The *Enquirer* separately predicted his divorce from Shriver over photos showing "grope-happy Arnold" with his hands all over a British television interviewer. Though he denied the affair with Goyette, Schwarzenegger announced that he would not run for governor that time around. In a follow-up, the *Enquirer* bragged that he had quit the race "because he didn't want even more scandals uncovered if he made a bid for public office!"

But a year later, circumstances had changed. When Governor Gray Davis, a Democrat, was reelected in late 2002, Schwarzenegger gained a powerful friend at the very company that had dashed his hopes before. In late November, American Media announced that Pecker and Evercore had agreed to spend $350 million to purchase Weider Publications, a collection of muscle and fitness magazines founded by Joe Weider, the bodybuilding expert who had brought Schwarzenegger to the United States in 1968 and helped to launch his celebrity career.

American Media had far outbid other suitors in an auction, paying a hefty price for Weider's seven magazines, which included *Muscle & Fitness, Flex, Shape,* and *Men's Fitness.* Pecker hoped the muscle mags would stanch the ongoing loss of newsstand sales in the tabloid market.

"We have a tabloid division and now have a consumer magazine division, with Weider as its crown jewel, combined with our own distribution system," he said. "This is a transforming event."

Schwarzenegger had become a crucial asset to American Media. A fitness icon and Weider's protégé, he had regularly appeared on the magazines' covers for decades. After Weider brought Schwarzenegger to Los Angeles from Austria, he supported the bodybuilder, who barely spoke English then, paying him $100 a week to write articles in the fitness magazines—with substantial assistance—that helped to sell supplements Weider marketed. Schwarzenegger won a string of Mr. Olympia and Mr. Universe contests, sponsored by the International Federation of BodyBuilding & Fitness, founded by Weider and his brother. Schwarzenegger's columns, earlier titled "Ask the Champ," continued as "Ask Arnold" after he became famous enough to be referred to the world over by his first name alone.

As the years went on, Weider and Schwarzenegger regularly did informal deals; the bodybuilder would appear on covers or let Weider use photos he had from the 1970s, around the time of *Pumping Iron,* a legendary weight-lifting docudrama featuring him, Lou Ferrigno, and others. In return, Weider would pay Schwarzenegger or give him ad space in the magazines, while sponsoring his Arnold Classic fitness weekends in Columbus, Ohio, and his bodybuilding competitions.

As the eighty-three-year-old Weider prepared to formally relinquish his beloved magazines to American Media, he brought up the *Enquirer*'s previous negative coverage of Schwarzenegger at a dinner with Pecker and their wives at the Peninsula Hotel in Beverly Hills, wanting to know if it would continue. He recommended that Pecker bring Schwarzenegger aboard at American Media in a public-facing role. It could be a formal continuation of the informal business arrangement Weider had with Schwarzenegger. Pecker was receptive and said the salacious stories the *Enquirer* had run in the past were "old news." He promised not to dredge them up again. Weider left with the impression that Pecker had told him the *Enquirer* wouldn't dig up any dirt on Schwarzenegger *at all.* The deal closed in January 2003.

By then, at the start of Gray Davis's second term, the governor's popularity was plummeting as Californians blamed him for an energy crisis that had driven up the cost of electricity. A move to recall Davis from office took shape, and Schwarzenegger's eyes turned to politics again. Unlike in a regular campaign, he wouldn't have to deal with a traditional party primary; this was a free-for-all. While deciding whether to recall Davis, voters on the same ballot would select their choice for his replacement from a long list of candidates of all parties who'd jumped into the fray.

That summer, Pecker met with Schwarzenegger for the first time at his production office in Santa Monica. He proposed a collaboration along the lines of what Weider had suggested—that he take on a formal role with some of the magazines. Schwarzenegger, who'd been briefed by Weider about Pecker's promise not to attack him in the tabloids, had already called associates to ask their advice about working with the publisher. They chatted, and Pecker told Schwarzenegger about his friendship with John Kennedy Jr., who was his wife's cousin. Schwarzenegger told Pecker he needed more time to think about working with American Media. He decided quickly about his political future, however, declaring that he would run in the recall election during a taping of *The Tonight Show with Jay Leno* on August 6, 2003.

"I know they're going to throw everything at me, and they're gonna, you know, say that I have no experience and that I'm a womanizer and that I'm a terrible guy," Schwarzenegger told Leno.

Pecker did more than lay off Schwarzenegger in his pages. He moved to protect his investment. As the celebrity's Leno announcement drew a wave of interest, Pecker issued an edict to buy up stories that would embarrass Schwarzenegger. At one Friday editorial meeting, Pecker instructed the *Enquirer*'s then editor in chief, David Perel, and another senior editor, Steve Plamann, to acquire the rights to Gigi Goyette's story—permanently.

When reporter David Wright reached her, Goyette was about to embark on a trip. But she agreed to make this second deal before leaving. Perel dispatched Jerry George, the *Enquirer*'s West Coast bureau chief, to Malibu, where he met Goyette at a café and presented her with the contract. George told her that American Media wanted exclusive rights to her life story for possible "future development." He mentioned that the company had a book division and television projects. Goyette liked the idea that American Media would help her publish a book on her life. She signed.

In the contract, titled "Confidentiality Agreement" and dated August 8, 2003—two days after Schwarzenegger had announced on *The Tonight Show*—American Media agreed to pay Goyette $20,000. In exchange, she agreed not to disclose her "conversations with Schwarzenegger, her interactions with Schwarzenegger or anything else relating in any way to any relationship [she] ever had with Schwarzenegger" to anyone but American Media, "in perpetuity."

George knew that the sole purpose of the agreement was to silence Goyette. Later in August, American Media signed Judy Mora, a friend of Goyette's who also knew about the relationship with Schwarzenegger, to a similar contract, giving her $1,000 in cash. The next month, the company agreed to pay $2,000 to a Los Angeles man, Thomas Wells, to buy his copy of a videotape of a twenty-year-old film shot in Rio de Janeiro in which Schwarzenegger was shown grabbing a dancer's buttocks, before she pushed his hands away, and in which he proclaimed that his favorite body part was "the ass." The contract also prohibited Wells from discussing the movie, even though other copies were available for sale on the Internet.

At American Media, employees dubbed the secret payments "the David Pecker Project."

During the campaign, the *Enquirer* made little mention of anything negative about Schwarzenegger, though an item that ran online—and in a shortened version in print after the election—repeated allegations about a love child reported by a British tabloid, the *Daily Mail*. (The *Enquirer* had earlier investigated that story but had not published anything, and ran it only after the *Mail* published it.) Meanwhile, American Media released a 120-page glossy magazine called "Arnold: The American Dream." In its pages, it glamorized Schwarzenegger and Shriver. *Star* urged voters to choose Schwarzenegger. The *Weekly World News* ran an "exclusive" with the headline "Alien Backs Arnold for Governor!"

Schwarzenegger won the recall election on October 7, 2003. The next month, two days before he was sworn in, he quietly inked a consulting agreement to launch the partnership he had previously discussed with Pecker, which they had finalized at meetings in Los Angeles and Las Vegas. The company agreed to pay him an estimated $8 million over five years. He would receive 1 percent of the advertising revenues of the Weider magazines. The company would also give $1.5 million to a fitness council created by Schwarzenegger, who, in turn, agreed to "help in various ways to further the business objectives of the Weider business."

After the election, the *Enquirer* published a series of puffy stories promoting Schwarzenegger and his presidential aspirations. As governor, Schwarzenegger would go on to use his veto to block legislation that would have established new regulations in California on the supplement industry, a significant chunk of the magazines' advertising base. At the Arnold Classic, Pecker and the governor announced in front of a huge crowd that Schwarzenegger would serve as executive editor of *Muscle & Fitness* and *Flex,* and that American Media would contribute to the fitness council. But neither made public the full scope of their arrangement.

Pecker, interviewed by a *Los Angeles Magazine* writer in 2004, sounded starstruck when talking about Schwarzenegger and the Arnold Classic. "I can tell you that to see 87,000 people in this convention center and then Arnold walks in—I never saw anything like that in my entire life. In the bodybuilding industry, people visualize him as an icon," he told Ann Louise Bardach.

Asked whether he was protecting Schwarzenegger, Pecker said, "Will I send 50 reporters to dig up something on my partner? . . . No. I'm not going to do that. But if anything that's newsworthy comes up, something that we know will sell, we'll publish."

After inquiries by reporters in 2005, American Media made public the details of their contract in a regulatory filing that referred to Schwarzenegger as "Mr. S." Ethics watchdogs accused the governor of a conflict of interest. Schwarzenegger dismissed the criticism but resigned from his role at the magazines and terminated the consulting arrangement. Soon after, the *Los Angeles Times* revealed the three catch-and-kill contracts American Media had executed during the recall campaign. The governor's representatives denied that he'd known about the deals, or that there had been any link between the favors American Media had done him and his paid promotion of the fitness magazines.

The hoped-for transformation of American Media that Pecker had trumpeted with the Weider purchase hadn't materialized. A month after the deal, in February 2003, he had vowed to "pursue even bigger targets" when Evercore and Thomas H. Lee Partners of Boston injected new capital into American Media. The two firms put down $508 million, paying off the investors who'd helped buy it in 1999 and giving Pecker more money to spend on the business, even as he sliced it. Pecker chopped more than a hundred jobs from Weider's magazines after buying them, including the entire editorial staff of *Natural Health*, so he could reinvent it and sell it in Walmart.

Pecker cut another seventy tabloid jobs that fall. Then he lost out on his next big mainstream target, the prestigious *New York* magazine.

A couple of years later, American Media's finances were still eroding. Ads at *Men's Fitness* were way down, as was the *Enquirer's* circulation. By early 2005, the company's net income had dropped by more than $20 million from a year earlier. Ominously, the company's $1 billion in debt was downgraded to negative. "We had a tough year," Pecker acknowledged to *The New York Times,* though he remained outwardly optimistic.

He and American Media escaped at least one potentially devastating problem. The money the company had spent to help Schwarzenegger in the recall hadn't been disclosed as a campaign-related expenditure, but prosecutors could have argued that it should have been. Worse, if the government had obtained evidence that the payments to Goyette and others had been coordinated with Schwarzenegger's campaign, criminal prosecutors could have tried to make the case that the money amounted to an illegally large contribution. But no one made an issue of it.

7.

THE CONDO BOARD

■ ■ ■

DONALD TRUMP'S IMAGE rehabilitation stalled in the new millennium. To many New Yorkers, he'd become a lurid curiosity, more of a campy salesman than a major developer. The Trump name had lost much of its buzz outside the city.

He rarely appeared in the *National Enquirer* or other American Media publications anymore. His fading popularity was only partially to blame. David Pecker had given his friend protection. Negative stories about Trump, he informed his editors, would not be tolerated. Positive stories about Trump, his editors knew, didn't sell.

Mark Burnett, the producer of the hit reality show *Survivor,* gave Trump a second wind in 2003. In *Survivor,* contestants were dropped into the wild with few provisions and eventually pitted against one another in various mental and physical challenges. The winners remained on the show, while the losers got the boot. Burnett, after watching a BBC documentary series about life inside large companies, was inspired to apply the *Survivor* conceit to a reality show about corporate strivers. He needed a tycoon to anchor the show, a natural showman who would decide which contestants would advance and which would go home. Donald Trump, whom Burnett christened "the last big mogul," was available.

Burnett built the show around an illusion of the businessman as a Lazarus-like emblem of the American success story: wiser, stronger, and wealthier for overcoming the odds and making it back to the top as an international celebrity. The last contestant standing, after various business challenges, would secure a six-figure job as an executive at the Trump Organization. *The Apprentice* was an instant hit. Trump's catchphrase—"You're fired"—was just another part of the myth Burnett had woven; in reality, Trump was loath to personally fire employees. He typically delegated the task.

Tips about Trump began to flow into the *Enquirer* as his star ascended with the success of *The Apprentice*. Editors summarily rejected story pitches that would paint Trump in a bad light, knowing Pecker wouldn't allow them. They ignored tips about Trump's romantic life. After a while, reporters simply gave up trying to write about Trump.

Occasionally, Pecker would order up a puff piece on Trump to run inside the *Enquirer*. The task of writing it sometimes fell to editor Larry Haley, who had long managed Trump's relationship with the tabloid. The *Enquirer* ran blurbs promoting Trump's board game and hair-care products. "The ga-jillionaire was inspired to create hair follicle enhancing products after his Donald Trump cologne proved a success," the tabloid reported in 2005. Later that same year, the *Enquirer* revealed that Trump, despite his gruff *Apprentice* persona, was "more of a pussycat than a snake."

Even positive stories about Trump were scrubbed of any potentially offensive language and cleared with Trump's people. Sometimes Trump stories would have changes labeled "per Pecker" that seemed aimed at flattering Trump, such as identifying him as a "ga-jillionaire" instead of merely a billionaire.

With his surging celebrity, Trump turned to profiting off his name, through his reality show and the licensing of the Trump brand to building projects across the United States and, soon, the world. But he still oversaw an empire of businesses and apartment buildings.

The last big mogul still had to deal with condo owners.

THE CHURCH OF the Holy Family, on Manhattan's East Side, sat in the shadow of Trump World Tower, a seventy-two-story skyscraper full of luxury condominiums. The modernist gray design of the church clashed with the $300 million skyscraper's dark paneling and glass.

Developed and managed by Donald Trump's company, Trump World Tower was briefly the tallest all-residential building in the world after its completion in 2001. Tallest or not, the building dwarfed the church and loomed over the nearby United Nations complex. If Holy Family, built in the 1960s, was bothered by its gigantic neighbor, it didn't let on. Indeed, the church loaned Trump World Tower the use of its basement for the building's 2006 condo board elections.

The elections were generally poorly attended, but the March board vote drew a crowd so large that residents joked about selling tickets. Everyone knew there had been an uprising by the board. And Trump himself was coming to put it down.

While Trump had built his brand around the art of the deal, the developer involved himself in even the most parochial aspects of his empire. At the heart of the condo board insurrection was a nearly $100 million tax break that Trump had obtained for the building.

The Trump World Tower condo board had agreed in 2003 to pay Trump $30 million in compensation for expenses and other money he'd left on the table during a legal fight with the city over the tax abatement. Trump's compensation was to be raised through an assessment on owners that amounted to tens of thousands of dollars in extra fees per unit.

Some owners felt like they'd been fleeced by Trump, who had marketed the abatement as a perk of buying into the building, and a few board members were reluctant to hand over the money. They hired their own lawyers and tax experts, who advised them that $30 million was too much. The board ultimately reduced Trump's compensation to $14.8 million, in an agreement with the developer finalized in December 2003.

But the matter wasn't settled.

Opponents of the assessment gained a stronger foothold on the board, and in late 2005 they undertook a new review of the agreement with Trump, this time appointing a special committee that included board chairman Stephen Wolf, a former airline executive, and Jerry Rotonda, a Deutsche Bank executive. The committee also hired a consultant to investigate structural deficiencies in the building—among them a front door that was difficult for residents to open because of differences in air pressure inside and outside the high-rise. The final straw, perhaps, was a measure under consideration that would remove the Trump name from the building.

Trump's response was disproportionate and severe. He sued six of the board's seven members in February 2006, accusing them of squandering tens of thousands of dollars of condo funds on "baseless witch hunts."

Ostensibly, the lawsuit was about a breach of fiduciary duty. But Trump used the complaint as a vehicle to dredge up embarrassing details about Rotonda and another committee member, Barry Jacobson. Trump's lawsuit recounted how Rotonda, while in Boston in the 1990s, had hurled racist slurs at a meter maid who put a ticket on his Audi. "I'll slap that stupid n—— grin off your face," the meter maid, Shirlene Pierce, said Rotonda had told her. "Don't come to Kenmore Square where decent people live, city n—— scum. Go back to Dorchester where monkey n——s live." The Massachusetts attorney general's office obtained an injunction in 2000, barring Rotonda from coming within 150 feet of Pierce.

The lawsuit also revealed that Jacobson, a real estate broker, had been convicted in 1983 of burning down his house to collect insurance money. Inevitably, the *New York Post* spotted Trump's lawsuit in New York Supreme Court and highlighted the past misdeeds of Rotonda and Jacobson in a story under the headline "The Donald's Faulty Towers—Wacky Board in Rebellion."

Trump had allies in the building. He'd invited George Sorial, a lawyer at the New Jersey law firm DeCotiis, FitzPatrick & Cole, to Trump Tower in the fall of 2005 and asked Sorial to put together a group of owners to counter the condo board. Sorial, who lived at Trump World Tower, was eager to protect his investment from condo board actions he feared could devalue the property. Another tenant, a lawyer named Michael Cohen, learned of the board dispute from Donald Trump Jr., who had become friendly with Cohen the previous year while selling him a block of apartments in another building, Trump Park Avenue. The younger Trump asked if Cohen could help Sorial restore order on the Trump World Tower board.

Cohen and the other owners met regularly at the apartment of Sherry Bertner, a money manager, and sometimes at Trump Tower to strategize on how to oust the condo board, which they felt was burning money in a crusade against the developer. Trump himself usually presided over the Trump Tower meetings. The core group included Sorial, Cohen, Bertner, and George Howard, an insurance executive. They leafleted the building, calling out the board and escalating the conflict, which guaranteed that a big crowd showed up to the upcoming board elections. The group worked hand in glove with Trump's building manager and attorney Marc Kasowitz and his firm, which the developer had hired to sue the board members. They shared information that could be used to turn residents against Stephen Wolf and his faction.

Cohen was gung ho—the loudest of the group. The man revered Trump. *Art of the Deal,* he proudly told people, was the only book he'd read more than once.

Donald Trump took note.

OUTSIDE HIS SCHOOL one day, before he'd turned ten, Michael Dean Cohen witnessed something that didn't sit right. His teacher sat inside an old car, struggling to get it started. The next day, Cohen sought the man out in private. "Sir, when I grow up, I will get a job, work hard, and buy you a new car," the boy said.

Though Cohen's persona wasn't yet fully formed, the episode foreshadowed so much of the man he'd become. For one, the idea that someone who should command respect would drive a run-down car. And then there was the offer to help, and in so doing to become indispensable to a person in power. Cohen impressed his teacher, who recounted the incident glowingly when his parents came in for a conference. "In all the years of teaching, I have never encountered a child with so much heart and soul," the teacher told them. His parents beamed.

Cohen grew up with the trappings of wealth in the upper-middle-class Jewish enclave of Lawrence, in the Five Towns, a suburban section of southeastern Long Island close to the edge of the New York City borough of Queens. His father, Maurice, had been born in Poland in 1935. When Maurice was four, Hitler's onslaught turned his childhood into a nightmare of bombings, bullets, and hunger before his family escaped to Canada and his world stabilized. He'd gone to medical school in Toronto and then to graduate school in New York, becoming a head-and-neck surgeon, opening a practice in Brooklyn, and marrying Sondra Levine, a nurse. Michael, the second of their four children, was born on August 25, 1966.

At Woodmere Academy, a small prep school, Michael Cohen ran with a crowd of kids who showed off family money by wearing flashy brands. As a boy, he had an instinct for making a quick buck; Cohen had a connection to score hot concert tickets, which he'd hawk to other kids at a profit. Some classmates found him unkind, but to those in his social circle he was fun, loyal, and generous. After receiving his driver's license, he'd chauffeur his sister and her friends around. One night, while at a club with a friend, Cohen found a wallet with more than $1,000 and a driver's license inside. The license had no picture on it, so he walked around the club for more than an hour, going table to table, until he found the rightful owner.

The young Cohen straddled the bourgeois world of his upbringing and the grittier scenes of New York City, where he spent time in high school hanging out with other children of immigrants in ethnic Russian neighborhoods. Through a mutual friend, he met Laura Shusterman, his future wife. Her father, Fima Shusterman, had been born in Ukraine, spent a couple of years in Israel, then moved to Queens and went into the taxi business. Through mutual friends, Cohen met Russian-born Felix Sater, whose buddies included the sons of Italian mobsters; Sater's father, Mikhail, had been partners in a storefront glass business in Brooklyn with Ernest "Butch" Montevecchi, a Genovese crime family soldier who became like an uncle to Felix. Likewise, Cohen's uncle by blood, his mother's brother Morty Levine, was a doctor in Brooklyn whose patients included members of the Lucchese crime family. Cohen spent time at a beach club Levine owned there and sometimes tooled around in his uncle's Bentley.

At American University in Washington, D.C., Cohen made friends with an eclectic group that included Jews, Muslims from Syria and Lebanon, and Italians, emerging as a natural leader who didn't drink and went to bed early. After graduating in late 1988, he enrolled at Western Michigan University Cooley Law School, which had some of the lowest admission standards in the country. In Lansing, which felt isolated to Cohen compared with New York, he befriended some football players at nearby Michigan State, acted as their designated driver when they'd been drinking, and let them use his apartment as a crash pad. To some of his fellow law school students, Cohen seemed gregarious and boastful, but not particularly interested in school. He'd drive around in a Jaguar and appeared focused on returning to New York.

Cohen did just that after finishing law school in 1991. He went to work for a lower Manhattan personal injury lawyer who within a few years of Cohen's arrival was arrested for bribing insurance adjusters through an intermediary. His boss eventually pleaded guilty to misdemeanor charges of bribery and scheming to defraud and lost his law license for six months. Cohen emerged unscathed. He reconnected with Laura Shusterman, with whom he'd lost touch before college, and struck up a romance. They married in 1994. Laura's father had recently pleaded guilty in a tax fraud conspiracy.

Following in the footsteps of his father-in-law, Cohen launched into a new business trajectory that ran on an upward arc through the 1990s: acquiring New York City taxi medallions, some of them with his wife, through holding companies with names like Mad Dog Cab Corp., Sir Michael Hacking Corp., and Lady Laura Hacking Corp. He continued his personal injury work in a spartan office above the grimy Queens taxi garage of Simon Garber, a Ukrainian immigrant who came to the United States as a boy and had begun buying taxi medallions to help pay for college. Garber had a temper, based on his criminal history. New York police had charged him in 1994, when he was twenty-eight, with assault and criminal possession of weapon: a black, handheld Kenwood radio that the victim said Garber had used to strike him in the face four times, giving him a bloody and swollen lip and a scratched and swollen left cheek. Garber fought the charges, but was convicted. In 2008, Garber reached plea agreements in New Jersey after he was charged with multiple incidents of trespassing, criminal mischief, and burglary. He was accused of, on a single day, entering one neighbor's home through a window he broke, running into the glass door of another, and leaving bloodstains in the bathroom of a third's home after showering there.

Garber would amass a fortune by running taxis in New York, Chicago, and Moscow. Cohen had met Garber while working as a lawyer. When Garber's partner ran into financial trouble, Cohen saw it as an opportunity and invested in the taxi business. It was a natural move, given that his wife already had some taxi medallions by virtue of her father. Garber took Cohen under his wing.

While amassing medallions, Cohen, smooth-talking and with a mop of wavy brown hair, recruited clients who had been in car accidents by leaving his business card at body shops. When contacted, he'd sometimes promise a lucrative settlement. "I'll take care of it," Cohen told them. "You won't have to do anything." The payouts were sometimes less than promised, but the pitch worked.

Eventually, he spent less and less time at the Queens law office, where two other lawyers Garber found to take his place were disbarred for splitting profits from their personal injury cases with him, a violation of legal rules.

Over the next few years, Cohen practiced law and did business deals out of an office on Fifth Avenue near Rockefeller Center belonging to the jeweler Bruce Winston. He shared the space with his brother. At that address, Cohen was listed as the legal contact for a medical corporation whose sole shareholder was a doctor who would twice plead guilty in fraud schemes.

By the early 2000s, with the value of his taxi medallions soaring, Cohen's restless gaze had turned to other types of ventures, including real estate. And one developer, naturally, drew his eye. He had briefly met Donald Trump a few years earlier, when the mogul held a fundraiser at his apartment for the ill-fated reelection campaign of Republican New York attorney general Dennis Vacco. Trump was brash and tough-talking, just as Cohen saw himself. His glittering building, with its facades of gold and glass, screamed luxury.

In 2001, Cohen and his wife, his in-laws, and his parents simultaneously purchased condominium units at Trump World Tower. Cohen had convinced them all to buy in together after deciding, correctly, that the units Trump was offering as the condominium's sponsor were underpriced.

The high-rise's lavish marble lobby, floor-to-ceiling windows, and views of the U.N. and the East River attracted a range of wealthy and famous residents and investors. Besides Kellyanne Conway and her husband, New York Yankees shortstop Derek Jeter had an apartment in the building. Cohen's was a $1 million apartment on the fifteenth floor. His parents bought the apartment directly beneath it. Cohen's in-laws, Fima and Ania Shusterman, owned apartments on the twenty-second, forty-second, forty-third, and fifty-seventh floors of the building. Cohen and his wife invested later that year in an apartment at Trump Palace, on East Sixty-ninth Street, as well, flipping it a year later for a $160,000 profit.

Cohen was looking for other opportunities. He invested in a Florida gambling cruise business with two Ukrainian-born men. The business, variously called Atlantic Casino or MLA Cruises, took customers outside U.S. territorial waters so they could legally gamble. The venture fell apart quickly, leaving unpaid bills and lawsuits in its wake. MLA Cruises, where Cohen said he was chief executive, was named in some of the legal complaints, but most were directed at his partners and a company they controlled.

His ambitions for public life came into focus in a 2003 race for New York City Council. Cohen had previously been registered as a Democrat, but he mounted an aggressive challenge as a Republican against the incumbent, Eva Moskowitz. His biography in the New York City voter guide said that, besides working as an attorney, he co-owned a fleet of two hundred taxicabs—apparently referencing the number he helped manage with Garber—and the casino cruise business. Cohen also wrote that he'd been appointed by New York governor George Pataki to an advisory board for the state's transportation authority, "where I serve as a public watchdog against corruption in government."

"I know firsthand how important quality-of-life issues are," Cohen wrote. "When the coffee shop in my neighborhood got lazy about its trash, I hectored them into obtaining a state-of-the-art disposal system. And when an undesirable commercial tenant wanted to move nearby, I researched and gathered evidence regarding the potential impact to the community, and sent them elsewhere. I'm not afraid to speak up when something needs to be said."

When a local free weekly newspaper accidentally left his full-page ad out of its edition the week before the election, Cohen called up the publisher, Tom Allon, screaming that he had cost him the race. Allon made fifty thousand photocopies of the ad and placed them in piles next to the newspaper bundles. Still, Cohen lost.

The next year, he was back with the Democrats. He told Greg Ehrlich, a former music promoter and Democratic Party supporter who knew Cohen socially, that he could help raise money for Patrick Kennedy's Rhode Island congressional campaign in 2004, in part because he wanted to go to a clambake fundraiser at the Kennedy compound in Hyannis. Cohen chartered a small plane and flew up with several other people. At the fundraiser, grinning widely, he posed for a photo with then-Senator Hillary Clinton.

Around this time, Cohen got to know Donald Trump Jr. He had taken an interest in buying into Trump Park Avenue, the former Hotel

Delmonico, which the developer had acquired in 2002 and converted into luxury condos. Trump Jr. was heavily involved in the project.

Over a meal at a Japanese restaurant on Manhattan's Upper East Side called Geisha, Cohen and Donald Jr. negotiated a deal. Cohen purchased multiple units in Trump Park Avenue that were then combined into one apartment, where his family would live. Cohen and his wife closed on their new $5 million home in February 2005.

By the next year, Cohen had upgraded his law practice, moving with his brother to the white-shoe law firm Phillips Nizer LLP as a partner. But his eyes were fixated elsewhere, on Donald Trump.

ON THE EVENING of the Trump World Tower board elections in March 2006, Trump paced the back of the basement of Holy Family church in an overcoat, his tie poking out, while the board members sat at a dais in front of the cavernous room. The board members introduced themselves to the large crowd, followed by the candidates to replace them, who were scattered among the audience.

Cohen, who spoke longer than any of the other candidates, was bombastic, much like the man he was trying to impress. He recapitulated allegations in Trump's lawsuit and took them further. He accused the board of taking kickbacks from a landscaper—without providing any evidence to support his claim—and condemned what he described as runaway spending by the special committee tasked with reviewing the board's agreement with Trump. The savings from the tax abatement would more than make up for the extra fees owners had to pony up for Trump, he said.

Trump was also given a chance to speak. He was confrontational. Wolf, the board chairman, had been the chief executive of US Airways in the years leading up to the company's 2002 bankruptcy.

"What does he know? He ran his airline into the ground!" Trump yelled.

Some attendees gasped. As board members spoke, Trump dismissed them with hand gestures.

Trump's allies, including Cohen, won seats on the condo board handily. With its new composition, the board disbanded the special committee and honored its 2003 agreement to pay Trump about $15 million for his efforts on the tax abatement. Rotonda and another board member, whose terms were not yet up, entered into a confidential settlement with Trump: The developer dropped the lawsuit against them and, in return, they stepped down from the board.

Afterward, the property manager called attorney George Conway, an owner who had offered guidance and support to the pro-Trump slate, and asked if he'd take one of the vacant seats on the board. Conway was reluctant, but his wife, Kellyanne, volunteered to serve on the board in his place. Through her new assignment, she got to know Donald Trump. Their relationship would eventually help propel them both to the White House. But for now, Trump was enjoying a more provincial victory: The condo uprising was crushed. And Michael Cohen had proved himself useful.

8.

THE CENTERFOLD AND
THE PORN STAR

■ ■ ■

I<small>T</small> <small>WAS A</small> lofty title for Karen McDougal, who'd grown up in small-town Indiana (Merrillville, population 16,000) and smaller-town Michigan (Sawyer, population a handful). Her mother, Carol Greene, had three boys—Jeff, Robert, and David—with her first husband, a trucker from Indiana named Robert Long. They'd married when Carol was seventeen years old. McDougal had a half sister, Tina McBain, from her mother's second marriage to another trucker, John McBain, and two stepsiblings from a third marriage. The year McDougal took *Playboy*'s top honor, Tina's eight-month-old son died of a skull fracture. The baby's father, David Flick, was convicted of second-degree murder. A pathologist concluded the baby had suffered three blows to the head.

McDougal's *Playboy* bio in the December 1997 issue said she was a preschool teacher who moonlighted as a swimsuit model, worked out daily, and hoped to have at least three children and open her own pre-K learning center by the time she was thirty-six.

McDougal embraced her *Playboy* backstory as the girl next door. There was truth to it.

"I was always wholesome little Karen. In high school my nickname was Barbie, as in Barbie doll—the nice, sweet, perfect girl. That sort of girl isn't expected to be seen in the most-looked-at men's magazine in the world," McDougal said in her profile in the magazine.

She was also the captain of the high school cheerleading squad, went stag to her prom, played the clarinet (yes, she went to band camp), and took Bible-study classes. Fellow students pronounced her the classmate with the "prettiest eyes" in the 1989 high school year-book.

According to the bio on her personal website, she moved to a De-troit suburb after college to teach. A friend encouraged her to enter a local swimwear-modeling competition. McDougal won the state fi-nals, securing her ticket to the Venus Swimwear International Model Search in Florida, where she met a *Playboy* photographer. He arranged for her to pose for a test shoot for the magazine, which quickly led to her first centerfold.

That was a sanitized version of her life. She had attended Ferris State University, in Big Rapids, Michigan, from September 1989 to May 1992, studying for an associate's degree in child development, but she never finished the program. She married Shannon McDougal, a fitness buff like her, in 1993, and divorced him three years later, keeping his name. McDougal had worked as a stripper in Michigan. *Playboy* gen-erally excluded exotic dancers from the ranks of its centerfolds, but it made an exception for McDougal. Her past was a badly kept secret among the company's public relations staff.

McDougal tried to parlay her success at the magazine into an acting career. She was cast in a B movie called *The Arena,* in which she played a scantily clad gladiatrix, and had uncredited roles in the more main-stream *Joe Dirt* and *Charlie's Angels.* She made the semifinals of a 2004 televised competition to become a World Wrestling Entertainment "Diva," as its female performers are known. But her acting career had stalled by the time the thirty-five-year-old met Trump at the Playboy Mansion in June 2006. McDougal was recently separated from her second husband, James Grdina, an Arizona entrepreneur, who would file divorce papers later that month after five years of marriage. She had spent a lot of time traveling for events, and Grdina had grown tired of her itinerant lifestyle. McDougal had felt as if nothing she did was good enough in the relationship. She was down on herself when Trump came along.

It was clear to McDougal that Trump immediately took a liking to her. He kept seeking her out and telling her how beautiful she was. A *Playboy* promotions executive, seeing Trump fawn over McDougal, joked, "I think you could be his next wife."

(Trump and McDougal had in fact overlapped once before, sharing acting credits in a softcore *Playboy* movie released in 2000. Billed as a "documentary," the movie focused on twin sisters who were also *Playboy* centerfolds. Trump made a cameo, breaking a bottle of champagne on a *Playboy*-branded limo, surrounded by Playmates.)

At Trump's request, McDougal gave her phone number to his bodyguard, Keith Schiller. Trump surprised her with a call soon after the filming at the Playboy Mansion. They made plans to meet for dinner the following week at the tony Beverly Hills Hotel.

Schiller picked McDougal up six days later at her Beverly Hills apartment and parked on a side street near the hotel. McDougal had thought she and Trump were going out to dinner, but Schiller escorted her around the back of the hotel to Trump's bungalow instead of taking her through the lobby, to avoid prying eyes.

They dined in. Trump had steak and mashed potatoes. They talked about Trump's three-month-old son. Melania had come up with the name Barron, he told her. "It's a great name," Trump said.

Then they stopped talking.

When they were dressed, Trump offered McDougal $4,000.

"Is that good enough?" he asked.

McDougal took offense. "I'm not that kind of girl," she told him. "I slept with you because I like you."

"Oh, you're really special," Trump said.

McDougal cried in the car as Trump's bodyguard drove her home. But she continued to see him—at his bungalow at the Beverly Hills Hotel; at his Trump Tower apartment in New York; at his golf course in New Jersey; and at a particular Lake Tahoe hotel in July 2006, where Trump would meet another woman that same weekend.

THE AMERICAN CENTURY Championship, held annually in July, was by day a celebrity golf tournament on the banks of Lake Tahoe and by night a let-it-all-hang-out party at which entertainers and athletes of various stages of fame gambled and drank. Donald Trump wasn't one of them. He played golf during the day but didn't like to stay out late. He amused himself in other ways at night.

On the course, Trump met Stormy Daniels, the star of *The Witches of Breastwick* and *Porking with Pride 2*, who was working the event for the porn production company Wicked Pictures. They rode in a golf cart together for a hole, and later Trump sought her out in the gift room, where celebrities could collect free merchandise and, the brands hoped, drive sales when normal people saw their idols wearing or using the products in public. Trump found Daniels, asked for her number, and then invited her to dinner. "Yeah, of course!" she said. Daniels wasn't a Trump fan, but she found him interesting. Trump told her to meet him at his hotel that evening.

Like McDougal on the night of her first date with Trump, Daniels expected him to take her out for a nice meal. She was dressed for a night on the town, in her favorite gold dress and gold strappy heels, when she arrived at Trump's room in the penthouse at Harrah's. Schiller was standing outside. "He's waiting for you inside," he told her. Daniels found Trump sprawled on the couch in black pajamas and slippers, watching television. They were dining in.

"Ha, does Mr. Hefner know that you stole his outfit?" Daniels asked.

"Oh, I just thought we would relax here," Trump told her.

They ate dinner and talked. Trump was curious about her business; he wanted to know how much she made from royalties. Daniels teased him about his hair. He showed her a magazine with him on the cover and told her she should be on *The Apprentice*.

"Well, it's never going to happen. NBC is never going to let a porn star on," she said.

"I can make it happen."

"You can't. I dare you."

Trump seemed serious. Daniels had never seen the show, but she let herself consider the possibility of a career-boosting turn as a contestant. They continued to talk about it. Daniels excused herself to use the bathroom, and when she returned, Trump was sitting on the bed.

"Come here," he said.

Here we go, Daniels said to herself.

TRUMP FINISHED SIXTY-SECOND out of eighty-two golfers at Lake Tahoe. Soap opera actor Jack Wagner shot an even-par 72, making him the first non-pro athlete to win the event.

Karen McDougal had booked her flight and hotel to visit Trump in Lake Tahoe. Trump always reimbursed her travel expenses in cash—to avoid a paper trail, he said. On July 16, the last day of the tournament, they ended up at a nightclub inside the casino, sitting at a booth with

Drew Brees, the quarterback for the New Orleans Saints, and others whom McDougal didn't know. Trump, perhaps flattering McDougal, leaned over and told her that Brees had recognized her as the Playmate of the Year. "See, baby, you are popular," he said.

Soon Schiller escorted Trump up to his hotel room, while McDougal stayed behind to maintain the fiction, however thin, that she and Trump weren't an item. The bodyguard then returned to collect McDougal and take her to Trump's suite. She didn't know Stormy Daniels, let alone that Daniels had been with Trump earlier that weekend in the same hotel, on the same bed.

McDougal marked down liaisons with Trump in a daily planner that she kept long after the relationship ended, scrawling "D.T." in her early entries, and later simply "T." She visited him at the Beverly Hills Hotel when Trump traveled to Los Angeles. Trump told McDougal he loved her. He took her to events, like the Miss Universe pageant at the Shrine Auditorium, where she and a friend sat behind Trump, who introduced her to music producers Quincy Jones and David Foster. McDougal spent time in New York at the Trump Tower residence while Melania and Barron were away. He showed McDougal a closet with Melania's clothes and shoes. McDougal was surprised at how small the kitchen was in the otherwise palatial penthouse. They had sex in Melania Trump's separate bedroom.

In January 2007, Trump and his family attended a party at the Playboy Mansion for *The Apprentice*. McDougal was working the event as a Bunny and took pictures with the Trumps. Trump told McDougal that he'd asked his middle son, Eric, to point out the most beautiful woman at the party. Eric, Trump said, had gestured toward McDougal. "He has great taste," Trump told her.

McDougal put a stop to the affair in April 2007. She felt guilty about being a woman on the side, knowing her mother would disapprove, and had come to view Trump as possessive and occasionally offensive, like when he called her friend flat-chested. He once asked her to have a threesome with another woman. (It never happened.) Another time, he told her she could be a contestant in his Miss Universe pageant, if only she were younger. Trump also said odd things like "I so want to make you pregnant." (In fact, McDougal had a pregnancy scare during their relationship; they never used protection.) McDougal had given Trump a set of cuff links and a crystal Versace wine stopper as Christmas gifts. Trump had told her that her gift was an apartment in New York, but that it was being remodeled.

McDougal didn't see a future for them.

"I know my mom knows about you, but she would be really, really devastated if she found out we were having a relationship and being intimate together," she told him.

"What, that old hag?" Trump said.

McDougal reminded Trump that he was nearly the same age as her mother.

9.

THE TRUMP ORGANIZATION EMPLOYEE

■ ■ ■

FRESH OFF THE condo board victory at Trump World Tower, Michael Cohen's relationship with Trump blossomed. The developer asked for Cohen's help smoothing over a problematic licensing deal that Donald Trump Jr. was overseeing. He then sought Cohen's advice on Trump Entertainment Resorts, Trump's long-suffering casino business, which had filed for bankruptcy in 2004. The company was trying to negotiate a buyout. Cohen, who had no expertise as a bankruptcy or transactional lawyer, nevertheless pored over stacks of documents to find answers for Trump.

The two men formed a mutual appreciation society as they grew closer. In early 2007, Cohen told a *New York Post* reporter that "Trump properties are solid investments." Trump repaid the compliment. "Michael Cohen has a great insight into the real-estate market," he said. "He has invested in my buildings because he likes to make money—and he does."

After Cohen lent a hand with the casinos, he visited Trump for the last time as an outside adviser. The two of them were sitting in Trump's office when the developer asked Cohen if he was happy at his "sleepy old firm." Cohen said that he was.

"Would you rather work for me?" Trump asked.

"Are you offering me a job?"

"Yeah."

They negotiated Cohen's role and salary. He never returned to his law office.

• • •

Top executives were told that Cohen, as an involved investor in Trump buildings, would be the boss's "eyes and ears" and represent his interests to condo owners. He was given an office and the title of executive vice president, but the precise nature of his job wasn't clear to others in the organization, including other lawyers. They knew Cohen owned taxi medallions, was a partner in a well-known corporate law firm, and had significant personal wealth. Why did he want to work there?

Almost immediately after he joined the company, Cohen's unique style came across in encounters with potential business partners. Trump tapped Cohen as his point man to buy an unfinished golf course development called Running Horse, in Fresno, California, that was enmeshed in bankruptcy proceedings. Lawyers for the developer who controlled the project were bewildered as Cohen, who seemed to them as if he had been Trump's consigliere for years, tried to coax them into a deal on unfavorable terms.

Cohen aggressively promoted Trump's message with radio appearances in Fresno and visits to the area with Trump. The two told the media, local politicians, and residents that they could turn Fresno around, while threatening to walk away and vilifying the developer and his lawyers for refusing their offers. Their approach seemed heavy-handed for the Central Valley of California.

"No one in the world other than Mr. Trump could make this project a success," Cohen told *The Fresno Bee*.

After Running Horse's owner, Mick Evans, rejected Trump's first offer, Evans's representatives went on a local talk show to discuss the deal. Cohen called in to the show and, while live on the air, nearly doubled Trump's offer to $40 million. But still the deal wasn't moving fast enough for Cohen. So he tried to cheat. Cohen offered the attorney for Evans, Harry Pascuzzi, a job at the Trump Organization as West Coast counsel, hoping to switch his allegiance to Trump. Pascuzzi said he'd consider the position after he finished representing his current client.

"No, it's got to be right now," Cohen told him, before withdrawing the offer when he realized Pascuzzi had no intention of wading into a massive conflict of interest.

Cohen's rush to wrap up a deal, any deal, made him a punch line with the other attorneys. Once, when Pascuzzi and Trump's California lawyers decided to break off the negotiations for the day, Cohen blew up and demanded they continue until a deal was reached. He was still ranting on the speakerphone, having called in to the meeting from New York, as the lawyers left the room.

Even after all the drama, the parties eventually struck an agreement, only to have Trump back out, saying the local redevelopment zone wasn't big enough to make the deal worthwhile.

Cohen then helped the Trump family with another condo board revolt at 220 Riverside Boulevard, a forty-nine-story luxury condo residence on the Upper West Side of Manhattan, one of seven buildings that made up a $3 billion development overlooking the Hudson River called Trump Place.

The previous year, one resident, Eugenia Kaye, had sent hand-signed letters to each owner criticizing the board for lax oversight of Trump's management company. She'd then canvassed the condo building for votes to unseat the Trump-aligned board members, including Donald Jr., who was treasurer. At a November 2006 meeting, Kaye shocked board members when she pulled out a sheaf of proxy votes she'd collected from owners—enough to oust the entire board, Donald Jr. included, and replace it with her own slate. "You're fired, Donald Trump Jr.!" began a *New York Post* article about the coup.

Donald Trump was so incensed he made a surprise visit to the condo holiday party, arriving with two bodyguards, and confronted Kaye, wagging his finger in her face.

"See this woman? This is a person bringing down the value of your apartments," Trump said. "I'm going to sue you. No, I already sued you today."

In fact, Donald Trump Jr. and the other ousted board members had sued Kaye in New York state court earlier that day, alleging that she'd won the election through fraud and demanding millions of dollars in damages. The next day, the building manager filed a police complaint against Kaye. He said she'd punched him at the Christmas party. She wasn't charged; the police officer who investigated the alleged assault later said that the building manager had been "pressured by the Trump organization to beef up the complaint against Ms. Kaye to have her arrested, because she had Donald Trump Jr. ousted as a board member of the building."

The Trump lawsuit against Kaye was thrown out, but Kaye filed a lawsuit of her own in December 2007, describing herself as the victim of a coordinated campaign of harassment in retaliation for moving against Donald Trump's oldest son. Cohen brought the case to his former firm, Phillips Nizer, which successfully defended the Trumps against Kaye's claims. Cohen wasn't listed as counsel, but he could claim credit for the win with his new boss. Kaye, by this time, had moved out of Trump Place, and Donald Jr. was restored to the condo board.

Back at the Trump Organization, Cohen appeared starstruck around Trump, so much so that colleagues came to believe that his priority, more than doing his job effectively, was to please the boss. He was secretive about the work he was doing, keeping others in the legal department in the dark about his projects and, unlike most of his colleagues, locking the door to his office at Trump Tower when he wasn't there.

Some colleagues were puzzled by Cohen's unending—and largely unrequited—affection for Trump. He helped negotiate several high-profile Trump deals, including a 2008 branding pact between Trump and Affliction Clothing, an apparel line that was branching out into fight promotion. And for a while, Cohen seemed on track to lead several Trump projects in the former Soviet Union.

But all the deals Cohen led ultimately fizzled, and it didn't take long for Trump to grow skeptical of Cohen's legal skills. He doled out projects he had previously assigned to Cohen to others and asked other lawyers to review documents Cohen had drafted.

"Why does someone else have to look at my work?" Cohen asked colleagues.

In 2009, Trump summoned lawyer George Sorial, who had also joined the Trump Organization after prevailing in the Trump World Tower condo dispute, to the developer's twenty-sixth-floor office in Trump Tower. Trump handed him an unpleasant task: He wanted Sorial to persuade Cohen to resign. He'd had it with Cohen, who wasn't getting things done and no longer seemed like a good fit at the Trump Organization.

"What's he doing here?" Trump asked.

Sorial returned to his own office and called Cohen for a meeting.

When Cohen arrived, Sorial was plain with his friend. He told Cohen he had spoken with the boss, who had asked Sorial to convince Cohen to leave.

What should I do? Cohen wanted to know.

Sorial advised Cohen to speak with Trump and tender his resignation.

But Cohen didn't resign, even as other members of the legal department relayed a similar message to him. Trump eventually dropped the issue, but not before dealing another blow to Cohen by way of a big pay cut, slashing his annual income of more than $400,000 roughly in half.

Still, Cohen redoubled his efforts, taking on ever more thankless work. One of his responsibilities was conveying to lawyers and vendors, many of them small business owners, that they could expect severely reduced fees or none at all for the services they provided Trump. The boss reveled in hearing Cohen recount how he'd gotten Trump's bills erased.

In one case, Cohen demanded a 70 percent discount from a law firm the Trump Organization hired in a legal dispute involving its winery in Virginia. Eric Trump, the second son of Donald and Ivana Trump, had tried and failed to get the law firm president, David Hopper, to cut the fees. Hopper's firm stopped work and asked a judge for permission to withdraw from the case when it became clear that the Trumps weren't going to pay voluntarily. Cohen followed up with Hopper on the phone. He was friendly enough at first, but he quickly turned threatening. Cohen told Hopper and another lawyer at the firm, Gary Cook, that unless the firm agreed to cut and cap its fees and resume its work for the Trumps, the attorneys could expect some bad publicity.

Soon, a local legal newspaper published a story in which Jason Greenblatt, the Trump Organization's general counsel, was quoted as saying of Hopper's firm, "We were very, very disappointed over their work quality and their billing practices. We needed to redo their work multiple times in-house."

Hopper and his firm later sued to recover their legal fees and accused Greenblatt of defamation. The parties reached a confidential settlement and released a joint statement, clarifying that Greenblatt's comments in the legal newspaper "were not intended to be a negative reflection on the business practices or quality of services performed by" Hopper's firm.

COHEN'S TOUGH-GUY ROUTINE, while useful for him and for Trump, contrasted with the generous nature seen by co-workers and even people Cohen met at random. That Michael Cohen went to great lengths to help people he knew and solve their problems, using connections in the huge Rolodex he had built with acts of kindness and a profound sociability. He had put hours into volunteering at his children's school and his son's baseball practice. In almost any restaurant, Cohen ran into someone he knew. While shopping for clothes with his family at Barneys, Cohen got off the phone and asked the young saleswoman, an aspiring fashion designer, "Who are you? I don't know you." Cohen handed her his card, launching a yearslong professional relationship in which he brought her clients and mentored her.

For those who knew him well, Cohen's enforcer persona could seem like a charade that was easily dismissed. On a trip to California, Cohen walked into Trump's residence with another man and found the bodyguard, Keith Schiller, blocking his way to the boss. *He's in a meeting. I'll let you know if he's available,* Schiller said. *Fuck this,* said Cohen, trying to brush past. Schiller, a former New York City police officer, threw him to the ground. *I told you, you're not going in,* Schiller said. With outsiders, though, his shtick could be effective. When Trump University, the mogul's real estate seminar business, had cash flow problems, Trump dispatched Cohen to work over vendors, who ended up getting twenty cents on the dollar for printing and other services they provided to the company.

Trump ordered his fixer to perform personal duties for him as well. Melania Trump's humidifier once overflowed and damaged the couple's ornate Trump Tower bathroom, with its frescoed ceiling. Trump asked Cohen to handle the insurance claim.

Cohen's portfolio at the Trump Organization also included media relations—a euphemism, in this case, that often meant trying to kill negative stories and persuade reporters to exaggerate Trump's wealth and power in positive or neutral stories. Trump continued to obsess about making the *Forbes* list of the wealthiest individuals each year.

Like Roy Cohn before him, Cohen fed the magazine's reporters profoundly rosy financial statements concocted with the Trump Organization's longtime chief financial officer, Allen Weisselberg. They'd take a Trump building and assign it the highest price per square foot they could find at another property in the vicinity. Or they'd use the gross rental income—the potential, rather than the actual, rent roll—as a starting point and create a multiplier, based on however Trump wanted to value the asset. Trump had as much as admitted that valuations of his net worth relied in part on whim.

"My net worth fluctuates, and it goes up and down with the markets and with attitudes and with feelings, even my own feelings," he said during a 2007 deposition in his lawsuit against author Timothy L. O'Brien, who had committed the sin of reporting that Trump was a mere millionaire in his book *TrumpNation: The Art of Being The Donald*. (A New Jersey court dismissed the lawsuit.)

Cohen found other ways to help Trump with messaging. He involved himself in public spats that Trump provoked or escalated, like his feud with talk show host Rosie O'Donnell. Cohen helped Trump compose tweets attacking O'Donnell as "an ass" and "a true loser."

What Cohen lacked as a dealmaker he made up for as Trump's designated bully and messenger, trafficking in threats and lies so Trump didn't have to do it himself. It was a niche that Trump very much needed to fill, and one for which Cohen was well suited. Through sheer persistence, he entered into his glory days at the company.

10.

WOODS AND EDWARDS

■ ■ ■

AMERICAN MEDIA'S TABLOID sales were in free fall. The *National Enquirer*'s circulation stood at about one million in 2005, less than half
what it was when David Pecker became chief executive of the publisher six years earlier. Prone to grand disruption, he had recently
cleaned house at the paper, hiring a veteran of the Fleet Street tabloids
in London, Paul Field, to revive the *Enquirer*. With Pecker's blessing,
Field replaced much of the tabloid's staff with twenty-two British tabloid reporters.

The overhaul was reminiscent of the Gene Pope era, when the tabloid imported many of its staffers from England. Pope had found particular inspiration in the *Daily Mirror*, a working-class tabloid in the
United Kingdom that covered crime and big personalities with abandon. He poached British reporters to avoid having to train an all-
American staff in the then-unfamiliar arts of tabloid reporting. By the
time Pecker followed suit, the United States had plenty of reporters
who knew the game and played it well. But he wanted change—and
fast.

Pecker also returned the *Enquirer* to its New York roots, leaving
Boca Raton behind. He settled the tabloid in a twenty-story office
building on Park Avenue in Manhattan. It was a fresh start. One of the
newly staffed tabloid's 2005 stories alleged that actress Cameron Diaz
had cheated on her boyfriend, pop star Justin Timberlake, with a television producer named Shane Nickerson. Diaz sued the *Enquirer* for
$10 million, accusing the tabloid of libeling her. (The parties eventually
reached an out-of-court settlement that Diaz's side described as "sub-

stantial.") Few celebrities saw the wisdom in publicly showing support for a tabloid in a defamation case. Donald Trump was an exception.

"Now I happen to know something about the *Enquirer* and I also know the man who runs it, owns it and everything else," Trump said in an online interview. "His name is David Pecker. He's a winner. He's a legitimate guy. He's smart as can be. And I have a feeling that when they print something, it's right on the button. And, Cameron, one last word of advice. You may just want to avoid hugging strange men in the bushes. Because you know what? David Pecker and the *National Enquirer* will get you every time."

Months earlier, the media executive had been a guest at Trump's wedding to his third wife, Melania Knauss, at Bethesda-by-the-Sea Episcopal Church, in Palm Beach. The couple held their reception in the $35 million ballroom at Mar-a-Lago. Pecker was also on hand for an Elton John concert at the Trump resort the following year. The famous pianist and songwriter changed the lyrics to his song "Daniel" to "Donald." As the now entrenched king of the tabloids, Pecker was not trying as hard to gain acceptance by the mainstream magazine world, though he had added personal lifestyle and fitness titles to American Media's stable. But Trump had welcomed Pecker into his orbit more and more as the years went by. Before long he'd have the opportunity to do important things for Trump in return.

No AMOUNT OF retooling lifted sales of the *Enquirer* or its sister tabloids. The publisher owned plenty of other titles, but the *Enquirer* had been the centerpiece of Pecker's plans to expand and conquer, with all the cash it had formerly thrown off. Revenue was declining quarterly. In August 2005, Standard & Poor's assigned American Media's nearly $1 billion in debt a negative outlook, citing declining operating performance and eroding tabloid circulation and profitability.

American Media was having bookkeeping issues, too. The company informed the United States Securities and Exchange Commission in early 2006 that it could no longer vouch for its most recent financial statements. It had been without a chief financial officer for much of the previous year. The need for a restatement had a cascading effect. Because its financial statements weren't up to date, American Media was technically in default on its bond agreements. That gave the company's bondholders leverage to negotiate new debt covenants that were far stricter and more onerous on American Media. The company was handcuffed.

Pecker was juggling the debt holders and an internal investigation of the misstated financial results, which was overseen by the audit committee of American Media's board. Pecker had to open his books to investigators and turn over employee emails. With financial pressures mounting, Pecker canceled the Fleet Street experiment. One day in April 2006, he summoned Paul Field upstairs and congratulated him on his achievements—the tabloid had recently broken a story about singer Whitney Houston's drug-strewn bathroom—but it wasn't enough. The Brits were too expensive, Pecker told him, adding that it would be best if Field left straightaway. Surprised, the editor walked out of the building and onto Park Avenue, calling his assistant to bring down his coat. Almost all of the tabloid's British workforce soon left, too. At the same time, Pecker moved the *Enquirer* back to Boca Raton to save money, a little more than a year after he had relocated the tabloid to New York, and reinstalled David Perel as editor. To free up more cash, he shuttered three of the company's magazines—*Celebrity Living, Shape en Español,* and *MPH*—and cut about eighty staffers.

Pecker seemed to have lost his famous bravado. He was preoccupied with the survival of the company and looking for support. He received some from his friend Trump, who sent Pecker a newspaper article telling of American Media's financial woes. Trump had scrawled an encouraging note over the newsprint with a Sharpie. Trump had been in Pecker's shoes. *You'll be on top again in no time,* he told Pecker. The media executive framed the note from Trump and kept it in his office, showing it to visitors with pride.

The internal investigation concluded that American Media needed to shore up its financial controls but found no intent on the company's part to deceive regulators or its bondholders. As American Media released its restated financials, the depth of the company's problems came into sharper focus. It recorded a $161 million loss in the fiscal year that ended in March 2006. Sales of the *Enquirer* had fallen again to 802,000, a sharp 20 percent drop from the year before. The *Weekly World News,* the last redoubt of alien and Elvis sightings, had tumbled to 83,000, nearly a quarter of its circulation when Pecker took over the company. He tried to cover the losses from plummeting circulation by raising the prices of the tabloids. The *Enquirer* now cost $3.29—more than double its cover price in 1999.

IN SEPTEMBER 2006, the *Enquirer* got a tip that golf sensation Tiger Woods was having an affair with a waitress from a Perkins Restaurant and Bakery in Windermere, Florida, near Woods's office. The waitress's name was Mindy Lawton, and on several occasions, Darryl Wrobel, a freelancer for the *Enquirer*, tailed her to Woods's gated home. But what he wanted was a photo of the two in the act.

One day, his tipster, a friend of Lawton's, told Wrobel that Woods and the waitress planned to meet at the Perkins parking lot before dawn the following Thursday. Wrobel arrived at 3:30 A.M., and waited. Soon, Woods pulled into the lot in a black Cadillac Escalade. Lawton arrived in her own car, following Woods after he flashed his lights. Wrobel watched them as they pulled out of the Perkins lot onto Conroy Windermere Road, made a U-turn around the median barrier, and headed to Woods's office, across the street from the restaurant. He took photos as Woods tried to use his key card to enter his office. It wasn't working. Woods was rubbing the magnetic strip of the card, blowing on it, but he couldn't open his own office door. Frustrated, he and Lawton got back in their vehicles and headed to a nearby church. They drove to the middle of a large field used for overflow parking, turned off their engines and lights, and got out of their vehicles, Wrobel watching them from a distance.

Wrobel debated how quickly to approach with his cameras—he had two of them around his neck—to catch them in flagrante. He reckoned about twelve minutes, but Lawton and Woods were back in their cars and pulling out of the field seven minutes later. He'd missed his chance. Soon Wrobel got a call from his source, who wanted to know if he'd gotten the photo he needed. After he explained what happened, she told him that she'd already spoken to Lawton, who had described having sex with Woods against the Escalade that morning. And there was another thing, the source said. Lawton had shared that she was menstruating—and that Woods had been undeterred by this fact. The tipster suggested that Wrobel return to the scene. He'd likely find his proof on the ground. Sure enough, Wrobel found a used tampon in the field where the cars had been parked. He stooped down and guided it into an envelope with a stick. Tabloid reporting was a dirty business.

Wrobel was patched in by phone to an editorial meeting at the *Enquirer* later that day. He told them his story. He had photos of Woods fumbling with his key as the waitress watched. He had photos of their silhouettes in the church field. He'd followed Lawton to Woods's compound at various times. He had a rather gross piece of evidence. If he didn't have the story, he was very close.

His handler at the *Enquirer,* a senior editor, gave him permission to call Woods and Lawton for comment. Woods hung up on him. When Wrobel reached Lawton, she didn't deny the affair, but she didn't confirm it, either. Still, Wrobel thought the story was on track. He called his editor regularly to see when it was running.

After weeks had gone by, the *Enquirer* editor called Wrobel. Did he still have all his notes and photos and the infamous tampon? she wanted to know. Of course he did, Wrobel said. The editor instructed him to destroy them all. Wrobel would be compensated for his work, she said, but the story needed to go away. When Wrobel asked for an explanation, the editor told him something was happening behind the scenes at the corporate level at American Media. She didn't precisely know, the editor said, but she had orders.

What Wrobel didn't know was that Pecker had traded the dirt on Woods for an exclusive interview with the famous golfer in the August 2007 edition of *Men's Fitness,* hoping to spur sales of American Media's workout and lifestyle magazine. Perhaps chastened by the Cameron Diaz lawsuit, Pecker used Wrobel's story as a chit. Gene Pope had done the same thing on many occasions, in the *Enquirer's* heyday. Usually the stories he traded away were off-brand for the *Enquirer*. The Tiger Woods story, however, was classic tabloid fare.

UNFORTUNATELY FOR JOHN Edwards, he didn't have anything to trade David Pecker. The telegenic former U.S. senator from North Carolina was making a second bid for the White House in 2007. He styled himself as a family man, but Edwards was having an affair with a woman he'd met the previous year at a New York bar. His political action committee had put the woman, Rielle Hunter, on the payroll in the summer of 2006 to produce videos about the candidate. As their affair progressed, the candidate's wife, Elizabeth Edwards, fought the cancer that would eventually take her life.

The *National Enquirer* broke the news of the affair in October 2007, without naming Hunter. Pecker wasn't excited about the story at first, but he allowed it. Edwards categorically denied the tabloid's report. "The story is false. It's completely untrue, ridiculous," he told reporters.

Even if Edwards's denials were to be believed, the story was low-risk for the *Enquirer*. The law shrouded news outlets in protections when reporting on public officials. To sue for libel, Edwards would have had to show, with "clear and convincing" evidence, that the *Enquirer* knowingly published falsehoods or acted with reckless disregard for the truth.

The *Enquirer* continued to build its case over the following months, methodically. Reporters rented a cottage in the gated community in North Carolina where they were told Hunter was staying. They'd heard she was pregnant with Edwards's child. The tabloid staked out the offices of nearby obstetricians for weeks. It worked: The *Enquirer* got a photograph of Hunter entering her doctor's office for an appointment. The love-child story ran in December 2007. Edwards again denied it. His ex–campaign aide Andrew Young claimed paternity.

Edwards withdrew from the presidential race in January 2008, having failed to gain purchase with voters in a competition that also included the rising star of the Democratic Party, Barack Obama, and one of its most recognizable faces, Hillary Clinton. But the *Enquirer* wasn't finished with him. Edwards's wife, Elizabeth, had announced in March 2007 that her cancer was terminal, but she was still battling it in July 2008, when reporters confronted Edwards as he tried to secretly visit Hunter at the Beverly Hilton hotel in Los Angeles. Refusing to answer their questions, Edwards fled to a bathroom in the hotel, where he hid until security personnel arrived and escorted him safely away from the muckrakers.

The tabloid revealed in its July story that Hunter had received "tens of thousands of dollars in hush money" from one of Edwards's wealthy political supporters. The next week, on August 6, the *Enquirer* published a photograph of Edwards playing with his baby at the Los Angeles hotel. Two days later, Edwards came clean about the affair in an

ABC interview, but he continued to deny paternity for another two months.

The *Enquirer*'s reporting annihilated Edwards's reputation and his standing on the national stage. The mainstream media took note— unaware, of course, that only a year earlier Pecker had short-circuited an investigation of what might have been another monster story, about the philandering Tiger Woods. The twin episodes showed that the *Enquirer* remained a powerful force no matter how it directed its resources—whether for journalism or to serve the aims of its CEO.

By 2009, DAVID Pecker and American Media had been defying predictions of their imminent financial death for two years. Pecker had finagled extensions and lifelines from banks and bondholders to avoid default. Early that year, he managed to (a) convince his investors to take a massive haircut; (b) convert bondholders into shareholders, relieving some of the debt pressure; and (c) keep his job as chief executive.

The bailout agreement reduced the company's debt by about $230 million. Evercore Partners, Roger Altman's New York investment firm, saw most of its 20 percent stake in the company wiped out. The company's largest shareholder, Thomas H. Lee Partners, had owned 59 percent of American Media—its $299 million investment was essentially written off, too. The company's bondholders became American Media's new owners, with control over a seven-member board.

American Media was still making money, and in some cases outperforming its peers racked by the same forces. The *Enquirer* in November 2009 proved its worth as a scandal sheet, again, by shattering the image of Tiger Woods as an off-the-course role model. Three years earlier, the tabloid had traded away a potential story, based on grainy photos taken at night and a used tampon, about Woods's alleged fling with a Perkins waitress. But now it had multiple sources confirming Woods's affair with another woman, a New York nightclub hostess named Rachel Uchitel. One of the sources, who said she was a friend of Uchitel's, had spoken to the *Enquirer* on the record. After reading the tabloid's report, Woods's wife, Elin Nordegren, had taken her husband's phone and found all the evidence she needed. On Thanksgiving night, Nordegren chased him outside of the house with a golf club.

Woods, woozy from sleeping pills and painkillers, crashed his Escalade into a fire hydrant while trying to escape. Soon, many other women came forward.

But the *Enquirer*'s scoop wasn't enough to reverse industry trends. Publishers were suffering from multiple chronic conditions: declining readership and advertising, increased competition, and the paradigm-shifting technology feeding all three problems: the Internet. The bailout agreement with bondholders gave Pecker some breathing room, but not much. "We can manage, we can compete, we don't have guns to our heads," he told *Crain's*. "I can't ask for anything more."

PECKER'S PROMISE TO transform the *Enquirer* into a more serious news organization had long ago given way to the financial realities of the industry. While the tabloid was sued less often, the *Enquirer* was still in the habit of fat-shaming and gay-shaming celebrities. It knew its audience and what would sell. But the tabloid enjoyed moments of mainstream glory, those investigations that reminded the snobs that tabloid reporters could occasionally also be real journalists with grit and ingenuity rivaling that of any of their peers in the news business.

In early 2010, the administrator of the Pulitzer Prize, the most prestigious award in newspaper journalism, admitted the tabloid into the annual competition for its coverage of the John Edwards scandal. Qualifying was no small thing. The *Enquirer* paid sources, something that was verboten at American newspapers, though not necessarily a barrier to entry into prize consideration. The larger question was whether the tabloid was a newspaper or a magazine; magazines weren't permitted to compete for the prizes yet. The *Enquirer* had alternately referred to itself as both over the years.

Though Pecker had initially been lukewarm on the Edwards story, he came to appreciate it. When the awards were announced in the spring, the *Enquirer* wasn't among the winners. It didn't even rate as a finalist. But its Edwards reporting continued to raise the tabloid's profile and esteem.

About a year after the winners were named, Edwards was charged, in a federal indictment, with accepting and failing to report hundreds of thousands of dollars in campaign contributions from two donors—money he had diverted to conceal his affair with Rielle Hunter. The tabloid, a scrappy outsider—something Pecker also fancied himself to be—had driven coverage of a serious story and commanded mainstream respect.

If Pecker needed more bucking up, his alma mater, Pace University, saw fit to bestow the executive with an award, naming him a Leader in Management. CNBC's Maria Bartiromo presided as master of ceremonies. Trump presented Pecker with the award. Pecker had joined the university's board of trustees and given lectures in the business school. His pearls of wisdom to students included "Never make your boss look bad" and "Have a work/life balance, but business must be a priority."

There was no question where Pecker's priorities lay. He kept to a work schedule that left little time for life as the financial crisis compounded his company's problems. American Media was still generating cash, but much of it was swallowed by interest payments on the company's still massive debt. Pecker tried to get his bondholders to go along with another debt-for-equity swap, as he had the previous year. It was either that or bankruptcy. Ultimately, the company couldn't rally its bankers and bondholders around a deal. American Media filed for bankruptcy in November 2010, exiting quickly with $355 million shaved from its debt. The company still owed about half a billion dollars that Pecker would add to and shuffle for years to come.

11.

MOMMY XXX

■　■　■

IN NOVEMBER 2010, Stormy Daniels received an intriguing email from a former porn actress. The woman, Gina Rodriguez, had recently left the business and reinvented herself as a talent agent with an unusual niche: representing former mistresses of famous men like Tiger Woods and helping them monetize their brushes with fame.

Rodriguez was also pursuing other projects. She told Daniels she was searching for actresses to fill out the cast of a reality show about the adult industry, tentatively titled *Adult Life*. The producers had already selected two of her clients and were looking for three more porn stars to round out the show. Daniels, a new mother who wrote, directed, and starred in porn movies, was an ideal candidate, Rodriguez said.

"I think you are the perfect person to show how far one can go in this industry," Rodriguez wrote in an email.

Daniels expressed immediate interest. She signed a talent agreement with the *Adult Life* producers in early 2011, with Rodriguez as her agent.

That same month, ABC News aired a feature on Rodriguez, describing her as "a queen of scandal." At the time she was representing Michelle McGee, the tattoo artist whose fling with Jesse James led to the collapse of his marriage to actress Sandra Bullock.

"What is this business?" asked ABC News's Neal Karlinsky.

"I'm managing the mistresses and all the people of scandal," Rodriguez said.

"What does that mean exactly?"

"I've taken these girls that were involved in these sex scandals and built them a career on their own."

The producers of *Adult Life* failed to find a buyer, but Rodriguez's mistress managing had given Daniels another idea. It was the start of an off-again, on-again relationship with Rodriguez that would last for years.

GINA RODRIGUEZ CAME to porn later than most women who enter the industry, as a mother of two in her late thirties. The business—and its stigma—had worn her down quickly and left her feeling soulless. Her heart sank when her own mother found out early on, sending her an email with her porn name in the subject line. On her block, neighbors posted flyers with pictures of her at a porn convention. Other parents didn't allow their children to come over. Her son had to be homeschooled because of harassment from students who put her pictures on his desk.

Born in November 1967, Rodriguez had been raised in the San Fernando Valley by her mother, Joyce, a woman of Italian descent who worked in life insurance. She barely knew her biological father, Michael "Micky" Anthony Delia Jr., a member of the Mexican Mafia who had opened a halfway house and been convicted of several murders. She met him when she was twenty-three years old. She was known as Gina Dice, after her adoptive father, Donald Oliver Dice, until she married.

As a younger woman, she studied acting, modeled for *Playboy* in 1992, and appeared in a couple of episodes of *Baywatch*. But her acting career stalled, and she began modeling and dancing in strip clubs. She'd been raising a son, Chris, and a daughter, Brandi, from her first husband, Richard Snail, who worked in movie and television production as "head of greens," which meant that he was responsible for the flora that appear on set. After a bankruptcy and a divorce, she married Rod Rodriguez, a veteran of the Los Angeles Police Department's elite Special Investigation Section who'd worked on the cop procedural *Robbery Homicide Division*. She showed up in an episode of that show, too. She had an affair and they divorced in 2002, but she held on to his name.

Rodriguez had gone to beauty school in 1987 and opened up a couple of salons in the early 2000s, in a desert suburb of Los Angeles and in Thousand Oaks, with hairstylists, tanning beds, a massage therapist, skin care specialists, and doctors applying Botox. She didn't believe it when a friend said one of her regular customers at Studio Tan was Randy Spears, one of the most prolific actors in adult films, with more than a thousand credits to his name.

"No," Rodriguez replied. "That's Greg." When her friend came in and slapped down a pornographic DVD with his picture on it, she knew it was true: Greg Deuschle was Randy Spears.

Rodriguez and Deuschle began dating, and soon they moved in together. Deuschle, now producing adult films, was planning to shoot a scene in their house. Rodriguez was not totally comfortable with him having sex with another woman under her roof, so she suggested that she perform the scene with him. With her long brown hair, caramel skin, and buxom figure, Rodriguez seemed like a natural for the role. So at thirty-seven years old, in 2005, she shot her first porn film as Demi Delia. As a newcomer in her late thirties, Rodriguez specialized in the "MILF" genre, starring in such titles as *My Friend's Hot Mom 8*. It seemed easy enough at first. By the time she celebrated her fortieth birthday, she had appeared in fifty adult movies.

Then a new opportunity came along.

Some producers were looking to make a reality show about children raised by parents in the adult film industry. An adult film actors' agency recommended three candidates who had children. Rodriguez was the most articulate and had the best personality, the producers thought. She was also a dedicated mother, and she didn't demand a lot of money. They settled on her, and Sony Crackle bought the project, committing to thirteen webisodes of a show they were calling *Growing Up X*. Before it aired in June 2009, a Sony executive changed the title to *Mommy XXX*.

In one episode, "Boob Job #11," Rodriguez's kids complained about her latest breast implants and discussed what her next ones would look like. After having her surgery filmed, she returned with her bandaged breasts to a giant WELCOME HOME sign that her son had made. "Get well soon," it said, with little dots transforming the two O's into a pair of boobs. "I don't look like a freak show," she said, as if trying to convince herself. In the roughly five-minute episodes, she received visits from her ex-husbands and her porn agent, harangued another actor to bring her a bagel, showed off her new website, and complained about neck pain after shooting a sex scene.

Rodriguez's children were the stars of her show. In "Female Parts," she brought her daughter, Brandi, who had begun dating, for a first visit to the gynecologist. Rodriguez bristled when the doctor implied that because she slept with men on camera, she was encouraging her daughter to have sex at a young age. Chris, a musician and a vegan with multiple piercings, offered a straight-faced, unrelenting critique of his mother's industry. "Porn stars are just disgusting people. They have no morals," Chris said. "I mean, I can speak—you know, *I know*. I've seen 'em all the time. They're just nasty. They carry diseases. We had an Easter party—they were having sex in the backyard."

Said Rodriguez: "They're not happy with the way I'm living my life right now."

The show was popular and did well, and a planned second season was to document Rodriguez's exit from the porn industry. Though it contained no nudity, the title that the Sony executive had given it led many people to think it was actually a porn project. Advertisers shunned it, and Sony didn't renew.

As *Mommy XXX* faded away, Rodriguez found new work. While watching television in late 2009, she learned that the porn actress Joslyn James had been publicly identified as one of eleven mistresses of golfing legend Tiger Woods. James, who had starred in *Gazongas 7* and other films—including, later, *The 11th Hole*—alleged she'd had a long-running affair with Woods. Rodriguez phoned her and said she could help. She flew James from Las Vegas to Rodriguez's home and drove her directly to the office of Gloria Allred, the media-friendly Los Angeles lawyer known for representing women who alleged that they'd been victimized. Rodriguez had known Allred since 1999, when the lawyer's office represented her in making a settlement with AT&T after a manager allegedly exposed himself to her.

In her new role, Rodriguez helped score James a big payday with an interview on *Inside Edition* and promoted her strip club appearance at the Pink Pony in Atlanta. To attract maximum attention, Rodriguez scheduled James's Pink Pony show to coincide with Woods's April 2010 return to the professional golf tour after a five-month layoff due to the sex scandal.

After Joslyn James, other Woods mistresses came to Rodriguez for help.

She realized she had discovered a niche. There was a market for publicizing women, and a few men, who had been thrust into the spotlight as the lovers of A-through-D-list celebrities. They could capitalize on their fifteen minutes of fame by appealing to the same public fascination with gossip that drove tabloid news, making their own celebrity sex tapes, public appearances naked or clothed, calendars, cosmetics, books, and the like. Rodriguez saw herself as a maternal figure to the women who sought her out. She wasn't exploiting them; the press had already done that. She was the net, catching them during their fall and empowering them to turn difficult circumstances to their own advantage. And after empowering them, Rodriguez would take 20 percent.

Her attempts at acting, running beauty salons, and appearing in porn had played themselves out, but Rodriguez had found a new and promising career arc that suited her. She understood these women, and she had the business sense and strategic vision to help them take advantage of their sordid experiences.

Another early client, Jessie Lunderby, was a twenty-one-year-old Arkansas jail worker who was put on leave after posing nude for Playboy.com. Rodriguez also represented the alleged mistresses of actor Mel Gibson and of Sandra Bullock's husband, and the boyfriend of Snooki from *Jersey Shore*.

Rodriguez had formally launched her talent agency as DD Entertainment, a reference to her porn name. That summer, she brought a collection of her mistress clients, calling them the "Girls of the Hottest Scandals of 2010," to Exxxtacy, an adult entertainment convention near Chicago's O'Hare airport. Then there was Mistresses Makeover Day, a collaboration with a plastic surgeon. Rodriguez negotiated free or discounted procedures in exchange for giving the doctor publicity. She thought it would help the women to have a fresh start with new and improved breasts, a slimmer nose, or tighter skin.

Rodriguez also recently had forged a bond with Michael Lohan, the father of actress Lindsay Lohan, who for years had been a target of tabloid stories about her substance abuse and family drama. On Facebook, Rodriguez messaged Lohan's father, whose brushes with the law and conflicts with his ex-wife, Dina, Lindsay's mother, made him a tabloid magnet as well.

BY CHANCE, RODRIGUEZ encountered a kindred spirit in 2010, a Beverly Hills lawyer who had built a practice that complemented her scandal business. She was picking up a check at Flash City, a West Hollywood photo agency, when the owners introduced her to another client, Keith Davidson. Now that Rodriguez was representing talent in the industry, she should get to know Davidson, an entertainment attorney with connections at TMZ and other gossip enterprises, they told her.

While Rodriguez tried to maximize the exposure of her mistress clients, Davidson tended toward quieter solutions. He represented clients who were in possession of dirt on celebrities, like sex tapes, embarrassing photos, or evidence of marital infidelity. Davidson helped his clients convert their information into cash, often selling the dirt to the celebrities themselves. His clients got paid and signed nondisclosure agreements, legally binding them to silence and preventing them from disclosing their dirt. The celebrities were spared embarrassment. Everybody won.

Rodriguez and Davidson exchanged numbers, and soon she was using him as her attorney for client contracts. Over time, she steered other work his way, including the small matter of a porn star who said she had slept with Donald Trump.

THE CIRCLES THAT celebrity scandal brokers operate in are surprisingly small. Davidson also found some business courtesy of the Lohan family at the end of 2010.

His client was Dawn Holland, an employee at the Betty Ford Center who had allegedly caught Lindsay Lohan and another patient sneaking back into the rehab clinic after curfew, reeking of booze. Holland claimed Lohan had pushed her and that when she called police, Lohan tried to grab the phone out of her hand, injuring her arm and wrist.

It was a messy situation, which Davidson had to navigate delicately. That was typical for his business. An editor at *TMZ* had let Davidson know about Holland. She hired him and told her story to *TMZ*, which paid her $10,000 through the attorney's client trust account. Betty Ford promptly fired her for violating patient confidentiality. Lohan, meanwhile, contended that Holland was the aggressor.

In the background, Davidson tried to arrange a deal with the Lohans, telling Holland that the celebrity and her family would likely pay huge sums if, in return, the clinic worker declined to cooperate with the Riverside County District Attorney's Office, which was investigating the incident. He said Holland was withdrawing the complaint she'd made to police and said she wouldn't press charges. Davidson often had to play to both sides to broker a settlement, catering to his client and selling a deal to his celebrity adversary. But in this case, the strategy didn't work. Holland, regretting the whole incident and the loss of her job, fired Davidson and hired another lawyer.

This wasn't the kind of law that Davidson had planned to practice when he started out. That he'd become a lawyer in the first place, let alone in Beverly Hills, had been a highly improbable eventuality, given his childhood on the outskirts of Boston. The expectations for Davidson's life had been epitomized by a moment in high school that had seared itself into his brain. He was in the car with his father, a firefighter, when the subject of his future came up. Davidson had harbored ambitions of a different sort of life, but his father urged him to go into firefighting, as several generations of their family had.

"You're not smart enough to go to college," his dad said.

Davidson had been born in April 1971 and grown up in Brockton, Massachusetts, a small city twenty miles south of Boston, along the Salisbury Plain River. Brockton schools regularly turned out great athletes; it claimed its fame as the home of boxers Rocky Marciano and Marvin Hagler. Thus Brockton's nickname, "City of Champions."

For a time, Davidson's family lived above a convenience store and he'd get woken up by early-morning milk deliveries. At Boston College, he couldn't afford a dorm room, so a friend let him bunk for free. Davidson, whose aunt was a nun, had an inclination toward public service. After his college graduation, in 1994, he went to work for the Massachusetts Legislature and as the community education coordinator for the Plymouth County District Attorney's Office.

Soon he left the cold New England winters behind, enrolling at Whittier Law School, in Costa Mesa, California, south of Los Angeles. The school was known for enrolling an ethnically diverse cross section of students who might not otherwise have had the opportunity to go to law school. Though many later struggled to land legal jobs and found themselves drowning in debt, Whittier had turned out some successes as well, including judges and a popular talk radio host.

Davidson fell in love with the warm climate and the flash of the L.A. lifestyle. He stayed in California, living as a young lawyer in the Hollywood Hills, and began his legal career with an assortment of cases, tilting toward representation of the less powerful. His aunt, the nun, had written him a letter reminding him not to forget the plight of the poor. He represented the interests of children who said they had been molested and plaintiffs who claimed that doctors had injured them in medical malpractice suits. Among his proudest moments was winning an acquittal for Lana Vasquez, a young woman who'd been charged with murder. Vasquez's mother paid Davidson in rolls of quarters.

Through a friend, Davidson met Freddie Roach, the legendary boxing trainer who hailed from a Boston suburb near Brockton and who worked with the Filipino fighter Manny Pacquiao, a young national hero in his beleaguered country. Davidson helped with legal advice when Pacquiao was unhappy with his Filipino managers, then ultimately joined Shelly Finkel and Nick Khan in replacing them. Besides making fight deals, he lived for a time in the fast-paced world of the boxing circuit. Davidson spent time at Roach's Wild Card Boxing gym in Hollywood, dined with Pacquiao in Las Vegas and Manila, and traveled with him by plane and Mercedes-Benz. Within two years, by the end of 2006, the mercurial boxer, ever juggling his handlers, had cut Davidson and his staff loose.

Davidson was already moving on to a new and potentially lucrative arena: peddling dirt on celebrities from his office on Wilshire Boulevard in Beverly Hills. He began to secure six- and seven-figure payments for their stories and materials—sex tapes, tales of tawdry affairs with prostitutes or porn stars, adultery, and more.

There was only a small crop of lawyers who handled such matters, leaving a wide-open market for Davidson. Some lawyers generally represented the celebrity in question, while others, like Davidson, usually signed up the person who had the dirt. Davidson found that he had a talent for navigating the complicated issues that arose in such circumstances and finding a path to a creative resolution. Plus, the work was exciting and fun.

The value of the case, Davidson came to see, resided in the potential damage to the celebrity that exposure might cause. Usually he'd first try to reach a "settlement" with the person about whom a client had compromising information, offering contractual silence in return for money. Or Davidson would sell his client's story and supporting evidence to the highest bidder among his network of contacts at celebrity publications that wrote checks to sources. It was work balanced on the knife's edge of legality. Davidson became, in his own estimation, one of the country's foremost experts on the laws surrounding extortion.

"Some lawyers are black-and-white," he'd say. "I think there's a niche for the gray." Davidson and his associates weren't giving celebrities an ultimatum by offering to help keep materials out of the press. They were offering these big shots a favor. (On more than one occasion, the materials that stars had paid to keep suppressed eventually came to light anyway.)

In one of his early deals, Davidson represented a mysterious client who he said owned the material, a trove of scandalous items that hotel heiress Paris Hilton had kept in a storage locker. The locker had contained Hilton's diaries, sexy videos, naked photos, and medical and financial records, all of which were auctioned off by the storage facility over an unpaid bill for $208. Davidson went looking for buyers.

Hilton's materials showed up online in 2007 on a website called *Paris Exposed*, which offered viewers the chance to view her private, intimate records for a fee. The site's operators were hidden behind an offshore domain registration and post office box. Though it was shut down after Hilton's lawyers obtained a court order, the site popped up again. The registrant this time was a shell company created in St. Kitts that was represented by Davidson.

Davidson wasn't shy about his profiteering, though he knew that too much greed could make a person sloppy. "Pigs get fed," he liked to say. "Hogs get slaughtered." But his penchant for walking on lines other lawyers stayed miles away from caught up to him in 2010. Davidson received a ninety-day suspension of his law license by the California State Bar for several client-related lapses. Among them: He deposited $750 a man had paid him to evaluate medical records into his general bank account rather than a client trust account, which was against strict rules about commingling funds, though he'd refunded the money. The light suspension was based on his clean record and cooperation and the character evidence he presented.

Work nonetheless kept coming in, and controversy followed. Davidson signed up musician Francis Falls, the ex-boyfriend of Tila Tequila, the model and reality star. Again there was a sex tape. In a lawsuit, Tequila accused Davidson of threatening to sell the tape overseas if she didn't cooperate in marketing it. She had refused to play ball. Davidson, denying the threat, then offered to give her the tape's copyright, which he said he'd obtained, in exchange for dismissal of the lawsuit and—in light of his recent suspension—settlement language protecting him from any allegation that he'd committed an ethical violation. They reached an agreement, keeping the terms confidential.

His next client would introduce a steady income stream from possibly the most lucrative celebrity target in the history of Hollywood gossipmongering: Charlie Sheen, known for partying with prostitutes and for his drug-addled outbursts. Capri Anderson, a twenty-two-year-old porn actress, had alleged that after a dinner in New York in late 2010, the star had melted down in his room at the Plaza Hotel, throwing a lamp after she asked him to stop choking her during a sexual encounter. She was found naked, locked in a bathroom. Sheen ended up at a hospital for a psychiatric evaluation.

Upon Anderson's return to Los Angeles, she retained Davidson. A month later, after discussions with Sheen went nowhere—she said he'd offered $20,000 via text message to keep quiet—Anderson and Davidson were interviewed together on *Good Morning America*. By then, Sheen and his representatives had begun suggesting that Anderson had concocted the episode for a payday.

"She's a victim of abuse at the hands of a very rich and powerful man," Davidson told George Stephanopoulos, promising a civil lawsuit.

But it was Sheen who struck first in court, accusing Anderson in a lawsuit of attempting to extort $1 million from him to remain silent. He also claimed she'd stolen a $165,000 Patek Philippe watch. Within a year, Sheen dropped the case.

As THEY DID with the Lohans, Davidson and the agent Gina Rodriguez shared a business connection to Charlie Sheen. After Davidson represented Capri Anderson, who never ended up suing Sheen and quietly settled his extortion lawsuit, Rodriguez took her on as a client, booking media appearances for the adult actress.

In the coming years, the agent and the lawyer would sometimes work for the same clients, as with Anderson, and sometimes not, as with the Lohans, where they were on opposite sides. For Davidson and Rodriguez, the lines of loyalty fluctuated. There were clients to be represented; and then there were professional relationships to be maintained; and then there was money. It all bled together. Sheen's ongoing antics would bring other clients Davidson's way, some of whom Rodriguez also assisted. Rodriguez picked up new clients herself, steering the media career of Nadya Suleman, who gave birth to octuplets and posed topless before declaring bankruptcy. She would bring Davidson new clients as well.

One of these clients, before too long, would be Stormy Daniels.

For on the other side of the country, in New York, Donald Trump had begun making noise, in 2011, about parlaying his *Apprentice* fame into a run for the presidency. As word of Trump's ambitions spread, Rodriguez would link up with Daniels again and learn of another potential opportunity.

12.

SHOULDTRUMPRUN.COM

■ ■ ■

IT HAD BEEN eleven years since Donald Trump first made a public show of considering a presidential run. But he'd maintained a voice in national affairs, through his media appearances and regular riffs on politics and pop culture that aired on hundreds of Clear Channel Communications stations under the name *Trumped!* A couple of years earlier, he'd even devoted one of his ninety-second radio segments to speculation about a "dream ticket" of Barack Obama and Hillary Clinton as they jockeyed in the Democratic primary in 2008.

"Well, I know her, and she'd make a good president or good vice president," Trump had declared of Clinton.

In October 2010, *Time* magazine published an online story about a mysterious telephone poll of New Hampshire voters that sought to test Donald Trump's appeal as a presidential candidate. The poll asked participants whether, for instance, they knew that Trump had made political donations to Democrats in the past and whether they thought his television celebrity would help or hamper him in a political race. *Time* couldn't determine who had sanctioned the poll or how Trump had fared among potential voters.

Trump said he didn't know who'd conducted the poll. Some pundits speculated that billionaire Michael Bloomberg, the mayor of New York City, was behind it, using Trump's political shape-shifting as a proxy for his own so that Bloomberg could gauge his own potential as a candidate.

Whatever the case, Michael Cohen saw the poll as an opportunity. He'd regained some of his standing with the boss, but Cohen was still eager to make himself useful. When he learned of the *Time* story, Cohen took it to Trump.

What if Trump did run? "Wouldn't that be something?" Cohen asked.

At first, Trump seemed hesitant. On October 4, the day after the *Time* report appeared, Trump filibustered when asked about his presidential aspirations. "It's not something I talked about or consider, but somebody has to do something or this country is not going to be a very great country for long," he said in a CNN interview.

By the following day, he had apparently changed his thinking.

"So are you going to make the run?" Fox News host Gretchen Carlson asked.

"Well, you know, for the first time in my life, I'm actually thinking about it," Trump said, casually omitting his very public White House contemplations in 1988 and 1999.

When Carlson mentioned his near candidacy in 1999, under the flag of the Reform Party, he said, "First time I am being serious about it. I've been asked for years to do it. And I had no interest," Trump lied.

Encouraged by Trump's response to the buzz about his potential candidacy, Cohen teamed up with Stewart Rahr, a friend of Trump's who was also known as Stewie Rah Rah. Rahr, a pharmaceutical billionaire, had gotten the nickname after he divorced his wife in a midlife crisis and began appearing in the gossip pages wearing colored sunglasses and dating young models.

Rahr and Cohen hired one of Mr. Cohen's friends to set up a website called ShouldTrumpRun.com, using their own money. "JOIN THE MOVEMENT," read a banner on the home page.

Cohen turned to David Pecker for help spreading the word. Pecker and Cohen had developed a relationship over the years that was independent of Trump's bond with the tabloid chieftain. They had dealt with one another so often in business and social matters that they couldn't agree on how they'd met. Pecker told people they'd been introduced by a furniture company executive at a bar mitzvah. Cohen thought they'd become acquainted through mutual friends.

Beginning in November 2010, the tabloid produced a series of increasingly obsequious stories hyping Trump's unofficial candidacy and directing readers to Cohen's website. The tabloid gushed about "the amazing groundswell of support emerging across America" for Trump and quoted Cohen as calling Trump a "self-made man and one of the worlds [*sic*] most successful businessmen in history."

Trump wasn't a natural Republican. He had, for example, expressed support for abortion rights in the past, but now, as he courted support for his run, Trump switched sides in the debate, casting himself as antiabortion. When a skeptical reporter asked about his change of heart, Cohen explained, "People change their positions all the time, the way they change their wives."

In March 2011, Cohen flew on Trump's private jet to Iowa, the first state to hold a vote in the presidential primary season, to explore the possibility of a Trump candidacy. He met with the state Republican Party chairman in Des Moines. Cohen said he talked with more than a dozen other GOP operatives, grassroots organizers, and finance officials.

"Every one of them expressed not just an interest but a fervent desire to see somebody like Donald Trump join the race in hopes that we can turn this country around," he told reporters.

Trump bragged that Cohen had been swamped by supporters during the trip.

Days later, an aide to libertarian Ron Paul, who was vying for the Republican presidential nomination, filed a complaint with the Federal Election Commission alleging that Cohen's Iowa trip violated restrictions on campaign contributions. The complaint said that Rahr, who had paid about $125,000 to cover the cost of the flight on Trump's jet, had given Trump an excessive campaign contribution. Individuals could contribute no more than $2,500. Cohen's work on the website and in Iowa was also illegal, the complaint said, if he had done it as part of his job at the Trump Organization. (Cohen said that he was promoting a potential Trump run in a personal capacity, independent of Trump.) Though Trump hadn't formally announced, he was "testing the waters" and bound by the same laws as a candidate, according to the complaint.

FEC staff later recommended that the agency pursue the matter, but the commissioners split along party lines—as usual—with Republican members voting against a full investigation. The commission's vice chairman, Don McGahn, chastised FEC staff for spending too much time on the probe.

• • •

SOON AFTER COHEN's return from Iowa, he and Trump descended an escalator into the atrium of Trump Tower, where a scrum of reporters waited for news of the businessman's political intentions. But it was a bait and switch.

"Good afternoon, everybody. My name is Michael Cohen. I'm an executive at the Trump Organization," Cohen said. "Seven months ago, at the request of a dear friend of mine, Giorgi Rtskhiladze, I traveled to the Republic of Georgia to explore several real estate opportunities on behalf of Mr. Trump."

Cohen then introduced President Mikheil Saakashvili of Georgia, and George Ramishvili, the chief executive of an oil transportation company called Silk Road Group. The company, made up of layers of far-flung subsidiaries, had begun branching out into the hospitality industry. Cohen had negotiated an agreement to license Trump's name to a new tower in Batumi, a Georgian city on the Black Sea. It was thoroughly Cohen's baby, and the news conference, featuring a head of state, signaled his improved standing with Trump. It was also a perfect way to parlay press interest in Trump's political future into business gain.

Trump would receive a million dollars to slap his name on the tower, even if it never got built. (It never got built, but Trump moved Cohen soon after the announcement from a small office with no windows to a larger one overlooking Fifth Avenue.)

Reporters were less interested in the project than in Trump's political aspirations. "Mr. Saakashvili, do you think Mr. Trump should consider running for president?" one reporter asked the foreign head of state.

"That's totally up to him. I mean, it's none of my business. If he decides to run for president in Georgia, he might win, I don't know," Saakashvili said.

Trump at first declined to discuss Cohen's trip to Iowa, but he couldn't help himself when a reporter asked whether he was encouraged by the response to Cohen's visit.

"Well, I certainly was. I mean, the response has been amazing, actually," Trump said.

The *Enquirer* dutifully reported the Georgian president's visit to Trump Tower, falsely stating that "the *Celebrity Apprentice* boss is investing $300 million to build a residential tower and a luxury hotel as part of Georgia's effort to bring tourists and businesses to the former communist country." Cohen was the source for the article.

In fact, Trump wasn't investing any of his own money, but he and Cohen hoped the Batumi tower was just the first of several licensing deals in the country.

"You see what's happened with the Republic of Georgia and you see what's happening to our country. You see what can be done with proper leadership," Trump told the tabloid.

TRUMP BEGAN TWEAKING his message after the news conference. He continued to harp on China and unfair trade practices. Still years away from coining his trademark campaign slogan, he complained that America was no longer great. And he now questioned whether the country's first black president had been born in the United States, as required by the Constitution, injecting new life into a conspiracy theory that carried more than a whiff of racism.

Trump revealed himself as a member of the "birther" movement in an interview with *Good Morning America* that aired on March 17, 2011, in which he wondered why details about Barack Obama's childhood in Hawaii were so scarce.

"The reason I have a little doubt, just a little, is because he grew up and nobody knew him," Trump said, falsely. Many Hawaiians had publicly described encountering Obama in his younger years, and Obama had released his short-form birth certificate.

Trump wasn't the first to hoist the far-right conspiracy theory into the mainstream, but he quickly became its most prominent purveyor. He found an eager audience among Obama's detractors. Many Republican leaders remained silent or declined to forcefully condemn a narrative that undercut Obama's legitimacy. It seemed to work: By April 2011, Trump was polling in second place behind Mitt Romney among potential Republican presidential candidates.

As Trump always had done when he found a message that resonated, he turned up the volume.

"I would like to have him show his birth certificate, and can I be honest with you, I hope he can. Because if he can't, if he can't, if he wasn't born in this country, which is a real possibility . . . then he has pulled one of the great cons in the history of politics," Trump said in an April 7 interview with NBC's *Today*.

Trump suggested that he had investigators searching for proof of Obama's birthplace, another falsehood. "They cannot believe what they're finding," he said.

The *National Enquirer* pounced on his comments. "Media mogul and White House hopeful DONALD TRUMP has hired a team of detectives to dig deep in the archives to prove that Barack Obama was not born in the United States and would be then ineligible to be President," the tabloid reported.

The *Enquirer*'s sister publication, the even more conspiracy-minded *Globe,* was fully invested in Trump's birther narrative. "OBAMA'S MELTDOWN OVER TRUMP" read one banner headline on *Globe*'s front page. "PRES TERRIFIED OF WHAT 'THE DONALD' HAS UNCOVERED." The story claimed that Obama had enlisted Oprah Winfrey to persuade Trump to drop his investigation of Obama's birthplace.

Enquirer editor Barry Levine dispatched one veteran reporter, Rick Egusquiza, to Hawaii, but his assignment had nothing to do with Trump's adopted conspiracy theory. Egusquiza was searching for dirt on Obama after one of his longtime friends, Robert Titcomb, was swept up in a prostitution sting. He found none. The reporter returned with photos of Obama as a child in Hawaii that he'd found at an apartment complex where Obama's grandmother once lived. The photos included one of Obama in a pirate costume.

With Trump stoking the birther movement, Obama released his long-form birth certificate in late April, announcing the move in a televised speech in the White House briefing room. His reelection campaign ramping up, Obama used the occasion to sharpen the contrast between himself and his opponents.

"We're not going to be able to solve our problems if we get distracted by sideshows and carnival barkers," he said, taking a dig at the celebrity businessman without using his name.

Obama wouldn't be as subtle the next time he addressed Trump.

The *Enquirer* spun the president's announcement as a capitulation to its favorite presidential hopeful, with a story headlined "TRUMP FINALLY GETS OBAMA TO RELEASE BIRTH CERTIFICATE."

. . .

A FEW DAYS after Obama's White House address, Trump was the guest of Lally Weymouth, the daughter of *Washington Post* publisher Katharine Graham, at the annual White House Correspondents' Dinner, a black-tie event where journalists mingled with their celebrity guests. The president usually attended and was expected to perform something like a comedy routine, poking fun at himself, his adversaries, and the press.

Obama used part of his routine to torch Trump.

"Now, I know that he's taken some flak lately, but no one is happier, no one is prouder, to put this birth certificate matter to rest than the Donald," Obama said. "And that's because he can finally get back to focusing on the issues that matter, like: Did we fake the moon landing? What really happened in Roswell? And where are Biggie and Tupac?" Obama deadpanned.

He was just warming up: "We all know about your credentials and breadth of experience. For example—no, seriously—just recently, in an episode of *Celebrity Apprentice*—at the steakhouse, the men's cooking team did not impress the judges from Omaha Steaks. And there was a lot of blame to go around. But you, Mr. Trump, recognized that the real problem was a lack of leadership. And so ultimately, you didn't blame Lil Jon or Meat Loaf. You fired Gary Busey. And these are the kind of decisions that would keep me up at night. Well handled, sir. Well handled."

As Obama joked, a team of Navy SEALs, on his orders, was preparing for a mission to kill Osama bin Laden.

Trump absorbed Obama's slights, smiling and waving. But then comedian Seth Meyers of *Saturday Night Live* took the stage. His jokes about Trump were sharper, and they appeared to draw blood. Trump sat stone-faced as Meyers quipped, "Donald Trump has been saying that he will run for president as a Republican—which is surprising, since I just assumed he was running as a joke."

Meyers made fun of Trump's Miss USA pageant and confronted him over the current of racism that ran through the birther movement. "Donald Trump said recently he has a great relationship with 'the blacks.' Though unless the Blacks are a family of white people, I bet he's mistaken."

Trump didn't laugh. When reporters asked him for his reaction after the routines, Trump said he felt honored to have been roasted by the president. He then left for the airport, skipping the after-parties.

Trump's elevated profile caught the notice of Stormy Daniels, who hadn't forgotten about his failure to follow through on a promise to put her on *The Apprentice*. She had slept with him seeing a business opportunity. Still, she felt used, and she wondered if Trump's celebrity might be worth something to her, too.

13.

STEPHANIE FROM
WICKED PICTURES

■ ■ ■

THE GIRL WITH the purple Camaro changed Stephanie Gregory's life.

She was seventeen, attending high school in Baton Rouge, Louisiana, and living with her boyfriend in a spare apartment with a mattress on the floor. They were out one night to see a rock concert in a local field when a nineteen-year-old named Amy pulled up in her shiny new car. Two years out of high school, she had bought it herself.

"I'm a dancer," she said, and invited Stephanie to visit her at Cinnamon's, the strip club where she worked.

Stephanie's childhood hadn't been easy. She was born in March 1979. Her father, Bill, a technician who set up control systems for industrial plants, dragged the family from one state to another as his jobs demanded when she was a kid, moving them around in a giant Suburban with his boat in tow. When the time came for her to enter school, she and her mother, Sheila, stayed at their permanent home, a ranch house in Baton Rouge, while Bill Gregory went to work in Alaska. He didn't come back for months. When he did, Gregory told his wife he was leaving her for another woman. Then he departed in the Suburban for good.

Stephanie's mother, a strawberry blonde who'd dated the actor Kurt Russell when she was younger, fell into a deep depression, chain-smoking, ignoring her daughter, and letting the house fall into disrepair. Stephanie watched Tanya Roberts, the shapely heroine of *Sheena, Queen of the Jungle,* and admired her strength and beauty. In real life, Stephanie's hair was unkempt and her clothes smelled of smoke. At a friend's house, she overheard the adults calling her white trash and predicting that she'd follow her mother's path.

She ran into the bathroom and got angry through her tears.

"Fuck them," she said into the mirror.

That became her mantra for the forces that had been and would be arrayed against her. She focused on the parts of her life that lifted her up. She bought a horse, Perfect Jade, for $500 and learned to ride. She dreamed of becoming a ballerina and learned to dance. And she focused on school, gaining entry into the Scotlandville Magnet High School, an engineering school with a focus on science and math. In high school, she also began to write, discovering her love for storytelling and her eye for detail. She took advanced placement English and became an editor of the school newspaper. She also discarded her first name, which she hated, in favor of Stormy. The new name fit her personality and had an added benefit: The bassist for Mötley Crüe, one of her favorite bands, had named his daughter Storm.

When she could no longer stand to live with her mother, she left home and moved in with her boyfriend, who tried to support them by delivering pizza. Two weeks after she stood in awe of Amy's purple Camaro, Stormy and her boyfriend were driving past Cinnamon's, Amy's strip joint, which was in a trailer. Inside, the dancers crowded around Stormy and encouraged her to dance a guest set. They dressed her up in a bustier and did her eyebrows and makeup. She was introduced as "Stephanie Stormy" and made $85 in less than ten minutes. From then on, she danced on weekend nights while finishing high school.

Eventually she moved to the Gold Club, a more upscale strip club, dancing sixty hours a week. On a trip to Cincinnati when she was seventeen, she visited her father, who still didn't know about her new career, borrowed his car, and secretly drove across the Kentucky line to dance there.

At twenty, she enlarged her breasts. The doctor made them larger than she'd asked, but she named them Thunder and Lightning and noticed an immediate increase in her tips. Soon she became a feature dancer, traveling to clubs in different cities and developing dance routines that told a story, using expensive props and sparkly outfits. Then she started modeling nude for magazine spreads, going by the name

Stormy Waters for a time. When she was twenty-three, she flew to Los Angeles with a friend and shot a girl-on-girl scene in her first adult movie, *American Girls 2*. In the film, shot at the Dry Gulch Ranch, in the Santa Monica Mountains in western Malibu, Stormy goes hiking with a friend, who sprains an ankle. Comforting her friend, of course, leads to a sex scene.

Told she could earn $15,000 a month in porn, she opted not to return to Louisiana. Instead she signed a contract with Wicked Pictures, an adult film studio, and adopted her official porn name: Stormy Daniels. She had seen a bottle of Jack Daniel's whiskey; it was a Southern favorite, and she figured she fit that bill. She'd get a new legal name as well, becoming Stephanie Clifford through a brief marriage to porn director Pat Myne, whose real name was Bart Clifford. But from then on, in movies or in real life, she called herself Stormy Daniels.

So began a career in adult movies that led to more than a hundred appearances, along with awards—she was *Adult Video News*'s Best New Starlet—and directing credits. Daniels still loved to write, and found that porn producers liked her creative story lines. She cracked the mainstream market with spots on *Real Sex,* on HBO, and cameos in *Pornucopia* and *The 40-Year-Old Virgin,* with Steve Carell. (Carell played virgin Andy Stitzer, who in one scene is watching one of Daniels's actual films, *Space Nuts,* when she appears in his bedroom.)

Even among porn industry stars, Daniels was notably unabashed about her career choice.

"I actually managed to find something that I'm good at and enjoy doing," she told a group of academic researchers in an interview in Los Angeles in June 2006, a month before the Lake Tahoe golf tournament where she met Trump. "I'm not talking about the sex—everybody likes to have sex. I'm just talking about creatively speaking. Creatively speaking, I enjoy the writing, the directing, and creating something." She added, "The money's good, and I have nice things. I set my own schedule. I could be digging ditches. I'm very lucky."

AFTER THEIR NIGHT together in Tahoe, Trump called Daniels every so often from a blocked number. She found it amusing and put him on speaker. She wanted others, including Mike Moz, her boyfriend and later husband, who also worked in the porn industry, to hear Trump calling her "honeybunch." She didn't mention to Moz that they'd had sex.

For a while, Trump maintained the illusion that he'd been trying to figure out how to get her on *The Apprentice*. She was skeptical but went along as these conversations dragged on for months.

Daniels saw Trump a few more times, though they never had sex again. In January 2007, he invited her to the launch party for Trump Vodka at Les Deux, a Hollywood club popular with celebrities. Trump kissed her on the lips and introduced her to his son, Donald Jr. Karen McDougal had also come to the party at Trump's invitation, but neither woman was aware of the other. In March, the porn star stopped up to visit him at his office in Trump Tower. He set aside tickets for her to the upcoming Miss USA pageant on March 23 at the Dolby Theatre in Los Angeles, though she didn't talk to him there.

At their final meeting, on July 29, 2007, Trump had invited Daniels to his bungalow at the Beverly Hills Hotel, on Sunset Boulevard, the same one where he would meet Karen McDougal. Moz drove her, and Keith Schiller, Trump's bodyguard, escorted her to Trump's cottage. The mogul had ordered a steak dinner, and brought up the upcoming season of *The Celebrity Apprentice*. He promised to work out her star turn. Daniels asked Trump to cut her steak for her, then he invited her to the couch to watch Shark Week.

As they cuddled, Trump sat entranced—and horrified—by *Ocean of Fear: The Worst Shark Attack Ever*. The sharks disgusted him. As they watched, Trump admitted to her that he'd been unable to get a porn star on *The Apprentice* after all. Someone had vetoed her. Finally, preparing to make his move, Trump turned his focus to her, observing that her nose resembled the beak of an eagle. As he stroked her, Daniels told him she had her period, which was a lie, and left. Moz returned to pick her up from the hotel.

Trump called a few more times, but Daniels had lost interest and stopped picking up calls from unknown numbers. One time when she did, in January 2008, Trump apologized that another porn star, Jenna Jameson, had been on his show because her boyfriend was a contestant. Daniels quickly hung up the phone.

. . .

WHILE TRUMP'S PROMISE to put her on *The Apprentice* hadn't materialized, Daniels still wanted more than porn. She toyed with politics, in the form of a run for the U.S. Senate in Louisiana, against Republican David Vitter. Vitter had become embroiled in a prostitution scandal with the "D.C. Madam" in Washington. A Democratic operative, Brian Welsh, responded to Vitter's sex scandal by launching a "Draft Stormy" campaign in 2009, recruiting political science students as volunteers and attracting considerable press. Daniels joked to reporters that she wanted *Hustler* publisher Larry Flynt to manage her bid. The campaign slogan, she said, would be "Screwing People Honestly." She launched a listening tour to big crowds, making sporadic appearances in the first half of the year.

When Welsh, who had become her campaign manager, asked her to look through her phone contacts to identify potential donors, Daniels scrolled through and picked out a daughter of Flynt, Jenna Jameson, and, eventually, Donald Trump. "He should give me some money, damn it," Daniels said. Later that day, she revealed the full story as they were driving between Lafayette and Shreveport for her second listening tour in a rented silver Chevy Malibu. She told Welsh about sleeping with Trump at a golf tournament, spanking him with a magazine that had his picture on it, and watching Shark Week. Daniels said she could understand that Trump wasn't able to get her on his show, but she was still angry because she felt that he had reneged on a promise to give her a condo. Welsh found it surreal.

Daniels, a native of Baton Rouge, had since married Mike Moz and moved to Tampa. Under federal law, she would have had to establish residency in Louisiana by the time she was elected.

Her potential candidacy had always been more about ruffling the establishment and public relations than public service, but a couple of incidents convinced her to drop the act. First, an Audi convertible belonging to Welsh went up in flames, and he speculated that someone may have tried to blow it up.

Two days later, Daniels had an altercation of her own. Though they'd been married only two years, her relationship with Moz had quickly disintegrated. Soon after she arrived at their home in Tampa, Daniels got upset that her father-in-law had done the laundry, including her undergarments, and over a bill that had come in the mail. She began throwing household items at Moz, including a plant and candles. Moz called the police and, when they arrived, said she had hit him. Daniels was arrested. The Stormy Daniels campaign was effectively over.

Moz dropped the charges, but their marriage was over, too. Even before the breakup, Daniels had begun to see someone else. She'd taken time off from her political exploration to go to Europe with Glendon Crain, a drummer for a band called Hollywood Undead. With Moz and Vitter in the past, they became serious quickly and moved to Las Vegas. Soon, Crain told her that he wanted a baby, and Daniels agreed on one condition: He had to do porn, so that if they ever split up, he couldn't use her career against her in a custody dispute. He agreed, and filmed sex scenes as Brendon Miller.

Daniels gave birth to their daughter, Caiden, in November 2010, not long before reports surfaced about the presidential ambitions of Donald Trump, who had dangled the prospect of Daniels's appearing on *The Apprentice* and failed to deliver.

As the year came to a close, Daniels was preparing for another reality show, *Adult Life,* the one Gina Rodriguez contacted her about. Rodriguez tried to get the new mother free Botox injections and laser treatment for Daniels's stretch marks, procedures Rodriguez had arranged for other clients in return for giving plastic surgeons press. But the doctor's office advised against the procedures because Daniels was nursing.

Though *Adult Life* would never get made, Daniels and Rodriguez soon were collaborating on a new project. In the spring of 2011, Daniels asked her friend Greg Deuschle, the recently retired adult film star known as Randy Spears, whether he reckoned she could monetize her five-year-old fling with Trump.

"Randy, do you think there's a story here where we could make some money?" she asked.

"Sure sounds like it to me," Deuschle responded.

Trump was famous and wealthy. He was in the news. Why not give it a try? He told Daniels to reach out to Rodriguez, who had made money for other women who had stories to tell about their affairs with famous men. Deuschle was separated from Rodriguez, but they were still close. He was living in Rodriguez's basement and helping her around the office.

Daniels then called Rodriguez, who was happy to take on the assignment.

AFTER HIS ROASTING at the correspondents' dinner in April 2011, Trump continued to bask in the buzz surrounding his possible candidacy, promoting the birther agenda on *The View* and *Good Morning America*. "Part of the beauty of me is that I am very rich," he said on the ABC morning show, suggesting he'd spend $600 million of his own money on the campaign.

In the mainstream media, few took him seriously, questioning how, notwithstanding the preposterousness of a reality-TV-star presidency, Trump could possibly succeed as a Republican, given the positions he'd taken in the past.

Others saw this as another feint by a serial White House wannabe, and probably a marketing ploy. "He's one of the great hucksters, and I say that admiringly. He's using this idea of running, milking it for all it's worth—and it's worth a lot," said former New York City mayor Ed Koch.

Michael Cohen and Stewart Rahr had been planning for Trump to make a late-May announcement of his intention to enter the presidential race, after the season finale of *The Celebrity Apprentice*. But NBC wanted his commitment for another season. The network planned to announce its fall lineup in May, and executives hoped to be able to tell advertisers that Trump was on board. A "maybe" would make it harder to secure sponsors.

Trump, faced with a decision, couldn't part with his show. His poll numbers were now scraping the ground. He was tied for fifth place with Ron Paul, whom Trump himself had deemed unelectable. Public Policy Polling, a Democratic shop, described Trump's collapse as "one of the quickest rises and falls in the history of presidential politics."

He put out a statement on May 16, 2011. "I have spent the past several months unofficially campaigning and recognize that running for public office cannot be done half-heartedly. Ultimately, however, business is my greatest passion and I am not ready to leave the private sector."

The *National Enquirer,* with Cohen's help, continued to push Trump's candidacy after he withdrew. "MILLIONS IMPLORE DONALD TRUMP

TO RECONSIDER NEW PRESIDENTIAL RUN," the tabloid reported that July. The evidence of this mass of support? Michael Cohen, whose ABC News blog item was quoted by the *Enquirer*: "Despite Mr. Trump's Republican withdrawal from the Presidential primary race, the never ending phone calls and e-mails to shouldtrumprun.com, demanding that I get Mr. Trump to reconsider, continue."

American Media's *Globe*, meanwhile, kept the birther conspiracy theory front and center, reporting in August in a front-page story that "President Obama is being investigated by top Arizona lawman Joe Arpaio on claims the birth certificate the White House released in April is a FAKE!" (Trump would later pardon Arpaio, the longtime sheriff of Maricopa County, erasing his conviction for criminal contempt of court—a conviction Arpaio earned by ignoring a judge's order to stop detaining people solely on suspicion of their immigration status.)

Mitt Romney, the front-runner for the Republican presidential nomination, apparently believed that Trump had enough clout left to make his support worth the lumps Romney took for associating himself with the celebrity businessman. In February 2012, days before the Nevada caucuses, Romney formally accepted Trump's endorsement at Trump International Hotel in Las Vegas.

Trump kept his remarks brief, a small blessing for Romney and his wife, Ann, who stood stiffly off to the side of the lectern, her face turning various shades of red as Trump spoke.

"He's not going to allow bad things to continue to happen to this country that we all love," Trump said of Romney.

Romney seemed to unintentionally reveal a sense of resignation to the realities of modern politics—to having to bow to a thrice-married reality television star who was promoting a racist conspiracy theory—when it was his turn to speak. "There are some things that you just can't imagine happening in your life," Romney said. "This is one of them."

He grimaced slightly as he shook Trump's hand at the end of the seven-minute event. Romney took no questions. As the campaign wore on, Romney maintained his ties with Trump, who taped a robocall and helped raise money for the Republican nominee, even as Obama's aides poked fun at their opponent's association with the "Birther-in-chief."

Cohen spent time with Romney's staff as well and attended fund-raising events. At one fundraiser for the Republican presidential nominee in New York, he mentioned to a Romney campaign aide that he had a gun strapped to his ankle. Then Cohen rolled up his pant leg to display a pistol. "You've got to get this out of here now!" the staffer exclaimed. Cohen went outside and stashed the gun in a car.

TRUMP'S DECISION TO abandon the race didn't deter Rodriguez from trying to sell the story of Trump's escapade with Daniels five years earlier. She had already arranged for a call between Daniels and Gloria Allred, but after hearing that Daniels had no proof of the affair, the lawyer said she couldn't help. Rodriguez turned to her contacts in the media.

On May 4, she emailed Gina Bacchiocchi, a senior editor for *In Touch Weekly,* a celebrity magazine owned by Bauer Publishing.

> Hi there,
> This is Gina Rodriguez from DD Entertainment, I wanted to see if you wre [*sic*] interested in a very big story with Donald Trump and a contract Porn star. He was with her several times right after his current wife had there [*sic*] baby.
> Interested?
> Let me know.

Bacchiocchi quickly responded. "Hi Gina, I'd say we're interested!" the reporter wrote. Minutes later, Rodriguez offered the outline of her client's story.

> This is the deal, I have the girl (Stormy Daniels) and she wants the story to come out as a source telling it. But she is willing to do a polygraph and she has a photo of her and The Donald together and details of staying with him in Tahoe, Beverly Hills, Vegas, etc. Also I have her ex husband who is willing to take a polygraph and go on the record telling the story as they were married when she was seeing Donald. This was 2 years ago right after Trump's current wife had there baby. He was promising Stormy he would get her on Celebrity Apprentice. She was never paid by him. I also have another source (a close friend of Stormy's-Randy

Spears) who will also do a polygraph and be a source in the story as she told him that she was seeing Trump while they were both signing together at AVN in Vegas 2 years ago. An interesting adition to the story is Stormy ran for Senator a couple years ago as well. :)

We donot have texts as he never texted her, She would call the office and speak to his assistant and then Donald would call her back from a blocked number. But she has the assistant name and the number she used to call as well as Trumps bodyguard name and cell that she would have to call to get in to see Trump.

Let me know! This would be a good one since he is all over the press right now.

That night, Daniels emailed Rodriguez a narrative of her relationship with Trump.

Met at Celebrity Golf Event in Lake Tahoe in Aug/ he invited me dinner/ went up to his room and was surprised he meant we'd be having dinner in his suite/he showed me a magazine cover he was on/we chatted/he had lots of questions about the business aspect of porn/I asked him about his hair and he told me he was afraid to cut it or he'd lose his money (I made a few jokes about his expense)/he said I was smart and he was surprised I was so business oriented and did porn/he said he'd try to get me on Celebrity Apprentice/ he kissed me/we went to the bedroom and had sex (one position, no condom (idiot) . . .

Daniels went on to describe Trump's genitalia, in detail, and wrote that, after sex, she and Trump hung out at a hotel club with Pittsburgh Steelers quarterback Ben Roethlisberger, who eventually escorted Daniels to her room, at Trump's insistence.

She then enumerated her interactions with Trump in the months after the Lake Tahoe golf tournament, offering her ex-husband, Mike Moz, as a witness.

* Trump said he'd call and he did many times and always from a
   blocked number/I'd put him on speaker phone (in front of Moz
   and once in front of a photographer)/ he always said he'd seen
   me in some story or show/called me "Honey Bunch" repeatedly

during every call/ kept saying we should get together to discuss my part on the Celebrity Apprentice

* I would contact him by calling Rona on his office line 212-832-2000 or his bodyguard Keith 646-942-2216. He always took my call.

* I went to NY for an appearance and Trump insisted I come see him at his office. My assistant and I went. We were welcomed right away into his office by his secretary who said he was "expecting me" when I told her who I was. He greeted me with a hug and kiss.

* He invited me to the Miss USA pageant and left tix for me and my assistant at will call. Moz drove us./this was March 2007

* He invited me to the launch party for Trump Vodka at LeDeux in Hollywood. (there are red carpet photos of me there). My assistant was with me. He greeted me warmly with a hug and kiss and had me join him in the VIP area. Was only there for a few minutes./he wanted to get together later but I believe I had flight early next day.

* July 2007 he had me come meet him at the Beverly Hills Hotel/ Moz drove me and his bodyguard walked me to his bungalow and back out to my car/We had dinner in his bungalow/He wanted sex/I wanted to know what was up with Celebrity Apprentice/ Shark Week was on television and he was strangely obsessed with watching it (he REALLY hates sharks..lol)/He kept kissing me but I wanted to talk business/finally he admitted NBC had turned me down/I left/this ending or 11 month regular correspondence

* He randomly called a few more times/I stopped answering blocked numbers

Rodriguez pressed Daniels for more details to fortify her story. What bath products did he use? Rodriguez wanted to know. Did they talk during sex?

"I just remember laughing to myself that someone with so much money wore Old Spice. I didn't talk during sex. He had Old Spice in his bath products. Very cheap," Daniels responded in an email.

Ultimately, *In Touch* dropped the story, but Rodriguez had emailed a reporter at another Bauer publication, *Life & Style*, who also expressed interest in Daniels's story. On May 16, the same day Trump announced that he wouldn't run for president, reporter Jordi Lippe sent Rodriguez a source contract promising Daniels $15,000 for her story upon publication.

Daniels spoke to Lippe over the phone and was matter-of-fact as she recounted the tale of her dalliance with the mogul. Daniels said she had viewed it as a business decision, because she wanted a spot on his reality show. Since then, she said, Daniels had wondered "if he was just flat-out lying the whole time."

"I didn't have any unrealistic expectations of actually being on the show. I figured my chances were 50-50 . . . So now I wonder if the whole thing was just a fucking lie."

"Just to impress you to try to sleep with you?" Lippe asked.

"Yeah," Daniels said. "And I guess it worked." She also said she didn't feel bad at the time that Trump had been cheating on his wife. "But now that I have a baby, that's the same age as his was at the time, I'm like, 'Wow,'" she said.

At *Life & Style*'s request, Daniels, Deuschle, and Moz all took—and passed—polygraph exams about their knowledge of the Trump encounter. Daniels had told Deuschle and Rodriguez about Trump in 2006, while they were eating craft services on the set of one of Daniels's movies. Moz, who took his test in Los Angeles, said Daniels had never told him about having sex with Trump, but he had come to suspect it. The report found him truthful about listening to Trump's phone calls with Daniels: "Question: Did you overhear Donald Trump call Stormy Daniels Honey Bunch on the speakerphone? Answer: YES."

Daniels told Las Vegas polygrapher Ron Slay that she'd had unprotected sex with Trump and been promised a spot on *The Apprentice*, but "she doubted he would be able to do that 'because of who I am,'" Slay wrote in his report.

"Ms. Clifford presented herself well in outward appearance of credibility. There were no observable indications of intent to deceive." Slay added, "In the opinion of this examiner, Ms. Daniels is truthful about having unprotected vaginal intercourse with Donald Trump in July 2006." The test was inconclusive, however, as to whether Daniels was telling the truth about Trump's promise to get her on *The Apprentice*.

On the same day that Slay finished his report, May 19, 2011, Lippe submitted her interview with Daniels to *Life & Style*.

But when the magazine contacted the Trump Organization for comment, it was Michael Cohen who returned the call, dialing the publisher's general counsel and threatening to sue.

At *Life & Style*, executives reasoned that a Trump affair wasn't a huge deal and wouldn't drive sales. A reality star past his prime didn't exactly titillate readers. Moreover, Trump and his allies at *The Apprentice* could occasionally be helpful in the celebrity gossip trade. The publisher killed the story. Lippe emailed Rodriguez: "I think they're going to pass. I'll keep you posted."

Life & Style soon informed Rodriguez that it was passing on the story for legal reasons. Cohen, who had learned that Rodriguez was the one shopping Daniels's story, called her and left a message with Deuschle, who was still living in Rodriguez's basement. "You tell Gina if she ever wants to work in this business again then she needs to call me immediately," Cohen said.

Rodriguez immediately contacted Keith Davidson, who advised her to back off, because Daniels lacked hard proof of her story, other than the names of Trump's bodyguard and one of his assistants, and because the going price for the story—$15,000—was too small to justify a potential legal battle with Trump.

In October, some of Rodriguez's clients appeared on the podcast of Nik Richie, a colorful gossip jockey who ran a blog called *The Dirty*, which published tips about celebrity scandals. Off the air, Rodriguez told him about Daniels's story. Intrigued, he spoke with Daniels and told her he'd run the story on his blog. He said he didn't care if Trump tried to sue.

On October 10, Richie had his colleague Anthony Kotzev post an anonymous note (written by Daniels and forwarded by Rodriguez) describing an affair between Trump and an unnamed woman after "one of his golfing events." *The Dirty* revealed in the same post that the woman was "Stephanie Gregory Daniels aka Stormy Daniels."

This was a typical tactic for exploiting a celebrity story: Offer a dribble of gossip to entice the celebrity news outlets that would pay handsomely for the details, and then pull it back. Almost immediately, Richie received a cease-and-desist letter from Keith Davidson asking him to remove the post because of the "unauthorized use of [Daniels's] name and celebrity." While accusing *The Dirty* of commercially exploiting the porn star's "name and likeness," Davidson made no claim that the story was false.

The next day, Davidson got on the phone with Cohen. The Trump lawyer unleashed a string of expletives and threatened to sue if the *Dirty* post wasn't removed, saying he would pursue Daniels and her representatives "to the ends of the earth." Davidson told Cohen that Daniels's representative had asked him to get the blog post taken down. Cohen softened at the news.

But after the *Dirty* post, *Life & Style* decided to publish a story about the alleged encounter, preparing a two-page spread under the headline "Did Donald Cheat?" It featured photographs of Daniels and of Trump with his wife, with past examples of alleged infidelities during his previous two marriages. Cohen, alerted to the story, emailed a legal threat to the publisher's general counsel, Greg Welch, with Davidson's cease-and-desist letter to *The Dirty* attached. "I again am hereby demanding that the story be removed from your magazine." But by the time Welch received the email, the issue with the story had already gone to press.

Responding to the report that had surfaced online, Daniels told *E! News* that the story of her affair with Trump was "bullshit."

KEITH DAVIDSON LEARNED of another business opportunity in October 2012. An editor at *TMZ*, a source of clients for the lawyer, connected Davidson with a man who said he had obtained videos of wrestling icon Hulk Hogan having sex with the wife of his onetime best friend, radio shock jockey Todd Clem, also known as "Bubba the Love Sponge." Hogan, whose real name is Terry Bollea, also made racist remarks while he was unknowingly being filmed.

A few months earlier, in March, *TMZ* had reported about the existence of the tape, and then *The Dirty* posted a still image from it, in an item that vaguely alluded to Hogan's racist comments. The two gossip items had been fueled by a former associate of Clem's, Matthew "Spice Boy" Lloyd, who claimed to have purchased the Hogan sex videos inadvertently at a garage sale fundraiser. (Lloyd said he thought he was buying some regular movies.) But after the initial items, publicity died down until October, when *Gawker* published an excerpt from a sex tape of Hogan and Clem's wife, Heather, obtained from a different source.

TMZ sprung into action again, agreeing to pay Lloyd $8,500, funneled through a friend, for clips and a transcript of the tape. *TMZ* then quoted the tape but left out the racist remarks, thus preserving damaging material of value that Hogan might still pay to suppress. That was when the editor referred Lloyd to Davidson.

Quickly, Davidson broached the subject in an unsolicited email to Hogan's lawyer, David Houston.

October 10, 2012, 2:14pm
Subject: Hulk Hogan Tape

Please call me regarding above.

Hogan and Houston, who saw the approach as a brazen attempt at extortion, tipped off the Federal Bureau of Investigation. They began cooperating with federal agents in an attempt to bust Davidson and his client, who was Lloyd's friend acting again as his cover. During phone calls in the subsequent weeks, Houston recorded Davidson, who was typically careful not to step into territory that might qualify as extortion. Davidson told Houston that he didn't want to "hold anybody over the fire."

"I hope I'm part of the solution here," Davidson said, avoiding Houston's efforts to bait him through some of the settlement terms. "You're almost asking my client to admit that she's an extortionist," Davidson said at one point.

After the faux negotiations resulted in a tentative $300,000 settlement agreement, Davidson and the "client," Lori Burbridge, met Hogan and Houston in a room at the Sandpearl Resort, in Clearwater Beach, Florida. They signed a contract, and Davidson gave them DVDs containing the Hogan videos. After Houston handed Davidson a settlement check, federal agents poured into the hotel room, which had been outfitted with hidden listening devices and cameras.

Burbridge, panicking, kept asking if she was the butt of a practical joke, while Davidson remained outwardly calm. An FBI agent confronted him with the fact that he'd been recorded, trying to get him to make an admission of wrongdoing, but he didn't engage. When she asked him if he wanted to hear what he'd said on the tapes, hoping that might provoke some kind of response, Davidson agreed. She and her colleagues fumbled around before finding the clips they wanted. He was pretty sure he'd not crossed any lines, but he was curious what they might have.

As they played one clip after another, Davidson made mental notes. *That's not extortion,* he silently told himself after hearing the first one. *That's not extortion, either,* he thought after the second. He was almost certain the FBI had nothing that indicated he'd broken the law.

When he was free to go, Davidson walked out of the resort, gazing out at the huge white-sand beach and the ocean and thinking that his family would have loved to vacation there. But he knew he'd never come back. He got in a cab to the airport and began to make a call but suddenly grew worried that his driver, too, might be an undercover federal agent. Instead, he changed course and got dropped at the office of a defense lawyer who had once led the U.S. attorney's office in Tampa.

Hogan later launched a wave of civil lawsuits, one of which put *Gawker* out of business. Davidson wasn't charged criminally, and neither was Lloyd, Burbridge, or anyone else. But Hogan sued the lawyer in civil court for extortion and invasion of privacy, enmeshing him in litigation for years to come.

He was still free, and he was still in business.

14.

THE CANDIDATE

■ ■ ■

SINCE ABANDONING HIS last presidential flirtation in favor of his reality show, Donald Trump had kept his eye on the White House. Long after President Obama had gone to the extraordinary measure of releasing his birth certificate to give the lie to the birther conspiracy theory, Trump continued publicizing false claims about Obama's birthplace.

Michael Cohen returned to the kinds of side projects that had come to define his role at the Trump Organization. He arranged for Stewart Rahr, the billionaire who'd funded Cohen's 2011 Iowa trip, to act as a straw bidder at an auction of celebrity portraits held by ArtHamptons, an annual event on the East End of Long Island. Rahr pumped up the price of a portrait of Trump, who paid for the painting himself but pretended in a tweet that he'd had nothing to do with the sale. "Just found out that at a charity auction of celebrity portraits in E. Hampton, my portrait by artist William Quigley topped list at $60K," Trump wrote in the July 16, 2013, tweet.

Cohen also served as a liaison to the media during Trump's failed bid to purchase the Buffalo Bills, and worked diligently to preserve his reputation as a pit bull for the boss's entire family.

After the 2012 season of *Celebrity Apprentice,* Trump's company had received a call from *Us Weekly,* a Wenner Media magazine pursuing a story about an affair between Donald Trump Jr., who had been a judge on the show, and contestant Aubrey O'Day, a member of the singing duo Dumblonde. Cohen returned the call, swearing and threatening *Us Weekly*'s editors with legal action as they huddled around a speakerphone. He became so irate that they muted the call, laughing at his over-the-top New York shtick. In the end, the magazine dropped the story, deciding it wasn't worth the fight. They also didn't think gossip about Trump—or, in this case, his son—interested readers much, either, and he'd been helpful in *Apprentice*-related stories.

Cohen phoned up Tom Allon, an owner of *Avenue Magazine,* to convey Trump's displeasure at not making the society glossy's list of the 200 Most Influential New Yorkers. But that wasn't all: "He is pissed that you left Melania off the list of the 25 Sexiest New Yorkers," which had appeared in a previous issue. They reached a détente. After a meeting with Trump, Allon published a profile of Melania Trump, and he sold the mogul an ad contract.

Then Cohen called in to *TMZ Live* to demand an apology to Trump from Miss Pennsylvania USA 2012 or she'd face a lawsuit for "massive damages." Sheena Monnin, who had sought the Miss USA title, had angered Trump by posting on Facebook that the pageant was "fraudulent, lacking in morals, inconsistent, and in many ways trashy." She resigned her state title while criticizing the pageant's acceptance of transgender contestants. Cohen yelled at Monnin's father, saying that if she refused to take down her posts and apologize, it would be "Game on," before slamming down the phone. Trump, who said on *Good Morning America* that Monnin was angry because she'd lost, filed a $10 million defamation suit and obtained a $5 million default judgment in arbitration. They later reached a confidential settlement.

At the same time, Cohen remained Trump's chief political adviser. His experience in politics dated back to his work volunteering for Democrat Michael Dukakis's 1988 presidential campaign and interning for Congressman Joe Moakley of Massachusetts, also a Democrat. He had deepened his political expertise with his losing campaign for city council in 2003, as a Republican, and an abbreviated New York State Senate bid in 2010, as a Democrat. Cohen was still a registered Democrat as he counseled Trump on his next move.

In 2013, New York Republican State Committee operatives wooed Trump as a potential challenger to Governor Andrew Cuomo, the incumbent Democrat who'd soon be up for reelection. One of the operatives, Michael Caputo, was close to Roger Stone, who set up a meeting with Trump. Trump was intrigued and agreed to meet with local Republican political leaders from all across the state. After that initial meeting, Cohen privately mused to Caputo about his own desire to run for mayor of New York City. On another occasion, Cohen—apparently having forgotten his mayoral aspirations—suggested to Caputo that he'd be ideal to run for lieutenant governor on Trump's ticket, even though he was a Democrat. Cohen was pushing the mogul to challenge Cuomo, while Stone and his disciple Sam Nunberg, who'd been advising Trump on politics, urged the mogul to focus on the presidency. Trump coveted what he called "the bigger thing" and decided against entering the governor's race.

TOGETHER, TRUMP AND Cohen focused on trying to remake the reality star's image as a candidate to be taken seriously, given the ridicule he'd taken in the past. They saw an opportunity when CNBC announced an online poll to select America's top business leaders. Surely Trump should make the list, they thought.

But to hedge his bets, Cohen sought help from a man he'd come to regard as his personal tech guru over the past several years. He asked John Gauger, a technology officer at Liberty University, an evangelical Christian school in Virginia run by Jerry Falwell Jr., to rig the CNBC poll in Trump's favor.

The men had met in 2012, when Falwell invited Trump to give an address to Liberty students. Cohen had accompanied Trump and forged a connection with Falwell and his wife and others at the school. Afterward, a colleague of the thirty-two-year-old Gauger introduced him to Cohen, who was forty-six by then and needed help setting up his Instagram account. Gauger had started his own technology consulting and search engine marketing firm on the side, called RedFinch Solutions. He walked Cohen through the steps and gave him his number in case he needed more help.

Cohen took him up on the offer, calling Gauger periodically for personal technology issues like help with cloud storage. He tasked Gauger with creating positive content on Cohen's Wikipedia page and posting negative information on the page of his former business partner, Simon Garber, with whom he'd been feuding. Cohen didn't pay RedFinch for these services. But he promised to land the eager Gauger work worth millions of dollars providing technology services for Trump golf courses and hotels, none of which Cohen ever delivered.

Cohen did pay Gauger occasionally, and seemingly at random, after asking him to do work for people he knew. One of them was Sharen Turney, the chief executive of Victoria's Secret. Turney had just met him for the first time at a party in New York to raise money to help people with autism. She was talking about trying to establish an online profile that reflected the philanthropic work she was doing to help children. *I know somebody that can help you,* Cohen said.

Around the same time, Turney was dealing with *New York Post* reports that she'd had a "torrid affair." She hired Cohen, who asked Gauger to help Turney elevate positive search results about her online and push down the negative ones. RedFinch set up a website for Turney, helped her people post links and pictures to it, and ran her Twitter account.

Gauger found Cohen mercurial and strange. He also wanted all of their dealings to be clandestine. Cohen never mentioned Trump's name, referring to him only as "the boss." Before setting up a call with Sharen Turney's people, he told Gauger to use a fake name and not to identify his company.

"None of this is sketchy," Gauger protested.

"Don't worry, it will make it sound more important if they don't know who you are," Cohen said. Gauger introduced himself as John.

When CNBC set out to identify the country's top business leaders, it used online polling to help an expert panel narrow the field from two hundred to one hundred and then to the top twenty-five. Trump made the cut of the first two hundred and canvassed for votes on Twitter. "Honored to be named as one of business's 'Top Leaders, Icons and Rebels' by @CNBC," Trump wrote in a January 24, 2014, tweet. "Vote Trump!" Five days later, he again solicited votes: "Thanks to everyone for your support on @CNBC's 'Top Leaders, Icons and Rebels.' Thanks for voting Trump!"

It wasn't uncommon for Trump's assistant, Rhona Graff, to email employees telling them to vote for Trump in online polls. In this case, Trump had left Cohen a printout that said "Michael C," with an arrow pointing down at information about the CNBC contenders. Cohen went to Trump's office to offer assistance. "There are ways that you could play with these online polls by using bots and algorithms," Cohen told him. "There's a company that I know that can actually do it."

"How good do you think that they can do this?" Trump asked. "I want to be number one."

"Well, that would be kind of suspicious, don't you think?" Cohen asked. "How about if we just go for number nine?" Since that would still put him in the top ten, Trump agreed.

Cohen called Gauger and asked him for help rigging the poll. Gauger asked a friend to create computer script that he hoped would flood the poll with votes for Trump. The gambit didn't work. Trump failed to make the top one hundred, at least in part because the judges didn't respect his business acumen and also frowned on his history of corporate bankruptcies. Even though they'd cheated, Trump was apoplectic when he called Cohen to his office again. He lashed out at CNBC.

"Stupid poll should be canceled—no credibility," Trump wrote in one of two angry tweets on March 10. Believing that he had been wrongfully eliminated by the judges, Trump coordinated with oilman T. Boone Pickens, who also believed he'd been cut out of the top one hundred by the network, in taking their complaints to CNBC. Cohen called a CNBC executive and threatened to sue the cable channel for "ignoring the will of the people," before dropping the matter.

By the beginning of 2015, Trump was still craving the attention that his 2011 electoral fling had generated and still smarting from some of the mockery he'd endured on account of it. He was finally ready to step away, at least temporarily, from his television career. He geared up to announce his candidacy, traveling to the Iowa Freedom Summit in January and criticizing potential rivals, including Romney and former Florida governor Jeb Bush.

In February, Cohen and Gauger went back to work, trying to game another online poll. This time it was a Drudge Report survey of the potential Republican candidates. Again, Gauger attempted to use computer code to boost Trump's popularity. The mogul came in fifth, with about 24,000 votes, 5 percent of the total. Still, Cohen declared victory. Trump had scored ahead of Bush, former Texas governor Rick Perry, and a sitting Florida senator, Marco Rubio.

"Mr. Trump's impressive showing is an affirmation that the American people are looking for a new type of leader," Cohen told *The Washington Times*. "His no nonsense and direct approach is being well received by citizens across the country who are fed up with the failures of their elected officials. Mr. Trump is a visionary who is unafraid to say and do what would be needed to make America great again."

Cohen had asked Gauger what he owed for the poll-rigging efforts. Gauger told him it would cost $50,000, considering all his baked-in expenses to run proxy servers and the like. In reality, it hadn't cost nearly that much, but after doing free work for years in the hope of winning Trump contracts that never materialized, Gauger had come to doubt that he'd ever collect anything from Cohen. On a trip to New York, he reached out and was surprised when Cohen invited him up to his office in Trump Tower to get paid.

When Gauger got upstairs, Cohen ushered him into his office. There, he handed the technology executive a Walmart bag containing more than $12,000 in cash. Cohen acknowledged that it wasn't all he owed, but it was a start. Gauger remarked on a poster Cohen had on his wall for Affliction Entertainment, the mixed martial arts venture he'd once worked on for Trump. Then Cohen presented Gauger with a gift: a single boxing glove that he claimed had once been worn by the Brazilian mixed martial arts fighter Vitor Belfort. After leaving the bizarre encounter, Gauger sent his wife pictures of the boxing glove, which was signed by Belfort, and the bag of cash.

Cohen had also been vowing to help Gauger secure work with Trump's campaign, which would far exceed what he owed for the poll rigging. As the campaign swung into motion, Cohen set up a couple of calls for Gauger, including one with newly installed campaign manager Corey Lewandowski. When Gauger followed up, Lewandowski ignored him. Periodically, Gauger inquired about the remainder of the payment, and Cohen apologized. "You're the only fucking person in the world I owe money to," he said. But he assured Gauger that he'd get him the campaign work, because eventually, Cohen said, he would be running the show.

THAT DREAM NEVER came to pass. Over the past few years, Cohen had increasingly been dabbling in private real estate deals on the side of his Trump Organization work, flipping property using connections he'd made through Trump, and making a lot of money. He'd been considering leaving the company. But when Trump made it clear that he planned to run, Cohen decided to see the campaign through, given the role he'd played in the 2011 presidential effort.

To that point, Trump's confederation of squabbling political advisers had consisted of Cohen, Stone, and Sam Nunberg. Cohen and Stone, who was usually at his home in Florida, jockeyed for Trump's attention and disliked each other. Nunberg had met Stone when they worked to fight a proposed mosque two blocks from where al-Qaeda had knocked down the twin towers on September 11, 2001. Nunberg had been hired and then fired by Trump after convincing the mogul to cooperate with a 2014 *BuzzFeed News* profile that ended up mocking his political aspirations. "36 Hours on the Fake Campaign Trail with Donald Trump," it was called. But a few months later, Trump rehired him.

Now Trump wanted to be seen as more than a Republican carnival barker, and he knew his existing troika couldn't mount a full-scale presidential campaign. So he looked farther afield. On the advice of David Bossie, head of the conservative advocacy group Citizens United, he hired Corey Lewandowski. Lewandowski, a forty-one-year-old New Hampshire–based lobbyist, had been voter registration director for Americans for Prosperity, an organization backed by the Koch brothers, the conservative industrialists.

While he was not well known, Lewandowski's political pedigree ran deeper than Cohen's. He had waged a failed write-in candidacy for the Massachusetts State House while in college, worked as a congressional aide, served as a regional political director for the Republican National Committee, and managed the reelection campaign of New Hampshire senator Robert C. Smith.

Lewandowski also embodied the renegade, brawling qualities that Trump valued in an adviser. While working in his late twenties for Bob Ney, a Republican congressman from Ohio, Lewandowski had been arrested after bringing a laundry bag with a loaded pistol, three magazines, a holster, ammunition, and dirty clothes into a congressional office building. Lewandowski, who said he'd forgotten he had the gun in the bag, fought to get it back for four years until he was denied in a federal appeals court. After Ney was convicted on federal corruption charges, Lewandowski wrote a letter to the judge seeking leniency, saying the congressman had been a best friend and surrogate father to him.

The arrival of a carpetbagger might have been alarming to a less confident man than Cohen. But he and the rest of Trump's old guard believed that they would be able to manipulate the young New Englander and his team, leaving the grunt work of the campaign to them while continuing to exert their influence over the boss. It was a miscalculation. Lewandowski's aggressiveness and his work ethic won Trump over quickly. And he was a more resourceful and subtle operator than any of them realized.

Cohen didn't know that David Bossie had already warned Lewandowski about him. Before Trump mulled the 2012 presidential race, Bossie had written some memos and counseled Trump about the mechanics of waging a true national campaign. Cohen had called Bossie unsolicited. *I want to be involved. I am Mr. Trump's guy,* Cohen said. But because Trump hadn't told him to work with Cohen, Bossie ignored him. Soon he found Cohen working against him, intercepting his messages, trying to block his line of communication to Trump, and calling to berate him: *You have to go through me! You have to deal with me!*

Armed with this information, and the sense that Cohen didn't have the sharpest political instincts, Lewandowski determined to keep him away from the official campaign. Trump agreed. The decision was sold to Cohen, and he accepted it. He was told he'd remain in an important role at the boss's side as special counsel inside the Trump Organization. Others could deal with the nitty-gritty work of building a political organization across the states. Cohen could reach out to interest groups, like the spiritual community, where he already had a relationship with Jerry Falwell and his wife. When problems arose, he could fix them.

COHEN SETTLED INTO his role back at home while Trump traveled to South Carolina and New Hampshire and announced an exploratory committee. He served as a mouthpiece and a bulldog with print reporters covering the campaign. He still identified himself as Trump's chief political adviser, despite Lewandowski's hiring. Making frequent appearances on cable news, Cohen was an aggressive surrogate, aping Trump's combativeness and backing up his public statements, no matter how wacky.

After *Forbes* assigned Trump a net worth of $4.1 billion, Cohen argued that he could still relate to regular people. Cohen peddled the false narrative Trump had been selling for decades, that he was self-made, ignoring that he'd launched his career on the success of his father. (At the same time, Trump once again disputed *Forbes*'s findings and insisted that he was really worth $10 billion.) "Mr. Trump intends on making America the superpower it once was and ensuring prosperity for all Americans," Cohen told *The Boston Globe*. "Just as he did with his own company, he will build it from startup to greatness."

Behind the scenes, Cohen worked to squelch potential threats, often through intimidation. Reporters had begun looking for Trump's academic records, and Cohen moved quickly to prevent them from getting out. The instinct to suppress Trump's records wasn't surprising, but it was ironic. Less than three years earlier, a month before the 2012 election, Trump had filmed a YouTube video trying to goad Obama into releasing his own records with "a deal that I don't believe he can refuse, and I hope he doesn't."

"President Obama is the least transparent president in the history of this country. There's never been anything like it," Trump had said. "If Barack Obama opens up and gives his college records and applications, and if he gives his passport applications and records, I will give to a charity of his choice—inner-city children in Chicago, American Cancer Society, AIDS research, anything he wants—a check immediately for five million dollars. The check will be given within one hour after he releases all of the records so stated."

Obama had ignored the challenge, and now Cohen was turning down reporters' requests for Trump's academic records. He also wrote to Trump's former schools. In a May 5 letter to Reverend Joseph M. McShane, a Jesuit priest who was president of Fordham University, in the Bronx, Cohen warned of "jail time" for anyone releasing the records without consent. Trump, who'd been a middling student, spent two years at Fordham before transferring to the undergraduate program at the Wharton business school at the University of Pennsylvania.

"We will hold your institution liable to the fullest extent of the law including damages and criminality," Cohen wrote. "Please guide yourself accordingly and contact me to inform me that the records have been permanently sealed."

He added, without irony, "P.S. Mr. Trump truly enjoyed his two years at Fordham and has great respect for the University."

Trump's camp also refused a request for his long-form birth certificate and passport records. *The Guardian* found the stance "confusing," because in 2012 the paper had asked for the same records and been rebuffed on the grounds that Trump wasn't a candidate. Back then, Michael Cohen had called the request "stupid."

"What's your point?" Cohen had said. "Mr. Trump's not the president of the United States and he's not running for the presidency."

Early on, Trump made it clear that Cohen's duties in the presidential race also entailed handling any publicity problems that might come up with women the candidate had been with—or tried to be with—in the past. In Trump's office, he sat with Cohen and Nunberg, laughing at how his fixer had handled a recent episode. "Michael just got me out of another one," Trump said.

NOW TRUMP WAS running. The only question was when the official announcement would be.

After getting the operation off the ground while shuttling back and forth between New York and New Hampshire, Lewandowski, in the spring of 2015, decided to take a break before the launch, knowing he'd have less time with his family afterward. He left with his wife and children on a trip to Aruba, which they'd planned before he took the job with Trump.

While he was away, Cohen got in the boss's ear and convinced Trump that he needed to announce his candidacy, and soon. Trump, who had been calling Lewandowski incessantly while he was in Aruba, put him on speakerphone to discuss moving the launch. In his bathing suit, Lewandowski heard Cohen's voice. "We've set a date," Cohen said. He'd already begun telling reporters that Trump's announcement would come on a Monday in late May. From his resort, Lewandowski argued that it was too soon, that Monday was a terrible day to make news, that he'd need at least five weeks to plan, and that without a proper rollout, Trump's campaign would die quickly. They compromised, settling on Tuesday, June 16, in the lobby of Trump Tower. Trump ordered Lewandowski to leave Aruba and get his ass back to New York.

The planning was equally contentious. Cohen advocated for a band, huge TV screens, and an elephant. Lewandowski wanted Trump to walk out and speak in front of the traditional American flag backdrop. But he opposed Trump making his grand entrance down the mirror-sided, gold-trimmed Trump Tower escalator. Trump had often done this before and liked doing it, but it had that cheese factor that risked him looking like something—a ringmaster at the circus (even sans elephant), the debutante at the ball, Zeus coming down Mount Olympus—other than a serious presidential contender. Couldn't he just take the elevator?

On the day he formally launched his presidential bid—for real this time—Trump followed his wife down the escalator to Neil Young's "Rockin' in the Free World" as hundreds of people cheered in the marble lobby of Trump Tower and on the floors overlooking it.

Fifty-five of them were actors who had been paid $50 each to cheer. Cohen had told campaign staffers that he was working with David Schwartz, a lawyer and lobbyist friend, to bring people to the event—indicating that he'd tapped into a wellspring of Trump fans who were agitating for the presidential run. But Schwartz, who'd built crowds before through his company, Gotham Government Relations & Communication LLC, couldn't find people. Trump had little support from state and local Republican groups, which could have steered members to the campaign launch. Most students at local college campuses, another ready supply of supporters, had left for summer break. So Gotham hired a casting company called Extra Mile to get bodies to Trump Tower without revealing the nature of the event, which had been suggestively described as "People for a Stronger America."

When the actors arrived, they were given MAKE AMERICA GREAT AGAIN T-shirts and signs before setting up at different locations around the venue. Schwartz paid the actors in cash on the day of the event. He had previously done some work for Trump, who referred to him as "the Screamer." Before the announcement, Schwartz was on hand in the lobby with a megaphone, riling up the crowd and telling people when to cheer.

"Wow. Whoa. That is some group of people. Thousands," Trump said in a vast exaggeration after arriving at the lectern, in front of the American flags Lewandowski had wanted. "This is beyond anybody's expectations. There's been no crowd like this . . . Some of the candidates, they went in, they didn't know the air conditioner didn't work. They sweated like dogs. They didn't know the room was too big because they didn't have anybody there. How are they going to beat ISIS?"

Trump criticized Obama's policies and previewed his campaign theme: "We are going to make our country great again." He promised to scrap Obamacare and build "a great, great wall" on the Mexican border. "They're bringing drugs. They're bringing crime. They're rapists. And some, I assume, are good people." He also vowed to self-fund his campaign, telling journalists, as he had four years earlier, "I'm really rich."

And, as before, few took him seriously.

Pollsters put his odds at less than 5 percent. *The Wall Street Journal* posted an online video with the title "Donald Trump: Presidential Hair Apparent," with images of Trump's bright orange-yellow hair blowing wildly off his forehead. A Democratic Party spokeswoman deadpanned that Trump "adds some much-needed seriousness that has previously been lacking from the GOP field."

A couple of days after Trump's announcement, *The Hollywood Reporter* revealed the presence of paid actors at the event. One had posted a picture of himself in a Trump T-shirt on social media, and the publication obtained a copy of an email the casting company hired by Schwartz had sent to its pool of extras, seeking people to work the event. Lewandowski was furious with Schwartz and Cohen when the story came out. The Trump campaign's lawyer, Don McGahn, lectured Cohen. *You don't have authority to do anything with the campaign,* McGahn told him. *And if you pretend to do so, you're going to cause trouble for the campaign down the road, and then we are going to have to unwind everything that you do.*

His words were prophetic. American Democracy Legal Fund, an advocacy group founded by liberal activist David Brock, soon asked the Federal Election Commission to investigate the hiring of the actors. The Trump campaign hadn't reported the expense in its first disclosure report to the FEC. In response, Trump's campaign issued a $12,000 check to Schwartz's company, and both denied hiring any actors. (Extra Mile had invoiced Schwartz's company, Gotham, for its booking fee for "participant/crowd casting" of fifty-five people, but Gotham's lawyer told federal regulators that they'd been hired as "administrative staff.") The election commission's staff said the late payment might have been an infraction, but the amount was small. The matter was dropped.

Cohen shifted into high gear. He told Sean Hannity on Fox News that the other Republicans "have the right to be afraid" of Trump, the "mega-billionaire, real estate developer, celebrity, author, movie star, et cetera." (Trump had made cameos as himself in a number of movies, such as *Zoolander* and *Home Alone 2,* and on television, in *Sex and the City* and *WrestleMania 23.*) Cohen said Trump wouldn't back down from mainstream Republicans who scorned his candidacy: "We're definitely not looking for a fight. But you bring a fight to Donald Trump, he's going to take that fight and he's going to finish it!"

Within a month of the campaign launch, Cohen's aggressiveness resulted in his candidate having to defend him, rather than the other way around. A *Daily Beast* reporter had called Cohen about Ivana Trump's statement that Trump had raped her while they were married. She'd made the allegation, as reported in *Lost Tycoon,* a book by Harry Hurt III, in a deposition during their divorce. In a statement appended to the book, Ivana Trump had walked back the claim, saying that she'd felt "violated" on one occasion in 1989 because the love and tenderness Trump normally showed her during sex was absent, but that she hadn't meant that she'd been raped "in a literal or criminal sense."

Cohen waded into perilous territory in his call with *Daily Beast* reporter Tim Mak, expounding incorrectly on the legal definition of rape. "You're talking about the front-runner for the GOP presidential candidate, as well as private individual who never raped anybody. And, of course, understand that, by the very definition, you can't rape your spouse," he said. (In fact, marital rape had been a crime in New York for decades, and in most U.S. states by the early 1990s.)

Then Cohen went on a rampage against the reporter, who was recording their call: "I will make sure that you and I meet one day while we're in the courthouse. And I will take you for every penny you still don't have," he told Mak. "And I will come after your *Daily Beast* and everybody else that you possibly know."

The longer they spoke, the angrier Cohen became, making threats that were over the top: "So I'm warning you, tread very fucking lightly, because what I'm going to do to you is going to be fucking disgusting. Do you understand me?"

The statements led to days of negative headlines. Lewandowski and other campaign aides distanced themselves and their candidate from Cohen's remarks and Cohen himself, taking pains to point out that he wasn't an official surrogate for Trump or the campaign. Lewandowski by now had begun to assert his influence over Trump, in part by appealing to his natural instincts as an outsider and harnessing his larger-than-life character rather than trying to rein him in. "Let Trump be Trump," he wrote on a whiteboard in the Trump Tower campaign office.

Despite his expanding reach, Lewandowski wasn't able to convince Trump to fire Cohen over the *Daily Beast* debacle. In an interview with CNN's Don Lemon, Trump at once defended Cohen and disavowed his commentary about spousal rape. "When I first saw it, I said, 'Wow, you know, it's something I disagree with,'" Trump said. "You know, he is speaking for himself. He is not speaking for me, obviously." Still, Trump said he had no plans to fire Cohen, who apologized while blaming the reporter for shocking him into making "an inarticulate comment" that he didn't actually believe. Trump privately told his aides that he was putting Cohen "in the penalty box." The candidate ordered him to stay off television and away from reporters. But Cohen soon got out of the box again.

MICHAEL COHEN WASN'T the only Trump adviser making news. Sam Nunberg, butting heads with Lewandowski, was fired again, over an email to a reporter, and then rehired again. He was fired for good after a news report about years-old racially charged Facebook posts. Less than a week later, Trump said he had fired Roger Stone. According to Trump's version of the parting, he had heard that Stone was about to make a noisy exit from the campaign to distance himself from Trump's attacks on Fox News's Megyn Kelly over her tough questions at a Republican presidential debate. But Stone said he'd been frustrated with Lewandowski and quit before Trump claimed to fire him. Reporters couldn't be sure who was telling the truth. News also broke that Trump's Arizona state director had posted doctored pictures on Facebook of President Obama in a turban with a beard, and alongside Adolf Hitler. Then the man released a recording of Lewandowski concocting talking points to describe the Arizona director as an "overzealous volunteer."

Even after being instructed to stop going on television, Cohen soldiered on as before, continuing to thrust himself into the limelight with incessant cable appearances. He'd lock the door to his Trump Organization office early in the afternoon on some days and bid goodbye to his colleagues, explaining he had something to do, then show up on the news a few hours later. On the road, Lewandowski would see Cohen onscreen and yell at Hope Hicks, the campaign's communications director, as if she could control him.

Cohen also attacked Hillary Clinton, who was again seeking the Democratic presidential nomination, for being involved in "cover-ups" and "the besmirching of women" who'd accused her husband of sexual improprieties. He denied that Trump had mocked a disabled reporter and defended Trump's evidence-free claim that he had seen thousands of Muslims in New Jersey cheering the September 11 attacks. "I can tell you that Mr. Trump's memory is fantastic, and I've never come across a situation where Mr. Trump has said something that's not accurate," Cohen told CNN's Jake Tapper, who struggled not to chuckle, replying, "Seriously?" Cohen befuddled Sean Hannity with the remark that Russian president Vladimir Putin looked at Obama as a "lamb chop" and would see Marco Rubio the same way if the Florida senator were elected. "What's a lamb chop?" Hannity asked. "It's something that . . . he has no respect for," Cohen replied. "And he's going to enjoy eating our lunch."

But behind the scenes, it was Cohen and Trump who were trying to curry favor with Putin. They wanted to build a Trump-branded residential tower in Moscow, a dream the real estate mogul had been chasing for years.

15.

THE DOORMAN

■ ■ ■

DAVID PECKER AND Donald Trump regularly drew from what Tom Wolfe called the Favor Bank over the course of their relationship.

After American Media boosted Trump during his presidential go-round in late 2011, Pecker had come to him for aid with a problem the *Enquirer* had created. The tabloid had sent a black reporter, Belinda Robinson, to the funeral of Jack Manigault, the murdered brother of onetime *Apprentice* star Omarosa Manigault. Robinson's story, a huge spread in the *Enquirer*'s October 31, 2011, edition, had a banner claiming an "exclusive interview," and the headline "Omarosa: My Heartbreak Over Slain Brother."

Afterward, a furious Omarosa hired lawyers and threatened to sue, saying Robinson had pretended to be a mourner, never identifying herself, and using quotes from her eulogy while falsely claiming she'd given an interview. Trump, asked by Pecker to intervene, called his former disciple urging her not to sue. Pecker was a friend of his, and he was willing to work with her, Trump said. "What do you want?"

Together, Trump and Cohen defused the situation by orchestrating a job offer from American Media in exchange for Omarosa's dropping her legal threat. Pecker personally called her to apologize. In December 2011, American Media named her the West Coast editor of *Reality Weekly,* a magazine about the reality show industry. Her duties weren't made clear to Jerry George, who ran the *Enquirer*'s Los Angeles bureau. He gave her an office far from the reporting staff, near the advertising department. Sometimes she'd show up with her mother, who was known around the office as "Mamarosa." After *Reality Weekly* shut down, Omarosa was moved to a job at *OK!* and then left after a two-year stint at American Media.

Trump's formal entry into the presidential race offered another opportunity for collaboration and mutual benefit.

Soon after Trump announced his candidacy, in June 2015, a small media company had approached Trump's office about old photos its co-founder had obtained of Trump holding a pen near a woman's bare breasts, as if to autograph them. The pictures had been discovered by Jeremy Frommer, a former Wall Street trader who co-founded Jerrick Media, which was focused on digital technology and was developing a social media platform. Frommer found the Trump pictures while sifting through a collection he'd purchased of personal art, pictures, and other items that once belonged to the late *Penthouse* publisher Bob Guccione.

Frommer wanted to see what they were worth to Trump. One of his employees emailed Trump's office. Hope Hicks, Trump's campaign spokeswoman, called back and argued that Jerrick would be in violation of copyright laws if the company published the photos. She ended the conversation by promising that the company would be hearing from Trump's lawyers. Within an hour, Cohen called Jerrick, asking for whoever was in charge. When Frommer got on the phone with Cohen, the lawyer immediately threatened a lawsuit. Cohen suspected that Frommer was trying to extort Trump. But his demeanor changed when he realized they had a mutual acquaintance: David Pecker.

Frommer had dealt with Pecker and American Media in 2013 in connection with another item he'd discovered in Guccione's collection, a photocopied image of a young Arnold Schwarzenegger naked on a couch. An *Enquirer* reporter learned of the photocopy, which occupied half of a letter-size sheet of paper, and soon Frommer was meeting with Pecker in his office. Pecker paid $20,000 to take the photo out of circulation just a few months after American Media had named Schwarzenegger an executive editor of *Muscle & Fitness* and *Flex* magazines. Pecker gave the photo to Schwarzenegger's longtime adviser Paul Wachter, and Pecker understood he would be reimbursed. When Wachter returned to Pecker, he told the publisher that Schwarzenegger wouldn't pony up for the "crappy picture," though Schwarzenegger would later deny ever making that comment. It wouldn't be the last time Pecker spent money to help a friend and had to eat the expense.

On the call, in the summer of 2015, Cohen suggested that Frommer take the Trump pictures to Pecker. Frommer, who hoped to make the *National Enquirer* archives broadly available to a digital audience and publish a book based on them, was enthusiastic about the idea. In an email, Frommer told Pecker that he wanted to talk to the *Enquirer* publisher about "our growing media company." They agreed to meet for drinks in early July at Cipriani, a Wall Street eatery frequented by the publisher.

Pecker made Frommer sign a nondisclosure agreement about their discussions. The American Media chief executive told Frommer that he'd smoothed over any lingering ill will between Frommer and Cohen, assuring the Trump aide that Frommer posed no threat to the boss. "I related the message to Cohen just as we discussed," Pecker texted Frommer before their meeting. "All Calm."

At drinks, they talked about a possible collaboration between Jerrick and American Media, as well as a video interview of Trump by Jerrick that Cohen would arrange. As for the pictures, Pecker told Frommer that American Media had no use for them.

Ironically, neither Frommer nor Pecker nor Cohen knew the true story behind the pictures of Trump preparing to sign the woman's breasts. Frommer believed they'd been taken at a Guccione event in the late 1980s. In fact, they'd already been printed in the *National Enquirer*, eight years before Pecker's arrival. The pictures were snapped at an Atlanta club called Petrus, after Trump showed up at a January 29, 1991, fundraising dinner. His then girlfriend, Marla Maples, a Georgia native, had hosted the event for Childkind, a charity that helped children with AIDS.

According to the *Enquirer*'s 1991 story, a stripper known as Pama "Precious" Powell had come up to Maples at the event and said, "Marla, I'm from your hometown. I don't have anything for Mr. Trump to write on. Do you mind if he signs my chest?" Maples replied, "I think that'd be really cute," and led Powell over to Trump. When he went to sign her chest, she dropped her top, shocking both Trump and Maples. "He started to write his name just above my cleavage when I dropped my top in a flash. I said, 'Welcome to Georgia!'" Powell told reporter Bennet Bolton, who'd joined the *Enquirer* after covering the Vatican for the Associated Press.

Even though Maples hadn't known about the prank, Trump growled at her angrily, "What have you done to me?"

Twenty-five years later, the implication was clear as Pecker and Frommer discussed the photos over drinks: If Frommer withheld them from publication, there might be something bigger in it for his media company. When Frommer later grew impatient and suggested that he might pass on a collaboration—thus putting the pictures into play—Pecker texted him: "I think you are making a major mistake . . . I think we can do a lot of business together." Frommer agreed, and responded that he wanted to work with Pecker and learn from him. They were still in discussions when Pecker met with Trump and Cohen at Trump Tower in August 2015 to talk about how American Media could prop up Trump's campaign and protect him.

As he invested himself in Trump's campaign, Pecker would try not to repeat the mistakes he'd made in California, where his efforts on Schwarzenegger's behalf eventually became public in the *Los Angeles Times*. This time Pecker would make sure that fewer employees knew what he was doing.

PECKER HAD BEEN in the top spot at American Media for sixteen years, a lifetime in the publishing industry. He was now more closely associated with the checkout-aisle publications—he called himself the "chairman of the tabloids"—than the glossy passion titles he'd overseen at Hachette Filipacchi. For a long time, Pecker had tried to transform his company into a mainstream publisher like the one he once led. He'd bought Joe Weider's fitness magazines. Later, he tried in vain for months to convince Jann Wenner to sell him *Rolling Stone;* Wenner refused to allow the classic music magazine he'd created to become an appendage to the *Enquirer*. Pecker had also explored merging American Media with Time Inc.

In 2013, Pecker's friend Ari Emanuel, a high-profile entertainment agent, secured him a meeting with Time Warner chief executive Jeff Bewkes. Emanuel had pitched Pecker as a savvy businessman who might bring the flagging newsweekly *Time* back to its former glory. Bewkes took the meeting as a favor to Emanuel. Despite his slick appearance, Pecker impressed the Time Warner CEO with his facility with numbers as he pitched merging their magazines and saving money by combining their distribution operations. But Bewkes never seriously considered allowing a gossip king with no real journalism credentials to control titles with the history of *Time* and *Sports Illustrated,* let alone combining them with the tabloids under one roof.

The *New York Post's* Keith J. Kelly had learned of the Time Inc. meeting and, in a resulting column, quoted an insider as saying that Pecker's hiring would lead to a mass exodus of *Time* writers, who disdained the checkbook journalism for which American Media was known. As usual, Pecker had one prominent booster. "David Pecker would be a brilliant choice as CEO of TIME Magazine—nobody could bring it back like David!" Donald Trump had tweeted.

Pecker seemed to have pigeonholed himself at American Media. Once he crossed over into the tabloid world, he'd risked banishment from the more staid corner of the publishing industry he had once occupied. If that were the case, he would continue to pursue respectability from his perch at American Media. He would hunt for withering media properties with big names, like *Time,* that he could acquire on the cheap, and forge stronger bonds with his powerful friends, a presidential candidate now among them.

American Media had recently undergone another financial restructuring that turned the company over to its two biggest creditors, Chatham Asset Management LLC and hedge fund manager Leon Cooperman. Chatham now owned 80 percent of the company, while Cooperman and Pecker each held 10 percent stakes. Three owners were better than a complex bondholders' group. Pecker had fewer people to answer to and more flexibility, and he was still CEO, after all these years.

COHEN DELAYED FROMMER for months with assurances that he could arrange an interview when Trump's schedule allowed, but he never delivered. Likewise, American Media waited until October before rejecting the proposed collaboration with Jerrick Media. (American Media ultimately made a deal with Harvey Weinstein's company to open its tabloid archives for development.) Frommer was bitter but did nothing with the pictures until much later, publishing one of them in a blog post before the 2016 election. It failed to make a dent in Trump's campaign. The photos were a small thing next to the tip that came into the *Enquirer* in late 2015.

Dino Sajudin was a doorman at Trump World Tower—the Manhattan residential building where Trump had quashed the condo-board uprising with Cohen's help—from 2008 to 2014. He'd been out of the job and living in East Stroudsburg, Pennsylvania, when he contacted the *Enquirer*'s tip line in late 2015.

His story was sensational: Sajudin told the tabloid that he'd learned from other employees that Trump had a brief fling with a woman who had worked at Trump Tower and at Trump International Hotel and Tower in New York—and that she'd had a child by him. The woman described herself in an online résumé as a concierge assistant. Her husband had been working as a chauffeur for Trump, his family, and his business associates since 1990. The driver's supervisor at the Trump Organization was Matthew Calamari, the company's chief operating officer. Sajudin named Calamari as one of the Trump employees he'd overheard saying that Trump had gotten the woman pregnant. Her daughter, Trump's purported love child, was now a young woman in her twenties, with a career in Northern California.

American Media entered into a source agreement with Sajudin on November 15. He would get paid $30,000 if the *Enquirer* published a story based on his information.

The *Enquirer*'s executive editor, Barry Levine, put at least four reporters on the story, including some who had helped break the John Edwards scandal. They staked out the Queens home of the mother of the child, hoping to get a photo. Once, they tailed her as she ran errands and followed her back to her house. An *Enquirer* reporter and photographer knocked on her door after she went inside, but she didn't answer. The reporters located her daughter and downloaded pictures from social media accounts. But they refrained from contacting the Trump Organization employees from whom Sajudin said he'd learned about the young woman, wanting to avoid tripping any alarms at Trump Tower.

Dylan Howard, American Media's chief content officer, outlined the team's steps in a memo to Pecker dated November 30, 2015. "Right now, we're arranging his poly," Howard wrote, referring to a polygraph test. "We have not made any moves on Dino's contacts because they could go right to Trump."

Sajudin took the lie detector test early the following month. Prompted by questions from the polygrapher, Sajudin said that he'd heard Trump had fathered the child from other employees and from residents of Trump World Tower.

"Did you overhear Matt Calamari saying that [the woman] got knocked up by the boss?" Michael Mancuso, the private investigator who administered the polygraph, asked Sajudin.

"Yes," Sajudin said.

"It is the professional opinion of this examiner based on the subject's reactions to the relevant test questions, that the subject was being truthful," Mancuso wrote in his report to the *Enquirer*.

Sajudin had no proof of the affair besides what he'd heard, and he had an ax to grind. After he was fired from his doorman job, he'd reached out to the woman for help. She'd told him she didn't want to get involved. He also had potential credibility problems. The year he lost his job, someone posting anonymously at DinoSajudin.com— a blog created to attack him—had accused the former doorman of trying to blackmail a resident of Trump World Tower. The post said Sajudin had once filed a false report online saying that the resident, Lawrence Penn III, had committed sexual assault. Sajudin had hoped to squeeze cash out of Penn, who had also recently been accused by the Securities and Exchange Commission of fraud, the anonymous poster said. (Penn later pleaded guilty to federal criminal charges in the $9.3 million scheme and was sentenced to six years in prison.)

But the biggest problem with Sajudin's story about Trump was also the most obvious: The child bore a strong familial resemblance to her mother's husband, the chauffeur. If this young woman was Trump's daughter, she looked nothing like him.

Impatient to figure out whether Sajudin's story held any truth, an *Enquirer* reporter called Rhona Graff, Trump's assistant, to ask whether the young woman was Trump's child. The reporter, Sharon Churcher, hadn't told her editors of her plans. Word of the call quickly made its way to Cohen, whose office was down the hall from Trump's.

Cohen then dialed Dylan Howard at American Media and pleaded with him not to publish the story. It was false and could hurt the boss,

Cohen said. "He is furious," Howard told other *Enquirer* editors after the call. But Howard and editor Barry Levine were still excited about the story. Cohen had sounded desperate, a sign that there might be some truth to the allegations.

After passing the polygraph in December, Sajudin pressed the tabloid to pay him immediately, threatening to walk otherwise. Levine asked Cameron Stracher, a general counsel for the company, to draft a revised source agreement and dispatched a New Jersey–based reporter, Robert Hartlein, to East Stroudsburg with the new contract, which provided Sajudin the $30,000 up front. Hartlein presented it to Sajudin at a McDonald's near the former doorman's house. "This is going to be a very merry Christmas," Sajudin said as he signed it.

It was a break with the tabloid's typical policy of paying for stories upon their publication, and a large sum relative to most source payments. But the *Enquirer* occasionally deviated from its usual practice if editors deemed a source's information important enough. In return for the $30,000, Sajudin agreed that he wouldn't disclose his story or his agreement with American Media to any third parties. "In the event Source breaches this provision, Source shall be liable to AMI and shall pay to AMI . . . the sum of $1,000,000," the contract said.

The *Enquirer*'s sources were often unsavory, the kind of people willing to sell out their friends and relatives. The liquidated damages provision made sure they wouldn't take the tabloid's money and disappear or blab to another publication. It was meant to scare them. No judge would make Sajudin pay $1 million for breaking a $30,000 agreement, but Sajudin didn't know that. He wasn't a lawyer, and he didn't hire one to review the contract before he signed it. He was as good as gagged.

Then the story died.

The *Enquirer* halted reporting completely after paying Sajudin. The editors told the reporters assigned to the story to move on. The reporters had been surprised that they were allowed to investigate Sajudin's claims in the first place, given Trump's protected status at the tabloid. They were left wondering why they'd been told to stand down. Even if there was no love child, the reporters suspected Trump had had a relationship with the mother.

Howard, who had been keen on the story, now told staff that Sajudin wasn't credible. The reporters suspected interference from Pecker, but they had no inkling of what Pecker had offered Trump in August 2015. Not even the top editors at the *Enquirer* knew.

Cohen would later say that Pecker had bought the story to figure out whether it was true and needed to be suppressed. Pecker might have thrown away his relationship with Trump in exchange for a massive scoop about the presidential candidate fathering a love child, a story that would have boosted *Enquirer* sales and esteem for the tabloid. But bottling up a story of a mere affair was worth more to Pecker in Trump's gratitude than a bump in newsstand sales. Even if no part of Sajudin's story was true, he could have sold it elsewhere had American Media let him walk. He'd passed a polygraph, after all. That didn't mean much in a court of law, but in the tabloid world it was proof. Stories had been published on less.

The practice of buying a story to prevent it from seeing the light of day was known in the tabloid world as "catch and kill." Sajudin's story was American Media's first big quarry of the campaign season. There would be another.

16.

PUTIN'S CHAIR, OR GOF.RU

■ ■ ■

As Trump's polls were rising that fall, Cohen began to work with Felix Sater, an entrepreneur he'd briefly met growing up, and a Russian developer, Andrey Rozov, to pursue a Trump Tower Moscow. Trump had been looking to develop a building with his name on it in the Russian capital since the 1990s, but nothing had materialized.

Sater knew of Trump's interest. In the mid-2000s, he'd been a partner at a development firm that worked with Trump and his children to develop Trump SoHo, a condominium hotel in lower Manhattan. At that time, Sater had also scouted projects for Trump throughout Eastern Europe, including in Moscow. He had chaperoned Ivanka Trump and Donald Trump Jr. there on a trip in 2006 and finagled a visit to Putin's office, where Trump's daughter, who was in her mid-twenties, spun around like an excited kid in the Russian leader's chair. (Putin wasn't there at the time.)

Sater had a criminal past. In his twenties, he had been convicted of assault for breaking a margarita glass on a man's face in a 1993 bar fight, doing a stint in jail. The episode also cost him his license as a stockbroker. After his release, Sater joined a stock fraud scheme that used members of Italian crime families for protection. The scheme unraveled in 1996, and the FBI later learned of Sater's involvement. He pleaded guilty and agreed to cooperate with the authorities in 1998.

But by that time, Sater had become a source for U.S. intelligence agencies, using a network he had developed in Russia and Afghanistan while looking for business deals. His value as an intelligence asset and his testimony against the mobsters and fraudsters he had collaborated with in the stock scheme allowed him to avoid prison.

After Trump SoHo, Sater had reconnected with Trump in 2010, as a commission-based consultant at the Trump Organization, suggesting potential projects. Sater had carried a business card with the title "Senior Advisor to Donald Trump" and had an office three doors down from the boss's own. The arrangement lasted less than a year and hadn't resulted in any deals.

But Sater remained on the lookout. He had met Andrey Rozov while pursuing some projects in Russia a few years earlier. Rozov had since begun to build residential apartment buildings in Moscow. Sater thought Rozov could be the vehicle for Trump to finally realize his dream of a Moscow tower. He suggested the idea to Cohen, whom he had coincidentally met as a teenager, in the fall of 2015.

By early November, Trump had signed a letter of intent for the Moscow project. The plan was for 250 luxury condominiums, a first-class hotel with fifteen floors, and commercial and office components. Trump's company would have received a $4 million fee up front, plus generous percentages of whatever income the building generated for years. After his missteps earlier in the campaign, Cohen desperately wanted to prove his worth by delivering something Trump himself had been unable to get done despite years of trying. Sater enthusiastically egged him on. "Michael I arranged for Ivanka to sit in Putins private chair at his desk and office in the Kremlin," Sater wrote in an email to Cohen on November 3. "Buddy our boy can become President of the USA and we can engineer it. I will get all of Putins team to buy in on this, I will manage this process . . . Michael, Putin gets on stage with Donald for a ribbon cutting for Trump Moscow, and Donald owns the republican nomination. And possibly beats Hillary and our boy is in."

By now, reporters had begun to write about Trump's past association with Sater, noting his criminal convictions as a young man. Trump said he barely remembered Sater, even as Cohen was engaged in new discussions with him. "Felix Sater, boy, I have to even think about it," Trump said to an Associated Press reporter in December.

In the coming months, Cohen briefed Trump on the project as they walked and talked on the mogul's way to campaign events. He also consulted with Ivanka Trump about hiring a big-name architect for the project, which was to include a "Spa by Ivanka Trump," and he talked to Donald Trump Jr. about his experiences in Moscow. Sater, meanwhile, looked for land and tried to arrange financing with Russian bankers, efforts that would require buy-in from the Kremlin. As a marketing tool, Sater suggested giving Putin a $50 million penthouse, which he thought would entice oligarchs to buy units in the building. And he spoke to Cohen about traveling to Russia to seal the deal. Cohen texted Sater a copy of his passport. Sater suggested that Trump should go, too. When Cohen asked Trump about it, the candidate said he was willing to go if it would help the project. He instructed Cohen to discuss it with Lewandowski, who told him to come back with actual dates.

The effort to obtain financing stalled, and the travel plans were put off. On December 17, 2015, Cohen forwarded Sater a Google alert of an article about Putin calling Trump "talented" and "colorful," with a note: "Now is the time. Call me."

But Sater continued to struggle to make progress, and Cohen grew frustrated, telling him he'd pursue the project on his own with other partners. "Not you or anyone you know will embarrass me in front of Mr. T when he asks me what is happening," Cohen wrote in a text message. He added, "You are putting my job in jeopardy and making me look incompetent." In a text on December 30, he told Sater he was "setting up the meeting myself."

Cohen took matters into his own hands. On January 11, 2016, he emailed the office of Kremlin press secretary Dmitry Peskov, a high-ranking Putin aide, and asked to speak with Putin's chief of staff, Sergei Ivanov. But Cohen misspelled the email address—he ended it with "gof.ru" instead of "gov.ru"—and it didn't go through. Three days later, he correctly emailed a different address. Cohen wrote:

Dear Mr. Peskov,

Over the past few months, I have been working with a company based in Russia regarding the development of a Trump Tower-Moscow project in Moscow City.

Without getting into lengthy specifics, the communication between our two sides has stalled. As this project is too important, I am hereby requesting your assistance.

I respectfully request someone, preferably you; contact me so that I might discuss the specifics as well as arranging meetings with the appropriate individuals.

I thank you in advance for your assistance and look forward to hearing from you soon.

On January 16, he again emailed Peskov and asked to speak to Ivanov. An assistant to Peskov, Elena Poliakova, emailed him a few days later, on January 20, asking Cohen to call her in Moscow. They spoke for some twenty minutes about the Trump Tower Moscow project and about Andrey Rozov and his company, I.C. Expert Investment Company. Cohen asked her for help finding land and obtaining financing. She agreed to follow up with others in Russia, but the discussion didn't lead to any progress. Sater also tried to get Cohen to visit Russia at the end of January, but he declined.

As THE PRESIDENTIAL primaries began, Trump translated his strong polling into an authentic surge with voters. He came in second behind Ted Cruz in the Iowa caucuses on February 1 but won the New Hampshire primary on February 9 and the Nevada caucuses on February 23. While the boss was knocking down victories, Cohen was finally finding his groove, a niche he could successfully occupy in the presidential campaign.

He'd been told again, firmly, to stay away from the campaign after a controversy surrounding Trump's first television ad, in early January 2016, which carried the banner "STOP ILLEGAL IMMIGRATION." After the ad ran, reporters discovered that the footage was from Morocco— and had nothing to do with illegal immigration to the United States. "No shit it's in Morocco," Lewandowski said, weirdly claiming that the Moroccan clips had been used intentionally to demonstrate the universality of the problem. Cohen, however, abruptly contradicted him, telling Chris Cuomo on CNN that he'd get to the bottom of the mistake. Though he walked back the comments, allies of Republican candidate Jeb Bush cited the imbroglio in a Federal Election Commission complaint suggesting that Cohen's "ambiguous" and "illicit" role with the campaign amounted to an illegal political contribution.

So Cohen turned to building coalitions for Trump behind the scenes. There had been some setbacks there, too. In the fall of 2015, he'd arranged for Trump to meet with Javier Palomarez, the head of the Hispanic Chamber of Commerce. But Cohen's efforts led to a public dispute between Palomarez, who said the candidate had backed out of a question-and-answer session with the chamber's members, and Trump, who insisted he had never committed. There had also been successes. That December, he'd asked Jerry Falwell Jr. to endorse Trump when the candidate spoke at Liberty University the following month. Falwell, who'd started his career as a lawyer and businessman, had assumed the presidency of Liberty in 2007 after the death of its founder, his father, Reverend Jerry Falwell. Despite never being ordained as a pastor, he'd become a leader among evangelicals. Falwell Jr. didn't want to back Trump for president on the campus of the nonprofit school—he'd been criticized for that in a previous presidential election—but he endorsed Trump soon after.

Cohen had also established a bond with Lynnette Hardaway and Rochelle Richardson, two sisters from North Carolina who made YouTube videos as Diamond and Silk. They'd once been Democrats but began filming colorful and campy videos in support of Trump. Cohen had also worked with Darrell Scott, a pastor from Cleveland he'd befriended who had put together a group of one hundred black clergy for Trump. The pastors met the candidate at Trump Tower in late November and some endorsed him. In the spring, Cohen helped Scott on another visit to announce the creation of a more broad-based group called the National Diversity Coalition for Trump.

Cohen's efforts for the campaign left him enough time, meanwhile, for a few side hustles.

John Gauger, the technology expert from Liberty University, was on vacation overseas with his family in early 2016 when he received a call from Cohen, who still owed him money for rigging polls years before, despite having paid part of the bill with a bag of cash. Cohen said he wanted to start a boutique marketing business, and he invited Gauger to work with him.

Cohen had been retained by a New Jersey–based assisted living company called CareOne Management LLC, which was paying him $50,000 a month for his "expertise in a multitude of areas," according to Cohen's contract with the company. Cohen had claimed he could help the company's chief executive, Daniel E. Straus, blunt the impact of negative stories that were showing near the top of Google searches of his name. In fact, Cohen wanted Gauger's company, RedFinch, to help him manipulate the online search results. Employing his custom-ary secrecy so that the client wouldn't know who was actually doing the work, Cohen arranged a call with Gauger but ordered him not to disclose his real name. He told Gauger to pretend he was a Russian. "Boris, are you there?" Cohen said after connecting the call.

RedFinch set up websites featuring glowing—and fake—articles about Straus that were intended to supplant the negative ones atop Google. Cohen collected $200,000 from CareOne for arranging the manipulation of the online search results. He paid RedFinch, which had actually done the work, $50,000 and kept the rest. Cohen didn't tell Gauger how much he'd made, nor would he pay taxes on the income. Like his efforts to build a Trump Tower in Moscow, it was a potential source of trouble for Cohen but one that was likely to go unnoticed, unless someone decided to take a close look at what he'd been doing.

With Trump's campaign building momentum through the spring of 2016, Cohen asked for one more favor from Gauger. He wanted him to create a Twitter account called @WomenForCohen, which would post about his good looks and business acumen. "Do this one thing for me, pal," Cohen had said. He didn't offer to pay, but Gauger decided to do it anyway, with the thought that someday Cohen might actually throw him some business. Gauger recruited a friend to help, and they created the account in May 2016. In the profile field, Gauger's friend wrote, "Women who love and support Michael Cohen. Strong, pit bull, sex symbol, no nonsense, business oriented, and ready to make a difference!"

So Gauger's friend began tweeting through @WomenForCohen into the summer and fall, posting Cohen's pictures and links to his media appearances and pontificating on his virility and masculinity. Cohen retweeted some of the posts and interacted with the account, grateful for the accolades.

TRUMP WAS CLOSING in on the Republican nomination in May when Sater reached out to Cohen again to try to jump-start the Moscow project. Sater told Cohen that Dmitry Peskov wanted to invite him to the St. Petersburg International Economic Forum that June, likening it to Russia's version of Davos, the renowned conference in the Swiss Alps. Sater, excited, said they'd meet with Peskov, and possibly Putin or

Prime Minister Dmitry Medvedev. Cohen accepted, and told Sater that Trump would be able to travel to Russia after formally accepting the Republican Party's nomination at the July convention in Cleveland.

In June, Sater forwarded Cohen an invitation from the Russian foundation organizing the forum, along with a visa application, and asked for passport photos. Cohen didn't see any indication on the documents that Peskov had actually invited him. He was skeptical about Sater's claims that the Russian officials were interested in meeting him. In the lobby of Trump Tower, Cohen told Sater he wasn't going to Russia. The pursuit of a Trump Tower in Moscow was finally over.

The Moscow effort had been emblematic of Cohen's relationship with Trump. The notion of a presidential candidate actively pursuing a business deal with a hostile foreign power in the middle of a campaign would have been anathema to any conventional political or business adviser. But Trump's presidential bid, sincere as it was, also rested on the assumption that he'd most likely lose and then return to his business. Viewed in that light, it made sense to advance the Moscow deal while Trump was running, when the effort might benefit from his candidacy. So Trump signed off, and Cohen once again, out of a desire to impress, proved willing to try to do what others around the boss surely wouldn't have. Together, they kept the deal a secret from others at the Trump Organization and pursued it quietly until the campaign had progressed so far that the opportunity would have to wait. Once again, as before, a deal Cohen had spearheaded had failed to materialize, though, to be fair, Trump's success in the campaign had complicated matters.

Neither of the men knew then whether he would win, or how it would look, if he did win, to have chased a deal with Putin while seeking the presidency. But if anyone raised an issue, Cohen could always lie his way out of it. And if he were to be caught lying, Cohen had kept Trump removed enough from the talks that the boss could deny any real involvement.

In late June, Corey Lewandowski's tenure as Trump's campaign manager also came to an end. Lewandowski had drawn negative news to the campaign as well, when he was briefly charged with assault after grabbing a *Breitbart News* reporter at a Trump campaign rally. The charges were dropped after authorities concluded that he'd been trying to protect Trump. More problematic, Lewandowski hadn't adjusted for the general election campaign and had been unwilling to widen the circle of people who had control. "I liked Corey very much," Trump said after the firing. "I've been very loyal to Corey." He already had Paul Manafort, Roger Stone's former lobbying partner, waiting in the wings to replace him. Trump had brought on Manafort, a longtime Republican consultant who had developed a specialty advising political campaigns in former Soviet bloc states, as an adviser a few months earlier.

Cohen was in the conference room when Donald Trump Jr. told Lewandowski he was gone, before he was escorted from the building. Lewandowski's departure didn't mean that Cohen would become campaign manager, but it did free him up to go on television again.

17.

RESOLUTION CONSULTANTS LLC

■ ■ ■

FOX & FRIENDS co-hosts Ainsley Earhardt and Brian Kilmeade sat on a cream-colored couch, their backs to a wall of glass that looked out on Sixth Avenue in midtown Manhattan. On television screens, a graphic below the hosts identified a guest who had phoned in: "DONALD TRUMP (R)/2016 PRESIDENTIAL CANDIDATE."

The May 3, 2016, interview began with the topic of evangelical voters and their relative affection for Trump and for Ted Cruz, who was—incredibly—Trump's last viable rival for the Republican nomination.

At a recent campaign event, Cruz's father, a preacher acting as the Texas senator's surrogate, had called on fellow evangelical Christians to support his son, "the candidate that stands on the word of God," warning that the "alternative"—Trump—"could be the destruction of America."

In the Fox News studio, Earhardt, her hands folded across her lap, asked Trump's disembodied voice to respond to Rafael Cruz's exhortation to the evangelical base.

"It's disgraceful that his father can go out and do that," Trump said. "And, you know, his father was with Lee Harvey Oswald prior to Oswald's being, you know, shot. I mean, the whole thing is ridiculous. What is this, right prior to his being shot, and nobody even brings it up. I mean, they don't even talk about that. That was reported, and nobody talks about it . . . I mean, what was he doing? What was he doing with Lee Harvey Oswald shortly before the death? Before the shooting? It's horrible."

About two weeks earlier, the *National Enquirer* had plastered Cruz on its cover, declaring in a large yellow font, "TED CRUZ FATHER

LINKED TO JFK ASSASSINATION!" The evidence was a single grainy photo of an unidentifiable young man standing next to Oswald, handing out pro–Fidel Castro literature in New Orleans in 1963, months before Oswald shot Kennedy to death. The *Enquirer*'s "experts" compared the photo to others of Rafael Cruz around the same time and concluded that, yeah, maybe he was the man beside Oswald. Such authoritative reporting had been enough to support an outlandish banner headline.

Trump had savaged Ted Cruz for weeks as the two presidential candidates clawed for delegates that spring. "Lyin' Ted," Trump called him at every opportunity. He mocked the looks of Cruz's wife, Heidi, posting a photo of her on Twitter next to a picture of his own wife, Melania, a former model. And now he took the *Enquirer* story and ran with it.

THE TABLOID LIFTED the JFK conspiracy theory from the weirder corners of the Internet, where it had been circulating for some time. The story would have been funny if it weren't so effective. Cruz campaign aides had to ask Rafael Cruz, with a straight face, if he had been involved in Kennedy's killing. (No, Rafael said.) But the campaign had to assume, before issuing a flat denial, that the *Enquirer* story was based on a peel of truth that the tabloid had stretched beyond recognition. They had to quiz Rafael on his whereabouts in the 1960s, to determine whether he had been in Louisiana at the same time as Oswald, and precisely where he was in Dallas when Kennedy was shot. Rafael had been eating lunch with co-workers at a restaurant along the motorcade route and walked outside to watch Kennedy as the young president rolled by, about fifteen minutes before Oswald shot him. He was red hot over the *Enquirer* story.

If there was a silver lining, the *Enquirer* had given the Cruz campaign some much-needed attention and an opportunity for the candidate to paint himself as a victim of Trump's unscrupulous allies in the media, just as voters went to the polls for Indiana's primary.

"Yes, my dad killed JFK, he is secretly Elvis, and Jimmy Hoffa is buried in his backyard," Cruz said at a campaign event.

The Cruz campaign had gone through a similar exercise months earlier, when the *Enquirer* reported that the Republican candidate had had extramarital affairs with five women. ("IT'S OVER FOR PERVY

TED," the tabloid enthused.) Cruz dismissed the allegations, and his staff believed him. The campaign had a thick file on the senator to guard against opposition research. (It contained no evidence of affairs.) But Cruz and his staff had to prepare his wife for the story, and they had to figure out who the alleged mistresses were. The *Enquirer* hadn't identified them when it sought comment from the Cruz campaign. Nor had the tabloid named the women in print; it published pixelated photos of faces, with black rectangles covering eyes. The campaign (and many others) saw through the digital disguises worn by the women in some of the photos. A campaign lawyer spoke with one of the alleged mistresses, who was as insistent as Cruz that the story was bogus.

Cruz's staff also fielded inquiries from—and haggled with—the mainstream press as reporters tried to corroborate the tabloid's reporting. They never did. But the story was a boon for Trump, throwing the Cruz campaign off-balance and forcing it to divert resources. It was like a concussion grenade. Afterward, the campaign got in the habit of dispatching an aide each week to Randalls, a supermarket on San Felipe Street, near campaign headquarters in Houston, to procure the latest issue of the *Enquirer* and scan it for more potential trouble.

Since the launch of his campaign, Trump had commanded the news cycle, earning billions of dollars in free media coverage. The *Enquirer*, with its sagging circulation of 364,000, was a marginal presence compared with the national newspapers, news sites, and television networks that reached millions of Americans. But it had power beyond its size. The tabloid's audience was made up largely of members of Trump's base, for one thing. That gave Pecker influence with Trump, who in turn promoted the *Enquirer*'s stories, making the tabloid seem like more of a player than it was. The *Enquirer* also had a track record of breaking political scandals. The paper served up plenty of tendentious slop, but its past scoops exposing the infidelity of John Edwards, Gary Hart, and Jesse Jackson—to name a few—made it difficult for politicians and the mainstream media that covered them to ignore the *Enquirer* entirely.

David Pecker stayed true to his word. The *Enquirer* had made sport of tarring Trump's political rivals since his meeting with Trump the previous August. A tabloid "investigation" revealed in October 2015 that Hillary Clinton would be "dead in six months," driven to an early grave by failing health and a "deadly thirst for power." But before she died, Clinton was headed to jail "for covering up the murder of her lover, Vince Foster!" the *Enquirer* promised later that month. The tabloid resurfaced its past coverage of sexual misconduct accusations against Bill Clinton, and Hillary Clinton's alleged role in suppressing them. It also claimed that Bill had brain damage and that Hillary was a lesbian. And the *Enquirer* hired Dick Morris, a former adviser to Bill Clinton turned sworn enemy, to write weekly columns and make online videos trashing the Clintons.

The other candidates fared no better, regardless of party. Marco Rubio was hiding a "bombshell drug scandal that could derail his bid for the Oval Office." Democrat Bernie Sanders was a Russian spy. In addition to his alleged mistresses, Ted Cruz was trying to cover up his past as a "boozer." Late in the primary campaign, when Carly Fiorina, the former chief executive of Hewlett-Packard, was named Cruz's running mate, the *Enquirer* quickly dismissed her as a "homewrecker" and called her the "fake face of ambition," claiming she'd had plastic surgery. A cover story about the presidential candidates headlined "WHAT THEY'RE HIDING!" reported that Rubio had frequented gay nightclubs as a teenager, that Cruz's wife was involved in a "suicide scandal," and that Sanders was caught up in a "child-sex probe."

Trump's secret? The candidate had "greater support and popularity than he's admitted to!"

And that was just a sample of the tabloid's coverage in the run-up to Trump's nomination. In all, the *Enquirer* had published more than sixty stories attacking his opponents, the Clintons most of all, followed by Cruz.

Meanwhile, the *Enquirer* had practically deified Trump, publishing a two-part "world exclusive" interview with him that explained how the "billionaire businessman has quietly donated a huge chunk of his fortune to charity—and still finds the time to remain a doting dad to his young son!" (The story, of course, was a complete fantasy. *The Washington Post*'s David Fahrenthold punctured the myth of Trump's generosity in the months before the election, reporting that he often showed up to charity events without giving a cent and almost never followed through on his public promises to donate money.)

• • •

Trump trounced Cruz in the May 3 Republican primary in Indiana, hours after his interview with *Fox & Friends,* capturing 53 percent of the vote to Cruz's 37 percent. The loss forced Cruz from the race, the sixteenth and final Republican candidate vanquished by Trump's populist campaign. Trump strode to the podium at his Trump Tower campaign headquarters in Manhattan to the Rolling Stones song "Start Me Up." The self-described billionaire was now the presumptive Republican presidential nominee, and he was gracious in victory.

"Ted Cruz, I don't know if he likes me or he doesn't like me, but he is one hell of a competitor," Trump told a crowd of cheering supporters at Trump Tower.

Flanked by his wife and his daughter Ivanka, Trump began to tick off the blocs of voters he said had rallied to his side in Indiana. He won the evangelical vote, he said. The Hispanic and African American vote, too.

"I won with women," Trump said, pausing a beat for effect. "I love winning with women."

The crowd laughed.

Four days after Trump's win in Indiana, an actress and former *Playboy* model named Carrie Stevens posted a tweet.

"I usually don't get involved in politics but why Bill Clinton can't [*sic*] get an extramarital BJ but @RealDonaldTrump can?" Stevens wrote on May 7.

Stevens, the Playmate of the Month in June 1997, was more specific in her next tweet: "#donaldlovesplaymates @karenmcdougal98."

Trump had been the presumptive Republican nominee for about a month when the woman referenced in the Carrie Stevens tweets, Karen McDougal, met with attorney Keith Davidson in Arizona. McDougal had left Los Angeles and the Playboy Mansion behind. Recently divorced from her third husband, she lived in Arizona and was temporarily staying with a friend, an ex-cop named John Crawford who ran UPS stores in the Phoenix area.

By her own reckoning, McDougal was a "different girl" than the model who had carried on a ten-month affair with Donald Trump a decade earlier. She had embraced Christianity. McDougal's Twitter feed was a mix of references to her faith, inspirational quotes, and advocacy against animal cruelty. She bore no ill will toward Trump. In fact, she openly supported his presidential campaign.

But the tweet from Carrie Stevens, a friend of McDougal's before they had a bitter falling-out, was a wake-up call. Trump's outsider campaign had caught fire. It dawned on McDougal that her affair with Trump was likely to become public as the spotlight of the election intensified. She'd received media calls over the years and had denied having a relationship with Trump, but that was before he'd become the most famous person on earth. If the story came out, she wanted to be in control of the narrative. If that control boosted her career, so much the better.

Crawford encouraged her to sell her story before someone else beat her to it. He reached out to an acquaintance, Jay Grdina, a businessman and former porn actor, for possible contacts in the media. Grdina put Crawford in touch with Davidson, whom Grdina had used in the past, a lawyer who had experience helping clients profit from dirt on celebrities.

Davidson and McDougal met at a Pita Jungle restaurant on Frank Lloyd Wright Boulevard in Scottsdale on June 15, 2016. McDougal said she was conflicted. She wanted to use the affair to help her situation, but she didn't necessarily want the details to become public. What would her mother think? Davidson told McDougal the rights to her story of an affair with Trump could be worth serious money. His fee would be 45 percent of whatever McDougal received, Davidson said, describing his cut an industry standard. (Plaintiffs' lawyers typically took a third, but Davidson's work was unique.) The attorney sent her a retainer agreement to sign later that day and told her to expect news within twenty-four hours. The agreement described Davidson's services for McDougal as assisting her with negotiating a confidentiality agreement or the sale of her story rights "related to interactions with Donald Trump."

TRUMP'S POLITICAL RISE gave the story of Stormy Daniels's fling with Trump in Lake Tahoe new currency, she figured. Five years had passed since Michael Cohen bullied the *Life & Style* publisher into killing its interview with Daniels, who'd passed a polygraph, affirming her claims of a sexual encounter with Trump. Daniels was fixing up a ranch for her horses and was in need of some extra money. "Just got the estimate for the building contractor for my stable. Currently breathing into a paper bag and shitting my pants," she wrote in a May 2016 tweet. The month before, she had contacted Gina Rodriguez, who was now representing reality television stars, and they made plans to shop her story again. Here was another chance, Rodriguez thought, to make far more than the $15,000 *Life & Style* had agreed to pay.

She approached the magazine again, as well as *In Touch* and the British tabloid the *Daily Mail*. Her asking price was $200,000 to $250,000, but none of the publications wanted to shell out for a story that Daniels had publicly denied. Rodriguez went to Dylan Howard at American Media, an old friend for whom she'd been a useful source on Charlie Sheen and other stories. (Howard had dogged Sheen and broken the story of the actor's HIV diagnosis.) She sent him the timeline and narrative of the Daniels-Trump affair in an April 7 email, but Howard told her the story was worth little, because it had already surfaced years earlier—in *The Dirty*, where Rodriguez herself had planted it. Daniels, he reminded her, had called the story "bullshit." American Media was a pass, too.

Howard had an altogether different reaction when he received a call from Keith Davidson on June 15, 2016, about Karen McDougal. Davidson was representing the former Playmate "regarding an alleged romantic relationship" with Trump, and McDougal was exploring her options, he told Howard. Was American Media interested?

After the call, David Pecker contacted Michael Cohen to warn him. Howard, meanwhile, arranged a meeting with Davidson in Los Angeles to hear McDougal's story.

McDougal brought her friend John Crawford to the meeting at Davidson's office. Jay Grdina, who had connected McDougal and Davidson, was also on hand. McDougal also knew Grdina—she had been married to his brother when she met Trump. Davidson had agreed to pay Grdina and Crawford consulting fees for connecting him with McDougal, as a workaround to ethics rules barring attorneys from splitting legal fees.

McDougal brought notes she'd recently written about the affair, containing dates when she said she was with Trump and telephone numbers she used to reach him. But she didn't have anything in the way of hard proof, and as Howard interviewed her, he sensed her reluctance to come forward. "I don't want to be the next Monica Lewinsky," McDougal said at one point. The former White House intern had been mocked and vilified after her affair with Bill Clinton became public. McDougal didn't want to end up as a punch line. Without stronger documentation, Howard said McDougal's story wouldn't be worth more than $15,000. McDougal suggested that she might have some corroborating materials in a storage locker. She promised to look for them.

After the interview, Howard agreed to let Davidson know whether American Media intended to buy the story by day's end. In the meantime, Davidson would refrain from shopping McDougal's information to another outlet. Howard got on a three-way call with Pecker and Cohen soon after leaving Davidson's office. He described her account of a relationship with Trump, pointed out that she had little to back it up—though she came across as credible—and related her Lewinsky comment. They agreed that the *Enquirer* would hold off on offering McDougal a deal. There was no reason to spend money on a story she didn't seem to want to tell.

That night, Davidson emailed Howard.

"Today we provided you unfettered access to Ms. McDougal wherein you interviewed her in an uninterrupted, direct and in-depth manner. You expressed, (as I believe), that Ms. McDougal was being completely honest regarding the subject matter discussed today," Davidson wrote. "Pursuant to our explicit agreement, the 12-hour exclusive negotiating period that we graciously extended you has now expired."

Howard was noncommittal in his response. "Understood. And please advise if your client might wish to continue discussions with me once your client obtains further information from her search of storage etc," he replied.

The implication was clear. American Media wasn't biting.

In her search for more evidence, McDougal found the 2006 datebook in which she'd marked her visits with Trump. McDougal had hoped to recover a minicassette tape with Trump's voice on it, from her old answering machine, but she couldn't find it.

Davidson was already considering other possibilities.

. . .

THE DANGER MAY have passed for the moment, but Trump took no chances. After the candidate learned of McDougal's story from Cohen, he phoned Pecker on June 27 to make a direct plea for the publisher's help. Pecker was in New Jersey at a meeting with American Media's largest shareholder, the hedge fund Chatham Asset Management, when he connected with Trump. *Can you make this go away?* Trump asked the publisher.

Davidson had been talking with bookers for ABC News who took an immediate interest in McDougal's story. They soon connected Davidson and McDougal with ABC News's investigative team. On July 7, Rhonda Schwartz, the lead investigative producer, met with McDougal, Davidson, and Jay Grdina at the Beverly Wilshire Hotel for a full-day interview. McDougal and Schwartz spent hours together over the next several weeks, forging a bond that Schwartz hoped would lead to an on-air interview of McDougal by Schwartz's longtime collaborator Brian Ross, chief investigative correspondent for ABC News. At the Arizona Biltmore Hotel, in Phoenix, they went through McDougal's datebook and discussed her relationship with Trump. ABC News entered into a confidentiality agreement with Davidson that barred the outlet from publicizing any of the information McDougal provided, unless or until she agreed to do the interview.

The pitch was soft: ABC News would present McDougal's story in a serious, focused way. Ross and Schwartz weren't looking for lurid details. She'd appear on *Good Morning America* and other ABC News segments. The exposure would be massive. But McDougal was still wary of stepping into the spotlight as Trump's former mistress, and ABC couldn't offer her money.

ON JULY 19, 2016, Republican delegates in Cleveland formally selected Donald Trump as their presidential nominee. Veteran politicians like former governors Jeb Bush, Chris Christie, and Mike Huckabee and Senator Marco Rubio had withdrawn months earlier. Only Cruz and Ohio governor John Kasich had remained in the race past April, and Kasich had merely been a spoiler, having won a single primary, in his home state.

Trump had dominated spring contests in Connecticut, Delaware, Maryland, Pennsylvania, and Rhode Island that were collectively nicknamed the Acela Primary, after the Amtrak train that services the Northeast Corridor. In the Indiana primary, Trump had collected another fifty-seven delegates. Kasich dropped out soon after.

Cruz, having endured Trump's insults and the *Enquirer's* barrage, refused to endorse the businessman at the Republican convention in Cleveland. Trump had taken aim at his wife's looks. The *Enquirer* had accused him of adultery and implied that his father was involved in the assassination of JFK. "I am not in the habit of supporting people who attack my wife and attack my father," he explained to an angry Texas delegation after withholding his support for Trump.

Trump responded by repeating the *Enquirer's* allegations about Rafael Cruz's association with Lee Harvey Oswald. "All I did is point out the fact that on the cover of the *National Enquirer* there was a picture of him and crazy Lee Harvey Oswald having breakfast," he said in a send-off speech the morning after the convention ended. "Now, Ted never denied that it was his father." (In fact, the man in the picture, who was never proven to be Rafael Cruz, was passing out leaflets next to Oswald. And Ted Cruz had called Trump "a pathological liar" for linking his father with the assassin.) Trump reminded his audience that the allegations had come from what he considered a very credible source.

"This was a magazine that frankly in many respects should be very respected," he said. Trump went on, "I've always said why didn't the *National Enquirer* get the Pulitzer Prize for Edwards, and O. J. Simpson, and all of these things?"

KEITH DAVIDSON PLAYED ABC News and American Media off each other as he sought a deal for Karen McDougal in July 2016. He told ABC that McDougal had another offer, one with considerable financial incentives. McDougal wanted to be on ABC's *Dancing with the Stars,* one of the most popular shows on television. Davidson nudged the news division to pull strings to get her on the show.

Meanwhile, Davidson told Howard that ABC was moving forward with an interview that would give his client prime-time billing. If American Media wanted to buy the story, it had better hurry, the attorney said. But McDougal wanted more than money. *If you want this story, you're going to have to come up with something that will revitalize her career,* Davidson told Howard.

Howard conveyed the news to his boss, Pecker. Naturally, Cohen soon learned of the ABC talks from the American Media executives and alerted Trump. They decided now was the time to buy.

"American Media Inc is very much looking forward to presenting a series of lucrative career and business opportunities to your client," Howard wrote to Davidson in a July 29 email. "These will focus around our health and celebrity titles—in addition to other endorsements."

Davidson and American Media negotiated the agreement over the first week in August.

The publisher would acquire the rights to McDougal's story but would never convert them into a tabloid scoop, Davidson told his client. American Media was in the tank for Trump.

The $150,000 contract guaranteed McDougal's appearance on at least two American Media magazine covers, giving her the exposure she wanted and granting the publisher the option of printing fitness columns under her name.

In a video call, Howard promised McDougal that her story would remain confidential and told her the magazine covers and fitness columns would help resuscitate her modeling career. She wouldn't have to sacrifice her privacy, and potentially her reputation, to build her brand.

McDougal had questions after reading the contract Davidson sent her. She wanted to know what would happen if the story got out through some other means. Could American Media penalize her?

"I understand I need to keep my mouth shut about the 'relationship' . . . and I will . . . but what if ABC or ANYONE else leaks it? If I deny, I'm safe?" she asked in an email.

"CORRECT IF YOU DENY YOU ARE SAFE," Davidson responded.

When McDougal asked for more time to review the particulars of the contract, Davidson nudged her forward. "WE CAN DISCUSS ANYTIME—HOWEVER WE REALLY DO NEED TO GET THIS SIGNED AND WRAPPED UP SO WE CAN TELL ABC THAT UOUVE [sic] CHOSEN NOT TO TELL YOUR STORY."

McDougal signed the contract on August 6. Davidson sent the signed document to Howard and American Media's lawyer, Cameron

Stracher, the following day. Davidson also emailed Rhonda Schwartz at ABC News to let her know the former *Playboy* model was backing out.

"After much introspection and after hours of consultation with friends & family, Karen has decided against publicly discussing any of her past life events with ABC or anyone," Davidson wrote in an email.

Pecker had sought the advice of an expert on campaign-finance laws before authorizing the McDougal deal. The executive knew well from the prosecution of John Edwards—a case fueled by the *Enquirer*'s reporting—that paying hush money for a politician was a dangerous game. Pecker had come away from discussions with the lawyer believing the contract with McDougal was legally sound. The publisher wasn't (merely) handing her hush money. American Media was paying her, ostensibly, to be a model and columnist for its publications.

Never mind that Section 3 of the contract granted American Media "all rights in and to the life story of McDougal regarding, (in the broadest possible way), any relationship she has ever had with a then-married man."

Davidson, as a courtesy, contacted Cohen to let him know the deal was done, but Cohen already knew, of course. So did Donald Trump, and he was grateful.

As McDougal's deal came together, Michael Cohen assured Pecker that he would reimburse him for laying out the $150,000 to keep her quiet. Together, they came up with a plan for shifting the expense. Trump would pay $125,000 for the rights to McDougal's story—less than the full payment, as American Media would retain the rights to McDougal's magazine covers and health columns. Separately, Cohen was pushing American Media to turn over all its archival material on Trump, in case Pecker left the company. Cohen and Trump didn't want a new chief executive with no loyalty to Trump to have control over it.

In the first weekend of September, Cohen briefed Trump on the talks. He was secretly taping the conversation on his iPhone.

"Um, I need to open up a company for the transfer of all of that info regarding our friend, David, you know, so that—I'm going to do that right away," Cohen said.

"So what do we got to pay for this? One-fifty?" Trump said.

Cohen said he would be paying for "all the stuff" that Pecker had on Trump.

"Yeah, I was thinking about that," Trump said.

"All the stuff," Cohen replied. "Because—here, you never know where that company—you never know what he's—"

"Maybe he gets hit by a truck," Trump ventured.

"Correct," said Cohen. "So I'm all over that."

On September 30, 2017, Cohen created a limited liability company in Delaware, calling it Resolution Consultants LLC, to use as a conduit for buying the rights to McDougal's story. Delaware was among the top destinations for companies to incorporate because of its favorable tax and secrecy laws. Owners of Delaware corporations could shield their identities by hiring a lawyer or an agent to be the named contact person. But Cohen listed himself on the incorporation papers, making him vulnerable to discovery, although the documents connecting him to the company weren't visible online. To see them, someone would have to pull the formation papers from the state's file.

Pecker took an extra measure to keep the transaction a secret. He turned to someone he trusted: Daniel Rotstein, the company's long-time human resources executive. Rotstein had come to American Media seventeen years earlier when Pecker bought the rival tabloid *Globe*. Over the years, when Pecker erupted at an employee and a departure became inevitable, he relied on Rotstein to calm the situation, negotiate severance, and ensure that the separation went smoothly. Rotstein was based in Florida, so if he appeared in New York, it signaled that someone's head was about to roll. He became known to staff as "Dr. Death."

Rotstein was no longer an American Media employee. He was now a well-paid consultant for the publisher, but he served in essentially the same role as he had before leaving. He was also a full-time human resources director for the city of Pembroke Pines, southwest of Fort Lauderdale. As Pecker had with other sensitive matters, he asked Rotstein to run the McDougal reimbursement through the consultant's own corporate entity to try to keep it confidential, even from Pecker's underlings at American Media. Pecker and Cohen executed a contract, and Rotstein issued an invoice through his shell company.

But the money never came. Cohen told Pecker that Trump was

dragging his feet because he was cheap and no longer wanted to pay. In the meantime, Pecker discussed the rights transfer with Stracher, his general counsel, who told the media executive that he'd be crazy to sell McDougal's story to Trump. The optics would be terrible if it ever came out. Pecker took the attorney's advice to heart. American Media would eat the expense of McDougal's story. It was a favor that Pecker could perhaps trade in the future.

In a phone call, Pecker told Cohen the deal was off.

"Tear up the contract," he told the Trump aide.

Cohen said he would, but he didn't.

GINA RODRIGUEZ AND Stormy Daniels had been out of touch for a few months in the summer of 2016. No one wanted the Trump story, at least not for the price both women thought it could fetch. The most they had been offered was $5,000—a pittance. They were incredulous. Why didn't anyone want a story about the Republican presidential nominee having an affair with a porn star?

The answer was likely twofold. The world already knew Trump had been unfaithful to his first wife. It wasn't exactly news that he might have had another affair. Nor was it surprising that celebrity publications would turn down a story of said affair, especially given Daniels's public denial and the prevalent belief that Trump was about to lose in a landslide. But Rodriguez was unwilling to accept defeat.

If the media wasn't interested, maybe Trump's camp would be willing to take the story off the market. Rodriguez had been keeping her friend and sometime collaborator Keith Davidson up to date on her attempts to sell the story. Davidson agreed to talk to Cohen to take his temperature on buying Daniels's silence, but Davidson didn't trust Trump's fixer. Cohen was volatile, and Davidson had learned to avoid his kind. He put distance between himself and Daniels when he spoke with Cohen in September, making it clear he wasn't representing her. Davidson told Cohen that he knew the porn star was shopping her story. If Cohen or Trump had any desire to reel in Daniels, Davidson could approach her and Rodriguez about a deal, he said in a phone call.

Hell, no, Cohen said. The story was ancient, and Daniels had denied it publicly.

Cohen warned Davidson that the Secret Service was now protecting Trump, and that Cohen wouldn't hesitate to sic them on Daniels and Rodriguez if they tried to extort the presidential nominee.

He also issued a legal threat. "Did you tell them they could get sued?"

On October 7, 2016, *The Washington Post* nearly derailed Donald Trump's presidential campaign. Someone had leaked an outtake from one of Trump's appearances on NBC's *Access Hollywood* to David Fahrenthold, the same *Post* reporter who had investigated Trump's claims that he'd given millions of his own money to charity. Trump could be heard on the *Access Hollywood* video, recorded in 2005 but never aired, chatting with host Billy Bush about his ardor for beautiful women and the liberties they permitted him because of his fame.

"You know, I'm automatically attracted to beautiful—I just start kissing them. It's like a magnet. Just kiss. I don't even wait. And when you're a star, they let you do it. You can do anything," Trump was re-corded telling Bush.

Bush: "Whatever you want."

Trump: "Grab 'em by the pussy. You can do anything."

Trump had shown remarkable staying power in the face of reports of his unsavory business dealings, his disregard for the truth, and his shabby treatment of business partners, vendors, and women in general. Trump's supporters stuck with him after he attacked the family of a U.S. Army officer killed in a suicide attack in Iraq and after he dismissed the heroism of Senator John McCain. ("I like people that weren't captured," he'd said.)

But the condemnation following the *Post's* story about the *Access Hollywood* tape was nearly universal. It plunged Trump's campaign into chaos.

Polls conducted by *The Economist*/YouGov and by Fox News had shown Hillary Clinton leading Trump by between four points and six points, respectively, before the video surfaced. Her lead in the polls jumped to ten points and eleven points in the days after the *Post's* scoop. Politicians lined up to register their disapproval. Many main-stream Republicans abandoned Trump.

"You either drop out right now or you lose by the biggest landslide in American political history," Reince Priebus, chairman of the Republican National Committee, told Trump as the candidate and his closest advisers took stock of the damage, in the candidate's residence on the sixty-fourth floor of Trump Tower.

But Trump ignored his warning. He would stay in the race and try to play a near-perfect game until November. Another scandal could be fatal.

18.

DD AND PP

■ ■ ■

THE ACCESS HOLLYWOOD video changed the math for Stormy Daniels as well as for Donald Trump.

Before it emerged, reporters had already focused on allegations of Trump making unwanted sexual advances and objectifying women. Afterward, more women came forward with stories about the Republican candidate's bad behavior. They told of incidents that could have been charted on a map like stops on a cross-country trip spanning the decades; women spoke of unpleasant and unwelcome encounters with Trump at the U.S. Open tennis tournament, at Mar-a-Lago, on the set of *The Apprentice,* at beauty pageants, during a flight, in a nightclub, and on and on, all consonant with the *Access Hollywood* revelation.

Trump denied all the accusations but issued a videotaped apology for the explosive report, saying that the words he had spoken on the tape "don't reflect who I am."

"I've said and done things I regret, and the words released today on this more-than-a-decade-old video are one of them," he said. "I said it. I was wrong. And I apologize."

The media frenzy breathed oxygen into Daniels's flagging efforts to sell the story of her own Trump tryst. Extramarital sex with a porn star, even one who'd slept with Trump willingly, would still damage his fading chances. Her agent, Gina Rodriguez, had already begun talks about Daniels with *Good Morning America.* They weren't advanced, but they were a card Rodriguez could now play.

On Saturday, October 8, following the worst day of Trump's campaign, Rodriguez, Dylan Howard of American Media, and lawyer Keith Davidson began a series of conversations about Stormy Daniels that would last into the night. They realized her story was more marketable now than it had been when Rodriguez first pitched Howard in April, before the *Access Hollywood* tape placed Trump's treatment of women in the national spotlight.

"Trump is fucked," Davidson texted Howard that afternoon. The editor agreed: "Wave the white flag. It's over people!"

A few hours later, Davidson emailed Rodriguez: "Have you heard from Stormy lately?" Howard followed up with her about a half hour later. He asked Daniels's manager to send him a pitch so he could elevate it to his boss, David Pecker.

"He likely will pay," Howard texted.

Rodriguez emailed him a brief description of her client's claims:

> Donald Trump had sex with Stormy Daniels while his current wife was pregnant. He flew Stormy to his Pageant and told her he would get her on Celebrity Apprentice which he never did. She met him while at a celebrity golf tournament and The Wicked girls were at the event.
>
> Stormy will take a lie detector and go on the record.

As the discussions about Daniels took shape, Cohen was visiting his daughter in London, where she had enrolled in a study-abroad program for college. He hadn't been in regular touch with Trump or Hope Hicks, the candidate's spokeswoman, in recent weeks. But now they sought him out as the *Access Hollywood* scandal roiled the campaign.

On that Saturday night in London, Cohen had a conference call with Hicks and Trump, followed by a call with Hicks alone. Hicks had heard from another campaign aide that a rumor was circulating of another tape, this one of Trump cavorting with prostitutes in Moscow during a trip there for the Miss Universe pageant in 2013. Hicks had been told that *TMZ* might have access to the tape, and she knew that Cohen was close to Harvey Levin, the gossip outlet's founder. Hicks asked Cohen to let her know if he heard anything from Levin. She also impressed on him, in the event he spoke to any reporters, that the campaign's messaging was that Trump's remarks on the *Access Hollywood* recording were merely "locker room talk."

The Moscow tape was bad, but it was just a rumor. Cohen had a more immediate problem. He learned from Pecker and Howard that

Daniels was still shopping her story. Cohen, Pecker, and Howard exchanged a series of calls after Cohen got off the phone with Hicks. Cohen lobbied Pecker to buy Daniels's story, and for a brief time that Saturday night it seemed as if American Media might repeat the favor the publisher had done for Trump by locking up Karen McDougal's story.

Less than an hour after receiving the pitch from Rodriguez that Howard had requested, he texted her to set a price.

"How much for Stormy?" Howard wrote.

"250k," Rodriguez replied.

She told Howard that *Good Morning America* and the British tabloid the *Daily Mail* were both hot for the story. The ABC show had expressed some interest but didn't pay sources. Rodriguez had fabricated the $250,000 offer from the *Daily Mail*, hoping to goad American Media into buying.

"Well I will buy it but I ain't got 250K! Lol. GMA can't pay her—they can license pix etc. I will tie it up ASAP if we can get a realistic price," Howard texted.

He told Rodriguez he could get her $100,000 for the story, an offer she rejected with an "Lol," before starting a rapid-fire negotiation by text.

"Ok what about 150k," Rodriguez countered.

"110," Howard replied.

"125k."

"120."

"Sold," Rodriguez wrote.

But it wasn't sold. Howard still needed approval from Pecker to buy the story. He told Rodriguez he'd be back in touch by the following morning.

Minutes after signing off with Rodriguez, Howard texted his boss.

"Woman wants 120k. Has offers from Mail and GMA want her to talk and do lie detector live. I know the denials were made in the past— but this story is true. I can lock it on publication now to shut down the media chatter and we can assess next steps thereafter. Ok?"

"We can't pay 120k," Pecker texted back.

Howard realized that Daniels would be Cohen and Trump's problem now.

"Ok. They'd need to handle. Perhaps I call Michael and advise him and he can take it from there, and handle," Howard said.

"Yes a good idea," Pecker texted.

AFTER SPEAKING WITH Howard once more, Cohen was ready to do a deal, but he didn't have anyone to deal with. Gina Rodriguez wasn't a lawyer, and anyway Cohen had already threatened to end her career and sue her and Daniels into oblivion. She wasn't going to negotiate with him directly. Howard, now the middleman, turned to Davidson, a friend with whom he shared celebrity gossip, but Davidson was still wary of Cohen. When Davidson had tested the idea of a deal for Daniels's story in September, Cohen responded with fury and threats. Davidson needed convincing that Cohen was willing to negotiate in good faith. Howard agreed to contact Cohen (again) to vouch for Davidson and to get Cohen's assurances that he wouldn't try to ambush Davidson. When they spoke, Howard told Cohen that Davidson was a friend. *Be nice,* he said.

Davidson soon relented and agreed to negotiate with Cohen.

Howard, having brokered the peace, first texted Pecker to let him know that Cohen had agreed to handle the story and leave American out of it.

"Spoke to MC. All sorted. Now removed. No fingerprints. I'll recap with you face to face," Howard said.

"Great work Thx," Pecker replied.

Howard then texted Cohen to let him know Davidson had come around.

"Keith will do it. Let's reconvene tomorrow," Howard said in a text to Cohen.

Cohen, for whom it was past 2 A.M., texted back after waking up.

"Thank you," he replied. He texted again a few minutes later to give Howard the name of his shell company, Resolution Consultants, which Cohen planned to use to funnel the money to Davidson.

Rodriguez kept up the pressure on October 9, telling Howard that she had another offer for Daniels's story, this one for $200,000, a lie meant to prod the deal along.

After waking up the next morning, a Monday, Howard checked in with Rodriguez and linked Cohen and Davidson via text, using coded language.

"Keith/Michael: connecting you both in regards to that business opportunity. Spoke to the client this AM and they're confirmed to proceed with the opportunity. Thanks. Dylan. Over to you two."

Davidson texted Cohen about an hour and a half later. "Michael—if we are ever going to close this deal—In my opinion, it needs to be today. Keith."

The two lawyers soon got on a call. Cohen wanted to buy the story, but he balked at Daniels's six-figure demand.

"You forget what I do. I know everybody in this business. This story isn't worth shit," Cohen said.

Davidson said $130,000 was as low as Rodriguez and Daniels were willing to go. Daniels wanted to get at least $100,000. After Rodriguez's commission and Davidson's $10,000 fee, she would get around $96,000—close enough.

"That's the drop-dead number," Davidson told Cohen.

He told Cohen that Daniels had a competing offer from a media company. Cohen pressed Davidson for details, but he pleaded ignorance. It was Rodriguez's deal, he said. Davidson told Cohen he knew only that the company had offered $130,000.

In fact, Rodriguez had no offer. She had invented it to use as leverage with Cohen, just as she had concocted the other offers she used to try to entice Howard.

It worked.

Three days after a video of Trump talking about grabbing women by their genitals entered the public domain, Cohen and Davidson had a deal. Cohen reluctantly agreed to match the offer he believed Daniels had from another company, and, in return, Daniels would sign a contract barring her from discussing her alleged one-night stand with Trump.

Davidson drafted the contract and used pseudonyms to conceal the names of the parties, a typical practice in deals of this kind. Trump was identified as David Dennison and Daniels was described as Peggy Peterson. Davidson had borrowed the name David Dennison from a guy he knew in high school; Peggy Peterson was also his creation. In the contract, the names were shortened to the initials "DD" and "PP," indicating that Trump was the defendant and Daniels was the plaintiff.

Cohen made his limited liability company, Resolution Consultants, a party to the contract as well.

Rodriguez and Davidson drove to Calabasas, a city at the edge of the Santa Monica Mountains, to present the contract to Daniels. She was directing *From the First Moment,* an adult film about a woman who is left at the altar and falls in love again. Daniels left the set and met Davidson and her agent in the driveway. She signed using her real name, Stephanie Clifford, on the trunk of Rodriguez's car. Rodriguez snapped a picture of Daniels with the contract and sent it to her boyfriend.

Daniels had been urged to go public with her story about Trump by friends who opposed him, including some photographers who'd shot DVD covers of her films and whom she considered her adopted "gay dads." But the deal, besides bringing her a chunk of cash, would mean Daniels wouldn't have to contend with the fallout of talking about Trump publicly. Also, her husband, Glendon Crain, was pushing her to close the deal with Cohen. She, Crain, and their daughter had moved from Las Vegas to the suburbs of Dallas. Daniels brought her horses, too, and spent time riding them.

Cohen, in New York, signed the agreement on a line above the name of his shell company. The signature line above Donald Trump's pseudonym, DD, remained blank. Cohen thought that putting his company into the Daniels contract would distance Trump from the agreement, but without Trump's signature, he'd given Daniels a legal foothold if she ever decided to challenge the validity of the deal in court. The contract bound DD and PP together, providing each with rights and responsibilities that Cohen's company didn't have as a third party. But no one expected the contract to ever be tested.

The only place that the actual names of Trump and Daniels appeared was in a side letter to the agreement, which documented the true identities of the parties. This type of side letter would traditionally be kept by lawyers for both sides, separate from the nondisclosure agreement, so that in the event a contract leaked to the media, it would be harder to decode who was behind the pseudonyms. In this case, Cohen insisted that only he be allowed to keep the side letter. He didn't want Daniels or Davidson to have a copy, and they agreed.

Initially, Cohen asked for ten days to make the payment, but Davidson balked. They had executed the agreement on a Monday. He gave Cohen until that Friday, October 14, to wire the settlement funds from

Resolution Consultants to Davidson's client trust account at City National Bank in Los Angeles.

"We good?" Davidson emailed him two days before the deadline. "Yes," Cohen wrote back, but he said Trump's offices were closed for the Jewish holiday of Yom Kippur. "I am in tomorrow but can speak for the next 3 hours via cell if necessary."

Cohen missed the deadline to pay Davidson, who granted him a three-day extension. In three-way calls, Rodriguez and Daniels yelled at Davidson to "close the fucking deal." Cohen was jerking him around, they said. They were convinced that Cohen was trying to delay paying until Trump lost the election, when the story would lose its value, leaving them with nothing.

Cohen blew the second deadline, too, offering more excuses for the delay. "My guy is in five fucking states every day," Cohen said. He also claimed to have found a problem with his shell company: A friend in Florida had a company also named Resolution Consultants, so Cohen didn't want to use it.

Daniels and Rodriguez told Davidson to tear up the NDA. They'd resumed talks with reporters, telling some of them about the contract with Cohen. Davidson was alarmed. He told Dylan Howard that Cohen was behaving like an idiot. And he'd lost control of Daniels and Rodriguez. He was worried the porn star and her agent would violate the agreement Daniels had just signed or veer into extortion territory. He decided it was time to extricate himself from these proceedings.

On October 17, half an hour after Cohen missed a deadline of 5 P.M. Pacific time to wire the funds, Davidson emailed him.

"Please be advised that my client deems her Settlement Agreement cancelled . . . Please be further advised that I no longer represent her in this or any matter," Davidson wrote.

Daniels had been communicating with *Slate*'s top editor, Jacob Weisberg, since August. Now she told him she believed that Trump was trying to stall on making a six-figure payment they'd negotiated until after his inevitable loss in the election, and that he would then renege when her story had lost its value. Daniels tried to make a deal with Weisberg's online magazine, sending him part of a draft nondisclosure agreement she had received from Davidson. Weisberg told her that *Slate* didn't pay for stories but encouraged her to come forward. Daniels was noncommittal.

Rodriguez had discussions with a Fox News reporter, Diana Falzone, who then pitched the story to her editors. Rodriguez confirmed the affair in her talks with Falzone and, as Daniels had done with Weisberg, gave her details of the proposed nondisclosure agreement. On October 18, Falzone gave one of her editors a rough draft whose main source was *The Dirty*'s Nik Richie. Although Falzone had let her editors know that Daniels was looking to be paid by Trump, this draft didn't mention the potential hush-money deal.

A porn star says a 2011 report claiming she had an 11-month affair with Donald Trump while he was married to his current wife is true—despite the fact her lawyers at the time issued a cease-and-desist letter threatening to sue the website that ran the story.

A representative for Stormy Daniels, who has appeared and directed in dozens of porn films since **WHEN**, told FoxNews.com the 2011 report in TheDirty.com, which detailed an alleged affair that took place in 2006 and 2007, was in fact accurate. "It's true," the spokesperson said, before adding Daniels "will not comment further" on the story.

Ken LaCorte, a senior vice president at Fox News Digital, didn't think they had enough. Falzone pushed back, but kept reporting. At the same time, Daniels was also talking to the *Daily Beast* about going public with her Trump encounter.

On the same day that Falzone submitted the draft of her story about the Trump-Daniels affair to her editor, William Bastone, a veteran reporter who ran a muckraking site called *The Smoking Gun,* published a lengthy story under the headline "Donald Trump and the Porn Superstar."

Bastone's main source was Mike Moz, the ex-husband of Stormy Daniels. The story described how Trump and Daniels met at a celebrity golf tournament in 2006 and remained in touch over the next year, and how, five years later, Daniels had tried to monetize her relationship with Trump. Moz told Bastone that he had driven Daniels to the Beverly Hills Hotel to meet Trump, but he didn't know if they'd had an affair. "It would be surprising but not shocking," Moz said.

After that story, Reince Priebus and the new Trump campaign chief, Steve Bannon, confronted the candidate about the affair allegations.

Trump told them the story wasn't true. He didn't mention anything about Cohen's agreement to make a hush-money payment.

DANIELS'S MEDIA STRATEGY wasn't panning out. She grew exasperated when Jessica Drake, an adult film actress from Wicked Pictures with whom she'd been feuding, held a news conference on October 22 with lawyer Gloria Allred, becoming the eleventh woman to accuse Trump of sexual improprieties. The two women had once been friends but had a falling-out over a man—a porn director Daniels had dated and Drake later married.

They'd been together in Lake Tahoe at the golf tournament where Daniels said she'd slept with Trump. The story Drake told made it sound like she, and not Daniels, had been the object of Trump's attention. Drake said that Trump had met her at the tournament and gone with two other women to his suite, where he hugged them tightly and kissed them. She also said that Trump or someone on his behalf later called and tried to get Drake to spend time with him alone, offering $10,000, which she declined. Daniels told people that Drake was lying; her story sounded like some twisted version of Daniels's own. Trump also called Drake's story "total fiction," mocking her.

"She's a porn star," he said. "Oh, I'm sure she's never been grabbed before."

Even though they'd canceled the deal with Cohen, Rodriguez and Daniels continued to lean on Davidson to get Cohen to pay what he'd agreed to. Davidson, in turn, leaned on the *Enquirer*'s Dylan Howard. By now it was late October. Davidson told Howard that Daniels was close to reaching an agreement with a media outlet to tell her story. On the evening of October 25, Howard texted Cohen, "Keith calling you urgently. We have to coordinate something on the matter [Davidson] is calling you about or it could look awfully bad for everyone."

After the text, Cohen got on a call with Howard and Pecker using an encrypted app. Howard let loose on Cohen. *Why are you dragging your feet?* he wanted to know. Rodriguez and Davidson were his friends and helpful with celebrity news, and he wasn't about to screw them over because Cohen couldn't close a deal. If Cohen didn't pay, Howard went on, Rodriguez and Davidson would certainly go public with the fact that American Media and Trump's lawyer had been working together to silence Daniels.

The conversation with Howard and Pecker seemed to motivate Cohen. "Fuck it, I'll do it myself," he told Davidson afterward.

The next morning, Cohen finally reached Trump. After two brief phone conversations with his boss, Cohen retrieved the filing receipt for Essential Consultants LLC, another shell company he'd created in Delaware, ten days earlier, to replace Resolution Consultants. He then opened a business account for Essential Consultants at First Republic Bank in Manhattan, describing the company's purpose as "domestic real estate consulting" on the bank's application documents. Cohen had a $500,000 home equity line of credit at First Republic and decided to use it to pay Daniels so that he wouldn't have to explain the transfer to his wife, who handled their banking.

Cohen drew down $131,000 from his line of credit—adding an extra $1,000 to cover fees—and moved it into the Essential Consultants account. Davidson wasn't going to take another contract to Daniels until he had money in hand. But Cohen was nervous about sending the payment before he had an executed agreement. So Davidson promised not to send the payment to Daniels until she had signed the new contract.

Howard brokered the payment terms between Davidson and Cohen. "Thank you both for chatting with me earlier," Howard wrote in an October 26 email to the two lawyers. "Confirming agreement on:— Executed agreement, hand-signed by Keith's client and returned via overnight or same-day FedEx to Michael,—Change of agreement to reflect the correct LLC,—Transfer of funds on Thursday AM to be held in escrow until receipt of agreement."

On October 27, he wired the $130,000 payment to Davidson, who then circulated a new nondisclosure agreement for the parties to sign.

Cohen updated Trump the following morning in a five-minute call. Later that day, Davidson reassured Cohen that all was proceeding according to plan. Daniels signed the contract with a notary at a UPS store in Texas on October 28.

"All is AOK. I should have signed, notarized docs on Monday. You should have them on Tuesday," Davidson said in a text.

Cohen thanked him but was still anxious. "I hope we are good," he texted Davidson.

"I assure you we are very good."

Rodriguez texted Daniels on Halloween to look for the incoming $96,000 payment. "For sure!! And thank you!" Daniels texted back. "I know this was a giant pain in the ass. I will let you know when I actually get the $."

Davidson wired the money to her account on November 1, after confirming delivery of the overnight package to Cohen containing the signed contract and the only copy of the side-letter agreement identifying the parties. Daniels lied to her husband, Crain, telling him she was being paid because Trump didn't want his wife to know he'd been in a hotel room with a porn star, even though nothing had happened.

Daniels didn't keep any of the paperwork. Davidson had only the nondisclosure agreement, without the side letter revealing the real identities of the contracted parties.

"As is my duty to do, I will retain the entirety of this agreement in the strictest of confidence," Daniels's lawyer wrote to Cohen on a cover letter to the contract.

As a bonus, Davidson emailed Cohen an audio file of Davidson interviewing Daniels about recent allegations by her fellow porn star Jessica Drake saying that Trump had hugged and kissed her against her will in a Lake Tahoe hotel room. In the interview, Daniels recited all the reasons she believed Drake was lying.

Cohen called Trump but couldn't reach him. He got a call back instead from Trump's then–campaign manager, Kellyanne Conway.

Seven days before the presidential election, the deal was done.

PART II

• • •

THE UNRAVELING

19.

THE SOURCES

■ ■ ■

THE REALITY OF Donald Trump's presidential campaign—the *actual viability* of it—had been slow to take root in the newsroom of *The Wall Street Journal*. Journalists tend to prioritize early on which candidates to take most seriously. Especially in presidential campaigns, which often begin as a free-for-all, most media organizations just don't have the resources to give the gadflies, the publicity seekers, and those who simply want their names in the mix the same attention as the people conventionally seen as true contenders. Nor do consumers of news necessarily expect granular coverage of candidates who aren't likely to hang around for long.

Trump, of course, had been in the public consciousness long before and probably would continue to be long after whatever came of his political ambitions. But his history suggested that he had decided to turn yet another presidential race into an episode of the reality show that had been his entire public life. So some news organizations were justifiably reluctant to be complicit in what appeared to be a publicity stunt. It was not until more than six months after Trump's campaign launch—when his standing atop the polls was well established and he began knocking down primary election victories—that the *Journal's* top editors looked up and said, *Hey, we need to take a hard look at this guy.*

As reporters, we learn to jump into the deep end with a new story, whatever the topic, and start swimming. That is the challenge and the excitement of the job. At the *Journal* and elsewhere, we had both written extensively about legal issues and law enforcement, often with a focus on business and white-collar crime, consistent with the newspaper's century-old focus. With respect to Trump, we and other reporters began by looking at his business practices, to see what those practices might reveal about the kind of leader he might be. That included the people around Trump, his relationships with organized crime associates, including the mob lawyer Roy Cohn, and his history of contributing to political candidates to influence them—all of which seemed especially pertinent given his vows to "drain the swamp" in Washington.

Other outlets had examined Trump's alleged misbehavior with women who said he had sexually assaulted or harassed them through the decades. The *Journal* had steered clear of this topic—until the *Access Hollywood* tape. After *The Washington Post*'s publication of Trump's recorded boasts about how he could grope women at will because he was a celebrity, old accusations from women took on new weight, and new ones rapidly came to light. We started searching for these women, asking them to tell their stories, while pursuing tips about others. But the one we were about to receive stood out.

On the afternoon of Monday, October 17, 2016, *Journal* editor Ashby Jones shared a tip he'd received from a source. A Los Angeles lawyer with the initials K.D.—the source didn't want to volunteer more—was traversing the country, paying hush money to women who'd been romantically involved with Donald Trump.

The election was weeks away. The *Journal* had little interest in a story about Trump having had consensual affairs. It would have been no great surprise, even if it proved true. (Again, Trump had personally promoted his affair with Marla Maples in the 1980s.) Besides, by this point in his campaign, more than a dozen women had come forward and accused him of various degrees of sexual harassment and assault. These were serious claims, which Trump had denied, and they made allegations of past affairs seem inconsequential by comparison. It was an irony of Trump's rise that his bad behavior was often overshadowed by allegations of worse behavior.

But hush money was indisputably newsworthy. It didn't matter what Trump was potentially paying to hide, really—only that he was. If the hush money was real, it could have legal implications for Trump and for his campaign. John Edwards had been prosecuted for something similar. And, of course, it could also represent a vulnerability: A public official willing to pay to conceal a matter could be blackmailed for it.

Jones, chief of the *Journal*'s law bureau, had gone back to his source and learned the first name of the attorney: Keith. It didn't take long to find a Los Angeles attorney with the first name Keith and a last initial of D who had experience with settlements between women and the famous men with whom they'd allegedly had extramarital affairs. Keith Davidson.

We checked the name with our source. *That's the guy.*

Jones's source seemed to think that Davidson was helping Trump but didn't know for sure. He usually represented the plaintiff, the one seeking a deal. But he had a connection to Trump that a Google search turned up immediately.

Davidson had represented Stormy Daniels in 2011, when reports of her alleged affair with Trump first surfaced. Daniels was featured on Davidson's law firm website, on the "Representative clients" page.

The day after the tip came in, William Bastone published his *Smoking Gun* story quoting Mike Moz about Daniels's meeting with Trump at the 2006 golf tournament and her attempts in 2011 to sell the story of their relationship. We learned that Daniels had been guided by a woman named Gina Rodriguez, a former porn actress who'd reinvented herself as a talent manager, and that Keith Davidson had represented Daniels.

DAVIDSON'S WORLD—A SWIRL of reporters at celebrity publications, scandal brokers, and others who peddled dirt or helped the rich and famous keep it buried—was foreign to us in the newsroom at the *Journal*.

Digging through Davidson's cases and news clips, the *Journal* created a database of known contacts, including friends, former coworkers, lawyers who'd faced off with him, and others to whom he might have let slip the Trump-related work he was doing. With the election two weeks away, there wasn't time to tiptoe around. Parachuting into a new subject, facing a hard deadline, the *Journal*'s essential tactic was "smile and dial," as Mike Siconolfi, the head of the paper's investigative group, put it. Call as many people as possible—and keep calling—until you catch a break.

Davidson soon learned of our efforts and phoned us. He wasn't paying anyone hush money for Trump, he said. When asked whether he was representing any women in settlements with Trump, he paused. "No," he said. (This was technically true: Daniels had recently backed out of her initial deal with Cohen, for his failure to pay on time, and McDougal's licensing deal was with American Media.)

Meanwhile, the *Journal* team canvassed the porn industry to find people close to Daniels. Alana Evans, a leader in the adult film industry's union and a friend of Daniels's, confirmed that she was in Lake Tahoe in 2006 and had been hanging out with Daniels hours before the porn star went to Trump's hotel room. Later that night, Daniels and Trump had called Evans three times, trying to get her to join them, she said. Evans declined. The next morning, Daniels had given her explicit details about her encounter with Trump. But Evans said she knew of no hush money. She assumed that Daniels had been paid off, given that the normally outspoken star hadn't made any comments about Trump as his campaign polarized the nation.

Within a few days, we convinced Gina Rodriguez to get on the phone with us. She relayed that Daniels was preparing to tell her story publicly. They were "working something out" with ABC's *Good Morning America* and a tabloid. She denied that Trump had offered Daniels money to keep quiet. In fact, she said, one of Trump's aides had made a "threatening call" to Rodriguez in 2011, warning her to stop shopping Daniels's story of the affair, or else.

Sources confirmed that Daniels's representatives had been in touch with ABC, but she wasn't booked to appear on *Good Morning America* or any other network show.

While reporting out the Daniels thread, we called several former models featured in the 2000 *Playboy* movie in which Trump had made a cameo. One of the women was the 1998 Playmate of the Year, Karen McDougal. A man who identified himself as her friend—John Crawford—returned a voicemail message for her and said that McDougal wanted nothing to do with any story that we might be working on. It was odd. We flagged her name.

The reporting was starting to bear fruit. On October 25, another source emailed: "I think I may have something for you to look into."

This source said a woman named Karen, a former Playboy Playmate who lived in Arizona, had also been in talks with ABC News about going public with her story of an affair with Trump. The source said that she'd suddenly backed out of the negotiations a couple of months earlier. She'd been dealing with ABC through her lawyer—Keith Davidson.

Nine women named Karen had been Playmates of the Month. But only one of them lived in Arizona: Karen McDougal.

The spreadsheet of potential sources had grown to more than a hundred people, but none of them knew about or were willing to discuss hush-money payments to Stormy Daniels or Karen McDougal.

On Wednesday, November 2, we reached out to Martin Singer, a Hollywood lawyer to the stars who had negotiated deals with Davidson in the past. Singer hadn't returned our calls, so we emailed to let him know the *Journal* was reporting a story about Davidson representing women linked to Trump, "presumably seeking settlements as he has in the past." Singer forwarded the email to Davidson, who sent a legal threat a couple of hours later.

"I told you that I had never represented Donald Trump nor anyone adverse to him," Davidson wrote. "Yet you persist to call anyone and everyone under the sun." Davidson went on to say that any assertion by the *Journal* to the contrary was "false, defamatory and otherwise actionable" and demanded that the *Journal* refrain from publishing a story.

"I expect an immediate email confirmation from you that you and *The Wall Street Journal* will comply with this demand. Failing that, I will be forced to take appropriate legal action to protect my rights, and you and *The Wall Street Journal* will be acting at your and its legal risk and peril. Govern yourself accordingly," he wrote.

(Davidson then forwarded the message to Michael Cohen at his Trump Organization email address. He wrote simply, "FYI.")

Rather than comply with Davidson's demand, the *Journal* continued reporting. On the evening of November 3, a new source called: "I think I may be able to help you with your story."

The source, who'd learned we had reached out to McDougal, asked if we knew anything about Trump's close relationship with the chief executive of a media company, which the source didn't name. Yes, in fact. Several people contacted by the newspaper had mentioned

Trump's long-standing association with tabloid publisher David Pecker. And we'd seen the *Enquirer*'s fawning coverage of the mogul and the fusillade of negative stories directed at his opponents.

"Very interesting," the source said, promising to get back in touch later that night.

KAREN MCDOUGAL HAD begun to realize that American Media was less interested in her anti-aging advice and modeling than in her silence. She'd expected the publisher to begin running columns under her name soon after she signed the contract in early August. But more than two months later, she hadn't appeared in any of the company's publications. She felt like American Media executives were blowing her off. That was the state of affairs when the source called back the night of November 3 and described McDougal's deal with the publisher. The source had a copy of the contract and promised to share it with us through an intermediary the following day.

On the morning of Friday, November 4, we met the middleman near the brass clock in Grand Central Terminal. He produced a brown folder with a ribbon tie containing McDougal's August 2016 "Name and Rights Licensing Agreement." Over the next nine hours, we verified the authenticity of the document, spoke with three of McDougal's friends whom she had told about her relationship with Trump, and confirmed that American Media never intended to publish a story about the affair. The company had bought the rights to it for the sole purpose of burying it.

Trump's aides and Pecker's employees found out about our forthcoming article when we contacted them for comment that afternoon. McDougal's contract didn't name Trump, but the *Journal* had also received the model's retainer agreement with her lawyer, Davidson. It described the scope of his services as "negotiating a confidentiality agreement and/or life rights related to interactions with Donald Trump." We summarized our reporting for Trump's representatives and emailed them a list of questions:

> Did Mr. Trump have an extramarital affair with Karen McDougal?
>
> Was he or anyone close to him aware or involved in this contract between AMI and Ms. McDougal?

What is the nature of his relationship with David Pecker? (We understand, and it has been widely reported, that they are longtime friends.) Did he discuss this arrangment [*sic*] or Ms. McDougal's story, or their alleged affair with Mr. Pecker?

Has Mr. Trump or any of his representatives, had any dealings with Ms. McDougal's lawyer, Keith Davidson, in this matter or any other matters?

We also sent questions to American Media. David Pecker, Keith Davidson, and Michael Cohen had known for weeks that we were investigating the matter, but now, four days before the election, we had enough to move forward with a story. It could have been much worse for Trump. The *Journal* didn't have reporting tying the Republican nominee or his special counsel, Cohen, to the McDougal deal. We knew only that Trump and Pecker had a relationship, and that the *Enquirer* had gone full tilt for Trump during the campaign season.

As we hurried to bulletproof our story, Friday afternoon phased to evening and then to night, the ideal time for bad news to drop, if the bad news happened to be about you. Readers would be unplugging for the weekend. Cohen, using two phones, cycled through calls with Pecker, Howard, Davidson, and Hope Hicks, the press secretary for Trump's campaign. Cohen hoped to get a statement from McDougal rebutting the *Journal*'s reporting, but Davidson couldn't reach her.

Trump was angry, and Cohen was frantic.

"She's being really difficult with giving Keith a statement. Basically went into hiding and unreachable," Cohen texted Howard.

"I'll ask him again. We just need her to disappear," Howard responded.

"She definitely disappeared but refuses to give a statement and Keith cannot push her."

"Let's let the dust settle. We don't want to push her over the edge. She's on [our] side at present and we have a solid position and a plausible position that she is rightfully employed as a columnist."

Howard tried to soothe Cohen. "I think it'll be ok pal. I think it'll fade into the distance," he texted the Trump attorney.

"He's pissed," Cohen responded, referring to Trump.

"I'm pissed! You're pissed. Pecker is pissed. Keith is pissed. Not much we can do."

Cohen and Hicks cobbled together two draft responses to send the *Journal*. Their first effort read:

> We have no knowledge of this false story allegedly being shopped around, although it comes as no surprise—yet another publicity hungry individual with a get rich and famous quick scheme at the expense of Mr. Trump. We suggest you reach out to the parties involved as we have nothing to do with this final attempt by the liberal elite to disparage Donald Trump and stop this historic movement.

The second draft was largely the same as the first, except it began with the "liberal elite" sentence. When Hicks took the drafts to Trump, the candidate dictated a tighter, less indignant response, which the spokeswoman then conveyed to the *Journal*.

"We have no knowledge of any of this," Hicks said. The campaign professed ignorance of the American Media contract and denied McDougal's story of an affair.

In its own statement to the *Journal*, American Media denied paying McDougal to protect Trump. The company had made a deal with McDougal to have her appear on magazine covers and write health columns, the publisher said.

American Media provided a separate response from Pecker. "It is no secret that Donald Trump has been one of my friends for the past 25 years and I greatly admire his achievements both professionally and politically," Pecker's statement said, exaggerating the length of his relationship with Trump. "However, it was The National Enquirer under my management at American Media Inc. that set the agenda on Donald's Marla Maples scandal."

That was also false. Pecker had become chief executive in 1999. His arrival came after the *Enquirer*'s aggressive coverage of Trump's affair with Marla Maples, their marriage, and finally their split. He went on to say that American Media's surveys showed that readers were more interested in Trump than any other candidate; thus, the *Enquirer*'s coverage of Trump was what they had "come to expect from the publication of record on presidential scandals." No matter how much *Enquirer* readers liked Trump, Pecker's statement was perplexing. We couldn't imagine that readers expected the publication of record on political sex scandals to be covering them up.

THE *JOURNAL* STORY appeared online after 9 P.M., under the headline "National Enquirer Shielded Donald Trump from Playboy Model's Affair Allegation." It ran in the newspaper the following day, on the fifth page of the front section.

The story began, "The company that owns the National Enquirer, a backer of Donald Trump, agreed to pay $150,000 to a former Playboy centerfold model for her story of an affair a decade ago with the Republican presidential nominee, but then didn't publish it, according to documents reviewed by The Wall Street Journal and people familiar with the matter."

Our report also revealed that McDougal's lawyer, Davidson, represented another woman, Stormy Daniels, and that she had been in contact with *Good Morning America* about giving an interview to discuss an alleged affair with Trump. Like McDougal, she had cut off contact with media and gone quiet. The *Journal* story didn't say whether Daniels had been paid off. We didn't know that only the week before, Cohen had wired $130,000 to Davidson through a shell company, in return for Daniels's silence.

For a story that broke late on a Friday and ran on the inside of the newspaper, it did well online, with more than 800,000 page views in the first twenty-four hours. But other mainstream U.S. news outlets mostly ignored the report.

Cohen was thrilled at the lack of traction.

"So far I only see 6 stories," he texted Hicks.

"Same. Keep praying!! It's working!" replied Hicks, who was traveling with Trump on the campaign trail.

"Even CNN not talking about it," Cohen gloated.

Better still for the Trump campaign, no media outlet had followed up on the *Journal*'s reporting on Stormy Daniels. Cohen told Hicks that, just in case, he had a statement from Daniels "denying everything."

"I wouldn't use it now or even discuss with him"—Trump—"as no one is talking about this or cares!" Cohen wrote.

· · ·

THE McDOUGAL SCOOP was quickly swallowed up in the final churn of what had been a historically negative and charged campaign. Two days after it was published, FBI Director James Comey, who had informed Congress eleven days before the election that an investigation of Hillary Clinton's email had been reopened, revealed that no significant new evidence had turned up. Comey's unprecedented pronouncements on an ongoing investigation dominated headlines as the candidates crisscrossed the country and polls showed Clinton's lead narrowing.

Still, pollsters broadly predicted that she would win going into Election Day, Tuesday, November 8. But that evening, Trump took an early lead and never relinquished it.

Dylan Howard, the editor of the *National Enquirer,* had been watching the results roll in at home on television, incredulous that Trump seemed poised to win. He began texting a relative in Australia, where it was already the afternoon of the next day. The editor's family members didn't like Trump.

"Jesus. He's in with a massive chance," Howard texted at 10:20 P.M.

"Oh no. When will we know," came the reply.

"Probably an hour or so. But he's flipped states no one expected him to do. Or they're neck and neck," Howard said.

"At least if he wins, I'll be pardoned for electoral fraud," he added, in a bit of gallows humor that deflected the role he had played in aiding Trump's campaign.

By 11:30 P.M., Clinton's road to the White House had dwindled to an almost impossible string of unlikely swing-state wins. In Brooklyn, people who'd gathered in front of a giant television at the intersection of Clinton and President Streets melted away, while those who'd embraced Trump's populist message in the South and across the middle of the country rejoiced.

As the result became clear, Howard called Michael Cohen, who invited him over to join Trump's celebration at the New York Hilton in Times Square. Howard arrived with one of his reporters, James Robertson.

At around 1:30 A.M., Howard continued texting with his relative.

"Trump victory imminent," the relative wrote.

"I just turned up for the spectacle," Howard replied.

"Once in a lifetime opportunity," he wrote. "Come on . . . Who wouldn't turn up."

"I don't think I would."

Half an hour later, Howard wrote that Trump had been named president-elect.

"Oh dear," came the answer.

At around 3 A.M., after Hillary Clinton called Trump to concede, he emerged to give his victory speech. Trump seemed shocked, and uncharacteristically humble, though not without humor. "I pledge to every citizen of our land that I will be president for all Americans, and this is so important to me," he said. "For those who have chosen not to support me in the past, of which there were a few people . . . I'm reaching out to you for your guidance and your help so that we can work together and unify our great country."

Once Trump was finished speaking, Howard received another text from his relative: "I was hoping he didn't thank you or pecker in his speech."

"He did not," he said. It was after 4 A.M. in New York. "At least now we get pardoned."

"Why Wouldn't the FBI investigate?"

Howard responded, "He has ultimate power to override anything."

In the following weeks, Howard and his colleagues scrambled to publish health advice under Karen McDougal's name, assigning a reporter to act as her ghostwriter. Now that the deal had become public and American Media had denied that the contract was a vehicle for buying her story of an affair with Trump, the company had to make good on those columns and magazine covers. If Trump had lost the election, nobody would have likely cared what American Media had done to help him. But now he was going to be president of the United States.

DAVID PECKER RETURNED to Trump Tower in December 2016 to briefly offer his congratulations to the president-elect of the United States. It was their first meeting in more than a year. Ahead of the visit, Cohen had asked Pecker for a favor: He wanted him to urge Trump to pay Cohen more money. (Cohen frequently complained about not getting paid enough for his work.) Trump also hadn't yet repaid his fixer for the Stormy Daniels deal. When Pecker raised Cohen's request, Trump was unmoved.

"You don't know how much money he's got," Trump said.

The next time Pecker was at Trump Tower, in January 2017, Trump thanked the tabloid publisher for buying Karen McDougal's story and burying it.

20.

THE PRESIDENT'S LAWYER

■ ■ ■

THOUGH HE'D BEEN dead for thirty years, Roy Cohn's legacy had shadowed Donald Trump as he sought and then won the presidency.

When he moved to the top of the Republican field, Trump's relationship with the red-baiting McCarthy aide turned mob lawyer became fresh fodder for reporters trying to understand Trump and his rise in national politics.

A narrative began to take shape: Trump had adapted Cohn's gutter philosophy to his own purposes. Cohn had taught him how to get in the mud, bend the truth to his whims, and declare victory despite all evidence to the contrary. But the reality was more complicated than that. Cohn had had a great influence on Trump, but the two had been simpatico from the outset; Cohn had merely taken Trump's natural inclinations and refined them.

Reporters chronicled the matters Cohn had handled for him, including the harsh prenuptial agreement he'd negotiated before the candidate's marriage to Ivana Trump. And they unearthed examples of Trump's poor treatment of Cohn, who often didn't bill him, toward the end of his life: how he moved cases to other lawyers and sought to collect rent for housing he'd provided to Cohn's former lover who was dying of AIDS. The diamond-encrusted cuff links Trump had given Cohn in a Bulgari box in lieu of payment for work turned out to be knockoffs, another former lover of Cohn's told *The New York Times*.

When the attorney started appearing in news stories during the campaign, Trump sometimes presented an alternative narrative, with its own distortions, that minimized Cohn's influence in his life.

"He was my lawyer," he told the *Journal* during an interview at his Trump Tower office in May 2016. But hadn't Trump been closer to Cohn than most clients and their attorneys?

"So was Si Newhouse. So was George Steinbrenner. So were many other of the biggest people in New York during the time that Roy was alive. He was my lawyer."

Trump once had bragged about using Cohn's framed picture to intimidate the often mob-connected contractors and union leaders he negotiated with as a developer. But as a presidential candidate, he denied it.

"Here is my office now," Trump said, gesturing around the room as if to demonstrate that the picture had never been there, even though it was a different office and Cohn was long dead.

"These are tough people," he said of these business partners. "They don't scare so easily. They don't get scared by holding up a picture."

Among friends, Trump was more sentimental about Cohn. On the night he won the presidency, he couldn't help but reminisce. Decades after the dinner party where Cohn told Cindy Adams that his protégé would one day own New York, Trump stood with her at 10 P.M. on Election Night, watching television sets that showed the Upper Midwest glowing MAGA-hat red. He leaned over to remind her of Cohn's prediction on that long-ago evening. This was far better than owning New York.

Soon after, still basking in the glow, Trump connected with Roger Stone and brought up Cohn again. "We sure miss Roy, don't we?" Trump asked him.

Dining with friends at Mar-a-Lago in late December, three weeks before he'd assume the presidency, Trump shared yet another memory. This one perhaps was evoked by the resort and Cohn's last visit there, a few months before he died of AIDS. Trump recalled to his guests that after Cohn had left, "I had to spend a fortune to fumigate all the dishes and silverware."

THE DAYS IMMEDIATELY following Trump's election might have been the happiest period of Michael Cohen's life. Probably more than anyone else, he had been a loyal foot soldier willing to do almost anything for his boss—and in fact, he had. But his exclusion from the official campaign foreshadowed his fate as Trump prepared to move into the White House.

In the months before the election, when Trump reshuffled his campaign for a second time and named Steve Bannon as campaign chief, Cohen told associates he had expected to be tapped for the role. He'd also been saying for a while that he expected to be named White House chief of staff. After all, he was Trump's special counsel, his consigliere. And wasn't that the job of chief of staff? Strategizing. Bringing enemies to heel.

Cohen had averted two major crises in the waning months of the election, stopping McDougal and Daniels from adding to Trump's women problems and paving the way for his victory.

But he had also continued attracting ridicule. Not long after the McDougal deal in August, Cohen was interviewed by CNN's Brianna Keilar about Trump's naming of Bannon to replace Manafort as campaign chief.

> KEILAR: You say it's not a shakeup, but you guys are down, and it makes sense that there would—
> COHEN: Says who?
> KEILAR: Polls.
> COHEN: Says who?
> KEILAR: Most of them. All of them?
> [Long pause] COHEN: Says who?
> KEILAR: Polls. I just told you. I answered your question.
> COHEN: Okay. Which polls?
> KEILAR: All of them.
> COHEN: Okay. And your question is?

Then, a day after wiring payment to Stormy Daniels, Cohen was on Twitter appealing for help finding a homeless woman who had protected Trump's star on the Hollywood Walk of Fame from vandals, saying, "Mr. Trump has a gift for her."

Two days after that, on October 30, Cohen received a text from Giorgi Rtskhiladze, his friend with whom he'd worked on an unrealized plan to build a Trump Tower in Batumi, in the Republic of Georgia near the Black Sea. "Stopped flow of some tapes from Russia but not sure if there's anything else. Just so u know . . ."

"Tapes of what?" Cohen responded.

"Not sure of the content but person in Moscow was bragging had tapes from Russia trip." They were supposedly tapes of Trump with prostitutes made in Moscow in 2013 during his trip for the Miss Universe pageant. These were the same rumors that Hope Hicks had called Cohen about after the *Access Hollywood* tape surfaced.

"I'm sure it's not a big deal but there are lots of stupid people," Rtskhiladze wrote.

"You have no idea," Cohen replied.

After the election, Keith Davidson called to congratulate Cohen and to catch up. Cohen briefed him on the latest issue: There was talk in the press about a tape of Trump hitting his wife in an elevator. A Los Angeles lawyer had offered it to the gossip outlet *TMZ*. Before *TMZ* founder Harvey Levin and his lawyer could view it, the lawyer told them that her client, with whom she'd spoken only by phone, had vanished with the tape, which she'd never seen.

Cohen complained that he'd been unable to get his daughter a ticket to the inauguration, but he told Davidson how excited he was to go to Washington. He didn't know that Trump and people close to him, including Trump's daughter Ivanka and son-in-law, Jared Kushner, thought Cohen shouldn't be given a job at the White House. Trump privately had described him as a bull in a china shop.

When Cohen spoke to Davidson again in early December, the excitement of their last call had given way to depression as Cohen complained that he still hadn't been asked to go to Washington to work in the new administration. They spoke for a long time. Davidson, who had taken the call while shopping in an electronics store, had developed a sort of camaraderie with his Trump counterpart in their dealings over the past few months. He tried to console Cohen, who was still upset, on top of everything else, about the money he'd personally shelled out to silence Stormy Daniels.

"Can you fucking believe it? After everything I've done for him, I wasn't even paid back the $130,000!" he said.

Cohen had other plans to make money off the Trump presidency. For starters, he planned to write a book about his life and his work for Trump. Davidson didn't think it was a good idea. Lawyers should stay in the background, he said. Cohen didn't take the advice to heart.

While he waited for Trump to approach him with a White House offer, the presidential transition that he'd been excluded from went on just outside the door to his Trump Organization office. But Cohen kept busy. He made contacts, scheduled meetings, and made impromptu pitches for money—whether fundraising for Republicans or trying to generate business for himself.

On January 5, 2017, two weeks before the inauguration, Cohen still hadn't received any direction from Trump on his future. He sat in his twenty-sixth-floor office, a few doors away from the president-elect, surrounded by mixed martial arts paraphernalia. Cohen juggled two phones. He tried to sound indifferent when *Journal* reporter Alexandra Berzon asked about his still uncertain role in the Trump administration.

Trump, Cohen said, "doesn't operate with timelines." He corrected himself. "I am not a timeline item. He knows that an hour before he leaves, if he calls me and says, 'I need you in D.C.,' I'll be there."

About a week later, Cohen let his frustration show when he spoke with Berzon again. "I still don't know exactly what I'm going to do, whether I need to stay here for a while or go to D.C.," he said. "It's crazy we're talking about this three, four days before which everybody starts heading down and I have no idea."

Though he'd been given no job offer, Cohen was thrust into the media glare ten days before the inauguration when *BuzzFeed* published a dossier about Trump's alleged connections to Russia that had been circulating among major news organizations. The dossier was made up of raw intelligence, had been compiled by a former British spy, Christopher Steele, and included the false claim that Cohen had traveled to Prague in the late summer of 2016 for a secret liaison with Kremlin officials. A *Journal* profile of Cohen the next day focused on his role as Trump's troubleshooter and drew from comments he'd made to Berzon. "I am the fix-it guy," he'd told her. "Anything that he needs to be done, any issues that concern him, I handle."

COHEN HAD ALREADY begun laying the groundwork for an alternative to the White House in which he would stay on the outside in New York, advise Trump as he had always done, and garner lucrative consulting fees. Trump was so far removed from the Beltway culture, and his election had been so unexpected, that executives and lobbyists for corporate America were in a panic. They didn't know how he worked or how to access him, and they needed people who did. Former Trump campaign manager Corey Lewandowski and adviser Barry Bennett announced that they were setting up a consulting shop to "navigate our government" for clients, according to their website, and they were in high demand. Cohen, Trump's special counsel, had been by his side for a decade. He knew the boss and Trump World better than any of them. That was his pitch, anyway. Best of all, Cohen already had a company set up, and with the perfect name: Essential Consultants. He spoke about pitching foreign governments, in the Middle East and Asia. "Big guys are going to hire me," he told one associate.

In early December, Cohen offered his services to a top official at the Qatar Investment Authority, the oil-rich nation's sovereign wealth fund. Over a meal at a restaurant in the Peninsula Hotel in Manhattan, Cohen and the official, Ahmed al-Rumaihi, discussed infrastructure investments the Qataris were contemplating in the United States. Cohen, who'd met al-Rumaihi days earlier at a fundraising breakfast for the Trump transition, suggested that the Qataris hire him for a fee of $1 million—plus profits on projects. Though the men saw each other again when Qatari officials visited the president-elect at Trump Tower, Cohen didn't close the deal.

Meanwhile, Trump had found a role for Cohen outside of Washington. Just ahead of the January 20, 2017, inauguration, Cohen announced that he would leave the Trump Organization and serve as the president's personal attorney, based in New York. The priority for Cohen, however, was finding clients for himself, a goal he pursued at the inauguration, where Trump seemed to keep him at a distance, relative to others in the new leader's world. Cohen's guests weren't given priority access to events. Nor was Cohen seated behind the president-elect with the other VIPs when Trump was sworn in. Cohen wore the hurt on his face.

On the night before the inauguration, he attended a dinner for Trump in Washington's Union Station and chatted with a would-be client he'd been cultivating for a few months: Andrew Intrater, the American cousin of Russian oligarch Viktor Vekselberg. Intrater ran

Columbus Nova, a firm that invested money for Vekselberg's Renova Group, a Russian conglomerate, and other clients. Intrater and Cohen had met less than three weeks before the election at the Polo Bar, in New York, through a mutual friend. Intrater had been dining with the friend, who spotted Cohen in the dining room with his family. Cohen sat down at their table and stayed for half an hour. "Do you think Trump has a chance?" Cohen asked, and they talked about how both of their fathers were Holocaust survivors. Cohen's family went home, but he stayed. As he walked uptown with Intrater later, Cohen pitched him on investing in distressed taxi debt, without mentioning that he was carrying plenty of distressed taxi debt with his own depreciated medallions.

Intrater emailed Cohen the next day to follow up, and they stayed in touch. On the day after Trump's victory, Intrater texted Cohen to congratulate him.

They met a couple of other times before the inauguration in January. Intrater had scheduled a meeting at Cohen's Trump Tower office to discuss the taxi debt, and he invited Vekselberg, who was in town, to come with him. Cohen was in the process of cleaning out his office and taking everything off the walls. They talked about the investment idea and, briefly, about Russian-American relations. On another day, Intrater shared a meal with Cohen and noticed the stream of people approaching in the restaurant to kiss the ring of Trump's lawyer. Cohen spoke of having many wealthy friends who might invest with Intrater's firm. "I have people who want to put billions and billions of dollars somewhere," Cohen said.

As they stayed in touch by text, Cohen told Intrater that he hadn't decided on his next move once Trump went to the White House. Intrater thought about hiring him as a consultant. If Cohen could bring in just a few investors, the fees would far outstrip the cost of retaining him.

Intrater received two tickets to Trump's inauguration by virtue of a $250,000 donation to the committee organizing it, and he brought Vekselberg along. A few days later, Columbus Nova signed Cohen to a $1-million-a-year consulting contract. Cohen used Essential Consultants LLC, the entity he had created to pay off Stormy Daniels, in the deal.

With that deal in hand, Cohen began reaching out to other U.S. and foreign companies with a blunt pitch. He didn't know who was advising them, but they "should fire them all," Cohen told executives.

"I have the best relationship with the president on the outside, and you need to hire me," Cohen told them.

With this aggressive approach, Cohen notched other consulting deals, worth millions of dollars, to provide services on a broad range of topics about which he had no experience or expertise. AT&T had been alarmed by Trump's election and his subsequent declaration that he'd oppose the company's proposed acquisition of Time Warner for more than $80 billion. Time Warner owned one of the president's most disfavored purveyors of "fake news," CNN. In late January, Cohen began discussions with Bob Quinn, AT&T's senior executive vice president for legislative affairs in Washington, and in early February he discussed a potential contract by phone with Tom Synhorst, a global public affairs consultant for the company. "Just had Cohen call. Oh my. All good. Eager to tell you about it," Synhorst texted Quinn afterward.

A few days later, the consultant emailed Quinn a memo, saying Cohen had told him he was in Washington for a meeting with the president. He added that Cohen "made the point several times that he doesn't list clients, doesn't talk about clients and hopes we won't be publicizing that he's working w/ us. I assured him. And I hope he means it."

AT&T awarded a $600,000-a-year consulting contract to Cohen through Essential Consultants, "to creatively address political and communications issues facing AT&T" at the executive and legislative branches of government, including corporate tax reform and the Time Warner merger.

Through his friend Irwin Simon, the founder of natural foods company Hain Celestial, Cohen was introduced to Joe Jimenez, the chief executive of Switzerland-based pharmaceutical giant Novartis, which also wanted insight into the Trump administration. In contract negotiations, Cohen told Novartis executives that his work should be described as advice and consulting only, because he wouldn't be registering as a lobbyist. He also marked up the contract to make the description of his services vague. "He has pared it back substantially so that it no longer provides details as to precisely what he will do for us," one Novartis executive emailed to another. "I pushed him on this, but in his view it would be safer for both of us to say less."

In mid-February, Novartis agreed to pay Essential Consultants $1.2 million over a year, starting March 1, to advise the company on Trump's efforts to repeal and replace Obamacare, formally known as the Affordable Care Act. The chief executive, Jimenez, who had an exaggerated sense of Cohen's proximity to Trump and his administration, emailed a subordinate about the hiring on February 18:

> Confidentially I have put Michael Cohen on retainer to
> Novartis. . . . He will provide access and advice for us, but will not
> lobby. . . . I want to use him to set up meetings when I am in
> Washington in May. . . . Please think through who we should
> meet and let me know. I will contact Michael and ask him to set
> up meetings.

Next, Cohen set up a solo legal practice, Michael D. Cohen & Associates. He turned again to John Gauger, the tech guy at Liberty University whom he had asked to rig polls for Trump. Gauger's company, RedFinch Solutions, helped Cohen set up a new Web domain and email address. Cohen didn't pay for the services or reimburse Gauger, who still hoped for bigger business from him down the road, for domain registration or Web hosting fees.

Gauger was also providing technology advice to 4C Health Solutions, a startup in Midlothian, Virginia. He connected Cohen with the chief executive, David Adams. Adams was hoping to sell companies and government agencies on a software program that could reduce health care claims by detecting fraud. Cohen told Adams that he knew many corporate executives who might give 4C business. Among the company's prominent board members was Tommy Thompson, the former Republican governor of Wisconsin and secretary of the Department of Health and Human Services under President George W. Bush. Cohen negotiated a deal that would pay Essential Consultants 5 percent of all business he brought into 4C and the potential for equity.

The company also announced that Cohen would be joining its board, a development *The Wall Street Journal* covered in a story headlined "Health-Data Watchdog Company Has a Powerful Adviser." 4C didn't disclose to the *Journal* that Cohen had a consulting contract that could generate hefty fees if he could bring in federal business. Cohen dismissed the *Journal*'s questions about whether his relationship with the president might pose a conflict, saying in an email that they were "fundamentally flawed and biased." But after the article came out, 4C quietly abandoned the plan to put Cohen on the board.

In April, Cohen and Squire Patton Boggs, an international law and lobbying firm, announced a "strategic alliance." Squire Patton Boggs agreed to pay Cohen $500,000 a year. Cohen would get a cut of the fees from clients he referred to the firm, and Squire Patton Boggs could in turn parade him around to existing or prospective clients as its resident Trump connection. Cohen worked out of the firm's twenty-third-floor office at Rockefeller Center in New York, just down the street from his old Trump Tower digs, but he insisted on having his own computer server and a lock on his door, for which only he had the key.

He continued to scout for business. In early May, Korea Aerospace Industries, a South Korean defense contractor seeking to develop a trainer jet for the U.S. Air Force, also hired Cohen, paying Essential Consultants $150,000 a month to advise the company as requested.

Then, at a May 5 dinner party in New York, Cohen was introduced to Kenges Rakishev, the controlling shareholder of BTA Bank in Kazakhstan. Rakishev was looking for help recovering billions of dollars stolen from the bank by its former chairman. Cohen, who had little experience with cross-border asset recovery, pitched himself as the man for the job. *I'm the best,* he said. Cohen emailed Rakishev later that night to say what an honor it had been to spend the evening with him. "There are definitely a lot of mutual relationships between the two of us that require our assistance," he wrote. In his Squire office the next day, he told Rakishev that he could assemble a team of lawyers, investigators, and forensic experts. Within days, they worked out an agreement under which Essential Consultants would be paid monthly installments totaling $1.8 million over a year.

Trump had promised to drain the swamp of Washington. Now Michael Cohen, the man he left behind in New York, was practically surfing atop the muck.

"I'm crushing it," he told an associate. Cohen figured he would clear upwards of $5 million a year from consulting and nearly a million more from his law practice.

Not everyone bit on his sales pitches. He tried to market 4C's anti-fraud program to his friend Mark Cuban, the billionaire Dallas Mavericks owner and *Shark Tank* host, who turned him down. "I want you to know I'm out looking for deals," Cohen told him, in case Cuban had any other ideas.

Cohen explored a real estate consulting gig with Imaad Zuberi, a Los Angeles venture capitalist and former Democratic donor who jumped on the Trump bandwagon after the election, giving $900,000 to the inaugural fund. Cohen sent Zuberi a contract, and Zuberi gave him a $100,000 check, but Cohen didn't cash it and they never consummated the deal. Ford Motor Company refused Cohen's entreaties. So did Uber, which thought his ownership of taxi medallions posed a conflict. When he was rebuffed, Cohen reminded the bemused Uber executives that he was "the president's lawyer."

Cohen advertised his relationship to the White House in the signature line of emails he sent to corporate clients, even those with business before the Trump administration. Below his name, Cohen identified himself as "Personal Attorney to President Donald J. Trump." That kind of bold-faced, potentially line-crossing declaration might have seemed dangerous to other lawyers. For Cohen, it was a selling point.

FOR MONTHS, COHEN had stewed about not having been reimbursed for the $130,000 he had laid out to pay Stormy Daniels. Trump had rejected Cohen's appeal, through David Pecker, for a bonus. Cohen had been so frustrated that he'd even considered defecting from Trump, he told one associate.

Now, as Trump assumed the presidency, a plan was taking shape that—finally—would make Cohen whole.

The repayment plan was engineered by Allen Weisselberg, the Trump Organization's chief financial officer. It wasn't as simple as cutting Cohen a check with "porn star hush payment reimbursement" in the memo line. The money would be accounted for in a legitimate-seeming manner, under the process Trump Organization executives put in place. Cohen had announced he was leaving the company to become Trump's personal lawyer, which meant he could be repaid under the guise of providing legal services. In reality, Trump had not given Cohen a retainer agreement, nor had he asked him to perform any legal work.

Nonetheless, the executives decided to pay Cohen $35,000 a month for a year—$420,000 in total. They calculated the amount this way: $130,000 for Stormy Daniels plus $50,000 Cohen had falsely claimed he had paid RedFinch, John Gauger's company, for technology services related to the Trump campaign. To validate the Daniels payment, Cohen furnished Weisselberg with a bank statement showing the transfer to her lawyer, Keith Davidson. He scrawled the request for the $50,000 for RedFinch by hand.

Since Cohen's base payment of $180,000 would be reported to the Internal Revenue Service by him and by Trump as legal fees rather than the reimbursement it actually was, he would have to pay income taxes. So Trump's executives added another $180,000 to cover his taxes, and $60,000 more for a bonus, for a total of $420,000.

On February 14, Cohen sent Weisselberg his first false invoice, requesting payment for January and February 2017 pursuant to his nonexistent retainer agreement. Weisselberg instructed another employee by email: "Post to legal expenses. Put 'retainer for the months of January and February 2017' in the description."

In the beginning, the reimbursements were drawn from a trust that held Trump's corporate assets and accounted for as legal expenses. Weisselberg and Donald Trump Jr. signed those checks. After that, Cohen was paid from the president's personal checking account. Trump signed the remaining checks at the White House, and they were sent to Cohen in New York.

21.

THOUGHT STARTERS

■ ■ ■

Donald Trump's presidency ushered in heady days at American Media. David Pecker had fulfilled his promise to use his publications to help Trump's campaign, and now he—and his company—knew they had a friend in the White House. With the news of his catch-and-kill deal for Trump having passed seemingly without consequence, American Media continued to promote him on the covers of its publications.

McDougal had kept mum about her affair with Trump since her agreement became public in November 2016, though she had no legal obligation to do so. During the presidential campaign, Ted Boutrous, one of the nation's top media lawyers, had offered free representation to any woman sued by Trump for accusing him of wrongdoing. A friend of McDougal's reached out to him, and Boutrous then helped McDougal negotiate an amendment to the contract that permitted her to respond to "legitimate press inquiries regarding the facts of her alleged relationship with Donald Trump." McDougal was still barred from selling her story to another media company, and she needed written consent from American Media before sitting for interviews.

American Media was surprisingly accommodating. Howard told McDougal that the company wanted to continue its partnership with her and offered to hire a public relations team to bring in endorsements for McDougal and create a new brand for her "in the fitness space." She appeared on the cover of the spring 2017 edition of *Muscle & Fitness Hers,* her first of two guaranteed American Media covers. And she held out hope for more.

If it wasn't an explicit trade, McDougal knew that she stood a better chance of advancing her career through American Media if she kept silent about the affair, even when she received "legitimate press inquiries." When *The New Yorker*'s Jeffrey Toobin was working on a profile of David Pecker in June 2017, he contacted McDougal about her contract with American Media. She forwarded the request to the company, which crafted a benign "no comment" for her. She emailed Toobin: "I don't really like to talk about things other than my interests and passions—and that's health, wellness, etc, etc!!"

The New Yorker published arty black-and-white pictures of the tabloid king, by now sixty-five years old and wearing his mustache a little less bushy after a few decades. His mane, still slicked back, had gone silver. The headline pulled no punches. "The National Enquirer's Fervor for Trump," it read, with a blunter subhead: "The tabloid is defined by its predatory spirit. Why has it embraced the President with such sycophantic zeal?"

Pecker, who spent hours with Toobin, was candid about slanting coverage for the president, whom he called "a personal friend of mine," although he misled the writer about the McDougal deal. "When her people contacted me that she had a story on Trump, everybody was contacting her," Pecker told Toobin. "At the same time, she was launching her own beauty-and-fragrance line, and I said that I'd be very interested in having her in one of my magazines, now that she's so famous." He added: "Once she's part of the company, then on the outside she can't be bashing Trump and American Media."

This narrative was almost completely false. McDougal began talks with ABC News only after Howard had passed on her story. American Media had come back to her only after McDougal's lawyer made it clear she intended to go forward with a televised interview about her affair with Trump. There was no beauty or fragrance line, though McDougal wanted one, and American Media had only upheld its end of the bargain to put McDougal on magazine covers and publish fitness columns under pressure. Not surprisingly, Pecker didn't tell Toobin about his pledge to boost Trump's campaign, or that he had coordinated the deal with Michael Cohen and nearly sold Trump the rights to McDougal's story. As to the last statement, it was true that McDougal's original contract prevented her from discussing the Trump affair, but she had never intended to "bash" the president; she still spoke fondly of him.

Toobin also spoke to Gus Wenner, who was taking over Wenner Media from his father, Jann. Earlier in the year, the younger Wenner had negotiated a deal to sell *Us Weekly,* the entertainment magazine that competed with some of Pecker's titles, to American Media for $100 million. Wenner said that as they negotiated the deal, Pecker "was painting Donald as extremely loyal to him, and he had no issue being loyal in return. He told me very bluntly that he had killed all sorts of stories for Trump," a statement Pecker denied making.

With the purchase of *Us Weekly* and another Wenner magazine, *Men's Journal,* a few months later, Pecker returned to the strategy of trying to right American Media's wobbly finances by acquiring new publications and stripping them down to maximize profit. "They have a young audience and a terrific digital platform," he told *The Wall Street Journal* of *Us Weekly.* "They also have an incredible database, plus 500 advertisers we don't have."

As the summer of 2017 approached, Pecker had his sights set on a much bigger target, one he'd been eyeing for years: Time Inc., with its flagship newsweekly *Time* and its celebrity magazine *People.* He needed investors, though. Through Ari Emanuel, the entertainment agent, he had met Kacy Grine, a French businessman and an adviser to the wealthiest Saudi Arabian royal, Prince Alwaleed bin Talal. Under Crown Prince Mohammed bin Salman, the Saudis had forged a close connection with Trump and his son-in-law and adviser Jared Kushner. They were looking for U.S. investments.

In July, Pecker and Grine together visited Trump at the White House. Their group also included Howard; Daniel Rotstein, the consultant Pecker had asked to be a conduit for Trump to reimburse American Media for the Karen McDougal payment; Anthony Melchiorre, the founder of Chatham Asset Management, the primary holder of American Media's debt; hedge fund manager Leon Cooperman, who also had a stake; and Melchiorre's and Cooperman's wives. The group stopped in the Oval Office, and the president led them on a tour of the Lincoln Bedroom and the executive residence in the East Wing. They also dined with Trump, who addressed Howard as "editor man" and sought affirmation of his popularity, asking how *Enquirer* issues with stories about him sold compared with ones featuring other celebrities.

Not long after their White House visit, Grine accompanied Pecker as his adviser on a trip to Saudi Arabia, where the tabloid publisher met with the crown prince. Pecker knew by then that Time Inc. was no longer available, but he hoped to secure financing for other acquisitions and to expand American Media's brands and bodybuilding events into the Middle East.

PECKER'S BOOSTERISM OF Trump's presidency complicated life for his company in the president's first year. On the last day in June, Mika Brzezinski and Joe Scarborough, the hosts of *Morning Joe* on MSNBC, described an offer they said they'd received from the White House. "We got a call that, 'Hey, the *National Enquirer* is going to run a negative story against you guys.' And it was, you know, 'Donald is friends with—the president is friends with the guy that runs the *National Enquirer*,'" Scarborough recounted. "And they said, 'If you call the president up, and you apologize for your coverage, then he will pick up the phone and basically spike this story.'"

Trump shot back on Twitter: "Watched low rated @Morning_Joe for first time in long time. FAKE NEWS. He called me to stop a National Enquirer article. I said no! Bad show." Scarborough said he had not called Trump at all, and he had phone records to prove it.

The confrontation had been brewing for months. Over the years, Scarborough and Brzezinski had been close to Trump, but they had become sharply critical of him since his election, saying he'd changed. Scarborough had begun to question his mental fitness. Then in the spring of 2017, the *Enquirer* had begun making calls—to Brzezinski's children and her nanny—for a story about the romantic relationship between the hosts. The tabloid surveilled her house as well.

Scarborough, observing the *Enquirer*'s aid to Trump during the campaign, became alarmed at what seemed like an obviously coordinated retaliation. He called Jared Kushner, the president's son-in-law and adviser.

"If this story runs, I am not going to blame Pecker, I am going to blame Donald. You don't want to go there," Scarborough said.

"Maybe you should call him and apologize," Kushner responded. "Maybe he can make it go away."

Scarborough, who refused to apologize, fielded desperate requests from two other White House officials pleading with him to do so. One call came in from the West Wing in May as he juggled baseball equipment at his son's Little League practice. "You don't know how bad this story is. Just for your own sake, call Donald," the Trump aide said, to no avail.

In an early June edition, the *Enquirer* wrote about the *Morning Joe* hosts' relationship, and the tabloid also claimed that they'd rushed into an engagement because of the forthcoming story. Scarborough, the story went, had proposed to his "President Donald Trump–bashing sidekick" on a trip to France.

Still, the TV hosts didn't publicly reveal the White House's requests for an apology until Trump unleashed a Twitter tirade against them on June 29, calling Scarborough "Psycho Joe," and Brzezinski "low I.Q. Crazy Mika," and saying he'd seen her "bleeding badly from a face-lift." The pair struck back a day later with their allegations that the White House had tried to use the *Enquirer* to bully them into submission. (They also said Brzezinski had "tweaked" some skin under her chin but never had a face-lift.) Besieged with media inquiries, the *Enquirer* disavowed any involvement in the feud between Trump and the cable hosts. "At no time did we threaten either Joe or Mika or their children in connection with our reporting on the story," the tabloid said in a statement.

There was also a behind-the-scenes flare-up between Pecker and actor Joe Manganiello, best known for playing a werewolf in *True Blood*. By virtue of American Media's ownership of the muscle magazines and the Mr. Olympia competition, Pecker was trying to help Trump recruit members for the President's Council on Sports, Fitness, and Nutrition. He was struggling; many celebrities wanted nothing to do with Trump. Manganiello would do; he had played three varsity sports in high school before he was sidelined by injuries and turned to acting. Manganiello had also become close to Arnold Schwarzenegger, Pecker's off-and-on business associate, after they co-starred in the action movie flop *Sabotage*. Schwarzenegger had returned to an editing role at two American Media fitness magazines in 2013.

Pecker invited Manganiello to join Trump's council, but the actor demurred. At the same time, editors at American Media's *Star* magazine noticed a picture of Manganiello's wife, Sofía Vergara, the star of *Modern Family*, in which the actress was walking around without the enormous engagement ring that had drawn plenty of attention when the couple had married, less than two years earlier. Unaware of Pecker's proposal to her husband, the editors went for broke, using a cover photo of Vergara pressed up against another man at an awards event in Rome and declaring, "Divorce Shocker." Pecker approved the cover without mentioning his invitation to Manganiello and seemingly oblivious that it would kill any remaining chance of the actor joining Trump's council.

"Sofia & Joe . . . IT'S OVER!" the headline screamed. "SOFIA CAUGHT CHEATING IN ROME . . . *Her wedding ring is off . . ."

Vergara and Manganiello took to social media to accuse *Star* of photoshopping the ring off her finger in the cover photo and attack its editor, James Heidenry. The man in the picture, she said, was her friend Andrea Iervolino, who was producing a movie she was shooting in Rome. "The editor of this magazine is an idiot . . . if he is going to have my ring removed to created a 'fake' 'news' [sic] he should have made sure that he removed from social media all the other pictures of that award night in Rome where Im wearing it," she wrote on Instagram. The photo of her without a wedding band hadn't been altered. It ran inside the issue of *Star* and showed Vergara shopping in Beverly Hills while wearing only her engagement ring. The picture of the actress with Iervolino in Rome, to which she'd referred on Instagram, appeared on the magazine's cover to support the claim that she was cheating. In his own post, Manganiello wrote that the magazine was "run by malicious trash."

Manganiello privately emailed Pecker, irate that the publisher would ask him to join Trump's council and then publish a story about his marriage.

In another minor kerfuffle, soon after buying *Us Weekly*, American Media ran a cover story in that magazine about Ivanka Trump, with the headline "IVANKA TAKES A STAND: WHY I DISAGREE WITH MY DAD," outlining how the president's daughter had tried to influence him on issues from gay rights to the Paris climate accord, which he had abandoned despite her objections. The issue, though flattering to Trump and his daughter, prompted Twitter users to mock her supposed stand against her father with memes likening her to Luke Skywalker, Frankenstein's monster, and Tyrion Lannister from *Game of Thrones*. Publicly, Ivanka Trump said the article confused her because she'd never spoken to *Us Weekly*. The editors, who had extrapolated the headlines from others' reporting about her disagreements with Trump, had to explain themselves to one of her aides and run a "makeup" cover later in the year, headlined "My Life at the White House."

As Trump continued to rail against Hillary Clinton, so did the *Enquirer*. In a "world exclusive investigation" after revelations of a 2016 Trump Tower meeting that Donald Trump Jr., Paul Manafort, and Jared Kushner had attended with a Russian lawyer promising dirt on Clinton, the tabloid blamed . . . Clinton. "HILLARY FRAMED TRUMP FAMILY!" an *Enquirer* headline blared, saying she'd "set up" Trump Jr. with "dirt file emails." The story advanced an unfounded theory that Democrats were behind the meeting by trying to connect the dots. The Russian lawyer, Natalia Veselnitskaya, had previously worked with Fusion GPS, the research firm behind the Steele dossier, on a money-laundering case. Fusion's opposition research had been funded by Clinton's campaign. Fusion said it had nothing to do with the meeting.

Before 2017 was over, American Media also found itself in the middle of the scandal engulfing movie producer Harvey Weinstein. Reporting by *The New York Times* and *The New Yorker* revealed that he'd preyed on women for decades, using his sway in Hollywood to harm the careers of those who rebuffed him. The stories helped launch the #MeToo movement. Weinstein, the *Times* reported, was also a Friend of Pecker, who had been protected by American Media's scandal sheets. Weinstein had collaborated with the company's publications on various projects, including a talk show with *Radar Online* and a television production unit.

According to the *Times,* while working with Weinstein, American Media had tried but failed to buy an Italian model's story about the producer groping her. The company dispatched reporters to interview Weinstein's accusers and gather information about them; the women included actress Rose McGowan, who had accused him of rape. Howard then shared the reporting on McGowan with Weinstein. Howard told *The New Yorker* that he'd done so in his role as a business partner, not as a journalist, at a time when the producer was denying all the assault allegations against him. Howard said none of that reporting would have been published anyway.

Weinstein's dealings with American Media and its executives had overlapped with the publisher's efforts on behalf of Trump during his presidential campaign. The revelation of American Media's hush-money deal with McDougal on its own had damaged the company's reputation, but the black eye had been fading with time.

Now the disclosures about Weinstein had revived and amplified the narrative about Pecker's use of his business to protect his friends. The story line had gone beyond one about a tabloid publisher aiding a longtime friend as he sought the White House. The Weinstein maneuvers made clear that there was a culture at Pecker's company that was antithetical to its stated mission: journalism. This hit would be difficult for Pecker and American Media to surmount. Worse problems were still to come.

THROUGH TRUMP'S FIRST year in office, American Media continued to promise McDougal exposure above and beyond what her contract had provided. The company went through Keith Davidson, with whom the model had stayed in touch, to arrange an August 2017 meeting with her in New York. She wondered whether it was some kind of a setup to take advantage of her.

"LOL—I know it sounds weird saying this," Davidson wrote to her, "but . . . Dylan & his boss @ the national enquirer are actually men of their word. No set up. They are powerful guys in media & close to buying Time, Inc."

McDougal and Davidson had lunch with Howard and Pecker at Il Postino, a restaurant near the United Nations. As Pecker sipped white wine, he and Dylan Howard bandied about ideas for stoking McDougal's career. Earlier in 2017, the model had undergone surgery to have her breast implants removed, believing they were making her sick, and she had become interested in raising awareness about illnesses caused by breast implants.

Pecker and Howard talked about the possibility of working with McDougal on a documentary about the health impacts of implants. They discussed having her host fashion and awards coverage. McDougal mentioned a potential skin care line, which excited her most of all. Howard told her these ideas were "thought starters" for her budding relationship with American Media. But the conversation over lunch was the beginning and end of any further relationship with McDougal, because the publisher never followed through on anything the group had discussed.

22.

BOSS, I MISS YOU SO MUCH

■ ■ ■

THE DIZZYING ARRAY of transactions in Michael Cohen's various accounts had by the summer of 2017 drawn the interest of federal investigators for Robert S. Mueller III. Mueller was the special counsel investigating Russian interference in the 2016 election—and whether Trump's campaign had played any role in that interference. Mueller's team took an interest in the payments into his Essential Consultants account, which had been set up under the guise of domestic real estate investment consulting. Of particular suspicion were transfers from companies with ties to Viktor Vekselberg, the Russian oligarch.

Mueller had been appointed by Deputy Attorney General Rod Rosenstein on May 17, nine days after Trump fired FBI Director James Comey. Comey had deflected Trump's demands for loyalty. And he had not complied with the president's wishes that he make clear publicly that Trump was not personally under investigation. In his life as a real estate mogul, Trump had always been able to find people to serve his interests, dubious as the tasks might be. In the White House, he discovered, some of the people the president thought he commanded simply ignored his questionable whims. They had established careers independently of Trump and were mindful of preserving their reputations, of not crossing moral or legal lines, or some combination. Attorney General Jeff Sessions had also enraged Trump when he announced, in March, his recusal from the investigation because his participation in Trump's campaign posed a conflict.

White House counsel Don McGahn had been pushed by Trump to convince Sessions not to recuse himself. After Sessions recused himself anyway, Trump was furious. "I don't have a lawyer," he complained after calling McGahn into the Oval Office following the recusal. He told McGahn that he wished that the long-dead Roy Cohn were his lawyer. "Where's my Roy Cohn?" Trump said angrily. McGahn interpreted the rant as an indictment of his own inability to accomplish what the president wanted.

Trump had been romanticizing Cohn a lot of late. He'd told Reince Priebus, his chief of staff, that Cohn had produced incredible victories for him against long odds. The president had also brought Cohn up with Steve Bannon, who'd moved from the campaign into a strategy job at the White House, describing him as a winner and fixer who could get things done.

But the fixer Trump had called on in recent years was Michael Cohen, and Cohen was now an early person of interest to investigators in the Russia probe. His name had been prominently scattered throughout the pages of the dossier that *BuzzFeed* had published in January 2017. The collection of unconfirmed intelligence dispatches had been assembled by former British spy Christopher Steele during the campaign. Fusion GPS, a research firm founded by former *Wall Street Journal* staffers, had hired Steele. Fusion had been paid to dig up information on Trump first by a conservative publication and later by the Clinton campaign and the Democratic National Committee.

Steele briefed the FBI on his findings. Cohen's alleged liaison with Kremlin operatives in Prague stood out as particularly sensational among the dossier's anecdotes about Russian connections to Trump and his associates. The dossier claimed that Cohen had gone to Prague to engage in damage control after reports emerged of Manafort's lucrative political consulting for pro-Russian forces in Ukraine, *and* that he discussed covert payments to Russian hackers. Cohen vehemently denied that he had ever visited Prague, showing reporters pages of his passport.

Then there was his involvement in the Trump Tower Moscow deal, which was reported in February by *The New York Times,* along with news that Cohen had played a role in a brief, strange attempt early in the administration by Felix Sater and a Ukrainian lawmaker to broker a peace deal between Ukraine and Russia. Cohen gave varying explanations to different reporters. He told one that, when visiting the president at the White House, he left the peace plan on the desk of Trump's since deposed national security adviser, Michael Flynn. He told another he'd thrown it, unopened, into the trash at his apartment in New York. To top it off, Cohen's in-laws hailed from Ukraine.

On July 18, Mueller's investigators obtained a warrant for the contents of Cohen's Gmail account dating back to the beginning of 2016. In the coming months, they returned for additional warrants, telling a judge they had probable cause to believe Cohen had made false statements to a financial institution, committed bank fraud, and acted as an unregistered foreign agent.

In Cohen's emails and his Essential Consultants bank statements, which they'd subpoenaed, the investigators found records of his communications with and payments from his consulting clients. Although he hadn't registered as a lobbyist and had set up his company for domestic real estate work, the investigators pointed out, his clients included foreign companies such as Novartis and Korea Aerospace Industries. The FBI, mentioning KAI's bid to develop a U.S. Air Force jet contract, said it had found an email Cohen sent with the subject heading "K Project," and a consulting contract attached entitling him to a total of $1.2 million over eight months for undescribed advisory services.

The warrants also focused on his work with Columbus Nova because of its connection to Vekselberg, the oligarch who, an FBI agent noted, "has been involved in various symbolic acts seen to be in the Russian national interest, such as the purchase and repatriation of historic Faberge eggs." Mueller's team in its warrants quoted the *Journal* story from January 2017 that included Cohen's interview with Alexandra Berzon in which he called himself "the fix-it guy" who cleaned up Trump's messes.

On October 20, Rod Rosenstein, the Justice Department's number-two official, formally granted Mueller's team authorization to investigate Cohen, among others, and to follow leads related to his creation and use of Essential Consultants.

As the probe dug into Cohen's bank records that fall, Stormy Daniels's lawyer got an unusual inquiry from his bank. A client manager at City National Bank in Los Angeles had asked Keith Davidson the purpose of the wire transfer he had sent to Daniels almost a year earlier, and what the source of the money was. Davidson told the bank that the payment had originated with Essential Consultants, and that it was for a legal settlement.

Concerned, Davidson called Cohen. Millions of dollars moved through Davidson's client trust account. Strange that the bank would single out this one relatively small transaction, Davidson said. He suspected that the bank's questions were prompted by a federal investigation, possibly Mueller's, though he didn't share his hunch with Cohen, who was more concerned that someone pretending to be a bank employee had tried to get Davidson to divulge the nondisclosure agreement. Cohen didn't seem to grasp the potential peril. He did, however, secretly record their phone call.

THE RUSSIA INVESTIGATION didn't seem to Cohen to pose much of a threat. The dossier struck him as mostly fiction, because he knew he'd never been to Prague. He lied to reporters about the Trump Tower Moscow project when news of it broke, saying he'd decided on his own to terminate the discussions in January 2016, before the Iowa caucuses. That was a politically convenient timeline. It would allow Cohen—and Trump—to claim that they had not engaged in any discussions of a business deal with Russia during the official election season. Doing so would have been ethically murky, given that Trump could have leveraged the possibility that he'd soon be the leader of the free world in negotiations with a foreign power to benefit himself. But the narrative Cohen chose avoided an inconvenient truth—that he had continued to explore the Russia deal and briefed Trump on it even as the candidate stepped on his Republican rivals and clinched his party's nomination.

This messaging was consistent with what he'd seen from Trump during the campaign. While the boss had privately asked for updates on the Moscow project—and told him he'd be willing to travel to Russia if Cohen could "lock and load" the deal—Trump publicly, including five times at one news conference, said he had "nothing to do with Russia" except for selling real estate to some Russian buyers. After visiting Moscow in 2013 for the Miss Universe pageant, Trump told the media, he'd flirted with a project there but decided against it.

Afterward, Cohen had asked Trump why he'd misled the reporters. Trump told him there was no need to disclose what hadn't been finished. "Why mention it if it is not a deal?" he said.

Congressional investigators in early May asked Cohen for documents and testimony, neither of which worried him. Cohen declined the invitation to testify. Then he and Jay Sekulow, a lawyer known for expanding the rights of religious groups, whom Trump had added to his legal team for the Russia investigation, went to the White House to discuss the situation with Trump. "Why did you say no? Just cooperate," Trump said. "There's nothing here. There's no Russia. There's no collusion. There's no business dealings. Why didn't you cooperate?"

It was Sekulow who told him not to testify, Cohen explained, but Trump didn't understand why. "Well, they sent an invitation, and like to a bad bar mitzvah, you just don't go," Cohen said. But he understood the subtext of Trump's coded message. Without explicitly telling him to lie, Trump had instructed Cohen to stay on message, the one the president himself had been delivering. The message was that the Moscow discussions had been fleeting and never amounted to a deal.

Soon congressional investigators subpoenaed Cohen to testify, and he began a series of discussions with Sekulow about what he'd say. By then, Cohen and Trump had a joint legal defense agreement, and Cohen's legal fees were being paid by Trump's company and campaign. Cohen and Sekulow decided that he would say the discussions on the project had ended in January 2016, based on his frustrated text messages at that time telling Felix Sater that they were done working on it together. Cohen would also say that his outreach to Dmitry Peskov, the press secretary for Russian president Vladimir Putin, had gone unanswered. (The Trump Organization employees working on the production of emails to Congress didn't include the communications between Cohen and Peskov's assistant, which would have disproved that assertion.)

As Cohen's October date to testify in Congress drew closer, Sekulow reinforced the mission of staying on message. "The president loves you," he told him. Cohen would be protected, unless he went rogue.

The statement Cohen drafted for Congress included the lies he'd been telling the press about when the discussions of the Moscow project ended and his interactions with Russian officials. He also falsely said he had never thought about asking Trump to go to Russia and that he'd spoken to the boss about the deal only three times. When Cohen told Sekulow that he'd spoken to Trump more times than the statement indicated, and that he'd communicated with Russian officials, the lawyer told him it didn't matter. *Stay on message. Don't muddy the water.*

Keep it short and tight, Sekulow told him. *This will be over soon.* Cohen also spoke to Trump about the importance of staying on message.

Cohen submitted his false statements about the Moscow project to Congress on August 28. As he did so, reporters printed details of the embarrassing emails that Felix Sater had written as he tried to sell Cohen on the Moscow deal—the notes about putting Ivanka into Putin's chair and how the Moscow deal would help elect Trump. Cohen, in his submission to Congress, dismissed Sater's messages as braggadocio.

A few days later, waiting to give his testimony in person, Cohen sat down for breakfast in the Hamptons with Emily Jane Fox, a writer for *Vanity Fair*. He lamented that, based on legal advice, he'd been unable to speak with Trump, the first lady, or the Trump children for several weeks. He showed her his two phones, explaining that the black one was just for the White House. Appearing to well up, Cohen said he felt guilty that he wasn't at the Oval Office, where Trump was basically alone—surrounded by people who didn't understand the meaning of loyalty.

"I'm the guy who stops the leaks. I'm the guy who protects the president and the family," Cohen said. "I'm the guy who would take a bullet for the president." He and his family—including his children—had taken abuse for his association with Trump, Cohen told Fox. No matter the personal cost, he said, "I'd never walk away."

Cohen released the opening statement of his planned congressional testimony to the media on September 19. Afterward, Sekulow told him the president was pleased. He appeared before the House and Senate intelligence committees over two days in late October, calling Sekulow again after his testimony on both days.

DESPITE THE BOASTS of proximity to the White House that he had made to his consulting clients, Cohen became increasingly frustrated with the president throughout 2017 after he failed to land an administration job. He was also still smarting about the difficulty he had getting reimbursed for the Stormy Daniels deal.

Early in the year, he told friends that he felt undervalued and was considering making a break from the president. But soon after, he'd moved in the other direction. In February, he visited Trump in the

Oval Office. He was named deputy finance chairman of the Republican National Committee in April. Cohen also made calls to raise money for a legal defense fund for White House aides who were subpoenaed by investigators, though he hadn't been asked to do so and didn't bring in any money. In the summer, Cohen tweeted that he was "so proud" of Donald Trump Jr. for being honest when, in response to news reports, the president's son released emails about his June 2016 meeting with Russians who promised damaging information about Hillary Clinton.

Still, Cohen struggled for the president's attention, which he craved. So he took steps to get it back. After Cohen had lunch with Mark Cuban, the Dallas Mavericks owner and Trump critic, at Freds restaurant, in New York, a gossip item appeared in the *New York Post*. When they had breakfast another day, at the Time Warner Center in November, paparazzi showed up, prompting Cuban to conclude that Cohen was arranging their meetings to get Trump's attention.

The second meeting, as reported by *TMZ*, had the desired effect. Trump called Cohen to complain.

"No, boss, I had breakfast with him to set him straight. I told him he has to respect the office, to respect you," Cohen told him. "Boss, I miss you so much," he said later in the conversation. "I wish I was down there with you. It's really hard for me to be here."

In calls with other Trump associates, Cohen asked, "Have you heard from the boss?" He complained to one acquaintance he saw at a restaurant that Trump wasn't calling or helping him.

Cohen's consulting business hadn't produced much, if any, return on investment for his clients, some of whom were bailing. In the months after AT&T hired him, he told executives when he expected to have meetings with Trump, and they in turn produced talking points to give Cohen to discuss with the president. On May 12, an AT&T consultant emailed him, "Hey Michael, have heard anything new re merger?" But despite his hiring and AT&T's $2 million donation to the inauguration, the Trump administration came out against its merger with Time Warner.

Cohen hadn't brought in any clients for 4C Health Solutions. He'd done nothing to help the financial recovery efforts of BTA, the Kazakh bank, except make a referral to an associate of Marc Kasowitz, one of Trump's go-to lawyers, but the firm couldn't take the work because it conflicted with another client's interests. After making two install-ments totaling $300,000, the Kazakhs cut Cohen off, without inform-ing him. For months, Cohen would continue sending them desperate requests to get paid.

Novartis executives concluded after a meeting with Cohen in March that he likely would not be able to deliver much for them, but the con-tract didn't allow them to terminate the $1.2 million agreement except for cause, so they kept looking for value and continued paying him. Cohen reached out to the CEO, Joe Jimenez, on occasion over the next six months about proposals to lower drug prices, litigation over the opioid crisis, and other matters, but the discussons didn't lead any-where.

KAI, the Korean defense contractor, paid Cohen for at least four months, totaling $600,000, of the $1.2 million he had been seeking.

Andrew Intrater, from Columbus Nova, had decided not to invest in taxi debt without being able to predict how far it might fall in value. Cohen had also talked to him about putting money into a rebar facility in Michigan. "We could make a billion on rebar," Cohen had said, though that idea didn't go any further. He put Intrater in touch with a friend who was putting together a deal to consolidate oil and gas assets in Oklahoma, but after some research, Intrater determined the invest-ment wasn't quite as advertised.

Cohen connected Intrater with FrutaPOP, a maker of alcohol-infused ice pops. The company had been co-founded by his old college roommate, the artist Laurance Rassin. Intrater thought the product had promise, and Cohen said casino magnate Steve Wynn wanted to bring the ice pops to his facilities. But Rassin and Intrater couldn't come to terms, and Rassin didn't produce the marketing plan Intrater had requested to justify the investment of $250,000 to $1 million that FrutaPOP was seeking.

Cohen also put in a call to David Shulkin, Trump's secretary for veterans affairs, whom he had known for years, after Intrater men-tioned that he had a personal investment in an electronic cigarette company and hoped to market it to veterans.

The main purpose for which Intrater had hired Cohen—introducing him to investors—never panned out. They had talked about making trips overseas, to Asia and Europe, where Cohen would connect Co-lumbus Nova to his wealthy friends. But as he was drawn into the investigation into Russian election meddling, Cohen kept delaying those travel plans. After seven months, Intrater asked him to waive the no-cancellation clause in his contract, and Cohen agreed. By then he'd been paid $580,000 of his $1 million contract. There weren't any hard feelings. Cohen raised $35,000 from Intrater for a Trump fundraising event in Washington in June and comped him at another such event at Le Cirque, in Manhattan, three months later.

Squire Patton Boggs was considering terminating Cohen's contract as well. He'd brought only five clients into the firm, including a lobbying contract with the U.S. Immigration Fund, a company with ties to the family business of Jared Kushner, Trump's son-in-law.

Cohen had told people at Squire that he could call Trump whenever he wanted. But unlike other long-standing Trump advisers who seemed to wander in and out of the White House in the administration's early days, Cohen rarely traveled to Washington. When he was in New York, he kept his office door closed most of the time.

He also wanted to leave Squire Patton Boggs, telling associates near the end of 2017 that he might want to move to another lobbying firm, like FTI Consulting or Baker Botts. Cohen thought Squire was taking advantage of his connection to the president without paying him enough. "Every one of these motherfuckers is going around the world and using my relationship in order to acquire clients, but I'm not being fairly compensated," he told Keith Davidson.

Cohen's earnings included one last hush-money deal with Davidson, who had been approached by another former *Playboy* model, Shera Bechard, through a mutual acquaintance, a doctor. Bechard said she had become pregnant by Elliott Broidy, a Los Angeles–based venture capitalist who, like Cohen, was a deputy finance chair for the Republican National Committee. Bechard said they'd had a nearly two-year relationship in which Broidy, who was married, paid her to have a sexual relationship exclusively with him.

Now she wanted to cut a deal with Broidy to keep his secret. Davidson, researching Broidy on the Internet, called lawyers he thought might know him, finally reaching Cohen. "Do I know him?" Cohen said. "We're besties!"

Cohen dialed up Broidy. "It's your lucky day, because you have a big problem, and I can help you solve it," Cohen told him.

Cohen and Davidson negotiated a deal under which Broidy would pay Bechard $1.6 million over two years for her silence. Though it wasn't spelled out in the contract, she also agreed to have an abortion. Cohen's fee was $250,000, and Broidy had the first payment of $62,500 sent to Essential Consultants through another shell company.

Cohen had parlayed his proximity to Trump into income of more than $4.3 million in the first year of the new presidency.

23.

ESENTIAL CONSULTANTS LLC

■ ■ ■

FROM THE MOMENT the *Journal* reported that the *National Enquirer* had caught and killed the story of Karen McDougal's affair with Trump, sources began telling us—even in the few days left until the election—about other stories David Pecker had suppressed for friends and celebrities whose gratitude might come in handy.

We heard from Murray Waas, a freelance investigative reporter who just the month before, in October, had published a long article online about the efforts that Pecker, Michael Cohen, and American Media made early in Trump's campaign to dissuade Jeremy Frommer, the head of the digital technology company Jerrick Media, from publishing old pictures of Trump preparing to autograph a woman's cleavage. In the same article, Waas had reported that Pecker had promised Trump that he'd use American Media's publications to aid his presidential campaign, just as the tabloid executive had done for Schwarzenegger before.

The McDougal deal, and the catch-and-kill tactics it entailed, had already shown that the president-elect's debt to Pecker went beyond gushing stories and attacks on Trump's enemies. Now it seemed as if that debt could be greater than we even knew. What might American Media still be holding back? How might it be repaid?

ONE TANTALIZING LEAD stood out among the tips. It had come in to *Journal* reporter Lukas Alpert, who worked with us on the McDougal story, as we were preparing to publish it on Friday, November 4, 2016. Lukas's source said American Media had paid a former Trump building doorman to kill a story about a daughter Trump had fathered with a female employee. In the initial days of pursuing what we came to call "the love-child story" or "the doorman story," our challenges quickly came into focus.

First, there was the matter of confirming the deal and the identities of the participants. Then there was the question of whether we could be confident that the child was actually Trump's. On the McDougal story, there had been discussions at the *Journal* about the ethics of revealing her assertion that she'd had an affair with Trump without determining if it was true. Although the point of reporting it was the payoff, the concern was about publicizing a salacious and possibly false allegation that might smear a presidential candidate. In McDougal's case, we had spoken to several people who had been around her during the time she said she'd been in a relationship with Trump, and we found her story to be credible, even though we wouldn't and couldn't report that it was true.

By the end of November, we had learned the names of the ex-doorman, of the employee he said had given birth to the child, and of the daughter herself. The doorman, Dino Sajudin, had called the *Enquirer*'s tip line near the end of 2015. He'd passed a lie detector test and had been paid $30,000 for the rights to his information regardless of whether anything would be published, which was a princely sum in the world of checkbook journalism and a departure from American Media's usual practice of paying sources upon publication. No story had ever appeared.

We learned about the unreasonably harsh $1 million penalty that Sajudin's contract said he'd have to pay the company should he disclose the information elsewhere. It seemed intended to scare him into silence.

We tracked Sajudin to Pennsylvania, where he was pursuing a second career as a nurse. A simple Google search turned up allegations that cast doubt on his credibility. He had been accused of trying to blackmail a resident at the Trump building where he once worked. We decided that, on the same day in mid-December, we would approach both Sajudin and the woman he alleged had given birth to Trump's child at the same time, to maintain an element of surprise in the event that word of our reporting spread. Along with Alpert and another

Journal reporter, Nicole Hong, we traveled to Sajudin's town in eastern Pennsylvania and to the woman's home in Queens.

In Pennsylvania, Sajudin couldn't be found, but he received a message we'd left and returned the call. Sajudin told Alpert that he thought American Media had bought his information to bury it. "I don't think they had any intention of doing a story," he said. "I think it was just about paying some money to make it go away." In Queens, the woman listened to our inquiry from behind a slightly cracked front door. She refused to talk.

Within a couple of hours of that December visit, Michael Cohen had been alerted and called the *Journal* unsolicited, trying to shoot down the story. He called Sajudin's tip "baseless." He also threw in that our McDougal story was completely false. At the time, we didn't know how deeply he and Trump had been involved in pushing the McDougal contract forward.

After learning of our conversation with Sajudin, American Media released him from the $1 million damage provision in his contract, allowing him to speak publicly now that Trump had been elected president. In mid-December, the publisher responded to our written questions about the love-child story with a statement from Pecker and chief content officer Dylan Howard:

> After a deep and thorough investigation, we established the supposed story to be not true. Mr. Sajudin was unable to provide one shred of information to support his fanciful claims beyond second hand rumor and conjecture.
>
> We implored Mr. Sajudin to provide further proof. He could not.
>
> We subjected Mr. Sajudin to a polygraph exam. It is true that he passed—but Mr. Sajudin passed on the basis of what he had HEARD and NOT any individual item of proof that Mr. Trump had fathered a love child.
>
> Anybody can accuse anybody else of anything, an accusation is proof of . . . nothing.
>
> AMI is in the business of publishing world exclusive stories— and, importantly, returning a profit for our investors. If Mr. Sajudin's supposed story was credible, it would have been a Page One

that garnered international attention and had a demonstrable effect on the presidential race. It would have sold as many copies of
The National ENQUIRER as this company did when Elvis Presley
died in 1977. We stood to make tens of millions of dollars.

Nevertheless, AMI is not in the business of publishing knowingly false stories, and the information presented to us by Mr. Sajudin did not meet the basic editorial standards for any journalistic
organization.

After sending their statements, American Media executives—
seemingly determined to push back harder than they had on the
McDougal story—invited us to their office, near Wall Street. Pecker
didn't attend, but Dylan Howard did, along with attorney Cameron
Stracher and media representative Jon Hammond. They continued to
deny that they had killed the story to help Trump.

But the timeline American Media provided raised more questions.
The company had initially given Sajudin a standard source agreement,
which promised him payment only upon publication. Then, after
weeks of reporting, and after he'd passed the lie detector test, American Media agreed to pay him immediately when he threatened to take
the tip to a competitor, the executives said. Almost immediately after
paying him, American Media stopped reporting, without ever having
spoken to the woman in question or her daughter. Why pay him and
stop reporting? If Sajudin's credibility was the issue, hadn't the tabloid's
aggressive reporters found the blackmail allegations against him before signing Sajudin up as a source? We had discovered them with a
simple Google search within minutes of learning Sajudin's name. And
yet American Media had still decided to bring him in and give him
$30,000.

We sent another round of written questions—we wanted to know
the difference between the decision to kill the Sajudin story, owing to
doubts about his credibility, and the decision to run a story it had published only a couple of months earlier, in September 2015, about Hillary Clinton having only six months to live. In response, outside lawyers
for American Media and Howard sent threatening letters. These letters
weren't an issue; the *Journal* received and responded to them all the
time and moved forward anyway after bulletproofing stories.

The more problematic issue for the *Journal* was that we'd found no evidence that the Trump love-child rumor Sajudin had passed along was true. We thought the woman he had named as Trump's daughter probably wasn't. That gave plausibility to American Media's claim that it had not published a story because its editors didn't believe Sajudin. The tabloid's decision to suddenly stop reporting out Sajudin's tip after writing him a check suggested to us that American Media had intended to stop him from spreading the love-child rumor to other outlets, true or not. But we didn't have proof of that. What we had was a far more nuanced set of circumstances to explain to our readers than the *Enquirer*'s catching and killing McDougal's story.

The *Journal* decided not to move forward. The love-child story was dead.

As THE FIRST year of Trump's news-heavy administration rolled on, we kept a toe in the lurid world that had brought us the tale of the *National Enquirer*, the Playmate, and the president.

We peered down a few of the many rabbit holes created by Trump's tabloid presidency. We investigated a rumor that a tape of Trump acting violently toward Melania Trump in an elevator had been put up for sale months before the presidential election. We learned that a Los Angeles lawyer had indeed contacted gossip outlets offering the sale of such a tape and had scheduled a meeting with *TMZ* before backing out. The lawyer said her client had disappeared and she'd never seen the tape herself. We heard from our sources that other reporters were pursuing the same tape—one reporter had told sources he was setting off to find an oligarch who had taken it to Eastern Europe—but we eventually came to suspect that the so-called elevator tape was a phantom.

It had been a year since the McDougal story when we got our next big break.

We hadn't forgotten about Stormy Daniels. We knew that, like McDougal, she had been represented by Keith Davidson, had contemplated a television interview about her alleged encounter with Trump, and had gone dark before Election Day.

It seemed clear that someone had paid her. But who? No one knew or would say.

Toward the middle of 2017, we started asking sources again.

Finally, several cocktails into a late-night dinner near the end of the year, one of our sources offered a clue: "Think taxis."

Michael Cohen.

THE NOTION THAT the president's personal lawyer had paid off a porn star before the election instantly focused our attention. The McDougal deal had clearly been a favor to Trump, a connection we had been able to make for readers by virtue of his relationship with Pecker and the *Enquirer*'s sycophantic coverage of him. But there was still a gap between the tabloid and Trump. There was no daylight, on the other hand, between Michael Cohen and the president. If it was true that Cohen had paid the porn star, it would be as if Trump had paid Daniels himself.

We knew the likelihood was small that we would be able to obtain a copy of any NDA Cohen might have executed with Daniels, as we had been able to do with McDougal's contract. So we began searching for a shell company that we had been told Cohen used to make the payment. The source said that Cohen had created one for that purpose, with an apropos name—something like "Damage Control LLC." But we didn't know its actual name, exactly when it had been formed, or in what state. Finding it before making phone calls to other potential sources would help corroborate the information we had received without alerting anyone—who might tip off a competitor—to the possibility that the president's lawyer had paid hush money to a porn star.

Cohen had created many companies over the years, sometimes with colorful names that played on his own or his relatives' names or movie characters. But most were registered to the address of his Park Avenue apartment, a clear connection to him. None of those companies had been created near the end of the 2016 campaign, and none had names similar to Damage Control.

Our search for limited liability companies focused on those created in states that allow owners to remain secret—primarily Delaware, a haven for corporate secrecy not far from New York where fifteen thousand new companies are created every month. Cohen had been connected to at least one shell company in Delaware before. But we also looked in Wyoming, Nevada, and New York, because those were the places he lived.

Doug Denison, a former reporter who had become the director of community relations for the Delaware Division of Corporations, assisted in the search, kindly granting our cryptic requests for records that might help us identify a company with a name like Damage Control. When we asked for lists of every Delaware company formed in the fall of 2016, Denison discovered a report the state produced for commercial purposes that contained that information. We studied the reports through September and October 2016, picking out dozens of names that might fit the bill, and eliminating them all for one reason or another.

As we pored over the records to no avail, another source suggested that a hush-money payment might be a "resolution" of a problem. There was a Resolution Agency LLC in New York, and several in Delaware: Accurate Resolution Services LLC, Re-Solution-TX Inc., Resolve Inc., and Judgment Resolutions Inc. Again, either the names or their dates of incorporation didn't correspond with the timeline the source had laid out.

Still, while searching for the shell company, we learned from other trusted sources that Cohen's deal with Daniels had occurred in mid-October 2016, that he had paid her $130,000, and that Cohen had wired the money to Keith Davidson's account at City National Bank in Los Angeles. The sources also said that City National had in the fall of 2017 made inquiries about the nature of the transaction, suggesting it might be under scrutiny by federal investigators.

By Wednesday, January 10, 2018, we had gathered enough to publish a story. That morning, at 10:39 A.M., we emailed Hope Hicks, who had recently become the White House communications director. The email's subject heading read, "Wall Street Journal comment request/ POTUS/adult film star/settlement payment."

> We are seeking comment for a story that could be published as early as this afternoon.
>
> We are planning to report that Michael Cohen executed an agreement with adult film star Stormy Daniels (Stephanie Clifford) in October 2016 in which he agreed to pay her $130,000 in return for her not publicly discussing her account of a sexual encounter or encounters with President Trump after they met in 2006 at the American Century Celebrity Golf Championship at

Edgewood Tahoe Links in Nevada. (Please note there is a picture of them together online at this event.)

This story will report, based on multiple sources, that Mr. Cohen negotiated the agreement and paid Daniels through a shell company by sending the funds to her lawyer's client trust account at City National Bank.

Eight minutes later, Hicks wrote back, ignoring the payoff completely and focusing only on the allegation of a sexual encounter. Hicks wrote, "I will review your inquiry and get back to you however I believe I already responded to you for a previous story you published." She then quoted her denial in our McDougal story that Trump had an affair with Daniels. Soon, another White House spokesperson, Raj Shah, called to ask for more time, because Trump was at events and couldn't be briefed until early afternoon.

At 2:08 P.M., Cohen, whom we'd also contacted, sent his statement by email. Like Hicks, he ignored the questions about the hush-money payment.

Quote for usage:

"This is now the second time that you are raising outlandish allegations against my client, You have attempted to perpetuate this false narrative for over a year; a narrative that has been consistently denied by all parties since at least 2011. President Trump once again vehemently denies any such occurrence as has Ms. Daniels."

(see attached letter dated January 10, 2018).

Attached to Cohen's email was a PDF with a statement, atop Daniels's rather extravagant signature.

TO WHOM IT MAY CONCERN:

I recently became aware that certain news outlets are alleging that I had a sexual and/or romantic affair with Donald Trump many, many, many years ago. I am stating with complete clarity that this is absolutely false. My involvement with Donald Trump was limited to a few public appearances and nothing more. When I met Donald Trump, he was gracious, professional and a complete gentleman to me and EVERYONE in my presence.

Rumors that I have received hush money from Donald Trump are completely false. If indeed I did have a relationship with Donald Trump, trust me, you wouldn't be reading about it in the news, you would be reading about it in my book. But the fact of the matter is, these stories are not true.

Daniels had ignored our emails to her and to a woman who sometimes worked as her publicist, but Cohen had obtained a denial from her. Notably, she wrote that she hadn't received hush money from "Donald Trump," but she never mentioned not getting any from Michael Cohen.

The story didn't publish that day. The *Journal* wanted more time to thoroughly vet and review it because of the sensitivity of the topic. We knew that our 130-year-old business paper wouldn't have published a story as salacious as this one about the president having sex with a porn star. But we made clear that this was about money and a payoff. And the masthead editors agreed.

With the story in a holding pattern, something finally clicked on the shell company list. Resolution Consultants LLC had been created in Delaware on September 30, 2016. That seemed a little too early, but it was close. In Delaware, actual incorporation documents aren't available online, but Denison had offered to pull the papers for specific companies we identified. By now, we trusted him enough to reveal that he should look for the name Michael Cohen. "Is that the Michael Cohen I think it is?" Denison asked. He still didn't know why we were looking. But he dug out the incorporation documents and called back within minutes, excited.

"That's it!" Denison said. "It's him."

Although Cohen didn't have to do so, and could have paid a lawyer so he could remain anonymous, he had put his own name on the corporate formation documents. The records showed that the company had been dissolved on October 17, 2016, less than three weeks after it was created.

Confronted by phone with the assertion that this was the company he'd used to pay Daniels, Cohen said, "You include whatever you think you need to include. I have had enough of your antics. Anything you want to send to me, you send to me by email."

That night, after he was emailed the incorporation records for Resolution Consultants with his name on them, Cohen called back. He said that he hadn't even opened a bank account for Resolution Consultants, that it was a company he'd created for a real estate deal that didn't pan out, and that it had never been used for anything. This was troubling. It was the first thing, other than Trump's affair with Daniels, that Cohen had explicitly denied.

Hitting the Delaware records again that night, a group of *Journal* reporters and editors combed through the list of companies that had been created in October 2016, and specifically those formed on October 17, when Resolution Consultants was dissolved.

An entity called Essential Consultants LLC had been created that same day, by the same registered agent in Delaware who'd opened Resolutions Consultants. Googling, we found that on an obscure document-sharing website, someone had anonymously posted a consulting contract between Essential Consultants and 4C Health Solutions, the Virginia startup. (As it turned out, an employee at 4C had inexplicably posted the document online.) Cohen's name was on the contract.

The next morning, Doug Denison confirmed that Essential Consultants had been created by Michael Cohen two minutes before he dissolved Resolution Consultants. Challenged with this information, Cohen didn't deny that he'd used Essential to pay Daniels, but he didn't confirm it, either.

By Friday, editors and lawyers at the *Journal* had reviewed the story. We decided to withhold for the time being our reporting that Cohen had used a shell company to pay Daniels. The *Journal* put the story online at 3:13 P.M.: "Trump Lawyer Arranged $130,000 Payment for Adult-Film Star's Silence."

The story exploded online and on television, and in print the next day. The two New York tabloids paired the story on their covers with revelations that Trump had, in a meeting with senators that week, referred to the "shithole countries" of the Third World. "S#!T Stormy," blared the headline of the New York *Daily News,* under pictures of Trump and Daniels.

The New York Times, in the first paragraph at the top left corner of its front page, cited reporting by *The Wall Street Journal* in its story about the hush payment. The *Times* reported that Jacob Weisberg, editor of *Slate,* had spoken with Daniels in the summer and fall of 2016, before the hush-money deal, and that she'd told him a Trump lawyer named Michael had agreed to pay her. She'd also texted Weisberg a portion of an unfinished draft contract in which pseudonyms had been used. But then she had abruptly cut Weisberg off, and he had not pursued the story further.

A few days later, we reported that Cohen had used Essential Consultants to pay Daniels.

THE STORIES PROMPTED the publisher of *In Touch Weekly* and *Life & Style* to dig out its 2011 interview with Stormy Daniels about her liaison with Trump. It was the same interview that Michael Cohen had once successfully killed with a legal threat. The long-dormant Daniels interview was published five days after we revealed her nondisclosure agreement in the *Journal.*

"The sex was nothing crazy. He wasn't like, chain me to the bed or anything. It was one position. I can definitely describe his junk perfectly if I ever have to. He definitely seemed smitten after that. He was like, 'I wanna see you again, when can I see you again?'" Daniels was quoted as saying.

The interview flatly contradicted Daniels's statement to us and others denying the affair, and it elevated the story of the payoff. Cohen wanted to get Daniels on the air to push back against our story and the *In Touch* interview.

"I have her tentatively scheduled for Hannity tonight," Cohen said in a text to Davidson on January 17.

"She cannot don't [sic] today. She is flying to LA tomorrow. I'm trying to get her to commit for tomorrow," Davidson replied.

Cohen sent a series of text messages throughout the afternoon, pleading with Davidson to get Daniels on *Hannity* that day. "By doing tomorrow you just create another news cycle instead of putting an end to this one."

The plan to put Daniels on Fox News fizzled within hours that evening, after Cohen consulted with a group he called the "wise men," presumably referring to Trump and his advisers, and resumed texting with Davidson.

"Keith, the wise men all believe the story is dying and don't think it's smart for her to do any interviews. Let her do her thing but no interviews at all with anyone," Cohen wrote.

"100%," Davidson replied.

"Thanks pal."

"Just no interviews or statements unless through you."

"Got it."

24.

THE PLAINTIFF'S LAWYER

■ ■ ■

WITH HER HUSH-MONEY agreement in the open, Stormy Daniels maintained her silence on the topic of Trump, but she wasn't keeping a low profile. She launched a nationwide "Make America Horny Again" strip club tour. During her routine, Daniels danced in (and out of) a red-white-and-blue outfit. She'd adopted the theme from an entrepreneurial strip club owner in Greenville, South Carolina, who booked Daniels's first live performance after our story revealed Cohen's payment to her.

The Trophy Club described itself as Greenville's only completely topless strip club that still permitted smoking inside. Inside, owner Jay Levy gussied up his club with patriotic bunting and red, white, and blue balloons. He'd created T-shirts for the event with a silk-screen photo of Daniels posing in a bikini, holding a drink. "HE SAW HER LIVE," the Trophy Club's flier said. "YOU CAN TOO!" Daniels's show, on the one-year anniversary of Trump's inauguration, drew twice the usual Saturday night crowd.

Daniels had found a recipe for success, but the tour also created tension in the fragile dynamic between Daniels and Cohen. The Trump attorney thought Daniels's branding, a clear reference to the president's campaign slogan, was disrespectful to the boss.

Daniels also began making television appearances. *Inside Edition* aired an interview with her on January 25, soon after her Greenville performance. Daniels smiled and said nothing when her interviewer asked whether she had slept with Trump. Five days later, late-night host Jimmy Kimmel announced that he'd have Daniels on his show on the day of Trump's first State of the Union address, January 30.

Cohen was in close contact with Trump as they tried to bottle up the story. He had a five-minute call with the White House on January 19, the day before Daniels stripped at the Trophy Club. He also called Melania Trump's cellphone several times between January 26 and 30. The attorney had a seven-minute call with the White House on the day Daniels was scheduled to appear on *Jimmy Kimmel Live!* He and Trump wouldn't stop her from going on the show, but they wanted something in return. Cohen got on the phone with Davidson and told him to convince Daniels to sign a second statement denying the affair.

Davidson met Daniels, Gina Rodriguez, and Rodriguez's boyfriend, Anthony Kotzev, at the Hollywood Roosevelt Hotel hours before Daniels was to tape *Jimmy Kimmel Live!* (In an interesting bit of symmetry, Kotzev had worked at *The Dirty* and had posted the initial 2011 piece about Daniels's encounter with Trump, at the direction of his then boss, Nik Richie.) Kimmel's show put Daniels up in the Roosevelt's Marilyn Monroe Suite (naturally), with its white furniture, open floor plan, and wraparound balcony overlooking the hotel's pool. The group was preparing for the inevitable questions Kimmel would ask Daniels about the affair. Davidson told her that Cohen and company wanted another denial. "They wanted to know if you'd sign another statement, because they are letting you go on the show, and they want you to go have fun," Davidson told her.

Davidson had brought his laptop and drafted the statement in the room, with input from the group. It read:

> Over the past few weeks I have been asked countless times to comment on reports of an alleged sexual relationship I had with Donald Trump many, many, many years ago.
>
> The fact of the matter is that each party to this alleged affair denied its existence in 2006, 20011 [*sic*], 2016, 2017 and now again in 2018. I am not denying this affair because I was paid "hush money" as has been reported in overseas owned tabloids. I am denying this affair because it never happened.
>
> I will have no further comment on this matter.

Daniels was excited for Kimmel's show. She signed the statement without complaint, but she changed her handwriting, as if in subtle protest. Daniels had signed the first statement in large, looping letters. Her signature on the second was small and crabbed by comparison. Rodriguez, told by Davidson that Cohen wanted the statement out before showtime, distributed it to reporters hours before Daniels sat for her interview with Kimmel.

As DANIELS WAITED in the dressing room for the Kimmel interview, a producer for the show entered with a message. A representative for pornography publisher Larry Flynt had called and said he would pay Daniels's legal expenses for violating the agreement if she told her full story on the air with Kimmel. Daniels considered it, briefly, but Rodriguez, who was with her in the room, talked her out of it. They could call the mischievous Flynt after the show.

On the set, Kimmel was every bit as persistent as they had expected him to be. He asked in a dozen different ways whether Daniels had slept with Trump and whether she was bound to silence by an NDA. At one point, he produced three carrots, asking Daniels to point to the one that most closely resembled the size of the president's genitalia. (She deflected: "Who wants a carrot?") Daniels was clever and funny as she parried. But it wasn't the performance the Trump camp wanted. While she didn't admit to the sex or the agreement, Daniels didn't deny anything, either.

"You can't say whether you have a nondisclosure agreement. But if you didn't have a nondisclosure agreement, you most certainly could say, 'I don't have a nondisclosure agreement.' Yes?" Kimmel asked.

"You're so smart, Jimmy," she replied.

Kimmel remarked on the differences between Daniels's signature on the first statement denying the affair and the hush money (the one Cohen sent us) and the second one Davidson had presented to her hours earlier. Had she actually signed the second statement? he asked.

Daniels played coy. "I don't know, did I? That doesn't look like my signature, does it?" she said.

Reporters deluged Rodriguez and Davidson with calls and emails after the show, asking about Daniels's seeming disavowal of the second statement. Rodriguez, for one, was angry, and she let her client know it. Why hadn't Daniels owned up to signing it?

Daniels was defensive. "I have been called a liar for weeks. I was super careful about what I said. I should probably just go home. This is crazy," she texted Rodriguez.

They reached out to Flynt about potentially indemnifying Daniels after the show. Rodriguez spoke with his representative, who told her no money for legal fees would be forthcoming. Rodriguez figured the offer had been a ploy to get Daniels to open up in the moment.

DANIELS WAS INCREASINGLY looking for a way out of her agreement. Rodriguez was trying to get her a book deal, but publishers were begging off, "unless you were telling the story that everyone wanted to hear" about her affair with Trump, Rodriguez told her. And no publisher wanted to be the one to help her violate the NDA and risk the legal consequences.

When Flynt disappeared, Daniels asked Davidson to contact California billionaire Tom Steyer, who was bankrolling a $20 million ad campaign calling for Trump's impeachment. Maybe he would cover her for a breach of the NDA. But Davidson told her he couldn't make the call. He had negotiated the agreement for her, a deal she had wanted at the time, and, like the publishers, he wasn't going to help her violate it.

Daniels and Rodriguez took Davidson's resistance to helping them engineer an escape from the NDA as evidence that he was in league with Cohen. They were already considering new counsel on February 13 when two events hastened Daniels's flight from the NDA. A *Daily Beast* report that day described a book proposal Cohen was shopping. The proposal said the book would explain Cohen's role in the "unfortunate saga" involving Stormy Daniels. (Center Street, an imprint of Hachette Book Group, offered Cohen $750,000 for the book, tentatively titled *Trump Revolution: From the Tower to the White House, Understanding Donald J. Trump.*)

Daniels and Rodriguez were indignant. So he was going to profit from his role in the agreement, while Daniels was supposed to remain silent?

"He will call me a liar and say whatever he wants because he thinks I can't defend myself because of the nda," Daniels said in a text to her agent.

She was also still sore about having to sign the second denial. The first statement had been partially true. Trump hadn't paid her hush money; Cohen had. The second statement was completely false. And Daniels blamed Davidson, whom she described as "too friendly with Cohen," for asking her to sign it.

"By commenting (which [is] what the statement was) it implies there is no NDA. And the statement says 'there was no affair' and I wasn't paid. Both lies," she said in a text to Rodriguez.

Daniels added that, until putting her name on that second statement, "I hadn't actually lied," ignoring that she had also categorically denied any affair with Trump in the first statement.

But she hadn't lost her sense of humor about the rapidly devolving situation.

"If everything comes out, SNL better have me on to chase Alec Baldwin around in his underwear," Daniels wrote.

MICHAEL COHEN HAD shown unswerving loyalty to Donald Trump and his family for more than a decade. He'd taken on the tasks that no one else at the Trump Organization would. He'd cajoled, threatened, lied—whatever it took to protect the man and advance the boss's interests in business and politics. In return, Trump had nearly fired him, slashed his pay, then kept him out of the formal presidential campaign (while letting him participate unofficially) and declined to offer him a job at the White House.

Still, after the *Journal*'s disclosure of the hush-money deal with Daniels, Cohen rededicated himself to insulating his boss. He told journalists he regularly spoke to that Trump hadn't known about the Daniels deal, and that in his capacity as Trump's lawyer he had had the authority to make the payment without permission. "I did it on my own," Cohen told CNN's Chris Cuomo, while recording their conversation, not bothering to consider the utter illogic of that statement.

We'd heard on the afternoon of February 13 that Cohen was about to file a response to a complaint submitted to the Federal Election Commission by a government watchdog group in Washington called Common Cause. Citing our report, the complaint asked the agency to investigate the payment to Daniels for potential violations of election laws. We wanted Cohen to tell us what his brief said, but he was ignoring our efforts to reach him. His response would have remained confidential until the FEC decided to start an investigation or dismiss the complaint, a process that could take years. But he assumed a government official would leak it. After filing the brief, Cohen released a public statement to *The New York Times.*

"I am Mr. Trump's longtime special counsel and I have proudly served in that role for more than a decade. In a private transaction in 2016, I used my own personal funds to facilitate a payment of $130,000 to Ms. Stephanie Clifford," the statement said. "Neither the Trump Organization nor the Trump campaign was a party to the transaction with Ms. Clifford, and neither reimbursed me for the payment, either directly or indirectly."

He concluded, "Just because something isn't true doesn't mean that it can't cause you harm or damage. I will always protect Mr. Trump."

Cohen had carefully worded the statement, after conferring with Trump and Allen Weisselberg, the Trump Organization chief financial officer. It pointedly avoided saying whether Trump himself had reimbursed Cohen for the payment.

The statement was far closer to the truth than an earlier draft that Cohen had been working on since January. In that version, Cohen had denied having been reimbursed by Trump, his company, or the campaign and said he never advised Trump of his "communications or actions" regarding the nondisclosure agreement. "As outlandish and unusual as this may appear, the Trumps have been like family to me for over a decade. It's what you do for family," Cohen had written.

Rodriguez spotted the story about Cohen's statement before Daniels. "Did you see that Michael Cohen admitted to paying you 130k himself?" she texted her client.

"No," Daniels responded. "What does this mean for us?"

"I'm sure he's going to lie about what it was for so it doesn't matter because you're about to talk."

When Daniels read the statement, she was furious. *Just because something isn't true?* Cohen was calling her a liar in front of the world.

"Isn't the NDA officially fucking void now?" Daniels wrote in a text to Rodriguez.

Daniels joked that the dress she wore on her date with Trump would end up in the Smithsonian one day. She'd dry-cleaned it, however, unlike the blue Gap dress that Monica Lewinsky wore during her assignation with Bill Clinton. No Ken Starr types would be testing Daniels's dress for the "genetic material" of Donald Trump.

In the span of a day, Cohen had managed to trigger Daniels twice. She and Rodriguez told Davidson to convey the message that they viewed Cohen's statement and book proposal as violations of the pact, and that they'd proceed accordingly.

The deal was off.

AFTER COHEN RELEASED his statement, Trump called his personal attorney, who was in a car on the way to Teterboro Airport in New Jersey. The first lady was also on the line.

"Michael, did you really pay $130,000 to Stormy Daniels?" Trump asked.

"Yes," Cohen said.

"Why'd you do that?"

Cohen hadn't been expecting the call, but he knew what he was expected to say. Trump didn't need to tell him to lie to Melania Trump. That wasn't how Trump operated, generally. Trump *suggested*. ("Isn't this the best hamburger you've ever had," he might say. And the answer, of course, whether it was true or not, was "Yes.") By now, Cohen was fluent in the code.

"Sometimes, you know, just because something's not true doesn't mean it can't hurt you," Cohen said, staying on script.

"Wow. Melania, do you believe that? He took $130,000 out of his own pocket," Trump said. "Why didn't you tell me about it?"

Cohen said he planned to tell Trump after the election if he lost. But he won. It was safer to keep him out of it. "I guess I'll just call it a cost of doing business," Cohen said.

"Man, you're the greatest," Trump said.

Cohen assumed the first lady saw through the lie.

COHEN'S PUBLIC STATEMENT inadvertently had given the story new life, confirming our reporting, which to that point had come from anonymous sources. His phones were abuzz. Emily Jane Fox, the writer for *Vanity Fair*, was interviewing Cohen in his office on February 14 when he got a call from Trump. Fox couldn't hear everything Trump was saying, but she understood Trump to be trying to coordinate public messaging.

In a call with Cohen that same day, Davidson conveyed his client's displeasure with Cohen's statement to the media and news of his book proposal. Daniels and Rodriguez thought that Cohen was in breach of the agreement, Davidson told him, and that Daniels was now free to tell her story as a result.

"I fucking didn't breach it! I said something about the money because I had to," Cohen said. He told Davidson that if Daniels were to speak publicly about having sex with Trump, the president would seek damages under the provisions of their nondisclosure agreement.

Later that day, Rodriguez texted Daniels to brief her on the call between Cohen and Davidson. Rodriguez told her that Davidson had warned Cohen that Daniels was about to speak out. Daniels was amazed that Cohen wanted her to keep quiet when he wasn't doing the same.

"He said he paid me. Is he retarded?" Daniels wrote. "Did Cohen threaten me?"

"No, he didn't," Rodriguez said.

Daniels told Rodriguez that she'd approached the Law Offices of Tacopina & Seigel, a New York firm, for advice on Cohen's public statements.

"They said he's def in breach but best thing to do is have a judge officially deem it dissolved," Daniels said in a text.

They'd decided Davidson was no longer on their side. Rodriguez said she planned to speak with Sean Macias, an entertainment lawyer in Los Angeles who represented Mel B of the Spice Girls. Stormy needed a new lawyer.

MORE BAD NEWS for Trump and Cohen arrived on February 16. *The New Yorker* published a story based on notes that staff writer Ronan Farrow had obtained from Johnny Crawford, Karen McDougal's ex-cop friend. The notes, written by McDougal, amounted to a detailed reconstruction of her ten-month affair with Donald Trump. Farrow emphasized the similarities between the accounts of McDougal and Daniels: the bungalow at the Beverly Hills Hotel, Trump's bodyguard, promises Trump made but hadn't kept.

Daniels had never met McDougal, but she remembered seeing the former Playmate of the Year at the January 2007 launch party for Trump-branded vodka in Hollywood.

"Trump literally kissed me in front of Karen," Daniels said in a text to Rodriguez after they'd seen Farrow's story. "He is truly retarded."

By now, McDougal knew that American Media had been stringing her along about the projects Dylan Howard had called "thought starters." Though Crawford said he'd turned over McDougal's notes to *The New Yorker* without her knowledge, American Media executives suspected she'd planted the story to send a message: If American Media wanted her to stay silent, it had to give her something.

Pecker was incensed by the story. He had been trying to negotiate a one-year extension to McDougal's contract. By keeping her in the fold, Pecker hoped she'd stay quiet.

McDougal had given an interview to Farrow for his story but declined to discuss her relationship with Trump. "At this point I feel I can't talk about anything without getting into trouble, because I don't know what I'm allowed to talk about. I'm afraid to even mention his name," McDougal said.

Her lawyer and friend Carol Heller emailed American Media's general counsel, Cameron Stracher, after the *New Yorker* story published.

> Cam,
>
> We want to raise a time-sensitive issue with you regarding the barrage of legitimate press inquiries that we have begun curating.
>
> We are besieged with questions about, among other things, how Karen came to AMI, her contacts with Mr. Davidson, Mr. Howard and Mr. Pecker, what terms were agreed to, what terms have been performed and when, and her payment.
>
> From Karen's perspective, it would be useful to give these interviews and clarify the record.
>
> There is of course, nothing in the current Agreement that would prevent her from doing so.
>
> Since we have previously touched on the possibility of renewing or replacing the current Agreement with different terms, I would now like to re-raise this opportunity.
>
> One possibility might be to introduce some non-disclosure or other obligation (if that is AMI's preference), in return for additional consideration; we are open to discussion.

If AMI is not interested in pursuing continued negotiations, I would like to start granting legitimate press interviews starting as early as next Monday.

As always, Karen remains committed to keeping her obligations as to your now public ownership of her Limited Life Story Rights and will refrain from discussing any relationships she has ever had with any then-married man.

Respectfully,
Carol R. Heller

In other words, McDougal was not contractually required to keep quiet, but she'd consider entering into a fresh nondisclosure agreement if American Media was willing to pay her more money. If not, she'd grant more interviews.

The *New Yorker* story generated outside interest in the rights to McDougal's story. American Media was fielding calls from biopic producers who wanted to purchase the rights. Stracher told Heller that the publisher was negotiating the sale of the story rights and warned her that additional "disclosures" could interfere with the process.

Carol—The barrage of questions your client is facing is a result of her own actions in sitting down for an extensive interview with the New Yorker. We are currently in negotiations for the sale of Karen's "limited life rights," and any further publicity related to that topic will not only damage and impede those negotiations, but will surely be prohibited by any buyer of those rights who will want to control the timing and extent of publicity. Therefore, any further disclosures would breach Karen's contract with AMI and cause considerable monetary damages.

We are open to renewing Karen's contract, but she must satisfy the terms of the current contract, which include a photo shoot scheduled for March 13 for the cover of Men's Journal, as you requested. Please confirm that date, and please have your client reach out to Dylan Howard to arrange the logistics. Thank you.

American Media seemed to be taking the position that McDougal was still gagged, though her contract amendment clearly stated otherwise. She soon decided she wanted her life rights back.

• • •

TRUMP WAS PLEASED with Cohen's public statements taking sole responsibility for the Daniels deal. Days after Cohen admitted making the payment, *The New York Times* published a story that described his efforts to suppress negative stories about his boss. He received a text from one of Trump's lawyers after the story appeared.

"Client says thanks for what you do."

But Trump was headed for a collision with Daniels. As Cohen had predicted, when the president learned that Daniels and Rodriguez intended to step outside the NDA, he instructed Cohen to enforce it. In a phone call, Trump told Cohen to coordinate with Larry Rosen, a New York lawyer who'd done work for Trump and his company, and with Eric Trump, who was running the Trump Organization with his older brother and CFO Allen Weisselberg while their father occupied the Oval Office.

"I'll take care of everything," Trump told Cohen. To Cohen, this meant Trump would have his back and pay his legal fees, a commitment the president had honored, to that point, in connection with the Russia investigation.

Trump had another phone conversation days later with Cohen and Rosen, who were at Rosen's office in the Trump Building, on Wall Street in downtown Manhattan. The plan was to seek a restraining order against Daniels in a private arbitration proceeding in Orange County, California, a remedy provided in the NDA.

The Trump camp filed a demand for arbitration on February 22. Davidson, Daniels, and Rodriguez didn't learn of the filing immediately. Under the terms of the contract, Trump's side could seek a restraining order from an arbitrator without giving Daniels any warning.

While Trump, his son, and his lawyers tried to maintain the gag on Daniels, the White House publicly refused to answer questions about the hush money. Raj Shah, the White House deputy press secretary, tried to shut down ABC News's Jonathan Karl, who inquired about the Daniels deal in a briefing the day that Trump's lawyers filed the arbitration demand.

KARL: Last week, the president's personal lawyer acknowledged giving a $130,000 payment to Stormy Daniels. Is the president aware that his lawyer paid that kind of money to a porn star to buy her silence? Does he approve of that?

SHAH: I haven't asked him about it, but that matter has been asked and answered in the past.

KARL: No, not since he acknowledged this. He acknowledged this last week. This is the first time we've had a chance to ask about it. So can you go back—can we find out if the president approves of the fact that his personal—

SHAH: I haven't asked him about that.

KARL: Will you ask him about that?

SHAH: I haven't asked him about it.

KARL: But will you ask him about it, Raj?

SHAH: I'll get back to you.

Five days later, a retired Los Angeles County Superior Court judge named Jacqueline A. Connor signed a temporary restraining order precluding "Respondent Peggy Peterson" from disclosing any information covered by her NDA with "Claimant EC, LLC," meaning Cohen's company, Essential Consultants.

Cohen didn't know where to send the order to ensure that Daniels adhered to it. When Cohen tried to serve Davidson, the attorney said he was no longer representing Daniels. Rodriguez had put Davidson on notice that Sean Macias, the Los Angeles attorney Rodriguez had mentioned to Daniels, was replacing him. Davidson connected Cohen and Macias by email. Cohen then emailed them both a copy of the order.

Gentleman [*sic*],

Please see below the executed TRO against your client. It is important that she be made aware of this immediately so as not to be in contempt of the Order. This document is itself to remain confidential and not to be disclosed to anyone per the terms of the Judge's Order.

Thank you.

Yours,
Michael D. Cohen, Esq.

But Macias, who had already parted ways with Rodriguez and Daniels, answered Cohen's email by saying, "I don't represent Stormy Daniels." (Cohen was upset to learn that he'd sent a confidential order to a perfect stranger.) Days later, Cohen and Rosen, still desperately trying to find someone to serve, had a three-way call with Davidson, who was at the Tampa International Airport in a first-class lounge.

Rosen told Davidson that they were going to mail him the temporary restraining order, whether he liked it or not. Davidson, usually mild-mannered, exploded.

"Why are you doing any of this? It's crazy. You represent the goddamn president of the United States," Davidson said.

Taking Daniels to arbitration would blow up in their faces, provoking her and giving the story much longer legs, he said. Davidson predicted that Daniels would sue him for malpractice, using the complaint as a vehicle to disclose the details of her relationship with Trump and the nondisclosure agreement. He reminded them that Daniels had publicly denied the affair in 2011. Trump could let her talk and then have his surrogates attack her credibility. He didn't need to try to tighten the muzzle, Davidson said.

"You guys are fucking idiots," Davidson told them. "This seems to be a perfect case where the cure is worse than the disease." He urged the Trump lawyers to walk away.

Cohen was calm and businesslike, leading Davidson to suspect that he was being recorded.

"I don't think you understand. Contracts have meaning," Cohen told him. "If you enter into a contract with Donald Trump, you will abide by that contract."

In his business, Trump routinely made current and former employees sign NDAs that barred them from disparaging him or his family. He took the practice with him to the White House, demanding that staff sign NDAs as well. Don McGahn, the White House counsel, carried out Trump's orders with an eye roll, assuring officials who signed the agreements that they were unenforceable. The Oval Office wasn't the private sector. The government couldn't abridge protected speech to spare the president embarrassment.

But it was the principle—the threat—that mattered: If Trump let Stormy Daniels out without a fight, who knew how many other people who were subject to Trump NDAs might be emboldened to break them?

Davidson warned the attorneys that if they mailed him the temporary restraining order, he'd simply return it unopened. Rosen and Cohen sent it to him by FedEx anyway.

DANIELS DID HAVE a new attorney, but neither the Trump lawyers nor Davidson knew it yet. After Rodriguez reached out to Sean Macias about potentially representing Daniels, he had called a friend for help, a skilled litigator named Michael Avenatti.

On February 26, the two lawyers met with Rodriguez and her boyfriend, Anthony Kotzev, at the couple's San Fernando Valley home for a job interview of sorts. They all sat on a sectional sofa, discussing Daniels's options.

What does she want to accomplish? Avenatti asked.

Rodriguez said Daniels wanted to be able to discuss the affair and profit from her story, since it was out in the open and Cohen had admitted to paying her. In the meantime, though, Rodriguez didn't want Daniels sitting for interviews. The manager knew and respected Gloria Allred and her daughter, Lisa Bloom, lawyers who used news conferences and media strategically and often to help their clients. But Rodriguez told Avenatti she hoped to avoid that kind of exposure for Daniels. Rodriguez was trying to sell the rights to Daniels's story for print and television. The less Daniels revealed for free, the better.

Macias thought Daniels could get what she wanted by pursuing settlement talks with the Trump camp. A court brawl with the president and his personal attorney wasn't in Daniels's best interests. Avenatti, however, argued that the best way—the only way—forward was through litigation. Trump wouldn't let Daniels walk, he told Rodriguez. They would have to ask a judge to unwind the nondisclosure agreement, he said.

Persuaded by the brash new lawyer, Rodriguez said she favored Avenatti's approach. Macias was out; Avenatti would represent Daniels alone.

In the street outside Rodriguez's home, Macias cautioned Avenatti against taking Trump on in court. It would bring the full force of the presidency down on Daniels.

"You don't know what you're talking about," Avenatti said.

Rodriguez texted Daniels after the meeting to let her know that Avenatti soon would be contacting her.

"He's going to give you the options," the agent wrote. Daniels could try to get Trump's lawyers to come to the table and negotiate a resolution out of court—the approach Macias had advocated—but Avenatti didn't think that was a viable option, Rodriguez said. "Or you say fuck it," she added. That would mean speaking out, waiting to see if Trump went after Daniels in court, and challenging the agreement. Plus, a civil suit could force Cohen and Trump to sit for depositions, something Avenatti thought they would want to avoid, Rodriguez said.

Avenatti arranged to meet Daniels that same evening. They met at the Waldorf Astoria Beverly Hills. Daniels had just finished work for the day. The two of them hit it off, though Rodriguez had no way of knowing it. Immediately after hiring Avenatti, Daniels stopped speaking to her, at Avenatti's suggestion. He told Daniels that Rodriguez was leading her into a bad deal, hoping to take her percentage on the sale of Daniels's story rights and walk away.

25.

THE LAWSUITS

■ ■ ■

DAVIDSON WAS MOSTLY right. The temporary restraining order, once it reached Daniels and Avenatti, restrained nothing. On March 6, Daniels broke her silence about her dalliance with Donald Trump—not in a media interview, as the Trump camp had feared, but in a blunt filing in Los Angeles County Superior Court, authored by Avenatti.

Instead of a malpractice lawsuit against Davidson, the complaint sought to invalidate Daniels's NDA, acknowledging in seven pages that Daniels had been paid $130,000, signed a "Hush Agreement," and slept with Trump in 2006. The strategy was aggressive: Avenatti argued that Daniels could say whatever she wanted, because the agreement was "never formed." Trump hadn't signed it. Even if he had, Cohen had breached the contract with his statements to media, excusing Daniels from its terms and obligations, Avenatti said. The arbitration, meanwhile, was "bogus," premised on an agreement that never was.

The civil complaint accused Cohen of using "intimidation and coercive tactics" to get Daniels to lie to the *Journal* and other media, and the lawsuit sought to tie Trump to the hush money and efforts to conceal it. "It strains credibility to conclude that Mr. Cohen is acting on his own accord without the express approval and knowledge of his client Mr. Trump," Avenatti wrote.

More important, the lawsuit named Trump ("AKA DAVID DENNISON") as a defendant, along with Essential Consultants. Avenatti would try to drag the president and his fixer into depositions if they insisted on taking the case to trial.

News media across the country reported on the lawsuit. Daniels's nondisclosure agreement was attached to the complaint as an exhibit. Now it was available for all to see, and the story was about to get bigger.

DANIELS'S NEW ATTORNEY had a made-for-television quality to him. Avenatti, forty-seven, had bronzed California skin, a square jaw, and a closely shaved head. He wore expensive suits that accentuated his dense build, drove sports cars, and liked to brag about obtaining more than a billion dollars in settlements for his clients.

Rodriguez knew nothing about Avenatti when she interviewed him for the job as Daniels's lawyer. She'd wanted someone who would ply the adult movie star's case without a lot of fuss. Avenatti was not that lawyer. He enjoyed trying his cases in the media. He treated reporters as tools to be manipulated to his advantage. If a journalist dared deviate from the narrative Avenatti wanted to promote, he or she was cut off. (We learned this firsthand.)

The son of an Anheuser-Busch executive, Avenatti moved around as a boy before his family settled in a suburb of St. Louis. Neither of his parents finished college. He got involved in politics as an eighteen-year-old in 1989, working for his local congressman, and then majored in political science at the University of Pennsylvania. After a semester, he took a leave of absence to make money to fund his education. His father, a middle manager, recently had been laid off after thirty-one years at the beer company. Avenatti found a job at a political consulting firm run by Rahm Emanuel, the future Obama chief of staff and mayor of Chicago, where he learned how to do opposition research— digging up dirt on opponents. He worked on political campaigns around the country, specializing in media communications.

After a few years of campaign work, Avenatti returned to the University of Pennsylvania part-time so he could continue his career in politics. He moved to Washington, D.C., after obtaining his undergraduate degree and entered a four-year law school program at George Washington University, attending in the evenings while he continued to work. Avenatti graduated six months early and joined the California-based office of the law firm O'Melveny & Myers, working out of the Newport Beach and Century City offices. He stood out among the young associates, a thirty-year-old who was married and had a career before law. Avenatti was handsome, dressed expensively, and drove a black Porsche. O'Melveny wasn't a firm that celebrated flash. Fellow associates found him smart but arrogant.

He left the firm after three years. Avenatti wanted to phase into plaintiffs' work. O'Melveny was a corporate law firm that generally played defense. He wasn't universally mourned by O'Melveny partners. While at the firm, Avenatti had gotten into an altercation at the airport with the son of a California judge and had pressed charges. O'Melveny's management team had no desire to be on the bad side of a local jurist. But Avenatti had refused to drop the matter.

Avenatti landed at the plaintiffs' firm Greene Broillet & Wheeler, developing a niche representing victims of financial fraud in lawsuits against tax advisers and auditing firms. His first big settlement, for $22.5 million, came in a lawsuit against KPMG, one of the world's largest accounting firms, on behalf of his client Targus Group International, a company that made computer bags. The lawsuit accused KPMG of malpractice for failing to catch tens of millions of dollars embezzled by a Targus executive.

Avenatti also turned up in celebrity disputes, representing actress Zeta Graff in a defamation lawsuit against Paris Hilton. Graff accused Hilton of planting an item in the New York Post's Page Six column that said the actress had ripped a necklace off Hilton's neck in a fit of jealousy. (Hilton was paired with Graff's ex-boyfriend at the time; they settled the case.) Avenatti also sued Mark Burnett, creator of The Apprentice, along with Donald Trump and NBC Universal on behalf of a producer who said Burnett stole the idea for the hit reality show. (The parties reached a settlement for an undisclosed amount.)

In 2007, Avenatti co-founded a boutique plaintiffs' firm, Eagan O'Malley & Avenatti, where he played the role of rainmaker, promoting the firm and scouting for big-ticket cases. The firm's website touted Avenatti as "one of the nation's foremost trial lawyers." In another malpractice case against KPMG, in 2008, he delivered a $32 million verdict, plus interest. With all his success at suing the Big Four firm, Avenatti got a vanity plate for his car that read THXKPMG. Avenatti made news with lawsuits against the NFL for selling more tickets to the Super Bowl than the seating accommodated, and against cosmetics companies Estée Lauder, Avon, and Mary Kay over alleged false claims that they'd halted animal testing. He secured an $81 million judgment against a cemetery for desecrating corpses.

Meanwhile, Avenatti also tried his hand as a businessman. In 2013, he and actor Patrick Dempsey (a.k.a. McDreamy from the TV drama *Grey's Anatomy*) bought a bankrupt local Seattle-area coffee chain for about $9 million. Dempsey soon sued Avenatti, alleging that the lawyer took out a $2 million loan against the assets of Tully's Coffee without telling him. The actor quickly withdrew the lawsuit as he and Avenatti negotiated Dempsey's exit from the partnership.

Avenatti, raised in the middle class, embraced a new lifestyle as he amassed more settlements and verdicts. His firm moved out of a three-story building where he and his partners had once worked without furniture to a marble-clad high-rise in Newport Beach, one of the toniest communities in the country. His corner office overlooked the ocean and was the biggest suite on a floor he shared with billionaire investor Bill Gross. Avenatti, a car aficionado who raced part-time, had a $6,000 Porsche office chair.

He and his second wife, Lisa Storie, flipped a $7 million home in Laguna Beach for $12 million. They moved into a $19 million lease-to-purchase mansion in Newport Beach with their son, paying $100,000 a month. Avenatti's firm had a full-time driver, and he owned a 50 percent share in a private jet. His wife had a retinue of nannies and housekeepers. Avenatti paid $176,000 to belong to an elite private vacation club and owned two Ferraris, one an antique and the other a 2016 Spider.

Avenatti's favorite pastime was commensurately expensive. He'd harbored a passion for motorsports since his father had taken him to his first race in Colorado as a ten-year-old. Avenatti raced at the Daytona International Speedway and teamed up with a Saudi prince to compete in the Le Mans endurance contest. Their Ferrari 458 Italia finished seventh in its class in 2015, an experience the lawyer described as a dream come true, despite a flash fire that sent one of his crew members to the hospital.

About a year before he met Daniels, Avenatti won his biggest verdict yet. A jury awarded his clients $454 million in a lawsuit against Kimberly-Clark Corporation and a spinoff, Halyard Health Inc., over surgical gowns. The jurors found that the companies made misleading claims about the protection the gowns offered against Ebola and

other infectious diseases. During the litigation, Avenatti appeared on
60 Minutes with Anderson Cooper, who had done an investigation of
the gown maker for the news show. A former marketing director for
Halyard, which produced the gowns, told Cooper that they often
leaked, especially in the seams, when pressure-tested. The companies
immediately sought to reduce the award.

Avenatti's aura of success masked a swirl of allegations of ethical
and financial misconduct around the attorney. By the time he took
Daniels on as a client, the Internal Revenue Service was investigating
his businesses for millions of dollars in unpaid taxes. Avenatti's law
firm was in bankruptcy. A former law partner was trying to recover
money he alleged Avenatti had stiffed him. And Global Baristas, the
company Avenatti formed to buy Tully's, was under a heap of civil
judgments for nonpayment of debts.

In early 2018, he and his wife had recently separated after six years
of marriage; she was seeking more than $200,000 a month from Av-
enatti to maintain a life of extravagance he'd provided even as he was
allegedly deep in hock to the IRS.

According to the IRS, Avenatti's law firm and coffee chain had
stopped paying payroll taxes in 2015, triggering collection cases. A revenue officer tried in vain to get the coffee business to cough up back
taxes before sending the case to the IRS Criminal Investigation Division in March 2018.

The last of the Tully's stores closed that same month. As the company collapsed, Avenatti told reporters that he no longer owned it, that
he was merely its general counsel. That wasn't true.

As IRS investigators searched for millions of dollars in payroll taxes
withheld from Tully's employees, they came to believe that Avenatti
had shuffled money through a web of corporate entities with confus-
ingly similar names to dodge creditors, liens, and levies while divert-
ing cash to personal expenses.

His personal tax practices were at least as problematic. Avenatti
hadn't filed an income tax return since 2011. Still, he'd managed to obtain loans from a Mississippi bank by sending bank employees false
returns, the IRS found.

But few Americans had any inkling of Avenatti's troubles when he
sued the president of the United States in March 2018. He was on the
verge of becoming one of the most famous lawyers in the country.

• • •

THE MORNING AFTER Daniels sued Trump and Cohen in Los Angeles, her new attorney went on NBC's *Today* show, the first of more than a hundred television appearances that would transform him from a lawyer little known outside of Los Angeles to one of Trump's biggest thorns and a hero of the left, which was desperate for a figure who could out-Trump Trump.

His inaugural performance offered the Trump camp a preview of the pain they'd have to endure over the next ten months. Avenatti suggested, without saying so outright, that Daniels had hard proof of her alleged affair with Trump.

The language of Daniels's NDA, which the world was only now seeing, barred disclosure of any "tangible materials" in Daniels's possession that related to Donald Trump, including letters, audio or video recordings, and images. But the language was part of a template Davidson used to craft nondisclosure agreements for his clients. It didn't mean any of these tangible items existed, and in fact they didn't.

"Does she still have photos, images, text messages, documents that verify this claim?" Savannah Guthrie, co-host of *Today,* asked Avenatti.

"That's a question that Ms. Daniels will have to ultimately answer," Avenatti said.

"Do you know the answer to that question?"

"I do know the answer, and I'm not at liberty to disclose it this morning."

Avenatti also hinted that he had evidence of Trump's involvement in the hush-money agreement.

"We certainly haven't disclosed all the facts and evidence that we're aware of in connection with this," he said.

Daniels and Rodriguez had wanted to scotch the nondisclosure agreement so they could pursue media deals, but Avenatti now portrayed Daniels as desiring to speak truth to power.

"Is she looking to sell her story?" Guthrie asked.

"No, she's looking to disclose the truth about what happened," Avenatti said.

It was the first hint of the revisionist tale that Avenatti would superimpose over reality. He recast Stormy Daniels as a woman silenced by Trump rather than someone who'd twice sought to profit from an alleged sexual encounter with him more than a decade earlier. Avenatti hadn't come up with the story line himself. He was taking some of his cues from Daniels, who had downplayed her own role in the deal.

From the start, Avenatti and Daniels brought different motivations to their partnership. Daniels wanted to be free of her nondisclosure agreement and capitalize on her newfound fame. Avenatti, the veteran of dozens of Democratic campaigns, saw the political potential of the case, seizing on an opportunity to damage Trump and elevate himself. Though Rodriguez was no longer in the picture, Avenatti acted in accordance with her wishes and limited Daniels's media appearances. But this was not because the exposure could detract from the value of the rights to Daniels's story; Avenatti worried that Daniels, with her Make America Horny Again strip tour, would be treated like a joke if she were on the air daily. He believed he gave her credibility as the public-facing representative of the case. And he believed that he was damn good on television.

THE PUBLICITY AROUND Daniels's lawsuit translated into more pointed questioning at White House press briefings. Trump's spokespeople had endeavored, with some success, to deflect questions about the hush money by focusing on the allegations of the affair, which, they pointed out, Trump had long denied. But evasion as a communications strategy was fast becoming untenable. Sarah Huckabee Sanders, the White House press secretary, took questions on March 7, hours after Avenatti's *Today* appearance.

Up to now, the details of Cohen's move in February to silence Daniels by launching a private arbitration proceeding, as provided for in their nondisclosure agreement, had remained confidential. The president had told Cohen to work on the arbitration with Eric Trump and the New York lawyer Larry Rosen. They'd obtained a temporary restraining order against Daniels in California to stop her from speaking, which Michael Avenatti had decided to ignore in helping her to sue the president.

But now, in front of a crowd of White House reporters, Trump's press secretary brought up the arbitration proceeding and the restraining order—unexpectedly, inaccurately, and without context, prompted by questions from CNN's Jeff Zeleny.

ZELENY: Did the president approve of the payment that was made in October of 2016 by his longtime lawyer and adviser Michael Cohen?

SANDERS: Look, the president has addressed these directly and made very well clear that none of these allegations are true. This case has already been won in arbitration. And anything beyond that, I would refer you to the president's outside counsel.

ZELENY: When did the president address, specifically, the cash payment that was made in October of 2016 to—

SANDERS: The president has denied the allegations against him. And, again, this case has already been won in arbitration. Anything beyond that, I would refer you to outside counsel.

ZELENY: But did he know about that payment at the time, though?

SANDERS: Jeff, I've addressed this as far as I can go.

ZELENY: I'm not talking about the actual allegations, but about the payment. Did he know about the payment at the time?

SANDERS: Not that I'm aware of.

Later in the briefing, another reporter, Kristen Welker of NBC News, picked up the thread.

WELKER: You said that there's an arbitration that's already been won. By whom and when?

SANDERS: By the president's personal attorneys. And for details on that, I would refer you to them.

WELKER: But you're aware of them, so what more can you share with us?

SANDERS: I can share that the arbitration was won in the president's favor, and I would refer you to the president's outside counsel on any details beyond that.

In the president's favor? In fact, the president hadn't "won in arbitration," as Sanders asserted. The restraining order was pro forma, issued by the arbitrator in an attempt to ensure that Trump wasn't damaged before the case had a chance to proceed. While Daniels's lawsuit had made brief mention of arbitration, Sanders had for the first time revealed the temporary restraining order, linked it to Trump, and made plain that the White House was closely tracking the proceeding. Why else would Trump's press secretary be aware of an order issued in an arbitration over a contract that Michael Cohen had described as a private transaction between himself and Daniels?

Within a week, the line the White House tried to draw between Trump and the hush-money deal eroded further. Avenatti had received the February 22 arbitration demand from Trump's lawyers. The documents listed the name of the counsel for Essential Consultants: Jill A. Martin, vice president and assistant general counsel at the Trump Organization.

Martin was the Trump Organization's Los Angeles–based lawyer. The thirty-eight-year-old had defended the company against claims that Trump University had preyed on consumers. Instead of helping them, lawsuits filed in California and New York alleged, Trump University pressured them to take on thousands of dollars in debt to pay for canned advice and worthless certificates. Trump settled the cases, without admitting wrongdoing, for $25 million after winning the presidential election.

Martin had no formal role in Trump's campaign, but she had vouched for him in a CNN interview after women came forward and accused the candidate of sexual harassment and assault. "Thousands of women have worked for him, including myself, and he's treated us with nothing but respect, and appropriately," she said.

More recently, Martin had defended Trump in a controversy surrounding the height of the hedges around his mansion in Los Angeles. Beginning in 2017, Beverly Hills fined the president of the United States several hundred dollars for foliage that exceeded the city's six-foot height restriction. Martin said in a letter to the city that the too-tall hedges were "necessary for the provision of property security" to Trump and his family, adding that the U.S. Secret Service would soon conduct "a threat and security assessment to determine the necessity of the hedges."

About a week before Avenatti gave us the Daniels arbitration documents signed by Martin, the Secret Service rendered its opinion on Trump's shrubbery. Martin forwarded a letter to the city signed by the special agent in charge of presidential protection.

"Please be advised that the U.S. Secret Service finds the height and density of the existing hedges to be of protective value as they provide a visual barrier that limits the line of sight into the property," the special agent wrote.

The hedges could stay.

Martin's participation in the Daniels arbitration had come at the request of Eric Trump. Larry Rosen, Trump's outside counsel, and his firm prepared the documents, but he needed permission to participate in the arbitration as an out-of-state attorney. In the meantime, Eric Trump had him reach out to Martin, who was licensed in California and could sign the documents immediately.

When the *Journal* contacted Martin for comment, she emailed Eric Trump to ask how she should respond. After some back-and-forth, they settled on a statement with input from Rosen and Alan Garten, the Trump Organization's chief legal officer.

They then emailed it to us:

> As previously reported, Lawrence Rosen, a New York attorney, is representing EC, LLC in the arbitration. The Trump Organization is not representing anyone and, with the exception of one of its California based attorneys in her individual capacity facilitating the initial filing pending the pro hac admission of Mr. Rosen, the company has had no involvement in the matter.

The statement was at best misleading, but we didn't know that Eric Trump had been working with Rosen on the arbitration. We included the statement in a March 14 story that revealed Martin's role. "Documents marked 'HIGHLY CONFIDENTIAL PROCEEDING' for the first time tie President Donald Trump's flagship holding company to the continuing effort to silence a former adult-film actress who says she had an affair with Mr. Trump," the story began.

Avenatti had no compunction about releasing the documents to the *Journal* and CNN. He maintained that the arbitration was illegitimate and felt free to violate the rules of the forum. But that was the last time he deigned to help us with a story.

AFTER FILING THE lawsuit against Trump and Essential Consultants in early March, Avenatti camped in an office at MSNBC, juggling requests from guest bookers eager to have him train fire on the president. In staccato commentary on television and Twitter, he seemed capable of a Trumpian level of rhetoric and showmanship.

While debating Cohen's attorney and friend David Schwartz on CNN, Avenatti pulled out a poster-size photo of Cohen's hangdog face. "Where is this guy?" Avenatti asked. "He's dodging the questions."

The next time Schwartz and Avenatti appeared together on CNN, Avenatti recalled that Cohen had told a reporter during the 2016 campaign that a man couldn't be convicted of raping his wife. "This is a legal genius. Completely false. The guy doesn't even know the law. He's a thug! Your friend is a thug!"

The two men then began shouting over each other.

"Thug! Thug! Thug! Thug! Thug!" Avenatti said.

"That's a million dollars! A million dollars! A million dollars!" Schwartz said, referring to the amount the nondisclosure agreement said Daniels owed for a breach.

CNN anchor Anderson Cooper and legal analyst Jeffrey Toobin, who were sitting with the combatants, smiled uncomfortably as Schwartz and Avenatti clawed at each other. Schwartz soon stopped appearing on television on Cohen's behalf.

On HBO's *Real Time with Bill Maher,* Avenatti said of Trump, "He has trusted a moron with his innermost secrets."

When allies of the president tried to portray Avenatti as a Democratic stooge, he insisted he'd sought no financing for the case from donors on the left, wanting to avoid politicizing the case. Then *The New York Times* reported that he had, in fact, tried to raise money from liberal activist groups, including American Bridge 21st Century, founded by Democratic operative David Brock. The group's nonprofit arm had invested $200,000 in a secret—and ultimately unsuccessful—effort to recruit women to go public with allegations of sexual misconduct against Trump during the 2016 campaign. "I can't tell you the name of every person that I have spoken to, or not spoken to, over the last three months, but what I can tell you is that we have not taken any political-associated dollars from anyone on the right or anyone on the left," Avenatti told the newspaper.

But American Bridge declined to help Avenatti wage a fight that was already playing out in the news media. Instead, Avenatti started a crowdfunding page for Daniels's legal defense and the potential penalties she might face for violating the hush pact, soon raising several hundred thousand dollars. He flew her to New York to tape an interview with Cooper on *60 Minutes,* though it didn't air immediately because the show's producers wanted to corroborate Daniels's claims.

In his many media hits, Avenatti crafted a sympathetic portrait of his client to counter the view of her as a mercenary porn star who had profited from a sexual encounter with the president. The new Daniels narrative went this way: She never wanted to sell her story, not in 2011 and not in 2016. Seven years earlier, Daniels's ex-husband, Mike Moz, had pitched a story of her affair with Trump behind her back to *Life & Style,* which in turn pressured Daniels into cooperating with the piece, according to Avenatti.

That version of events was contradicted by virtually everyone involved, including associates of Daniels and people at the magazine, and by emails and text messages we had obtained. Daniels had tried to sell her story, but she lacked proof of the affair. She and Rodriguez had enlisted Moz and her friend Greg Deuschle (the porn star Randy Spears) to back up the information she provided to *Life & Style.* Both took polygraphs attesting to what they'd seen and heard of her interactions with Trump.

Avenatti and Daniels took even greater liberties with the events of 2016. They falsely said she had been lured into the deal by her own attorney, Keith Davidson, who was working in concert with Michael Cohen to silence Daniels. She feared for her family's safety if she refused to go along, they said. In fact, Daniels and Rodriguez had been trying to sell her story for months before Dylan Howard of American Media persuaded Davidson to negotiate with Cohen. That's why Davidson received $10,000 instead of his typical 45 percent fee—he'd come late to the party. Once he'd arrived, Daniels and Rodriguez put near-constant pressure on Davidson to close the deal before the election, believing that Cohen was trying to stall until Trump lost to Clinton and the story had shed most of its value.

When the *Journal* reported the inconvenient narrative of Daniels's long-running efforts to profit from the story, Avenatti lashed out. "Unfortunately, and despite the prior WSJ reporting which was credible, this story is far more fiction than fact. Too many inaccuracies to count," he said in a statement to the *Journal.* (When we asked, he declined to identify any specific error in our report.)

While working on that story, we'd found the Las Vegas polygrapher, Ron Slay, who examined Daniels in 2011 for *Life & Style*. He had a video recording of her test. After we spoke to Slay, Avenatti bought the video from the polygrapher for $25,000, preventing us from obtaining a copy.

"The reason why we did that was because we caught wind of the fact that there were [a] number of third parties, some in the mainstream media, that were attempting to purchase the video and the file for use in what I would describe as nefarious activities," Avenatti told NBC News. "We purchased the materials and the video to make sure that they were maintained from an evidentiary standpoint for potential use in the case."

Avenatti knew, or should have known, that we'd offered no money for the polygraph. The *Journal* does not pay sources. Nor did we consider news gathering to be a "nefarious" pursuit. The reality was that by controlling the video, Avenatti could prevent us and other journalists from airing footage that might depict Daniels as willing and eager to peddle her story about Trump. He was constructing a political narrative as well as a legal one, and political narratives are as important for what they leave out as for what they include.

As THE SPOTLIGHT shone ever more brightly on Daniels, Karen McDougal stepped back into it with a lawsuit of her own on March 20, 2018. McDougal brought a case against American Media in the same Los Angeles court where Daniels had sued Trump two weeks earlier. Like Daniels's complaint, McDougal's lawsuit stated unambiguously that she'd had a "10-month romantic relationship" with Trump and accused her attorney, Keith Davidson, of "colluding with the other side."

McDougal's new lawyer, Peter Stris, argued that McDougal's contract was "contrary to basic principles of law, fairness and the public interest." For one, American Media and Davidson had led her to believe that the contract guaranteed McDougal fitness columns in the company's publications, when in fact it only gave the publisher the option of publishing columns under her name, the lawsuit alleged. The second grounds for voiding the contract was a more potent threat to Trump and Cohen—and to David Pecker and American Media.

Stris said the agreement with McDougal was nothing more than a vehicle for evading restrictions on campaign contributions.

If the company refused to let her out of the contract, Stris said, "we're going to litigate and prove there was coordination between American Media, Karen's own lawyer, and Michael Cohen and that this was an illegal contribution that renders the entire agreement void."

Later that week, CNN aired an Anderson Cooper interview with McDougal, who discussed her relationship with Trump, including her belief that they might one day marry, her guilt about his wife, and her feeling of being misled about what had really happened with her contract. She hadn't known of Michael Cohen's role.

"Why was he involved in my deal?" she asked. "And why wasn't I told that he was involved in my deal? That's not fair. And it's, quite frankly, illegal."

She was also perplexed about how Trump had managed to sleep with her and Stormy Daniels at the same Lake Tahoe golf tournament without her knowing it at the time. She'd spent most of the time by his side.

"Now, I do remember him saying, he came in one day and said, 'Oh, there are a bunch of porn stars out there. They were wanting pictures of me.' And I'm like, oh, that's funny, you know, that's cute, whatever," McDougal said.

Three days after the CNN interview aired, CBS broadcast Anderson Cooper's interview with Daniels.

WHEN IT AIRED on March 25, the *60 Minutes* interview drew more than twenty-two million viewers, the largest audience for the show in a decade and one of the year's biggest television events.

Daniels told Cooper that she'd received a threat after trying to sell her story in 2011 as she retrieved her daughter's diaper bag from her car in the parking lot of a Las Vegas gym. Daniels said a muscle-bound man told her, "Leave Trump alone. Forget the story."

The man then looked at her daughter, strapped in her car seat. "That's a beautiful little girl. It'd be a shame if something happened to her mom," Daniels recalled him saying. And then he was gone. Based on that experience, she believed that her family might be at risk if she had refused the $130,000 agreement in 2016, Daniels said.

Daniels had never told Rodriguez or Davidson that she'd been threatened in a parking lot in 2011 or that fear had motivated her in 2016. Far from it. She had always seemed eager to sell her story. But Daniels had discussed the parking-lot threat with one of her friends, the photographer Keith Munyan, soon after she said it happened. Munyan had backed up her story when he spoke to *60 Minutes*. The show also had two unnamed sources who said Daniels told them about the threat.

Soon after the interview aired, Avenatti hired a well-known sketch artist to draw a likeness of the "thug" he said had threatened Daniels, based on her description. He offered a reward for anyone who could identify the man. On Twitter, some users posted side-by-side pictures of the man Daniels had described and of her own husband, Glendon Crain. They bore more than a passing resemblance, Trump noted on Twitter.

Avenatti by now had become a ubiquitous figure on the cable shows and had the beginnings of a fan base. He'd quickly accumulated 100,000 followers on Twitter, where some users referred to him as #HottieAvenatti. Many Americans who watched him on CNN and MSNBC were in his thrall. He channeled their anger at Trump.

But Avenatti's financial and legal situation was deteriorating. The IRS investigation of his coffee company for unpaid taxes had turned criminal on March 19. He'd reached a settlement with the IRS and creditors in his law firm's bankruptcy, agreeing to pay the United States Treasury $2.4 million in taxes. His lawyers made the first installment of $1.5 million to the government on March 26, the day after Daniels's *60 Minutes* interview aired. IRS special agents later traced the payment to client funds held in a trust by Avenatti.

Avenatti's potential salvation—his cut of the nearly half billion dollars in damages in the surgical-gown case against Kimberly-Clark and Halyard Health—shrank on March 30 when a federal judge reduced the award to about $21 million, a nearly 95 percent cut. If he'd been counting on that money to pay down his debts, he'd have to find more income, and fast. Both sides lodged appeals.

As Cohen listened to White House statements shifting all the responsibility for the burgeoning Daniels scandal onto him, he began to worry that his loyalty might not be reciprocated. The Daniels scandal had taken its toll on his income as well. The consulting arrangements of the year before had terminated or lapsed, and the money had stopped rolling in. Some of those earlier clients had been surprised when the *Journal* revealed in January that Cohen had used Essential Consultants, the same entity they had been paying, to funnel a possibly illegal payment to a porn star. Squire Patton Boggs had also ended its strategic alliance with him in March, after the Daniels scandal broke.

Cohen's emotions boiled over on April 5, 2018, after Trump—who had remained uncharacteristically silent—addressed the Daniels controversy for the first time in a Q and A with reporter Catherine Lucey of the Associated Press aboard Air Force One.

> LUCEY: Mr. President, did you know about the $130,000 payment to Stormy Daniels?
> TRUMP: No. No. What else?
> LUCEY: Then why did Michael Cohen make those if there was no truth to her allegations?
> TRUMP: Well, you'll have to ask Michael Cohen. Michael is my attorney. And you'll have to ask Michael Cohen.
> LUCEY: Do you know where he got the money to make that payment?
> TRUMP: No, I don't know. No.
> LUCEY: Did you ever set up a fund of money that he could draw from?

This last question, which Trump ignored, was another source of aggrievement for Cohen. He had waited months for Trump to reimburse him for paying off Daniels. Now Trump, who had personally discussed his reimbursement checks with Cohen at the White House in February 2017, was claiming outright that he had no idea where the money had come from, notwithstanding that Cohen had supplied Trump's CFO, Allen Weisselberg, with proof of the payment. The president knew exactly where the money had come from.

On the day Trump made his remarks, Cohen was in Florida, spending the evening on the yacht of Franklin Haney, a new consulting client he'd managed to sign. The president's comments drew widespread media coverage. As Haney's other guests sipped their drinks, Cohen grew irate, swearing and unnerving the people around him.

Haney was a seventy-seven-year-old developer who had worked his way through college as a Bible salesman, run for governor of Tennessee in his twenties, and built a successful real estate business, taking advantage of government enticements such as tax-exempt financing. Haney had been a big Democratic donor during the Obama administration, then switched sides with a $1 million gift to Trump's inauguration. He'd hired Cohen to assist in the search for funding for his latest project, the redevelopment of a pair of nuclear reactors Haney agreed to buy from the Tennessee Valley Authority.

Haney had agreed to pay Cohen up to a $10 million success fee, plus a monthly retainer to help secure funding—the developer was seeking a $5 billion loan from the U.S. Department of Energy. In Florida, Cohen had arranged a meeting with Qatari investors who were holding a business road show at the Four Seasons Hotel at the Surf Club, near Miami Beach. He and Haney pitched the nuclear investment to the vice chairman of the Qatar Investment Authority, Sheikh Ahmed bin Jassim bin Mohammed al-Thani.

By Sunday morning, three days after Trump's comments on Air Force One, Cohen had calmed down and rediscovered his commitment to the president. He tweeted a CNN video that explored his role as Trump's fixer, albeit a somewhat inept one. Reporter Brian Todd quoted an unnamed Trump campaign official describing Cohen as "a less cool version of Ray Donovan, Showtime's fictional Hollywood fixer." If less cool, Cohen was "every bit as tenacious," Todd said. CNN included a clip of Avenatti calling the Daniels NDA "amateur hour" and celebrity attorney Mark Geragos, a friend of Avenatti's, commenting that "99.9 percent of the lawyers in America would never even contemplate doing this."

Above the video, Cohen posted a quote from a novelist who had written a memoir about her relationship with J. D. Salinger.

"A person who deserves my loyalty receives it."- Joyce Maynard
I will always protect our @POTUS @realDonaldTrump

IN THE PREDAWN hours of Monday, April 9, FBI agents filtered into a side entrance of the Loews Regency Hotel on Manhattan's Park Avenue and took the service elevator to the seventeenth floor. They knocked on the door to room 1728. When a surprised Michael Cohen answered, an agent asked if he had any firearms. Cohen led the agents to a drawer where he kept his gun, which they confiscated. The agents furnished a warrant to seize financial records, evidence related to the payments to Stormy Daniels and Karen McDougal, and information about his taxi business and loans from banks and credit unions. Cohen's wife, Laura, sat on a bed as the agents carted away materials from Cohen's hotel suite, where he was staying while his apartment underwent renovations after a flood.

At roughly the same time, another FBI team appeared on the twenty-third floor of 30 Rockefeller Plaza. They entered Cohen's office at the law firm Squire Patton Boggs and boxed up his files, placing them in a truck. Agents also searched Cohen's Park Avenue apartment and a safe-deposit box at TD Bank.

The haul was considerable: computers, smartphones, and tablets belonging to Cohen's whole family, cartons of documents, even the contents of his shredder—millions of items in all.

In an affidavit in support of search warrants, an FBI agent had told U.S. Magistrate Judge Henry Pitman that the government expected to find evidence of bank fraud, illegal campaign contributions, and other crimes in Cohen's possession. The judge had signed the search warrants at 7:54 P.M. the day before the raids.

As the searches were under way, agents arrived at the Greenwich, Connecticut, home of David Pecker and at the Manhattan apartment building of Pecker's top editor, Dylan Howard. The FBI had subpoenas for both men and search warrants authorizing the immediate seizure of their cellphones. Mr. Pecker, who was at the dentist when the agents showed up, returned home and turned over his device.

The criminal investigation of Michael Cohen had spilled into the open.

26.

THE FEDS

■ ■ ■

THE FBI SEARCHES of Cohen's home, hotel, and office represented an extraordinary use of government investigatory power. Federal agents rarely raid attorneys—let alone the personal lawyer for the president. Law offices make for hazardous targets. They hold scads of communications between attorneys and clients that the law protects from discovery. Federal investigators risk tainting their cases if they peek at emails or documents covered by the attorney-client privilege. Judges have thrown out criminal charges for less.

Better to first try a less intrusive investigative tool than a search warrant to gather evidence from an attorney, like a subpoena, which puts the onus on the recipient to turn over files and challenge any potential encroachment on client protections, if need be. That's what the U.S. Department of Justice's manual for federal prosecutors advises, anyway, "unless such efforts could compromise the criminal investigation or prosecution, or could result in the obstruction or destruction of evidence."

In this case, FBI agents and federal prosecutors in Manhattan believed that Cohen was liable to withhold or destroy files if they simply sent him a subpoena for the evidence they sought. They'd been investigating the attorney since February, after inheriting the case from special counsel Robert Mueller. Mueller's team had looked into the foreign funds flowing into Cohen's Essential Consultants account but found no nexus to the Russian influence scheme. The special counsel's office had unearthed evidence of other crimes, however, while picking through Cohen's emails and financial records. They suspected he'd lied to banks while trying to get out from under $22 million in debt he owed on loans he'd taken out against his taxi medallions.

The medallions, once a safe investment, had lost much of their value in the face of competition from ride-sharing companies like Uber. When Cohen refinanced his taxi medallion loans in 2014, he'd reported a net worth of more than $77 million. Three years later, he complained that he could no longer keep up with the payments on the loans, telling Sterling National Bank and Melrose Credit Union he had a net worth of negative $12 million. But he'd neglected to disclose hundreds of thousands of dollars pouring into accounts he'd opened for Essential Consultants and his law practice, and millions more in cash sitting in other banks, investigators discovered.

The bank fraud investigation was beyond Mueller's Russia-centric remit, so the special counsel had outsourced it to the U.S. Attorney's Office for the Southern District of New York. The *Journal*'s stories on Cohen's payment to Daniels and American Media's deal with Karen McDougal prompted New York investigators to expand their probe to include potential violations of campaign-finance laws.

In legal circles, the Southern District is sometimes called the "sovereign district," a tongue-in-cheek nod to the office's independence and high self-regard. It is one of ninety-four field offices for federal prosecutors across the United States and its territories, all of them part of the massive Department of Justice, but the Southern District has a reputation for conducting itself as if it's the only game in town.

Southern District prosecutors work in a federal building at St. Andrew's Plaza in downtown Manhattan, near City Hall. The office is a premier assignment. Top law firms and in-house legal departments at large public companies court assistant U.S. attorneys from the Southern District, paying them many times their government salary to switch sides, given the office's reputation for attracting the best of the best.

But the office's reputation and independence have limits. The United States Attorneys' Manual requires federal prosecutors in the field to consult with their overseers in Washington before asking a federal judge to sign a warrant to search an attorney's office. The agency's top leaders and policymakers reside in the Justice Department's headquarters, in Washington, D.C., known colloquially as "Main Justice."

Involving Main Justice is no small matter. Trump had shown no respect for the independence of the Justice Department. He'd already asked for and received a resignation letter from his attorney general, only to change his mind and pocket the letter. (*You were supposed to protect me,* Trump had complained to Sessions after Mueller's appointment.) And he'd directed his White House counsel, Don McGahn, to pressure the number-two official at the Justice Department to fire Mueller. McGahn had ignored the order. But who knew what would happen if the president asked another White House official to do his dirty work?

On Twitter and elsewhere, Trump's disdain for the Justice Department and the FBI was on public display almost daily. Mueller, a Republican who had served under presidents from both parties, led a team of "hardened Democrats" motivated by politics to dislodge the president through undemocratic means, Trump said. The FBI, too, was guilty of attempting a bloodless coup. Sessions was weak. Trump said he wished he'd picked someone else to lead the department.

How would department officials under siege by the president react to a request by New York prosecutors to execute search warrants on Trump's personal attorney? Rod Rosenstein, the Justice Department's number-two official and its day-to-day manager, had been telling the agency rank and file that Trump's barbs were a test for them. The president had a First Amendment right to express his views, but his tweets and the insults he transmitted through the press had no bearing on their operating instructions. *Ignore partisan considerations,* Rosenstein had been saying.

Late in the week before the FBI raids, the search warrant affidavit made its way from Robert Khuzami, the deputy U.S. attorney in the Southern District, to Rosenstein's office, one rung below the attorney general. Khuzami was overseeing the Cohen case for the same reason Rosenstein was in charge of the Mueller probe. Their immediate bosses, U.S. Attorney Geoffrey Berman and Attorney General Jeff Sessions, had recused themselves from matters involving Trump. Berman, a former law partner of Rudy Giuliani, had been appointed on an interim basis by Sessions in January and was awaiting a formal nomination by Trump as his 120-day term neared expiration. (Berman would soon be confirmed by the chief judge in Manhattan federal court, in the absence of a presidential nomination.)

Justice Department officials in Washington didn't need to approve the searches, not technically, but they had to be consulted to make sure procedures were followed. Rosenstein tasked senior prosecutors in his office to look at the document, and he personally reviewed it. Everyone agreed that it satisfied the law and agency policy.

The green light from Main Justice was a signal to the federal agents and prosecutors in New York that the Justice Department would support their investigation, wherever it led.

Rosenstein gave his boss, Jeff Sessions, a heads-up that federal agents were planning to conduct the searches at the beginning of the coming week, if a federal judge approved them. Sessions, perpetually on the brink of resigning or getting fired, needed to know that the Justice Department was about to make a move guaranteed to provoke Trump.

Monday is going to be a bad day, Rosenstein told the attorney general.

By coincidence, Rosenstein and FBI General Counsel Dana Boente were scheduled to speak with Trump at the White House on the day of the Cohen raids. The president had called the meeting after hearing complaints from Republicans in Congress that the FBI was slow-walking their requests for documents related to the investigation of Hillary Clinton's email server.

That was a small thing next to armed FBI agents carting away evidence from the office, home, and hotel room of Trump's personal attorney. We didn't know what, if anything, Trump said to Rosenstein about the searches at that White House meeting. But we knew he was angry.

"I just heard that they broke into the office of one of my personal attorneys, a good man, and it's a disgraceful situation. It's a total witch hunt," he told reporters after the raids.

THE FOUR ASSISTANT U.S. attorneys working the Cohen case were all thirty-somethings in the Southern District's public corruption unit, a corner of the office that had shifted its focus under the previous U.S. attorney, Preet Bharara, from frauds on the city to high-profile prosecutions of elected officials. In recent years, the unit had prosecuted Albany mainstays like New York State Assembly Speaker Sheldon Sil-

ver and Dean Skelos, the Republican majority leader of the state senate. The unit had investigated the fundraising activity of New York
Mayor Bill de Blasio for a year before declining to bring charges.

The Southern District has few career prosecutors in its criminal division. Most line assistant U.S. attorneys are young, between thirty and
forty, graduated from top law schools, and went on to clerk for federal
judges or toil as junior associates at prestigious corporate law firms, or
both, before assuming the extraordinary powers of a federal prosecutor. New assistants begin in the general crimes and narcotics units,
prosecuting smaller-bore cases, before moving on to units, like public
corruption, that run more complex investigations. After about five
years, give or take, many Southern District prosecutors return to private practice as partners in the same prestigious law firms that represent the white-collar criminals they brought to heel. New York is
expensive, and government pay goes only so far.

The Cohen prosecutors had pedigrees typical of the office. The first
two to join the case were Thomas McKay, thirty-two, and Nicolas
Roos, thirty-three. McKay, the youngest of the four assistant U.S. attorneys, had been in the public corruption unit longer than his three
colleagues. He had been the fourth prosecutor on the Skelos trial team,
the "law guy," responsible for mastering the legal aspects of the case.
McKay prepared to retry the former Republican majority leader, whose
conviction had been overturned on appeal, while investigating Cohen.

Rachel Maimin, thirty-eight, had been in the office since 2010, longer than any of her colleagues. Another recent hire to the unit, she had
spent years prosecuting cases aimed at crippling New York gangs like
the Trinitarios, a violent group of Dominican Americans whose signature weapon was a machete. The fourth prosecutor to join the team
was Andrea Griswold. She'd recently been a senior member of the office's securities unit, where she prosecuted insider trading and corporate fraud. Supervisors added Griswold, thirty-seven, to the Cohen
team for her expertise in financial crimes.

The four prosecutors collaborated on all aspects of the Cohen case,
but McKay took point on the campaign-finance investigation, while
Griswold led the bank and tax components. Some of the prosecutors
had worked together in the past, but none had been involved in anything like their current assignment. The crimes they were investigating
were typical for the unit. Public corruption cases, as a rule, took time

and effort, often relying on circumstantial evidence to show a quid pro quo. But the people involved (the president, his lawyer, a tabloid executive) and the facts (hush money to a model and a porn star) were anything but typical. The public interest in the Cohen case would magnify any prosecutorial missteps tenfold. It created extraordinary pressure to get things right. The president of the United States was already accusing them of destroying attorney-client privilege with the raids on his personal lawyer.

The team was assembled and overseen by Tatiana Martins, the forty-year-old chief of the public corruption unit, and her thirty-eight-year-old deputy, Russell Capone. A skilled investigator, Capone picked up the slack when Martins was juggling preparation for another trial and her other supervisor duties. The top managers in the office, Khuzami and Senior Counsel Audrey Strauss, kept a close eye on the Cohen investigation and sought frequent updates. The reputation of the Southern District was on the line.

THE SEARCH OF Cohen's law office was merely one of the unusual aspects of the Southern District's investigation. American Media, clearly in the crosshairs, was a publisher. Freedom of the press dictated that the government tread carefully. News organizations had a right to choose what to publish and—more important in this case—what not to publish. The company could dig in its heels, forcing the government to litigate complicated First Amendment issues and sapping its investigative momentum.

The first meeting between federal prosecutors and attorneys for American Media and company executives, on April 17, underscored the risks. The government was in possession of Pecker's and Howard's phones, and the assorted defense lawyers wanted to stop the government from rummaging through their contents. Pecker and Howard were at the top rungs of a company that was engaged primarily in journalism, even if some people questioned its public value. Many of Pecker's communications focused on business, but Howard's were largely editorial.

Pecker had hired as his personal counsel Elkan Abramowitz, a former chief of the criminal division at the Southern District in the 1970s who had gone on to become one of New York's most venerated white-collar criminal defense lawyers. The publisher had tapped a peer of Abramowitz's to represent the company: Charles Stillman, another Southern District alum who'd also been a go-to member of the white-collar bar for half a century. Stillman, who'd merged his namesake firm into Philadelphia-based Ballard Spahr LLP, was there with his partner Jim Mitchell. Howard's lawyer was John Harris, another experienced Manhattan litigator.

It seemed to the defense lawyers that the prosecutors didn't believe the *National Enquirer* and its executives were entitled to the same journalistic deference that the government would have given to *The New York Times*, the *Journal, The Washington Post,* or other mainstream publications. But they were wrong, the defense lawyers argued. John Harris, Howard's lawyer, gave an impassioned presentation about the First Amendment fight the government would have on its hands if it insisted on accessing the editor's phone, which included information relating to his confidential sources. It would unfold in public, where the publisher could present itself as the victim of prosecutors who had gone too far by seizing the phones without any real reason to believe— the lawyers argued—that Pecker or Howard would have destroyed evidence had the government relied on a less intrusive subpoena.

Media companies often rallied to the sides of their competitors in First Amendment cases. Any encroachment on the press freedoms of one publisher could weaken protections for the rest. But the American Media group couldn't be sure mainstream media outlets would jump to the aid of a tabloid that had aggressively slanted its coverage to back Trump. The lawyers let it be known that cooperation wasn't out of the question, but they suggested the company would be far more inclined to assist the U.S. attorney's office if the phone issue was resolved to American Media's satisfaction.

The prosecutors had no doubt that the *Enquirer* and its parent company enjoyed First Amendment protections; indeed, they hadn't sent the FBI with a subpoena to the company's offices. But in seizing the phones, the government had taken the posture that, while legitimate journalistic work was protected by the Constitution, "catch and kill" deals intended to protect politicians were not.

In the days after the meeting, the lawyers and the government came to an agreement. The government search warrants authorized copying the contents of both Pecker's and Howard's phones, but American

Media would be able to identify editorial-related communications it believed should be redacted. They would deal with a Southern District review team operating separately from the prosecutors investigating Cohen. Howard's lawyers created a log of phone numbers belonging to confidential sources, so that the review team could remove information pertaining to them from the files that investigators were pursuing.

Soon prosecutors convened with Abramowitz, Pecker's lawyer. McKay, who was decades Abramowitz's junior, had written to the defense lawyer four days after the FBI raids and asked for a meeting as soon as possible.

It was odd for prosecutors to immediately seek an audience with the chief executive of a company under investigation. They usually tried to flip more junior executives first and work their way up the chain of command. Pecker's defense team at Abramowitz's firm thought it was a good omen. If prosecutors were skipping to the top, they must have been in a hurry. It also suggested that American Media was a secondary target. And that meant that they'd be willing to cut Pecker a good deal in return for his information. Pecker had given his attorneys a simple instruction: "Get me out of this."

At their meeting, prosecutors gave Abramowitz a list of questions for his client, and they told the defense lawyer what they expected Pecker to be able to tell them. They already seemed to know, for instance, that Pecker and Trump had discussed the McDougal payment. Prosecutors weren't trying to make a case against Trump. The Justice Department's Office of Legal Counsel, a quasi-judicial unit made up of some of the agency's brightest legal minds, had long ago determined that a sitting president could not be prosecuted. The unit had evaluated the question twice: during Watergate and again in formulating an October 2000 legal opinion, eighteen months after the Senate acquitted President Bill Clinton in an impeachment trial linked to his efforts to conceal a sexual relationship with Monica Lewinsky.

But the Southern District still needed to prove that Trump or someone on his campaign knew about the payoffs if it hoped to make a campaign-finance case against Cohen or American Media. The Federal Election Campaign Act of 1971 required the prosecutors to show that the payments to Daniels and McDougal had been made "in cooperation, consultation or concert with, or at the request or suggestion of, a candidate's campaign." And though they couldn't bring charges against Trump, they could create a record of his involvement in the hush-money deals for others, including Congress, which had the power to impeach the president, should it ever come to that. Midterm congressional elections were only months away, and polls suggested Democrats stood a good chance of flipping enough seats in the House of Representatives to take control of the chamber. If that happened, Democrats would have the power to subpoena witnesses and evidence and even lodge articles of impeachment, the legislative equivalent of bringing charges against the president.

The record of the Cohen investigation could also be reviewed by future prosecutors in the Southern District. Should Trump fail to win reelection in 2020 and return to civilian life, he'd no longer be invulnerable to federal criminal charges. At that point, if the prosecutors were so inclined, they could look at the evidence on Trump and weigh whether they could—or should—try to make a case.

A SEVEN-YEAR-OLD CASE hovered over the criminal investigation of the payments to Stormy Daniels and Karen McDougal. Thanks in no small part to David Pecker and his *National Enquirer*, the Department of Justice in 2011 had charged former Democratic presidential candidate John Edwards with conspiring to use secret funds from his political donors to hide his mistress and love child, in violation of federal campaign-finance laws.

The case had no precedent. Never before had prosecutors treated money given to a candidate by political donors and used to conceal an affair the same as campaign contributions that politicians invested in political ads, brochures, and rallies. The Federal Election Campaign Act required candidates to report money they received and spent on campaign-related activities, so voters could see who might be trying to influence them. It also placed restrictions on how much money donors could give candidates—$2,300 per election in 2008—and barred corporations from contributing directly to candidates. The language of the law was broad, defining a campaign contribution as "anything of value" intended to influence a federal election, including "in-kind contributions," meaning goods and services provided without charge or at a discount.

Federal prosecutors from the Justice Department's Public Integrity Section, a national anti-corruption unit, had accused Edwards of taking nearly $1 million from two political donors for his mistress's housing, medical care, travel, and other expenses. Edwards, a successful plaintiff's lawyer and former U.S. senator from North Carolina, hadn't reported the donations, causing his campaign to file false reports, the government alleged. And even if he had, under the prosecution's theory, the donations would have been illegal, far exceeding the $2,300-per-individual cap.

The 2012 trial of the disgraced politician was a test of the government's interpretation of the Federal Election Campaign Act. Jurors were called on to decide whether prosecutors had proved, beyond a reasonable doubt, that the payments steered to Rielle Hunter were primarily "for the purpose of influencing any election for federal office," by keeping a personal scandal that might damage Edwards's electoral chances a secret. If the jury determined that they were, Edwards was guilty.

Abbe Lowell, Edwards's savvy lawyer, erected two main defenses over the course of the monthlong trial: He viciously attacked the credibility of the government's star witness, Andrew Young, a longtime aide to Edwards who testified that the presidential candidate had enlisted him to coordinate the payments to Hunter and keep her from going public with the affair. Lowell also persuasively argued that Edwards was consumed with keeping the affair from his wife, Elizabeth, before her 2010 death from breast cancer, rather than protecting his viability as a candidate. The timing of the payments worked in Edwards's favor. His donors had provided a large chunk of the money after Edwards left the presidential race in 2007.

"John lied about his affair to keep it a secret in 2006, 2007, 2008, 2009, and straight through to the beginning of 2010, when he finally admitted that Quinn was his daughter," Lowell told the jurors. "But the prosecutors want you to take one time period, from when Mrs. Hunter was—Ms. Hunter was pregnant to the time John ended his campaign, and say that was the purpose of the lies. It was for the election. The fact that he continued to try to keep it out of the media long after January of 2008 tells you that's not the case. This was not for the purpose of influencing an election."

David V. Harbach II, a senior prosecutor in the Public Integrity Section, reminded jurors that Elizabeth Edwards already knew about the affair when the checks from her husband's donors began flowing to Hunter, though Edwards had lied and told his wife it was a brief fling. Even after he withdrew from the race for the 2008 Democratic nomination, Edwards had his eye on a cabinet position—attorney general—if a Democrat won the presidency, Harbach said.

"There is no question that no one wants their spouse to learn of an extramarital affair, but the evidence in this case clearly demonstrates that John Edwards's primary reason for taking these contributions and hiding his mistress from the public was to prevent damage to his campaign," the prosecutor said in his closing argument.

Nevertheless, the jury acquitted Edwards of one charge and deadlocked on the rest, dealing the Justice Department a defeat in a case that remains controversial within the agency years later. Some Justice Department officials and election-law experts considered the prosecution an overreach. The government cut its losses and opted not to retry Edwards on the hung counts.

Prosecutors in the Southern District were well aware of the Edwards problem when they began investigating Michael Cohen in early 2018. To avoid the same pitfalls, they would need to marshal proof that the looming 2016 presidential election was the primary impetus for the payments to Karen McDougal and Stormy Daniels. They anticipated an Edwards-like argument from Cohen that he had made and coordinated the hush-money payments to keep the alleged affairs from Trump's wife, Melania, and Trump's family.

We learned soon after the raids that the search warrants executed on Cohen's properties also gave agents permission to scoop up materials related to *Access Hollywood*. By this time, our core reporting team had grown to include Rebecca Ballhaus, a White House reporter in Washington, and Nicole Hong and Rebecca Davis O'Brien, who covered federal law enforcement in New York. We were all puzzled by investigators' interest in the show. Obviously, it had something to do with the now famous *Access Hollywood* video of Trump discussing grabbing women by their genitals, a tape that nearly sank his campaign. Had Cohen tried to quash the recording before *The Washington Post* published it? Had he tried to buy it, as he had with the Stormy Daniels story?

No, it turned out.

Prosecutors had come to view the *Access Hollywood* tape as the fulcrum in negotiations between Michael Cohen and Keith Davidson over Stormy Daniels's story. Before the recording surfaced on October 7, Cohen refused to entertain any talk of buying the story. After the *Post*'s scoop—literally three days after—Cohen was negotiating with Davidson to put a muzzle on Daniels.

For prosecutors, Cohen's sudden change in demeanor was proof that he'd bought Daniels's story for the purpose of influencing the outcome of the election. If the case ever went to a jury, they could frame the Daniels deal as a direct response to the damage inflicted on Trump's campaign by the *Access Hollywood* tape. If Cohen and Trump merely had been trying to keep the affair from Melania Trump, why hadn't they taken the Daniels story off the market in September, when they had the chance?

IN THE AFTERMATH of the raids, Cohen, a man who thrived on relationships, had to start over. All his devices had been hauled away. It was disorienting. On a new phone, people texted from unrecognized numbers, and he'd respond, "Who is this?"

For help, Cohen called John Gauger of RedFinch. He told him the investigation was just about taxes and how he'd accessed money, and that wealthy people sometimes drew capital from different sources. "It's not a big deal," Cohen said.

Then he asked for a final favor. "They took my phone. I bought a new one and I don't know how to log into my mail." Cohen not only couldn't get into his Gmail account, but he didn't know how to sync his contacts to the new phone. So Gauger googled how to reset a Gmail password and read him the instructions.

Cohen was bombarded with messages from media and perfect strangers as many of his friends backed away. It seemed like the whole world was paying attention to him now—even Joyce Maynard, the novelist he'd quoted in reaffirming his loyalty to Trump in a tweet the day before the raid. She responded in kind as word of the FBI's action spread.

"Attorney Michael Cohen does not deserve my loyalty or anybody else's." --Joyce Maynard. 4/9/18

Within a few days, he received reassurance from Trump, who called Cohen to check in and see how he was doing. "It's terrible, for you and your family," Trump said empathetically. "Stay strong. Hang in there." The president assured him that everything would be okay. Cohen was encouraged as Trump's friends and associates also reached out. One said he was at Mar-a-Lago with Trump, who wanted the friend to pass along that "he loves you," and not to worry. "Everyone knows the boss has your back," another said.

In a conversation with one of Trump's lawyers, Cohen said he was feeling uneasy after the raids, with a criminal investigation closing in on him. Cohen said he'd been a loyal lawyer and servant. But what was in it for him to remain that way? he asked. The attorney told him to stay on message, that the investigation was a witch hunt, everything would be fine. The conversation comforted Cohen, who believed that if he did as he was told—if he stayed on message—Trump would pardon him or find a way to shut the investigation down.

Five days after the raid, Cohen truly entered the popular culture when Ben Stiller portrayed him on the cold open of *Saturday Night Live*. "That's right, it's Michael Cohen, attorney at law—and also sometimes not at law," Stiller said. First, Cohen's character visited with Attorney General Jeff Sessions and Vice President Mike Pence at the Justice Department. "This whole raid was a complete violation of attorney-criminal privilege," he complained.

Then, in an echo of *Meet the Parents,* Stiller/Cohen was polygraphed by Robert De Niro, playing special counsel Robert Mueller. Stiller admitted to making the payment to Stormy Daniels but lied about whether Trump knew about it. "It was supposed to be a surprise for Stormy, like a gift . . . Like a rock you throw through a window with a note tied to it that says, 'Stop talking,'" Stiller said.

De Niro/Mueller explained that he'd given code names to all the suspects his team investigated. Cohen's code name? "Dead man walking."

FEDERAL INVESTIGATORS SEIZED eight boxes of documents and millions of electronic files from Cohen. But they couldn't dive into the trove right away. Soon after the raids, Cohen's lawyers at McDermott

Will & Emery, who represented him in the Russia-related investigations, asked a federal judge in New York to keep a lid on the government's evidence until a neutral party appointed by the court could sift through it to make sure that any material protected by attorney-client privilege stayed that way. The review could delay the investigation by months, if not longer. Federal prosecutors wanted to handle the sorting internally, with a "taint team," a group of government attorneys who weren't involved in the case and could weed out any potentially privileged documents before passing the non-privileged material to investigators.

Trump inserted himself into the dispute to guard against any privileged communications between him and Cohen falling into the government's hands. Two days after the raid, he added Joanna Hendon, a well-regarded white-collar defense lawyer in New York, to his legal team. Hendon, who began her career as a federal prosecutor in the Southern District, contacted her old office the next day. Like Cohen, she objected to the use of a taint team to review the seized files and asked prosecutors to hold off until they could litigate the issue in federal court in Manhattan. Michael Avenatti also butted into the proceeding, claiming that his client's privacy interests were impacted by the raids.

Cohen's lawyers estimated that the seized materials contained thousands of pages of privileged material, but the government knew better. Though he was an attorney, Cohen hadn't practiced much law since his pre-Trump days. He'd represented three clients since leaving the Trump Organization, and two of them were already known: Donald Trump and Elliott Broidy, the Republican fundraiser Cohen represented in a nondisclosure agreement with a former Playboy Playmate. We had recently revealed Broidy's hush-money deal in the *Journal*. Cohen's lawyers named Trump and Broidy as his legal clients in a letter to U.S. District Judge Kimba Wood ahead of an April 16 hearing in her courtroom, but they told her a third Cohen client had directed them to withhold his or her name.

Daniels showed up to the hearing with Avenatti. She wore a pink skirt suit with a black button-down shirt and black stilettos, a sharp contrast with the blues and grays preferred by attorneys. Daniels tripped and nearly fell while ascending the courthouse steps, surrounded by cameras. (She and Avenatti staged a news conference after the hearing.) Cohen's lawyers at McDermott, Todd Harrison and Stephen Ryan, sat at the defense table, while McKay, Maimin, and Roos were arrayed around the prosecution table.

Judge Wood seized on the mysterious third client early in the hearing. Cohen's lawyers said the client wished to avoid any association with the search warrant. If the client was outed, it might make other people think twice about consulting an attorney, they said. Why risk seeking private counsel if you might later be identified in court for doing so?

The law in her court's jurisdiction supported disclosure, with certain exceptions, Wood said. Potential embarrassment wasn't one of them.

"I'm directing you to disclose the name now," Wood said.

"Do you want me to stand and say it?" Ryan, Cohen's attorney, asked. Or should he write it on a piece of paper and hand it to her?

"Whatever you are most comfortable with."

"The client's name that is involved is Sean Hannity."

Some members of the audience gasped. The Fox News commentator, a confidant of the president, regularly assailed the Mueller investigation on his television and radio shows. Even among the cable news channel's stable of Trump-adoring hosts, Hannity stood out for his unyielding support for and defense of the president. Hannity had been recording his radio show on the day of the FBI raids in New York and recalled Cohen telling him that Trump was oblivious to the hush money paid on his behalf.

"I do remember Michael saying it publicly and saying to me at the time that in fact he never told the president about this, that it was something that he had pretty wide discretion on his own to handle matters without bringing it to his attention," Hannity told listeners.

Later, on his prime-time show, Hannity had called the FBI searches of Cohen's property an "all-hands-on-deck effort to totally malign and, if possible, impeach the president of the United States."

Some journalists would have felt compelled to tell their viewers and listeners about an attorney-client relationship with Cohen, if they intended to use their platform to torch a federal investigation of Cohen's conduct. (Just as it was the *Journal*'s policy, anytime we wrote about

Fox News or Hannity, to remind readers that the cable news channel and the newspaper shared common ownership.) But Hannity insisted that his legal discussions with Cohen—he described them as primarily about real estate—never rose to a level that would warrant disclosure. He was quick to note that Cohen never helped him with a legal problem involving a "third party." In other words, Cohen hadn't paid any hush money for Hannity.

"I never retained his services, I never received an invoice, I never paid Michael Cohen for legal fees," Hannity said on his radio show after he was unmasked as Cohen's third client. "I did have occasional brief conversations with Michael Cohen—he's a great attorney—about legal questions I had, or I was looking for input and perspective."

With the Hannity sideshow out of the way, Judge Wood still had a decision to make. Should she grant Cohen and Trump's wishes and appoint a neutral "special master" to decide which items seized from Cohen were privileged and which the government could use in its investigation? Or leave the task to a taint team in the Justice Department, an outcome that defense lawyers often derided as the proverbial fox guarding the henhouse?

MICHAEL COHEN CLOSED the drapes in a second-floor conference room at the Loews Regency Hotel on Park Avenue, concerned that workers in the office building across the street might look in on his meeting with the two lawyers seated across from him, Jeffrey Citron and Robert Costello. Cohen and Citron had known each other for about a decade. They'd served together on an advisory board to Sterling National Bank, one of the banks that loaned Cohen money against his taxi medallions. They also had a connection through the prep school Cohen's kids attended. A civil lawyer, Citron represented Columbia Grammar & Preparatory School, while Cohen sat on the school's board of trustees.

Citron had reached out to Cohen after the FBI raids and offered to put him in touch with his law partner, Costello, a former supervisor in the Southern District. Cohen quickly agreed. The lawyers invited Cohen to come to their firm, Davidoff Hutcher & Citron, for the introduction. But Cohen said the pack of reporters outside his hotel would follow him wherever he went, and he didn't want to be seen entering their office. The reporters wouldn't recognize Citron and Costello if they came to Cohen at the Regency. Now the two lawyers sat at a conference table, hoping the meeting would lead to a retainer agreement. For defense attorneys, representing the president's personal lawyer was about as high-profile as it gets.

Cohen looked as if he hadn't slept much in the eight days since the raid. He paced the conference room as Citron introduced Costello, a criminal defense lawyer who'd once represented New York Yankees owner George Steinbrenner and Leona Helmsley, the businesswoman and tabloid villain known as the "Queen of Mean." She was famously quoted as saying, "We don't pay taxes; only the little people pay taxes." Cohen eventually took his seat opposite the lawyers and began to unload. Reporters were camped outside the hotel, waiting to track his every move, he said. His business was in ruins. His family was suffering. His friends wanted nothing to do with him.

"This pressure is overwhelming. Over the weekend, I was up on the roof of the hotel seriously contemplating jumping off," Cohen said.

Costello, who'd never met Cohen, stole a glance at his law partner. *Is he serious?* Citron was wide-eyed, clearly taking Cohen's words to heart.

"One thing I can tell you is that I'm never going to spend one day in jail. Never. I will do whatever the fuck I have to do, but I will never spend one day in jail," Cohen told them. It was a refrain he'd repeat during pauses in the two-and-a-half-hour conversation. Sort of like commercial breaks, Costello thought.

Costello told Cohen that the pressure he was feeling was by design. The FBI and federal prosecutors wanted him to believe he had no other option but to cooperate.

"But I am cooperating!" Cohen said.

He'd turned over documents to congressional committees investigating Russian interference in the 2016 election and allowed special counsel Robert Mueller and his team to review transcripts of his testimony. (He neglected to mention that he'd challenged an attempt by Mueller to obtain his Trump Organization emails and that he'd lied to Congress about the duration and extent of his efforts to close the Trump Tower Moscow deal.)

Cohen said he would have done the same for federal agents and prosecutors in New York who raided him. "All they had to do was ask, and I would have turned over whatever they wanted," Cohen said.

Cohen insisted that he had no exposure beyond his involvement in the hush-money deals with Karen McDougal and Stormy Daniels, but Costello suspected that federal agents had more on him. Would Main Justice really approve a search of an attorney's office premised on possible campaign-finance violations? The vast majority of election-related cases were handled civilly, not criminally, and resulted in fines.

"I swear to God, Bob. There's nothing that I did with the Trump Organization and nothing I did in the past that violated the law," Cohen said.

It wasn't unusual for a suspect in a criminal investigation to hold back during his first meeting with lawyers, even though the conversation was privileged. Sometimes it took two or three meetings before a new client would open up. So Costello pressed on, asking Cohen to talk about the nondisclosure agreement with Daniels and American Media's contract with McDougal.

Cohen said he'd participated in the deals to protect Melania Trump. He'd tapped his home equity line of credit to make the Daniels payment because he wanted to shield it from his own wife, who handled the family's finances, Cohen said.

He had questions for the lawyers, too. He'd been reading reports about the potential for Democratic state attorneys general, like Eric Schneiderman in New York, to bring charges against Trump aides who'd been pardoned by the president. As president, Trump could erase federal convictions and prison sentences at will, but he had no authority to forgive state crimes. Cohen seemed fixated on the possibility that he could be prosecuted in state court even if Trump protected him from the feds or if he got immunity from the Southern District for cooperating.

Costello told him that he believed state prosecutors would be barred from bringing charges against Cohen if he ultimately faced federal prosecution. The Fifth Amendment's double jeopardy clause ensured that an accused person couldn't be tried twice on the same facts, following an acquittal or conviction. But Costello promised to investigate the issue further.

If Cohen hoped for immunity, he'd have to have something that federal prosecutors desperately wanted. Costello asked him if he knew of any other criminal conduct that the U.S. attorney's office would be interested in pursuing.

Cohen had heard about unaccounted-for funds that donors had pumped into the committee set up to finance the festivities surrounding the president's inauguration, he said.

"Does that implicate the president?" Costello asked.

"No, I don't think he even knows," Cohen said.

Did he have *anything* on the president? Costello asked.

"No."

Well, there goes any hope for immunity, Costello thought to himself.

THE DAY AFTER Cohen's meeting with Costello and Citron, we sat down with another defense lawyer, eighty-five-year-old Jay Goldberg, in his Upper East Side apartment, where oversize windows looked out on Manhattan. Goldberg had reached out to us through his public relations firm, wanting to convince us of the illegality of the FBI raids on Cohen. He'd represented Trump in his divorces from Ivana Trump and Marla Maples, but Goldberg was no divorce lawyer. Trump had sought him out in the 1990s because of Goldberg's reputation as a crack trial lawyer, whose clients included notorious mobsters like Genovese capo Matty "the Horse" Ianniello, the king of the smut business in Times Square, and prominent entertainment figures like Miles Davis.

Trump had arranged to meet with Goldberg after reading a profile of him in *7 Days* magazine, part of a feature on "Courtroom Killers." The attorney played to Trump's affections. Goldberg was a showman and a brawler like his client. During that first matrimonial case, in the early 1990s, Goldberg, wiry and handsome, had stood on the steps of the courthouse holding aloft a poster-size check to Ivana Trump for $10 million, signed by her husband. "If Mrs. Trump doesn't accept the check, she will rue the day she rejected the offer," he said as television cameras rolled.

Goldberg had an abiding affection for Trump, whom he represented in various matters until the mid-2000s. The attorney's entryway was festooned with framed notes of appreciation from his famous client.

We listened with our coffee as Goldberg criticized the raids on Cohen as government overreach and cited case law that he said could be used to challenge the prosecutors' use of records seized with the search warrants. Then he explained that he'd recently passed on the information to Trump and his lawyer Ty Cobb. That got our attention. Mike Siconolfi, the head of the *Journal*'s investigative unit, had accompanied us to meet Goldberg. He leaned in. Goldberg had spoken to Trump about Michael Cohen's case? he asked.

Trump had called him four days after the raid. Little by little, Siconolfi drew out details of the call from Goldberg.

The attorney had been plain with the president in their fifteen-minute conversation.

Don't trust Cohen, Goldberg had told him. On a scale of 1 to 100, where 100 is fully protecting the president, Cohen "isn't even a one," Goldberg warned. "The mob was broken by Sammy 'the Bull' Gravano caving in out of the prospect of a jail sentence."

The idea of Cohen cooperating with prosecutors seemed far-fetched to Trump, who'd counted on Cohen's loyalty for years, even as he marginalized him.

"Michael is very strong," Trump said.

Goldberg had cautioned Trump to stop communicating with Cohen. He could wear a wire and record their conversations. "You have to be alert," Goldberg said. "I don't care what Michael says."

His warning to Trump turned out to be prescient. Within days of their call, Cohen told Costello and Citron that he'd do whatever it took to stay out of prison, and he had already surreptitiously recorded Trump discussing the McDougal deal in 2016. When we returned to the office, we wrote a story about Goldberg's phone call with Trump, recounting his admonition that Cohen would turn state's evidence if charged.

WE WROTE ANOTHER story that same day, when the news broke that American Media had capitulated in Karen McDougal's lawsuit. As part of a settlement, American Media would relinquish her story rights and let her keep the money the company had paid her.

"I am pleased to have reached a settlement with AMI on my own terms, which restores to me the rights to my life story and frees me from this contract that I was misled into signing nearly two years ago," McDougal said in a statement provided by her lawyer, Peter Stris. "My goal from the beginning was to restore my rights and not to achieve any financial gain, and this settlement does exactly that."

The publisher would maintain a financial interest in any resale of the rights, but McDougal could speak freely about her affair with Trump. American Media also insisted, as part of the settlement, that McDougal's second magazine cover guaranteed by the contract go forward as planned.

McDougal had no interest in appearing on the cover of *Men's Journal,* a men's lifestyle magazine that typically showcased male celebrities like Ben Affleck and Liam Neeson. The magazine staff didn't want her as a cover model, either. Its top executives appealed to Pecker to abandon the plan, arguing that the McDougal cover could hurt the magazine's reputation, making it harder to attract top talent for future covers and alienating hard-won advertisers. They were overruled.

McDougal declined to participate in a photo shoot or interview with *Men's Journal* staff, forcing the magazine's editors to use an old picture for the cover and to recycle archived content for a piece about McDougal's fitness routine. The photo of McDougal they chose, of her wearing a red two-piece sport swimsuit, annoyed the model. It had been taken before she had her breast implants removed.

COHEN SAW GOLDBERG'S comments about him flipping and wanted to get word to the president that he had no intention of proving the octogenarian attorney right. He was still banking on Trump's protection, and the Trump Organization was paying for his lawyers at McDermott Will & Emery, using corporate and campaign funds.

On April 19, the day after our interview with Goldberg, *The Washington Post* reported that Rudy Giuliani, the former mayor of New York and a friend of Trump's, was joining the president's legal team. Their relationship had spanned the decades. Despite Trump's support for his 1989 mayoral bid, Giuliani, a Republican, had lost. But he'd come back to win four years later, serving two terms with the pugilistic style he'd honed as a prosecutor. In the waning months of his mayoralty, Giuliani won national acclaim for his leadership after the September 11, 2001, attacks and the destruction of the World Trade Center. In his next phase, Giuliani launched a lucrative practice in legal and consulting work, including for foreign governments and other overseas clients, such as an Iranian interest group listed as a terrorist organization by the U.S. State Department.

Giuliani's own presidential bid ended early in 2008, but he embraced Trump's victorious bid and angled to become Trump's secretary of state until the president-elect handed the post to Rex Tillerson instead. Giuliani continued his consulting work and had now become, after Michael Cohen, the second presidential lawyer to simultaneously represent clients whose interests could be affected by Trump's administration.

Giuliani's return to Trump's team was good news for Robert Costello, who had known Giuliani for decades. Now Costello could make his relationship with Giuliani a selling point for Cohen, who still hadn't officially retained Costello and Citron.

Costello did his best to shore up Cohen's nerves. Goldberg's prediction had rattled him. "Pay no attention to the talking heads like Jay Goldberg or Stormy's lawyer," the lawyer emailed Cohen. "All of this is to increase the pressure on you, do not give in to that strategy."

But that same day, *The New York Times* reported that Trump's team was becoming resigned to the likelihood of Cohen cooperating with authorities. The newspaper, writing about Trump's one-sided loyalty, described his insults and general mistreatment of Cohen over the years. "Donald goes out of his way to treat him like garbage," Roger Stone, Trump's longtime political adviser, told the *Times*. Costello emailed two of his partners: "I guess the NY Times knows more than we do."

Trump himself attacked the *Times* and its White House reporter Maggie Haberman on Twitter for "going out of their way to destroy Michael Cohen and his relationship with me in the hope that he will 'flip.'" He wrote, "Most people will flip if the Government lets them out of trouble, even if . . . it means lying or making up stories. Sorry, I don't see Michael doing that despite the horrible Witch Hunt and the dishonest media!"

Cohen had authorized Costello in a phone call to reach out to Giuliani on his behalf. Costello emailed Cohen in the early-morning hours of April 21 to brief him on his first phone discussion with Giuliani.

Michael,

I just spoke to Rudy Giuliani and told him I was on your team. Rudy was thrilled and said this could not be a better situation for the President or you. He asked me if it was ok to call the President and Jay Sekelow [*sic*] and I said fine. We discussed the facts, Jay Goldberg's stupid remarks etc. he said I can't tell you how pleased I am that I can work with someone I know and trust. He asked me to tell you that he knows how tough this is on you and your family and he will make sue [*sic*] to tell the President. He said thank you for opening this back channel of communication and asked me to keep in touch. I told him I would after speaking to you further.

   Bob

On the phone that day, Cohen asked Costello to assure Giuliani that Cohen still played for Team Trump. Costello had another call with Giuliani later that evening. He emailed Cohen afterward.

I spoke with Rudy. Very Very Positive. You are "loved". If you want to call me I will give you the details. I told him everything you asked me to and he said they knew that. There was never a doubt and they are in our corner.
   Rudy said this communication channel must be maintained. He called it crucial and noted how reassured they were that they had someone like me whom Rudy has known for so many years in this role.
   Sleep well tonight, you have friends in high places.

   Bob

P.S. Some very positive comments about you from the White House. Rudy noted how that followed my chat with him last night.

Cohen was still racked with anxiety about the raids. He was spending his days with the lawyers at McDermott, picking through his own files, trying to figure out what prosecutors would use against him. In his conversations with Costello, Cohen asked the attorney to broach the subject of a pardon with Giuliani. Costello tried to avoid the issue.

He didn't want to bring up any pardons with Giuliani, thinking it premature. But Cohen returned to the topic.

"Michael, you haven't been charged with any offense. It would be crazy for them to discuss a pardon at this point. And if I ask, they are liable to get pissed off," Costello told him.

Cohen continued to press. "I want you to ask him. He's your friend. You should be able to discuss this with him," Cohen said.

Costello said he would. The next time he spoke with Giuliani, the attorney tried to introduce the topic subtly, asking Giuliani what the potential "endgame" was for Cohen. Giuliani either missed the cue or intentionally avoided it. He reiterated Trump's support and affection for Cohen.

Costello tried again in a subsequent call.

"Listen, Rudy, I realize this is premature, but Michael is insisting," Costello said. "Is a pardon on the table?" he asked.

Giuliani's voice seemed to stiffen. "The president will not discuss pardons with anyone right now," he said.

When Costello related the news to Cohen, he was subdued. Costello had told him what to expect. But Cohen held out hope that his McDermott lawyer, Stephen Ryan, would have better luck. He had also asked Ryan to explore the possibility of a pardon with Trump's lawyers.

By April 26, Judge Wood had decided that someone outside the Justice Department should take the lead in reviewing Cohen's seized files for potentially privileged information. She assigned the task to a former federal judge, Barbara S. Jones, who would release the materials to the government on a rolling basis. Cohen had by then found a criminal defense lawyer in New York, Guy Petrillo, a former chief of the criminal division in the Southern District, though he hadn't told Costello or Citron.

While Wood ruled against the request of federal prosecutors in New York to review the seized material in-house, they believed that a special master would still enable them to meet their self-imposed deadline. Justice Department guidelines advise against charging individuals with campaign-related crimes on the eve of an election, lest the agency be accused of trying to influence the outcome. Trump wasn't on the ballot in the upcoming congressional elections, but an indictment of his personal lawyer on the eve of the midterms could harm Republicans, who were campaigning on their support for the president. New York prosecutors needed to bring any charges against Cohen by September, at least two months out from the election, or wait until afterward.

They didn't want to wait.

27.

A TINY LITTLE FRACTION

■ ■ ■

FOR COHEN, THE writing was on the wall. Trump and his allies seemed to be intentionally isolating him. First, David Pecker chose Trump over Cohen, even though American Media was now embroiled in a federal investigation over the favor he'd done for the president. "Trump Fixer's Secrets and Lies," blared a late April cover of the *National Enquirer*. Asked by CNN if the cover was a message from the president, Cohen responded, "What do you think?"

Then Trump called in to *Fox & Friends*. He said Cohen was "a good person" but acted like he barely knew the guy, portraying the investigation as a problem of Cohen's own making.

"They're looking at something having to do with his business. I have nothing to do with his business," Trump said. "He has a percentage of my overall legal work—a tiny, tiny little fraction. But Michael would represent me and represent me on some things. He represents me—like with this crazy Stormy Daniels deal he represented me. And, you know, from what I see he did absolutely nothing wrong. There were no campaign funds going into this . . ."

Trump continued, "I've been told I'm not involved."

Cohen reacted the next day through his friend Donny Deutsch, the former advertising executive turned television personality, who appeared on *Morning Joe*.

"Whoever is advising Trump, the way he played and talked about Michael Cohen yesterday I think is a grave mistake for him," Deutsch said. "Terrible mistake to not be loyal to Michael Cohen."

· · ·

RUDY GIULIANI HADN'T been on Trump's legal team for long when he and the president, realizing that Cohen was in fact being investigated for campaign-finance violations and not just his private business deals, decided that it was time to air their own talking points. It was a continuation of the narrative in which Cohen had arranged everything on his own and Trump hadn't done anything. But they were ready now to reveal a significant new detail: that Trump had reimbursed his fixer for the settlement. Giuliani made the disclosure about the reimbursement in an interview on Fox with Sean Hannity on Wednesday, May 2. He seemed to take Hannity by surprise when, in response to questions about the Russia investigation, Giuliani brought up Cohen "paying some Stormy Daniels woman $130,000."

> GIULIANI: Which, I mean, is going to turn out to be perfectly
> legal. That money was not campaign money. Sorry, I'm giving you
> a fact now that you don't know. It's not campaign money. No
> campaign-finance violation.
> HANNITY: So they funneled it through a law firm.
> GIULIANI: Funneled through a law firm, and the president
> repaid it.
> HANNITY: Oh. I didn't know that. He did?
> GIULIANI: Yep.

Giuliani told Hannity that, while he didn't think Trump had been aware of the deal beforehand, "he did know about the general arrangement that Michael would take care of things like this." He said Cohen had been repaid in monthly installments of $35,000. Giuliani didn't seem to think the events he was describing were unusual.

"I take care of things like this for my clients," he said. "I don't burden them with every single thing that comes along. These are busy people."

Even if the payment to Daniels qualified as an illegal campaign contribution, violations of election law normally result in a monetary fine and not in "stormtroopers coming in and breaking down his apartment and breaking down his office," Giuliani said. (The FBI agents hadn't actually broken down any doors when they executed the search warrant.)

"I feel very bad he's been victimized like this. The president feels even worse."

Trump and Giuliani continued the blitz the next day. In three successive tweets, Trump wrote that Cohen "received a monthly retainer, not from the campaign and having nothing to do with the campaign, from which he entered into, through reimbursement, a private contract between two parties, known as a non-disclosure agreement, or NDA." Such agreements, the president added, "are very common among celebrities and people of wealth" and, with respect to Daniels, one "was used to stop the false and extortionist accusations made by her about an affair."

Within an hour of Trump's tweets, Giuliani appeared on Fox again. He praised Cohen for paying Daniels but seemed to acknowledge that the deal had been intended to protect Trump's presidential bid. "Imagine if that came out on October 15, 2016, in the middle of the last debate with Hillary Clinton," Giuliani said. "Cohen didn't even ask. He made it go away. He did his job."

Cohen learned from another interview Giuliani gave to ABC News that he was no longer Trump's personal attorney. The president hadn't bothered to tell him.

ON THE FIRST weekend in May, Stormy Daniels fulfilled her own prophecy, playing herself in a *Saturday Night Live* skit. She wore a sleeveless red dress as she spoke by phone with Alec Baldwin's Donald Trump. (She didn't get to chase him around in his underwear.)

"Come on, Stormy, stop making such a big deal about this. Everyone knows it's just an act," Baldwin/Trump said from the Oval Office.

"I work in adult films. We're not really known for our acting," Daniels said. After Baldwin asked how he could make things right, Stormy warned him, "I know you don't believe in climate change, but a storm's a-comin', baby."

"I've never been so scared and so horny at the same time," Baldwin said.

A few days later, it was her lawyer who unleashed a storm on Michael Cohen. Michael Avenatti publicly released records of Cohen's banking transactions from reports that were illegally leaked to him. Ever since the *Journal* reported that First Republic Bank had flagged the Daniels payment as suspicious to the Treasury Department, Avenatti had been publicly calling for so-called Suspicious Activity Reports about Cohen's transactions to be publicly released. Such records are legally protected from disclosure because they contain personal financial information, but Avenatti had eventually found someone who furnished the information to him.

As part of what he dubbed "Project Sunlight," Avenatti compiled the records into a "Preliminary Report of Findings"—it was actually the only one he'd issue—with the caveat that the information was true to the best of his knowledge and subject to change.

Avenatti's report revealed that Cohen had told First Republic Bank that Essential Consultants would be a real estate consulting company that would collect fees for investment consulting, with its income coming from U.S. companies. In fact, according to the transactions, Cohen's consulting income came from a much more diverse set of clients, including AT&T and foreign companies such as Novartis and Korea Aero. Seizing on the payments from Columbus Nova, Avenatti wrote that *"within approximately 75 days of the payment to Ms. Clifford, Mr. Viktor Vekselberg, a Russian Oligarch with close ties to Russian President Vladimir Putin, caused substantial funds to be deposited into the bank account from which Mr. Cohen made the payment."*

The disclosures sent Cohen's consulting clients scrambling to explain why they'd sent money to the same Delaware entity that paid Stormy Daniels. Andrew Intrater, from Columbus Nova, had learned a few months earlier that the same Cohen company he'd paid had funded the Daniels payment. After the *Journal* revealed Cohen's use of Essential Consultants for the hush-money deal in January, Intrater had met him for a meal. "People are going crazy about my company. The company I had. They said I made a payment," Cohen told him. Intrater was confused. "Michael, what are you talking about?" he asked.

When he returned to his office, Intrater went online and figured out what Cohen had meant. Then he asked his staff for the name of the company that Columbus Nova had paid. When they told him it was Essential Consultants, Intrater was stunned.

Now, with Avenatti's disclosure, reporters noted the financial relationship between Columbus Nova and Vekselberg, and that the oligarch was Intrater's cousin. They queried whether the Columbus Nova payments had some connection to Russian influence on the election.

They didn't, but representatives for Columbus Nova struggled to explain that it was an American company—one that sometimes invested the Russian oligarch's money. They wanted media accounts to reflect that it was Intrater's decision to hire Cohen, and it was his company—not the oligarch—that had paid him.

Avenatti's document dump hurt his efforts to insert himself into the criminal case against Cohen. (Daniels's lawsuit against Trump and Essential Consultants, the one seeking to free her from her NDA, was now on ice. A federal judge in Los Angeles had paused it to avoid any interference with the rapidly intensifying criminal investigation.) In "Project Sunlight," Avenatti had inadvertently revealed private banking transactions involving two wrong Michael Cohens—one a Canadian in Tanzania and another in Israel. Avenatti shrugged off the mistake, arguing that the transactions were for less than $1,000 each. At a hearing in late May, attorney Stephen Ryan, representing Cohen, told Judge Wood that the release of the records was a "drive-by shooting of my client's rights."

Wood told Avenatti that he wouldn't be permitted to use the court as a platform to publicize private documents or make pronouncements about Cohen's guilt, "which you do." She said, "You are entitled to publicity so long as—that is, I can't stop you, unless you are participating in this matter before me." He would have to stop his "publicity tour" if he wanted to officially join the case. After the hearing, Avenatti made a few more appearances on cable news shows and tweeted that he was withdrawing his request to join the case. The publicity tour would go on.

Behind the scenes, Avenatti had been frustrating prosecutors at the Southern District in their investigation of Cohen. Avenatti told them he was trying to convince Daniels to waive attorney-client privilege so that her former attorney, Keith Davidson, could speak freely to investigators. Davidson was a key witness, having negotiated the NDA with Cohen. But even as he said that, Avenatti had been trying to keep Davidson and Daniels's former agent, Gina Rodriguez, from talking to anyone about the porn star, including the government. Before the raids, a lawyer for Avenatti had sent a letter to Davidson, warning him to "immediately cease making any statements of whatever nature" about Daniels. He also tried to block Rodriguez from providing her communications with Daniels to federal prosecutors before he'd had a chance to review them. Prosecutors had come to believe that Avenatti was stringing them along. Avenatti saw no compelling reason to waive privilege, something an attorney rarely advised his client to do. Investigators didn't need Daniels to ask Davidson about his discussions with Cohen, which were central to the investigation and weren't privileged.

When the *Journal* reported these developments in May, Avenatti denied that he'd been uncooperative with prosecutors and launched a counterattack by tweet. He accused us of publishing a "hit piece" using unnamed sources and falsely claimed that we'd known about Cohen's payment to Daniels long before we published the story and that we'd held it, presumably to protect Trump. "The WSJ had the story in the closing days of the campaign but sat on it." His evidence, which he posted on Twitter, was a letter a *Journal* lawyer had sent to Keith Davidson in November 2016, after Davidson had threatened to sue us. Our lawyer, Craig Linder, had told Davidson that we planned to continue to report on a matter of public significance and would be sending Davidson additional questions about Karen McDougal and Stormy Daniels. According to Avenatti, Linder's mention of Daniels meant that we knew she'd been paid off. He carefully omitted the fact that we'd published a story four days before the election about Karen McDougal's hush-money deal, and that we'd referenced Daniels in that story only as a client of Davidson, which was all we knew at the time.

At the same time, Avenatti continued his wave of litigation against those involved in the hush-money deal. Earlier, he had added a second lawsuit on Daniels's behalf against Trump, accusing the president of defaming her in a tweet after she released the sketch of a man she said had approached her in a Las Vegas parking lot in 2011 and told her to "forget the story." Trump had written, "A sketch years later about a nonexistent man. A total con job, playing the Fake News Media for Fools (but they know it)!"

Then, as the criminal investigation continued, Avenatti sued Davidson and Cohen, too. He called Davidson "a puppet" of Trump and Cohen and accused him of breaching his duties to Daniels, with Cohen's help. Avenatti cited Davidson's communications with Cohen after the *Journal* revealed the deal, in which they discussed having her appear on Fox to try to tamp down the story. Davidson countersued, accusing Avenatti of defaming him with a tweet falsely saying he'd been arrested and should have been charged with extortion, an apparent reference to the sting the FBI conducted over Hulk Hogan's sex tapes. Davidson also sued Cohen for illegally recording a conversation they'd had.

Avenatti frustrated the Southern District prosecutors again when they finally arranged for Daniels to speak to them voluntarily rather than in response to a grand jury subpoena. The day before she was to come in, *The Washington Post* reported on the upcoming interview, so prosecutors canceled it.

"Such leaks are inappropriate in and of themselves, and more importantly, call into question your commitment to maintaining the required confidentiality of the substance of our meeting with your client," Assistant U.S. Attorney Nicolas Roos wrote Avenatti in an email the lawyer also gave the *Post*. "For these reasons we have cancelled our meeting, and will reassess how to proceed."

Avenatti slammed the prosecutors on Twitter for backing out just "because the press found out about the mtg and they can't handle a few cameras outside their offices." He asked, "If they consider this a big deal, how will they . . . ever bring any serious criminal charges against Cohen et al., let alone handle a trial, in such a high profile matter?"

The plaintiff's lawyer had worn out his welcome in the U.S. attorney's office. Avenatti deserved the credit he claimed for elevating the story of the Stormy Daniels payoff in the public sphere, but federal agents and prosecutors had been investigating the hush money without his help and would continue to do so. He bristled at critics who derided him as nothing more than a television lawyer. Avenatti was good in a courtroom, by all accounts. He had won multimillion-dollar victories in litigation. But when he had to choose between assisting in the legal process and continuing his crusade against Cohen and Trump on cable news and in the press, Avenatti chose television over being a lawyer.

COHEN'S PARDON INQUIRIES hadn't gone anywhere. After Bob Costello was rebuffed, Stephen Ryan made a presentation privately to Giuliani in early May. Ryan talked about the history of pardons and when they'd been granted before a trial or even before indictment. There were only a few "off-ramps" for Cohen in the investigation, Ryan told Giuliani. First, Cohen could be indicted, go to trial, and win. The second ramp, in which he'd plead guilty and get squeezed by the government, could pose a big problem for Trump. The third ramp, where Cohen wouldn't be charged, didn't seem likely. *We like Michael. We like him a lot. We don't want anything bad to happen to him*, Giuliani said. But he said now was not the right time to talk about pardons. It wasn't a firm no. Cohen and Ryan felt the door was left open, but nothing materialized.

Since then, the public statements by Giuliani and Trump about Cohen had left him feeling abandoned. His elderly father, Maurice, had been urging him not to continue to protect Trump. "I didn't survive the Holocaust and come to this country to have my name sullied by this guy," the elder Cohen told his son.

At a small restaurant near the Loews Regency Hotel on Park Avenue that spring, Cohen and his wife had dinner with Jerry Falwell Jr. and his wife, Becki. Inside, another guest snapped a picture of Cohen. The owner, whom Cohen knew, made the amateur paparazzo delete it. The two couples had developed a friendship over the past few years, starting with Becki Falwell, who stayed in touch after his 2012 visit with Trump to Liberty University. Cohen, warm and sociable, had nurtured the relationship. But Trump was surprised when Falwell told him at one point how much he and his wife liked Cohen. *Really? Really?* Trump asked, in a way that suggested he didn't think so much of the man.

During dinner, Cohen didn't seem like himself. Though he knew Falwell was close to Trump, Cohen spoke openly and viciously about his feelings of betrayal by the president and those in his circle, and he said he didn't understand why they hadn't protected him. Cohen spoke so angrily that his wife, Laura, kept glaring at him and kicking him under the table. It was clear that he was wounded and felt backed into a corner, and he said he'd lost his will to live. The Falwells were shocked at how Cohen's love for Trump had turned to hatred, and they left worried that he might hurt himself. Afterward, Falwell separately called Giuliani and Trump lawyer Jay Sekulow to share his concerns about Cohen's stability.

Cohen also told Bob Costello, the lawyer close to Giuliani who was *still* trying to get him to sign a retainer agreement, that the president and his people were "throwing him under the bus." Costello tried to talk Cohen off the ledge and stop him from breaking with the president, telling him that his adversaries—the media speculating about when he'd be arrested or flip, Michael Avenatti, the prosecutors—were rooting for him to turn on Trump.

"The whole objective of this exercise by the SDNY is to drain you, emotionally and financially, until you reach a point that you see them as your only means to salvation," Costello emailed him. "You are making a very big mistake if you believe the stories these 'journalists' are writing about you. They want you to cave. They want you to fail. They do not want you to persevere and succeed. If you really believe you are not being supported properly by your former boss, then you should make that position known."

But Cohen had become gruff with the lawyer and largely stopped engaging. Making it worse, Trump refused to answer when reporters at a White House press gaggle asked if Cohen was still his friend. "I always liked Michael Cohen. I haven't spoken to him in a long time," Trump answered, calling Cohen "a good person." Cohen was enraged by Trump's use of the past tense when describing his affection.

Cohen's mounting legal bills became another force driving him away from Trump. Trump's company and campaign had been paying McDermott Will & Emery, the firm that had represented Cohen in the Russia probe and was reviewing the records seized by the FBI. But Trump's lawyers balked at the size of McDermott's bills for the document review and disputed the notion that the president was responsible for all of it, noting that Cohen's private business dealings—his taxi business and banking transactions—seemed to also be a focus of investigators.

The notion that the president shouldn't pay because he wasn't benefiting from the document review struck Cohen and his lawyers as ridiculous—and cheap. Yes, it was expensive, but the president's lawyers were getting advance notice of any damaging evidence, like the recording Cohen had secretly made of Trump.

Costello learned in mid-June that Cohen had already hired a new criminal defense lawyer, Guy Petrillo, through a link Cohen inadvertently included in an email. Petrillo had been an assistant U.S. attorney in the Southern District in the 1990s, serving as chief of the narcotics unit and as the office's top appellate lawyer. He spent about a decade in private practice before returning to the office in 2008 to oversee the

Southern District's criminal caseload. He'd since left and co-founded a boutique firm. If you wanted a lawyer who knew the customs and norms of the Southern District, Petrillo was an obvious choice. He was respected and sharp. Before he got his law degree at New York University, Petrillo was a chemistry major at MIT. He had a graduate degree in political science. But Petrillo was also a fraught choice. Cohen had hired someone who was seen as having a close relationship with the U.S. attorney's office—a useful trait in an attorney whose client is considering cooperation as a defense strategy.

Costello's first reaction to Petrillo's hiring was that Cohen had been stringing him along for free legal advice. His next was to let Giuliani know that Petrillo had worked at the Southern District when James Comey was United States attorney there. "Does Cohen really want a friend of Comey as his lawyer?" Costello texted. Petrillo was part of an "anti-trump gang of lawyers," whose hiring "would be a monumentally bad choice for Cohen and your team," Costello added.

Petrillo's hiring soon hit the news, as did stories about Cohen's complaints that Trump wasn't paying his legal fees. While Cohen privately insisted he wasn't cooperating with federal prosecutors, he began to publicly signal his independence from the president. Cohen left his post on the Republican National Committee on June 20, using his resignation letter to criticize his boss for the first time. Cohen condemned the president's policy of separating immigrant parents entering the country illegally from their children. "As the son of a Polish holocaust survivor, the images and sounds of this family separation policy [are] heart wrenching," he wrote.

Around the same time, Cohen bumped into Tom Arnold, the Los Angeles–based comedian and actor who'd once been married to Roseanne Barr, in the lobby of the Regency Hotel. In fact, their June 21 meeting hadn't really been an accident. Arnold, who'd been friendly with Trump years earlier, was working on a show for Viceland called *The Hunt for the Trump Tapes,* about his quest for unaired *Apprentice* footage that he believed showed Trump making racist and misogynistic remarks. Arnold had been interviewing other Trump associates, like Felix Sater, with whom he posed for a picture that he then posted on Twitter. Arnold freely admitted that he wanted to get under Trump's skin.

Arnold had first interacted with Cohen in 2017, when the comedian tweeted that Chuck LaBella, a former *Apprentice* producer, had dirt on Trump from a beauty pageant in Russia. Cohen referred LaBella to Keith Davidson, who threatened to sue Arnold. Now Arnold was film-ing in New York and had decided to stay at the Regency because he knew that Cohen was living there. He finally spotted Cohen on a Thursday night, while sitting in the lobby with a *Rolling Stone* reporter who'd been trailing him. "He's literally fucking there," Arnold said.

The reporter, Brian Hiatt, took a picture of them together, and Ar-nold tweeted it with the caption "I love New York." Cohen retweeted the picture without comment. When reporters called Cohen, he re-ferred them to Arnold, who got back to an NBC reporter late that night. "I say to Michael, 'Guess what? We're taking Trump down to-gether, and he's so tired he's like, 'OK,' and his wife is like, 'OK, fuck Trump,'" Arnold told NBC, even though Cohen's wife hadn't been present. He said, "This dude has all the tapes. This dude has every-thing."

Trump did take notice, and told Giuliani to find out what was hap-pening. Frantic, Cohen called Arnold, pleading with him to fix the problems he'd caused with the White House. Giuliani reached out to Bob Costello, asking him whether Cohen was upset about Trump's camp quibbling over his legal fees. But Costello no longer had Cohen's ear. The next day, Arnold mollified Cohen by tweeting a retraction:

Michael Cohen didn't say Me & him were teaming up to take down Donald Trump! Michael has enough Trump on his plate. I'm the crazy person who said Me & Michael Cohen were teaming up to take down Trump of course. I meant it.

But in ensuing cable news interviews, Arnold pivoted again, saying he and Cohen had met six times already. "Did he say anything that made you think he was going to cooperate with prosecutors?" Nicolle Wallace asked him on MSNBC.

"He knows that Donald Trump—Donald Trump does not care about him," Arnold told her. "Michael Cohen is going to take care of his family and his country first. That's all you need to know." On CNN with Poppy Harlow, Arnold looked straight into the camera and said, "Donald Trump, Ivanka Trump, I am spending the weekend hanging out with Michael Cohen, and there's a lot going on." When Harlow pressed him on whether Cohen had said he would flip if charged, Arnold sat silent for twenty-five seconds on national television before declining to answer.

"Well that was horrible," he texted Cohen after the CNN hit.

"Tom," Cohen replied. "This has gone from being a cordial selfie to something completely inappropriate and untruthful. It is absurd that you would say on national tv that we are hanging out this weekend when that's simply untrue. And, we have not met 6 times, I have never discussed tapes and am not participating on your upcoming show. I am asking you politely to stop talking about me. And, you're right . . . the segment was horrible because you flat out lied."

After twenty-four hours, Cohen finally tweeted a denial.

Appreciate @TomArnold kind words about me as a great father, husband and friend. This was a chance, public encounter in the hotel lobby where he asked for a selfie. Not spending the weekend together, did not discuss being on his show nor did we discuss @ POTUS. #done #ridiculous

Tom Arnold would not be Michael Cohen's chosen vehicle for making his break with Trump real and irreversible, but that move would come in short order. By now, Cohen had concluded that Trump wasn't coming to his rescue with a pardon. He was in this fight on his own. He tweeted a picture of himself on Sunday night, July 1, sitting with ABC's George Stephanopoulos. "My silence is broken!" Cohen wrote. He declined to be interviewed on camera, but he let Stephanopoulos ask him questions and quote him on the record. On *Good Morning America* the next day, Stephanopoulos reported that Cohen had told him, "My wife, my daughter, and my son have my first loyalty and always will." Cohen said he would end his joint defense agreement with Trump, a pact that allowed their lawyers to share information and coordinate in their common interests.

"I will not be a punching bag as part of anyone's defense strategy . . . I am not a villain of this story, and I will not allow others to try to depict me that way."

28.

SO SAD!

■ ■ ■

NEARLY FOUR MILLION pieces of evidence seized from Cohen were reviewed throughout the summer by Barbara Jones, the special master appointed by Judge Wood. Only a tiny fraction, a few thousand in all, were designated by Jones as attorney-client privileged or too personal to release to the government.

Trump's lawyers had waived privilege on twelve audio files that Cohen made surreptitiously, thinking that they were good for the president. Those files included Cohen telling people that he'd done the Daniels deal on his own. One, however, was the recording Cohen had made of him and Trump talking in the fall of 2016, discussing how they could buy the rights to Karen McDougal's story from David Pecker.

After *The New York Times* reported the existence of that recording, Trump tweeted, "Inconceivable that the government would break into a lawyer's office (early in the morning)—almost unheard of. Even more inconceivable that a lawyer would tape a client—totally unheard of & perhaps illegal. The good news is that your favorite President did nothing wrong!"

Early the next week, Cohen, who had recently hired Democratic operative and former Clinton hand Lanny Davis as a communications adviser, released the Trump recording to CNN's Chris Cuomo. "It is a big night here," Cuomo said, leading off the broadcast. "We have one of the Michael Cohen tapes."

Before its release, Giuliani told reporters that Trump could be heard on the recording telling Cohen to make a payment by check, demonstrating his desire for transparency. But when it aired, Trump sounded as if he was suggesting a cash payment. Only after Cohen replied, "No, no, no," did Trump ask, "Check?" This seemed to be the opposite of what Giuliani had said. It was Cohen, not Trump, who apparently rejected a cash payment.

On the recording, Cohen also told Trump that he had discussed the transaction with the Trump Organization's chief financial officer, Allen Weisselberg, dragging another long and loyal Trump employee into the scandal.

Trump tweeted again about the tape a few days later. "What kind of a lawyer would tape a client? So sad! Is this a first, never heard of it before? Why was the tape so abruptly terminated (cut) while I was presumably saying positive things? I hear there are other clients and many reporters that are taped—can this be so? Too bad!"

A day after Cuomo aired the Trump tape, the *Journal* revealed that Cohen had secretly taped Cuomo, too, for more than two hours, earlier in the year. The revelations of Cohen's surreptitious recordings further alienated him from the circle he'd developed working for Trump. Fox's Sean Hannity sent notes to let Cohen know he was praying for him and his family. But, wary of being recorded, Hannity stopped talking to Cohen on the phone. Hannity also advised Jerry and Becki Falwell, his mutual friends with Cohen, that they could be a source of spiritual support for Cohen, but that they should know he might be recording if they spoke by phone. The Falwells decided for the moment to keep their distance.

No matter what his past and present friends thought, Cohen's camp remained on the offensive. Lanny Davis piqued Trump with a planted story about Trump's knowledge of a June 2016 Trump Tower meeting in which a Russian lawyer promising dirt on Clinton met with Donald Trump Jr., Jared Kushner, and Paul Manafort. Trump had said publicly that he didn't know about the meeting, but Davis confidentially told reporters that Cohen would testify to the special counsel that Trump absolutely did know. Cohen and Davis would later disavow that Cohen had any such knowledge, but in the meantime, Trump criticized Cohen for "trying to make up stories in order to get himself out of an unrelated jam." Behind the scenes, Trump's legal team warned Cohen about violating attorney-client privilege.

In reality, though Davis didn't disclose it, Cohen's information about the Trump Tower meeting was limited to his recollection of Donald

Trump Jr. walking into Trump's office in early June 2016 and going behind the desk to speak to his father. Cohen remembered the young Trump leaning over and saying, in a hushed voice, "The meeting is all set," to which he heard Trump respond, "Okay, good. Let me know."

AT THE SOUTHERN District, prosecutors on the Cohen investigation rebuffed Guy Petrillo's early attempts to meet with them. From the search warrant documents, Petrillo had an inkling of what the government was investigating, but he didn't understand the full scope of the probe. He wanted to come in to learn more about their focus—and, where possible, to try to dissuade them from bringing charges. The prosecutors in New York were still reviewing and absorbing the material. And they didn't want to give Cohen and his lawyer a chance to shape a story to fit the evidence by divulging what crimes they thought had been committed. "You ought to know," they told Petrillo.

The office was willing to entertain a meeting if Petrillo was willing to bring Cohen in to meet with prosecutors for serious discussions about him cooperating with their investigation. That would have entailed admitting to the crimes they'd discovered and disclosing any others they didn't know about. But Petrillo wasn't about to blindly subject Cohen to an open-ended meeting with prosecutors and the FBI without any idea where the conversation was going.

So prosecutors focused on building a case against him without his help. That included giving immunity to both David Pecker and Allen Weisselberg. Pecker had provided valuable information in a series of interviews with prosecutors throughout the summer. His defense lawyer wanted protection of a type known as statutory or formal immunity, which must be ordered by a judge, rather than informal immunity, which is granted by agreement with prosecutors. This way, Pecker would be able to say that he had been forced to testify.

Before they'd agree to make the application to a judge, prosecutors needed to know what information Pecker had to share. His lawyer, Elkan Abramowitz, conveyed the answers to the questions they had posed for Pecker. Then Pecker met in person several times with the four prosecutors and FBI agents.

He told them about meeting with Trump in August 2015 and promising to identify and stop stories about women, and about his conversations with the candidate and Cohen about the McDougal deal, and the appreciation Trump had shown him for taking care of it. Pecker was a credible witness linking the president directly to a scheme to violate campaign-finance law.

Weisselberg, the Trump CFO, testified about the Stormy Daniels deal and the phony plan to reimburse Cohen by characterizing the payments as legal fees. He said he didn't know about the hush-money deal until after it was done, and his testimony didn't implicate the president, either. According to Weisselberg, he had agreed to the reimbursement without asking too many questions, because he knew that Cohen handled personal matters for the boss and his family.

The prosecutors cut a wide swath through Cohen's orbit. They had two sit-down meetings with Keith Davidson. They sent a subpoena to Cohen's former accountant, Jeffrey Getzel, obtained records from banks Cohen borrowed from, interviewed John Gauger of RedFinch, and spoke to the "Taxi King," Evgeny Freidman, Cohen's partner in the medallion business, who was cooperating after pleading guilty to defrauding New York State in a tax case.

The Southern District also delved into Trump's inner circle. Hope Hicks, Trump's campaign spokeswoman and then White House communications director, was asked what she had discussed with David Pecker when she called him following our inquiries about the McDougal deal. She recounted to the government that Pecker had told her American Media was providing comment to the *Journal,* and he shared the substance of the response—that McDougal had a contract to provide editorial content—in advance of sending it to us. The Southern District asked Keith Schiller, the security chief at Trump's company who became director of Oval Office operations, about calls he'd received from Pecker, and whether Schiller had just been passing the phone to Trump.

COHEN'S LAWYER GUY Petrillo had secured a meeting for him with investigators for Mueller on August 7, to see what help he might be able to offer them. Even as he professed a willingness to cooperate, when the special counsel's office asked Cohen about the Trump Tower Moscow deal, he repeated the lies he'd been telling for a year, minimizing the duration of the discussions and his interactions with Russian officials, among other things. Petrillo, unaware that Cohen was lying, thought the meeting had gone well.

He'd started to worry that the Southern District, which knew of the Mueller meeting, still hadn't engaged. Were they just going to indict Cohen, Petrillo wondered, without ever giving him a chance to negotiate on his client's behalf? So he asked again to come in, submitting his request to the office in writing on Thursday, August 16. This time, the Southern District granted his wish.

Petrillo and his partner Amy Lester went to 1 St. Andrew's Plaza on the following Friday afternoon for a meeting in the Southern District's library with the office's top brass and the line prosecutors investigating Cohen. The defense lawyers aimed their presentation at Robert Khuzami, the deputy U.S. attorney presiding over the probe. Khuzami was joined by Audrey Strauss, chief counsel to the U.S. attorney. Russell Capone had been elevated from deputy chief of the public corruption unit after Tatiana Martins left the office in July. He was there with his new lieutenant, Edward Diskant.

By now, Southern District prosecutors had combed through Cohen's bank records, his tax filings, loan applications, emails and text messages relating to his taxi business, his private real estate deals, his consulting agreements, and his work for Trump—including the deals with Daniels and McDougal.

The office had already started drafting a lengthy indictment detailing campaign-finance violations for the Daniels and McDougal deals, tax evasion related to income Cohen had failed to report on loans he'd made and consulting he'd done, and bank fraud in connection with allegedly deceiving a lender on his taxi medallion debt while trying to refinance.

Petrillo and Lester were still operating without the full picture, but for an hour and a half the lawyers tried to debunk some of the prosecution's theories, as they understood them. Petrillo had gathered that they were considering bank fraud charges. He told prosecutors that some of the bankers involved with the taxi medallion loans had credibility issues, which would weaken a fraud case if the government tried to make one. He put forward arguments to counter the idea that Cohen committed criminal tax evasion. As to the hush-money payments, Petrillo suggested the government might lose a campaign-finance case at trial, based on the failed prosecution of the John Edwards case.

Summing up, Petrillo asked the government to consider not bringing charges, or at least giving him more time.

But when Petrillo followed up with an email, he was told his requests wouldn't be granted. The prosecutors planned to seek a grand jury indictment against Cohen the following week.

Cohen went into Petrillo's midtown Manhattan office on Saturday, August 18, and discussions unfolded over the next three days.

Cohen decided against seeking a formal cooperation agreement, eliminating his best chance at receiving a short sentence or avoiding prison entirely. Prosecutors can petition judges to give defendants a reduced punishment for providing useful information to the government in ongoing investigations, but defendants have to cooperate fully to get credit. In the Southern District, that means they have to bare their souls—to divulge any crimes they know about or have committed. Have they ever stolen cable television? Been arrested for shoplifting as a teenager? These are questions prosecutors sometimes ask to acquaint suspects with the meaning of full cooperation.

Cohen refused to go through the exercise. According to his lawyer, Cohen held back out of a desire to expedite his case, but prosecutors suspected he wanted to avoid divulging more potential crimes. Cohen also feared that a cooperation agreement would hinder his ability to write a book or otherwise sell the story of his life as Trump's fixer. In the past, the Justice Department had required some high-profile defendants to forfeit any profits they might receive from movies, screenplays, and memoirs that delved into their crimes, as a condition of their plea deal.

Without a cooperation agreement, Cohen could still plead guilty and provide whatever information he was willing to give the feds in New York, to Mueller's team, and to state agencies investigating Trump and others. That would be a middle ground, still likely to result in a lighter sentence than if Cohen were convicted at a trial.

One of Cohen's major concerns was his wife. The prosecutors had uncovered evidence that tied Laura Cohen to the transactions they were investigating. She had filed joint tax returns with him that had left out millions of dollars in income, and her name was on an account that received some of that unreported income, as well as on the home equity line of credit application he'd submitted to First Republic Bank without fully disclosing his debt. While the government hadn't threatened to charge her, she was extremely upset at the prospect of losing many of her assets. If Cohen was charged with bank fraud, the government could force him to forfeit the money in their joint accounts.

When the government sent Petrillo its plea offer on the evening of Monday, August 20, bank fraud wasn't among the charges it wanted Cohen to accept. The decision was taken as a victory for Cohen and his legal team, and a huge relief for his wife. In lieu of bank fraud, which would have involved a much broader set of facts and been harder to prove had Cohen gone to trial, the government inserted a simpler charge. He would have to plead guilty to making false statements to a bank in the application for the home equity line of credit he'd used to pay Daniels.

Petrillo tried but failed to convince the prosecutors that the tax evasion charges could be handled with civil penalties. The Southern District was moving too quickly—prosecutors had to bring the case well before the midterms—to allow Petrillo time to appeal to tax division prosecutors at Main Justice in Washington. (They had, however, already been looped into the case by the Southern District and seemingly went along with New York's approach.)

The plea would be to an eight-count criminal information, the formal name for the charging document. At twenty-two pages, it was much shorter than the indictment would have otherwise been, and included the two campaign-finance violations that Cohen had committed on behalf of "Individual-1," as prosecutors referred to Trump.

The document described how, in August 2015, "Chairman-1" (David Pecker), who led "Corporation-1" (American Media), which published "Magazine-1" (the *National Enquirer*), offered to coordinate with Cohen to deal with negative stories that might come up about Trump. That led to the deal involving "Woman-1" (Karen McDougal), which "Attorney-1" (Keith Davidson) negotiated with "Editor-1" (Dylan Howard), and after which Pecker and Cohen discussed the ultimately abandoned effort to reimburse American Media. The prosecutors went on to detail the negotiations over Cohen's deal to pay "Woman-2" (Stormy Daniels) and to arrange reimbursement with "Executive-1" (Allen Weisselberg) under the guise of legal fees for services Cohen hadn't actually performed. Cohen was also reimbursed $50,000 for technology services he had claimed, referring to the poll rigging he'd hired John Gauger and RedFinch Solutions to perform. He hadn't mentioned that he'd paid Gauger only a fraction of that, in cash.

That wasn't all. Cohen would also have to plead guilty to five counts of tax evasion from 2012 to 2016. Prosecutors found he'd failed to pay taxes on $3.7 million he made loaning money to taxi operators, $100,000 for brokering a real estate transaction in Florida for a member of Qatar's royal family, a $30,000 fee for arranging the sale of a Birkin bag by Hermès, and $200,000 in consulting income from a New Jersey assisted living company. (That was the company run by Daniel Straus, who had paid Cohen to improve Straus's Web profile.)

Cohen's team thought the tax charges could have been rolled up into a single count, but the government wanted separate counts for different components of its investigation. It wasn't consequential for either side, but a matter of optics, and the government got its way.

Cohen, however, had trouble getting to yes. The felony plea would automatically cost him his law license. And he continued to privately deny that he'd evaded taxes, blaming his accountant for failing to report income that had been on his bank statements. Prosecutors gave him until Tuesday, August 21, to decide whether to accept the deal. Cohen labored over the decision through that Monday night. He knew that the agreement allowed him to plead to a reduced set of charges— and a possible reduced prison sentence—from what he'd face if indicted. If he rejected the plea, he'd likely have been indicted by Thursday. And if he was charged with bank fraud, his assets—and his wife's—would be in jeopardy. So he decided to take the deal.

Later that afternoon, Cohen walked into the U.S. District Court in Manhattan, past a media swarm, in a dark suit and a gold tie, to admit to violating federal campaign-finance law in connection with the payments to both Daniels and McDougal. Peppered with questions by Senior U.S. District Judge William H. Pauley III, Cohen seemed calm. He said he'd not taken any drugs or medication, except for having a glass of Glenlivet 12 on the rocks the night before. He understood what he was doing.

The plea appeared pro forma, until the judge told him to describe the crime in his own words. Prosecutors had demanded that Cohen accept responsibility for the campaign-finance charges and his other crimes. Cohen wanted to go much further. He stood up in open court to implicate the man he had once idolized, the one for whom he had sworn to take a bullet. He didn't use Trump's name, but in the packed courtroom, in an overflow room of the courthouse where the hearing was televised, and on Twitter, where his statement was broadcast as it was made, jaws dropped as Cohen admitted that "a candidate for federal office"—clearly referring to the president of the United States—had instructed him to commit two federal crimes.

> On or about the summer of 2016, in coordination with, and at the direction of, a candidate for federal office, I and the CEO of a media company at the request of the candidate worked together to keep an individual with information that would be harmful to the candidate and to the campaign from publicly disclosing this information. After a number of discussions, we eventually accomplished the goal by the media company entering into a contract with the individual under which she received compensation of $150,000. I participated in this conduct, which on my part took place in Manhattan, for the principal purpose of influencing the election.
>
> Your Honor, as to Count No. Eight, on or about October of 2016, in coordination with, and at the direction of, the same candidate, I arranged to make a payment to a second individual with information that would be harmful to the candidate and to the campaign to keep the individual from disclosing the information. To accomplish this, I used a company that was under my control to make a payment in the sum of $130,000. The monies I advanced through my company were later repaid to me by the candidate. I participated in this conduct, which on my part took place in Manhattan, for the principal purpose of influencing the election.

Cohen's shocking performance reverberated in the courtroom and beyond, coming within hours of the criminal conviction of Trump's former campaign chief Paul Manafort on fraud and money-laundering charges. Now Cohen was on a campaign to save himself—he would cooperate with any government agency he could in order to spare himself prison time. In a statement, Lanny Davis said Cohen had "stood up and testified under oath that Donald Trump directed him to commit a crime by making payments to two women for the principal purpose of influencing an election." He added, "If those payments were a crime for Michael Cohen, then why wouldn't they be a crime for Donald Trump?"

Davis later said that Cohen would be "more than happy" to tell Mueller "all that he knows about the obvious possibility of a conspiracy to collude and corrupt the American democracy system in the 2016 election."

Cohen had been depressed for weeks. But after the plea, his spirits lifted. Overnight, his stock rose among Democrats and Never Trump Republicans, who saw his guilty plea and implication of Donald Trump in federal crimes as an act of redemption. He was deluged with emails and letters of support. The Southern District was no longer on his heels, and he was having productive talks with special counsel Robert Mueller's team, helping prosecutors with one of the highest-profile investigations in generations. That had to be worth something. Maybe Cohen would have to serve a short prison sentence, but he could see a life beyond this mess and beyond Donald Trump.

INDIVIDUAL-1 TOOK TO Twitter on the morning after the plea. "If anyone is looking for a good lawyer, I would strongly suggest that you don't retain the services of Michael Cohen!" Trump wrote. In a second message thirty-seven minutes later, he compared Cohen with the other former adviser who'd been convicted the day before.

> I feel very badly for Paul Manafort and his wonderful family. "Justice" took a 12 year old tax case, among other things, applied tremendous pressure on him and, unlike Michael Cohen, he refused to "break"—make up stories in order to get a "deal." Such respect for a brave man!

Trump separately told Fox News that he had become aware of the hush-money payments "later on" and had immediately inquired whether they'd come from his campaign coffers, "because that could be a little dicey." While Giuliani said the Cohen charges didn't allege that Trump broke the law, Lanny Davis on CBS called for the president to be "indicted and jailed." On NBC, Davis declared that Cohen would never accept a pardon from Trump—as if he hadn't already privately sought one or now had any chance of receiving one.

Just as Michael Avenatti had done for Stormy Daniels, Davis announced that he had launched a crowdfunding page for his client with a $500,000 goal. "The Michael Cohen Truth Fund is a transparent trust account, with all donations going to help Michael Cohen and his family as he goes forward to tell the truth about Donald Trump," it said.

Cohen was subpoenaed the day after his plea by investigators for the New York State Department of Taxation and Finance, in a probe of Trump's foundation.

With polls showing Democrats likely to take control of the House of Representatives in the upcoming midterm elections, the Cohen and Manafort convictions spurred talk of impeachment, which Trump dismissed, predicting on Fox that removing him from office would cause the stock market to crash. Trump, whose approval ratings held steady in the days after Cohen's plea, also told the network that "flipping" on someone else—as in *him*—to get a lighter sentence "almost ought to be illegal."

As THE CALLS for him to talk about Daniels on cable had waned in recent months, Avenatti seized on other high-profile issues. He announced he was representing mothers and children as a result of Trump's family separation policy. Then, in August, Avenatti showed up in Iowa, where the first caucuses would be held eighteen months later, to tour the state fair and declare that he was exploring a run for the presidency. He drew raves at the Democratic Wing Ding fundraiser. "When they go low, I say we hit harder," he said, turning Michelle Obama's call for civility on its head. "I think the party has yearned for a fighter—a fighter for good, if you will—for a significant period of time," Avenatti told *The Des Moines Register*. "And for many, I'm probably seen as that individual."

Soon Avenatti jumped into the battle over the confirmation of Brett Kavanaugh, Trump's nominee to replace retiring Supreme Court justice Anthony Kennedy. As the Senate investigated allegations from Christine Blasey Ford, a psychology professor who said Kavanaugh and another boy had assaulted her in high school, and from a second woman, Deborah Ramirez, Avenatti came forward with a sworn statement from a third woman, Julie Swetnick. Swetnick's statement alleged that she saw Kavanaugh and his friend at high school parties, drinking excessively, assaulting girls, attempting to spike their punch, and trying to "cause girls to become inebriated and disoriented so they could then be 'gang raped' in a side room or bedroom by a 'train' of numerous boys." Kavanaugh, who denied all the allegations against him, said through a White House statement that Swetnick's story was "from the Twilight Zone."

In an interview with NBC News, Swetnick didn't back away from her accusations, but she gave inconsistent statements and acknowledged that she hadn't witnessed Kavanaugh spike punch or rape anyone. A second woman whose statement Avenatti released to back up Swetnick's story, and whom he connected with journalists, told NBC that—contrary to the statement Avenatti put forward—she hadn't seen Kavanaugh act inappropriately toward girls.

Kavanaugh was confirmed. Senate Judiciary Chairman Chuck Grassley of Iowa referred Swetnick and Avenatti to the Justice Department for criminal investigation. Avenatti said he welcomed the investigation.

IN DISCUSSIONS WITH the Southern District, Cohen gave prosecutors a very different version of events surrounding the Stormy Daniels deal than they'd received from Weisselberg, the Trump CFO. Cohen said that Trump and Weisselberg had been intimately involved in the plan to pay Daniels. He said he'd delayed paying her in October 2016 as the three of them tried to figure out how to get the money to the porn star without it being traceable to Trump. After discussing it in Trump's office, Cohen said, he and Weisselberg had gone to Weisselberg's office. Cohen didn't want to put up the money, so he asked Weisselberg to do it, but the CFO said he couldn't. Weisselberg asked if Cohen knew anyone who wanted to throw a party or join one of Trump's golf clubs. They could pay Cohen personally, and the money could then be used to pay Daniels without ever hitting the company's books. Weisselberg and Cohen had been unable to work anything out before Cohen, under pressure, made the payment himself.

Cohen's narrative directly implicated Weisselberg and Trump in the campaign-finance scheme as it unfolded, but Trump's longtime CFO had disavowed prior knowledge of the deal in his grand jury testimony. Prosecutors had only Cohen's word that Weisselberg had been untruthful, and given that Cohen had lied time and again, prosecutors couldn't hang a case on his word alone.

On Tuesday, November 7, Democrats took control of the House of Representatives as predicted, while Republicans kept the Senate. Representative Nancy Pelosi of California, set to return to her past role as House Speaker, quickly warned against expectations that she'd pursue an impeachment of Trump, unless there was a bipartisan will to do so. But Democrats readied their subpoena pens as they prepared to investigate the president.

Atop their priority list, following in Mueller's steps, the Democrats wanted to know more about whether Trump's aides had coordinated with Russia during the election. Those in the most powerful posts, such as Representative Elijah Cummings of Maryland, who was taking over the House Oversight and Government Reform Committee, turned their attention to Michael Cohen as well. Representative Jerrold Nadler of New York, who was to become chairman of the House Judiciary Committee, where any proceeding to remove the president would begin, told CNN that, notwithstanding Pelosi's warning, if Trump were involved in campaign-finance felonies, "that might very well be an impeachable offense."

Cohen, ready and willing to speak to anyone who might be able to influence his sentencing, had recently changed his voter registration, becoming again what he'd been before Trump was elected president: a Democrat.

29.

THE SENTENCE

■ ■ ■

MICHAEL COHEN SEEMED to be in good spirits, considering. He sat in a thirteenth-floor courtroom in the Thurgood Marshall Federal Courthouse, in Manhattan, on November 29, 2018, chatting amiably with his lawyers as they and a roomful of reporters and onlookers waited for U.S. District Judge Andrew L. Carter to take the bench.

Anyone closely following Cohen's prosecution by the U.S. Attorney's Office for the Southern District of New York would have noticed that the government attorneys at the table across from Cohen's were not the same prosecutors who had charged him in connection with hush-money payments to Karen McDougal and Stormy Daniels. The three attorneys—Rush Atkinson, Jeannie Rhee and Andrew Goldstein— were members of special counsel Robert Mueller's team. Cohen had been feeding Mueller information for months in secret, spending more than seventy hours over seven meetings with the special counsel's team, hoping that his contribution would earn him leniency at his sentencing, now only two weeks away.

But first he had to admit that he'd lied to Congress.

Cohen's written statement to the House and Senate intelligence committees the previous year had contained several false claims. He had told lawmakers that he abandoned the Trump Tower Moscow project in January 2016, when in fact he continued pursuing it into June of that year. Cohen had said his discussions with Trump and others in the Trump Organization about the project had been limited, when in fact they had been extensive. And he'd told Congress that he and Trump never talked about making a trip to Russia to seal the deal, when in fact they had. He'd repeated these lies in August 2018, when he met with the special counsel's office for the first time at the request of his own lawyers.

Mueller's team was prepared to accept Cohen's help with its investigation and put in a good word with his sentencing judge in return for truthful, useful information. But prosecutors and agents in the special counsel's office knew that he had misrepresented his work on Trump Tower Moscow. The previous year, they'd interviewed Felix Sater, the Russian American real estate developer who partnered with Cohen on the unsuccessful project. Sater had electronic communications with Cohen that showed that his conversations with the fixer about the project had extended well beyond January 2016. Cohen finally had copped to lying in his second meeting with Mueller's team in September, after he'd pleaded guilty to tax, bank, and campaign-finance crimes in the Southern District case.

Now Cohen had to wipe the slate clean and confess in federal court to one count of making a false statement to Congress—otherwise, how could Mueller credit anything Cohen told him in the special counsel's investigation and forthcoming report on Russian interference in the 2016 election?

Judge Carter read the charge against Cohen aloud in court and apprised him of his rights.

"How do you plead to the sole count of the information—"

Cohen inadvertently cut him off. "Guilty, Your Honor."

Carter asked Cohen to describe his unlawful conduct in his own words. Reporters leaned forward in their seats, wondering whether Cohen would again implicate the president in a federal crime. Had Trump or his aides directed Cohen to lie to Congress?

From his chair at the defense table, Cohen read from a prepared statement.

As I had in the years before the election, I continued in 2017 to follow the day-to-day political messaging that both Individual 1 and his staff and advisers repeatedly broadcast, and I stayed in close contact with these advisers to Individual 1. As such, I was aware of Individual 1's repeated disavowals of commercial and political ties between himself and Russia, his repeated statements that investigations of such ties were politically motivated and without evidence, and that any contact with Russian nationals by Individual

1's campaign or the Trump Organization had all terminated before the Iowa Caucus, which was on February 1 of 2016.

Cohen then enumerated the false claims he made to Congress, concluding, "I made these misstatements to be consistent with Individual 1's political messaging and out of loyalty to Individual 1." Cohen stopped short of saying that Trump had directed him to lie, unlike in the hush-money case, when he had told the court, unequivocally, that he'd made and coordinated the payments to Stormy Daniels and Karen McDougal at the behest of his former boss.

Now Cohen had pleaded guilty to a total of nine federal criminal counts. Still, he looked cheerful as he left the courthouse. He fully expected his mea culpa and cooperation with Mueller to translate into a vastly reduced punishment for his other crimes.

FEDERAL PROBATION OFFICERS pegged Cohen's potential prison sentence at four to five years, based on federal sentencing guidelines, but Senior U.S. District Judge William H. Pauley III had the final say; he could deviate upward or downward from the guideline ranges as he saw fit. (The special counsel's case against Cohen for lying to Congress had been consolidated in Pauley's court with the New York campaign-finance case.) Pauley, an appointee of President Bill Clinton, suffered no fools. While he had shown mercy to disadvantaged defendants, he took exception to privileged defendants who abused positions of influence. The challenge for those facing sentencing in Pauley's or any other court was convincing judges they deserved a below-guideline punishment without seeming to minimize the crimes they had committed. The strongest sentencing memorandums, the briefs filed ahead of the day of reckoning, make convincing legal arguments for leniency and portray defendants in the best possible light, underscoring their cooperation with authorities (if applicable), remorse, and lifetime of otherwise good deeds.

Michael Cohen's attorney Guy Petrillo filed his sentencing memo in the federal trial court in Manhattan on November 30. It began with a recitation of Cohen's assistance in various federal and state investigations: Cohen had sat for seven interviews with Mueller's team; he met twice with prosecutors in the U.S. Attorney's Office for the Southern

District of New York, as part of the hush-money investigation; he met with representatives of the New York State attorney general, whose office alleged in a lawsuit that Trump's charitable foundation had acted as an illegal appendage of his 2016 campaign; and Cohen met with the New York State Department of Taxation and Finance, which was investigating his taxes, as well as the Donald J. Trump Foundation.

Among the investigators, the U.S. attorney's office in Manhattan carried the most weight over Cohen's case. After all, the Southern District accounted for eight of the nine criminal counts to which Cohen pleaded guilty. But Cohen had pointedly declined to enter into a formal cooperation agreement with SDNY; as a result, there was little chance the New York prosecutors would ask Pauley to give Cohen a big break. Cohen had to hope that his assistance to Mueller would make up for the credit he lost by skipping confession with the Southern District. Petrillo tried to convince Pauley that the lack of a formal cooperation agreement in no way signaled that Cohen wanted to keep information from federal prosecutors.

"Arising out of Michael's concern that his entry into a traditional cooperation agreement would likely delay his sentencing, as investigations and trials unfold and conclude, he respectfully declined to pursue conventional cooperation so that his sentencing proceeding would go forward as scheduled," Petrillo wrote. "This personal decision does not signal any intention on Michael's part to withhold information or his availability to respond to additional inquiry."

To the contrary, he said, Cohen intended to cooperate further, but he needed to get on with his life. His professional and commercial relationships had vanished, and Cohen, now fifty-two, could scarcely begin to rebuild until the case was behind him. Petrillo wanted the judge to focus on Cohen's cooperation with special counsel Robert Mueller, whose investigation was under unremitting assault by the president.

"In the context of this raw, full-bore attack by the most powerful person in the United States, Michael, formerly a confidante [*sic*] and adviser to Mr. Trump, resolved to cooperate, and voluntarily took the first steps toward doing so even before he was charged in this District," the memo said, referring to Cohen's August meeting with Mueller. "He took these steps, moreover, despite regular public reports referring to the President's consideration of pardons and pre-pardons in the SCO's investigation."

Petrillo was unaware that Cohen had sought a pardon through his former lawyer, Stephen Ryan at McDermott Will & Emery.

The sentencing memo described Cohen as "utterly devoted to his family," including his retired parents, with whom he spoke almost daily. His two children were his heart and soul. Cohen and his wife, the brief said, rarely spent time apart. He was a prodigious fundraiser for good causes, including Columbia Grammar & Preparatory School, and Operation Smile, an organization that aided children in need of surgery. He devoted time to charity work for St. Jude's Children's Research Hospital. And he put his fixer skills to work for his friends and acquaintances, helping them make connections to advance their careers, dispensing business advice, and even arranging for medical care, Petrillo wrote.

Petrillo went on to argue that Cohen's tax crimes were "exceptionally *un*sophisticated," compared with other criminal tax cases. Cohen had failed to report more than $4 million in income, but he made no serious effort to hide the money. It flowed into his bank accounts, the statements for which he provided his accountant. He hadn't tried to obstruct any IRS investigation. Many cases like Cohen's resulted in civil penalties, with no criminal charges, his attorney said. Floyd Mayweather Jr., the boxer, owed millions in back taxes, but the government allowed him to write checks instead of charging him. Country music legend Willie Nelson was once indebted to the IRS for about $17 million; he settled with the government and was never prosecuted.

(One example Petrillo did *not* cite was Trump's first fixer, Roy Cohn, who had been pursued by the Internal Revenue Service for a quarter century but never faced criminal tax charges. Cohn paid little or no income taxes. His law firm, Saxe, Bacon & Bolan, paid his expenses, and everything he used was owned by the firm, by corporations, or by his friends. He accepted gifts in lieu of payment, including a Jaguar convertible from his friend the *National Enquirer* owner Gene Pope, and a diamond-encrusted watch from Trump that was possibly a knockoff. Cohn called the IRS "inept and clownish" when, four months before he died, in 1986, he and his associates were sued in civil court by the U.S. attorney for the Southern District—one Rudy Giuliani—for $7 million in back taxes.)

As for Michael Cohen's false statements to First Republic Bank, Petrillo argued that his client's omission of liabilities from his application for a home equity line resulted in no loss to the bank. (Cohen re-paid what he'd drawn.) Finally, his involvement in the hush-money deals compared favorably with other election-related cases prosecuted in the Southern District. Cohen felt obligated to help Trump quash "narratives that would adversely affect the Campaign *and* cause per-sonal embarrassment to [Trump] and his family," his lawyer wrote.

"In this sense, Michael's conduct was different in kind from recent campaign finance charges brought before this Court, in which the charged individuals used straw donors to make illegal campaign con-tributions."

Taken together, the circumstances warranted a sentence that car-ried no prison time, the brief concluded.

Trump, in keeping with his campaign to diminish Cohen, advo-cated for something harsher.

"You mean he can do all of the TERRIBLE, unrelated to Trump, things having to do with fraud, big loans, Taxis, etc., and not serve a long prison term?" Trump wrote on Twitter. "He makes up stories to get a GREAT & ALREADY reduced deal for himself, and get . . . his wife and father-in-law (who has the money?) off Scott Free. He lied for this outcome and should, in my opinion, serve a full and complete sen-tence."

COHEN'S KEY CONSTITUENCY was Judge Pauley, who controlled his fate. But he wasn't the only one Cohen had to worry about. Judges generally place considerable weight on the recommendations of fed-eral prosecutors. Defendants need to take care not to provoke their accusers in the sentencing phase. Unfortunately for Cohen, the U.S. attorney's office took great offense at the overall tone of his attorneys' sentencing memo—and responded with a sharpness that surprised us at the *Journal,* as well as veterans of the Southern District.

The Southern District prosecutors wrote in their brief of Decem-ber 7, 2018:

Cohen, an attorney and businessman, committed four distinct federal crimes over a period of several years. He was motivated to do so by personal greed, and repeatedly used his power and influ-ence for deceptive ends. Now he seeks extraordinary leniency—

a sentence of no jail time—based principally on his rose-colored view of the seriousness of the crimes; his claims to a sympathetic personal history; and his provision of certain information to law enforcement. But the crimes committed by Cohen were more serious than his submission allows and were marked by a pattern of deception that permeated his professional life (and was evidently hidden from the friends and family members who wrote on his behalf).

While Cohen's lawyers framed his cooperation with Mueller as a matter of personal resolve, the New York prosecutors reminded the court that Cohen had approached the special counsel only after learning he was under "imminent threat of indictment" in the Southern District.

Cohen repeatedly minimized his tax avoidance, blaming his accountant for failing to spot income Cohen said was apparent in his bank statements. But prosecutors said Cohen had refused to pay his accountant for services beyond the scope of what they'd agreed to, and combing through his bank records for income wasn't one of those services. Even if Cohen had authorized his accountant to do a thorough search, he hadn't provided adequate documentation to allow the accountant to identify the income as such.

But the most important line in the sentencing memo, from our perspective, appeared on page 11, in the Southern District's description of the campaign-finance offenses.

"Cohen coordinated his actions with one or more members of the campaign, including through meetings and phone calls, about the fact, nature, and timing of the payments," prosecutors wrote. "In particular, and as Cohen himself has now admitted, with respect to both payments, he acted in coordination with and at the direction of Individual-1."

The language was a little tortured, but its import was unmistakable. The Southern District had now stated as fact that Individual-1—President Trump—had steered Cohen in the hush-money deals. We had reported as much earlier, in November, and Cohen had used similar language when he pleaded guilty to violating campaign-finance restrictions in August. But prosecutors hadn't ever described Trump's involvement so directly.

The Southern District recommended a modest reduction in sentence for Cohen's assistance in the Mueller investigation but encouraged Judge Pauley to make him serve "substantial" time.

Special counsel Robert Mueller, who filed his sentencing brief in Cohen's case on the same day, came across as the good cop to the Southern District's bad cop. Mueller's team told Judge Pauley that any sentence for Cohen's lying to Congress should run concurrent with his sentence for the other crimes, essentially nullifying the sentence. And the special counsel's office provided a generous account of Cohen's cooperation in its investigation of Russian interference in the 2016 election.

Contradicting Trump's insistence that Cohen was lying to save his skin, Mueller's prosecutors told Judge Pauley that Cohen had provided them with credible information that jibed with evidence they'd obtained from other sources in their investigation. "The defendant has provided, and has committed to continue to provide, relevant and truthful information to the SCO in an effort to assist with the investigation," Mueller's brief said.

Cohen's information had been useful in four respects, the special counsel's office said. He'd described his own contacts with Russian officials during his abortive efforts on Trump Tower Moscow, as well as attempts by other Russians to reach the Trump campaign. He'd provided information, gleaned from his conversations with Trump Organization executives, about "discrete Russia-related matters" core to the special counsel's investigation. Cohen had detailed his contacts with White House officials in 2017 and 2018, helping Mueller's team with its investigation of whether Trump obstructed justice. And he'd offered important information about the preparation of his own statement to Congress, which had been reviewed by Trump's lawyers.

The Southern District's memo seemed to portend a stiff punishment for Cohen at his upcoming sentencing hearing, but Mueller's filing gave him hope. He still expected to be rewarded for his service in the Russia investigation with a minor prison term, maybe a year.

As Cohen's sentencing neared, Trump primed his base to view the Southern District campaign-finance case as a backup plan by Democrats to destroy him, should the Mueller investigation fail to establish a conspiracy between the Trump campaign and Russia.

"So now the Dems go to a simple private transaction, wrongly call it a campaign contribution . . . which it was not (but even if it was, it is only a CIVIL CASE, like Obama's - but it was done correctly by a lawyer and there would not even be a fine. Lawyer's liability if he made a mistake, not me)," Trump tweeted on December 10.

"Cohen just trying to get his sentence reduced. WITCH HUNT!"

BY THE FALL of 2018, cracks had begun to show in Stormy Daniels's relationship with her omnipresent attorney, Michael Avenatti. About a month before Cohen's second guilty plea, a federal judge in California bounced her defamation lawsuit against Trump out of court. The complaint had accused Trump of making a "false factual statement to denigrate and attack Ms. Clifford," referring to Daniels by her legal name. Trump's offending statement had come in a tweet that he typed in response to a sketch artist's rendering of the man Daniels said threatened her in 2011 to stop trying to sell her story about Trump or else. Trump said that the sketch depicted a "nonexistent man" and that Daniels and Avenatti were "playing the Fake News Media for Fools."

U.S. District Judge S. James Otero ruled that Trump was entitled to voice opinions about Daniels, who, he noted, had styled herself as Trump's foe. "If this court were to prevent Mr. Trump from engaging in this type of 'rhetorical hyperbole' against a political adversary, it would significantly hamper the office of the president," Judge Otero wrote in his fourteen-page ruling. "Any strongly-worded response by a president to another politician or public figure could constitute an action for defamation."

Trump celebrated Otero's ruling with an insult on Twitter. "Great, now I can go after Horseface and her 3rd rate lawyer in the Great State of Texas," where Daniels lived, Trump wrote, publicly airing a nickname for Daniels that he'd been using privately for some time.

The dismissal itself had no significant impact on public opinion regarding Daniels or Avenatti, at least among their supporters. Daniels had recently published her book, *Full Disclosure,* with a foreword from Avenatti. The book cast her as a working mom nudged into a hush-money deal that, upon its public disclosure, gave her no choice but to stand on principle and go public as one of the president's chief antagonists. (Daniels also devoted space in the book to a vivid description of Trump's genitalia, gathered during their encounter at Lake Tahoe.)

But losing the case in California meant that Daniels would now owe Trump money. In dismissing her complaint, Judge Otero had granted Trump's anti-SLAPP motion, a vehicle for quickly repelling meritless lawsuits tailored to harass or intimidate. As a result, Daniels had to bear the costs of Trump's defense.

In November, the adult entertainer told the *Daily Beast* that Avenatti had filed the defamation lawsuit against her wishes and that he refused to give her an accounting of his spending from her legal defense fund.

"I have always been an open book with Stormy as to all aspects of her cases and she knows that," Avenatti said in response.

He hadn't received "a dime" in fees, he said. Avenatti tapped the fund for litigation expenses, but most of the money raised online— hundreds of thousands of dollars—had been consumed by Daniels's security costs, according to the attorney.

Daniels and Avenatti reconciled within days. "Pleased that Michael and I have sorted shit out and we know the accounting is on the up and up. We are going to kick ass together on two coasts tomorrow," Daniels tweeted.

During their break-up/make-up routine, Judge Otero had been considering how much Daniels would have to pay Trump in legal fees. On the eve of Cohen's sentencing, Otero issued his order: Daniels owed the president of the United States $292,052, more than twice what he had paid her in hush money.

Avenatti promised to appeal, but if he lost, Daniels was on the hook, and she'd likely have to sue Avenatti for malpractice to avoid having to pay. But by then he had larger concerns.

The previous year, Avenatti's firm had helped a client, inventor Gregory Barela, obtain a $1.9 million settlement in an intellectual property dispute with a company in Boulder, Colorado, that made synthetic turf for athletic fields. Barela had alleged in a 2015 lawsuit that the company, Brock USA, took a system of paving he had developed and claimed it as its own, without listing Barela on the company's patent application. As part of the settlement, Brock agreed to pay $1.6 million to Barela by January 10, 2018, and the remaining $300,000 in three annual installments beginning in 2019. But Barela's copy of the agreement, supplied by Avenatti's firm, incorrectly listed the payment date as March 10, 2018.

By the fall of 2018, Barela hadn't received the $1.6 million. He'd texted and emailed Avenatti for months about the status of the money, but the attorney had brushed him aside, blaming Brock for the delay and promising to sort out the problem. Barela had made investments expecting that money to come through and was in financial straits. Avenatti had been floating him small payments—advances, Avenatti called them—in the meantime, but Barela was tired of Avenatti blowing him off. In November he hired a new lawyer, Steven Bledsoe, who immediately contacted Brock's attorney to figure out why the company hadn't issued the payment in March.

The company's attorney wondered why Barela had a new attorney, and why he was asking about money that Brock had already paid. Not only had Brock fulfilled its obligation—the company had wired the funds in January 2018, as stipulated in the settlement agreement.

Bledsoe was incredulous. He sent a letter to Avenatti on November 17, asking him to state in writing that he hadn't received the initial payment of $1.6 million from the company. If he had received the money, Bledsoe wrote, "we ask that you provide an immediate accounting concerning such funds."

Instead of responding to Bledsoe, Avenatti tried to get Barela on the phone.

"Pls call me," Avenatti wrote in a text that night.

"What is this all about? Pls call me ASAP," he texted again.

Avenatti then called Barela twice and emailed him—a total of five attempts to reach his (now former) client, after largely ignoring Barela for months.

Barela, now aware he'd been duped, forwarded all the messages to his new attorney.

Bledsoe sent another letter two days later, this one signed by Barela, demanding that Avenatti wire the settlement funds and transfer Barela's client file to Bledsoe. Avenatti ignored it.

A third letter from Bledsoe, sent to Avenatti on December 3, explained that Barela was still willing to resolve the "unfortunate situation" without resorting to litigation. When Avenatti again failed to respond, Bledsoe called the FBI and reported the theft of his client's funds. A couple of weeks later, two federal prosecutors from the U.S. Attorney's Office for the Central District of California called him back.

They asked Bledsoe to provide Barela's communications with Avenatti and other documents. Up to that point, the criminal investigation of Avenatti had been focused on taxes. With Barela's information, federal authorities soon began to look into settlements Avenatti had brokered for his clients. Were there any others, like Barela, who hadn't gotten money promised to them?

On December 12, 2018, Cohen sat at a table in Judge Pauley's courtroom with his lawyers, Guy Petrillo and Amy Lester. He wore a white shirt and a periwinkle tie with his navy suit, his graying hair cut short for the occasion. Most of Cohen's family watched from wooden benches in the gallery, a large contingent that included his wife, Laura, and their son, Jake; his parents, Maurice and Sondra; his in-laws, Fima and Ania Shusterman; his brother and sisters; a niece; and a cousin. They were surrounded by attorneys, court staff, reporters, and anyone else who'd managed to secure a seat in the overstuffed courtroom for Cohen's sentencing hearing. Avenatti was among the faces in the crowd.

Addressing the court, Petrillo played his strongest hand at the outset of the hearing. Tall and thin, his hands gripping the podium, the defense lawyer portrayed Cohen's cooperation with special counsel Robert Mueller as an act of bravery that merited special consideration. Cohen had recognized that his assistance to Mueller could "help him in some fashion" in the Southern District investigation, Petrillo acknowledged, but Cohen's decision to cooperate had to account for the risks of crossing a vengeful president. He deserved more credit than the Southern District was giving him, Petrillo told the court.

> He came forward to offer evidence against the most powerful person in our country. He did so not knowing what the result would be, not knowing how the politics would play out, and not knowing whether the Special Counsel would even survive, nor could he anticipate the full measure of attack that has been made against him; not only by the President, who continues to say that people like Mr. Cohen who cooperate with the Special Counsel are weaklings and those who hold fast and clam up are heroes, but also attacks by

partisans and by citizens who happen to be aligned with the President. And those attacks have included threats against him and his family.

Petrillo sounded tired and angry. Mueller's investigation was "of the utmost national significance," no less than Watergate, he continued. Others who stood up to power needed to be able to take courage from Cohen's example. If Cohen were to receive a harsh sentence, what kind of message would that send?

Nicolas Roos, one of the Southern District prosecutors, threw the comment back at Petrillo. He reminded Judge Pauley that Cohen had declined to cooperate fully with federal prosecutors in New York, where he faced the most serious charges. Despite his contribution to Mueller's probe, Cohen "didn't come anywhere close to assisting this office in an investigation," Roos said. What message would it send to other defendants if the court cut him a break? If Cohen got off lightly on the eight counts to which he'd pleaded guilty in the Southern District case, it might dissuade others accused of crimes from helping federal prosecutors.

Now it was Cohen's turn to take the podium. He'd been working on his speech in the days leading up to the sentencing hearing, with his lawyers and his friend David Schwartz. He began to read from a piece of paper:

> I stand before your honor humbly and painfully aware that we are here for one reason: Because of my actions that I pled guilty to on August 21, and as well on November 29. I take full responsibility for each act that I pled guilty to, the personal ones to me and those involving the president of the United States of America.
>
> Viktor Frankl, in his book *Man's Search for Meaning*, he wrote, "There are forces beyond your control that can take away everything you possess except one thing, your freedom to choose how you will respond to the situation."
>
> Your honor, this may seem hard to believe, but today is one of the most meaningful days of my life. The irony is today is the day I am getting my freedom back as you sit at the bench and you contemplate my fate.
>
> I have been living in personal and mental incarceration ever

since the fateful day that I accepted the offer to work for a famous real estate mogul whose business acumen I truly admired. In fact, I now know that there is little to be admired. I want to be clear. I blame myself for the conduct which has brought me here today, and it was my own weakness, and a blind loyalty to this man that led me to choose a path of darkness over light. It is for these reasons I chose to participate in the illicit act of the president rather than to listen to my own inner voice, which should have warned me that the campaign-finance violations that I later pled guilty to were insidious.

Recently, the president tweeted a statement calling me weak, and he was correct, but for a much different reason than he was implying. It was because time and time again I felt it was my duty to cover up his dirty deeds rather than to listen to my own inner voice and my moral compass. My weakness can be characterized as blind loyalty to Donald Trump, and I was weak for not having the strength to question and to refuse his demands. I have already spent years living a personal and mental incarceration, which, no matter what is decided today, owning this mistake will free me to be once more the person I really am.

Your honor, I love my family more than anything in the world. My dad, who is here today; my mom; my in-laws; siblings; love of my life, my wife Laura; my pride and joy, my daughter, Samantha, my son, Jake. There is no sentence that could supersede the suffering that I live with on a daily basis, knowing that my actions have brought undeserved pain and shame on my family. I deserve that pain. They do not.

I also stand before my children, for them to see their father taking responsibility for his mistakes, mistakes that have forced them to bear a shameful spotlight which they have done nothing to deserve, and this breaks my heart. For me, the greatest punishment has been seeing the unbearable pain that my actions and my associations have brought to my entire family. My mom, my dad, this isn't what they deserve to see in their older age, especially when as a child they emphasized to all of us the difference between right and wrong. And I'm sorry.

Cohen had to pause and compose himself as he read. Petrillo slid a packet of tissues onto the right side of the podium. Cohen's daughter,

Samantha, a recent graduate of the University of Pennsylvania, wept from her chair behind the defense table. She'd recently had hip surgery and was using a crutch, preventing her from sitting on the hard wooden benches in the gallery with the rest of Cohen's family. Jake Cohen, a college freshman, brushed away tears with the sleeve of his jacket.

Cohen said he foreswore a formal cooperation agreement to speed the proceedings along, minimizing the pain to his family. "The faster I am sentenced, the sooner I can return to my family, be the father I want to be, the husband I want to be, and a productive member of society again. I do not need a cooperation agreement in place to do the right thing," he said, promising to continue his discussions with investigators after his sentencing.

Judge Pauley, who had been listening impassively, told Cohen to take his seat. As he left the podium, Cohen noticed his daughter was crying. He reached out and touched her face before tucking into the defense table.

"The question for this court is what is the appropriate and just sentence for these crimes and this defendant. Mr. Cohen pled guilty to a veritable smorgasbord of fraudulent conduct," Pauley said, before ticking off Cohen's crimes. "While this is his first conviction, the magnitude, breadth, and duration of his criminal conduct requires specific deterrence."

These were not words that Cohen and his attorneys wanted to hear before the court handed down his sentence.

"Tax and campaign-finance prosecutions are rare, but unlike the mine-run tax evasion or campaign-finance violation, Mr. Cohen's crimes implicate a far more insidious harm to our institutions, especially in view of his subsequent plea to making false statements to Congress," Judge Pauley said. "Thus, the need for general deterrence is amplified in this case."

Another bad sign.

Judge Pauley acknowledged the many letters he'd received from Cohen's friends and family that showed the attorney to be a loving father and devoted husband, and he said cooperation like Cohen's should be encouraged, even if he provided it outside of a formal agreement with prosecutors.

Finally, a ray of hope—but only a ray, and it was ephemeral.

"While Mr. Cohen has taken steps to mitigate his criminal conduct by pleading guilty and volunteering useful information to prosecutors, that does not wipe the slate clean," Judge Pauley went on. "This court cannot agree with the defendant's assertion that no jail time is warranted. In fact, this court firmly believes that a significant term of imprisonment is fully justified in this highly publicized case to send a message to those who contemplate avoiding their taxes, evading campaign-finance laws, or lying to financial institutions or Congress."

Judge Pauley told Cohen to stand.

"Mr. Cohen, it's my judgment, sir, that . . . you be sentenced to a term of thirty-six months of imprisonment to be followed by three years of supervised release," the judge said.

Cohen shook his head and closed his eyes as Pauley read the sentence.

Three years in prison. It was far more time than Cohen thought he'd have to serve.

He offered no reaction to reporters waiting for him in the anteroom between the courtroom and the hallway after the hearing.

"This is my last time talking to you guys," Cohen said.

Cohen and his lawyers lingered in the court lobby while Laura, Jake, and Samantha Cohen exited the courthouse and pushed through a curtain of photographers and television crews to a waiting black Infiniti QX60.

His family safely on the other side of the media swarm, Cohen, looking grim, stepped outside the courthouse and beat a path to the car.

WITH COHEN'S FATE decided, the Southern District of New York then illuminated another corner of its campaign-finance investigation. Prosecutors secretly had reached an agreement with American Media months earlier. In return for the company's help in the Cohen investigation and its promise to educate employees on the finer points of campaign-finance regulation, prosecutors would refrain from seeking criminal charges against American Media. The U.S. attorney's office publicly revealed the agreement on the afternoon of December 12, in a news release announcing Cohen's sentence.

The agreement contained two pages of facts admitted by American Media. The company acknowledged that its chief executive had met with Trump and Cohen in August 2015 and offered to catch and kill stories about Trump's relationships with women; that the "principal purpose" of American Media's contact with Karen McDougal was to suppress her story of an affair with Trump; that American Media had executed the deal "in cooperation, consultation, and concert with, and at the request and suggestion of" Trump and Cohen; and that Pecker had agreed to assign McDougal's story rights to Trump in return for $125,000, before thinking better of it.

Contrast that with what American Media had been saying publicly for two years. "AMI has not paid people to kill damaging stories about Mr. Trump," the company had told the *Journal* in 2016, when we reported McDougal's deal. In response to McDougal's lawsuit against American Media, company lawyers rejected her characterization of the $150,000 contract as a vehicle for an illegal campaign contribution, saying that "the purpose of the payment manifestly appears on the face of the agreement to have been for the purchase of journalistic services, content, and a valuable story right."

Now the publisher had confessed to federal prosecutors that the true intent of the payment was to help Trump's presidential campaign by concealing an embarrassing story about the candidate. The Southern District had already described American Media's motivations for buying McDougal's story in its charging document in the Cohen case, filed in August, but those were merely allegations. The non-prosecution agreement amounted to the company telling the nation, *Yes, it's true. All of it.*

Trump seemed to recognize the threat immediately. He could call Cohen a liar all he wanted, but now another party, a publication that spoke to his base, was on record admitting that its top executive had coordinated with Trump to make a payment that prosecutors said was a felony violation of federal law. He offered a tweet-as-legal-defense the day after Cohen's sentencing.

"I never directed Michael Cohen to break the law. He was a lawyer and he is supposed to know the law. It is called 'advice of counsel,' and a lawyer has great liability if a mistake is made. That is why they get paid," he wrote.

For the first time, Trump was tacitly acknowledging that he had participated in the hush-money deals, and that he could be exposed legally. Instead of pleading ignorance of the facts, he was now pleading ignorance of the law. How could he be guilty of a crime if he didn't know he was doing anything wrong? He wasn't *a lawyer,* after all.

The problem with that argument was that Trump was more familiar than most with campaign-finance regulations. He had even bragged about his knowledge publicly. "I think nobody knows more about campaign finance than I do, because I'm the biggest contributor," he had told Larry King in a CNN interview in 1999. The Federal Election Commission had investigated him as both a contributor and a candidate. He submitted a sworn affidavit in one case, in 2000, stressing his intimacy with laws governing corporate contributions. In 1988, he testified before a New York State integrity commission about individual contribution limits.

Taken together, the statements created a record that future prosecutors or congressional investigators could use to show that Trump was literate enough in campaign-finance laws to have willfully broken them. But that assumed hush money could be regulated by federal campaign laws. No federal appeals court had ever had occasion to weigh the matter.

30.

A CON MAN AND A CHEAT

■ ■ ■

COHEN HAD BEEN so shaken by the three-year sentence that some of his friends were worried about him. Immediately afterward, a couple of them asked Bernard Kerik, who had served as both New York City police commissioner and corrections commissioner, to give Cohen a call. Kerik knew Trump and people in his circle. He had never liked Cohen or bought into his macho shtick, but he agreed to reach out.

Kerik understood plenty about what Cohen was about to face. Not only had he run Rikers Island, New York's infamous jail, but he had served time in federal prison after pleading guilty to tax fraud and lying to White House officials when he was briefly a candidate to lead the Department of Homeland Security.

He connected with Cohen late on the night of the sentencing. Kerik knew that an impending prison term could drive some guys to self-harm. He tried to assure Cohen that no matter how bad things seemed, he would get through them and survive. He walked Cohen through the process of getting assigned to a prison and surrendering. They talked for more than an hour, and Cohen was all over the place, confident in one moment, panicky in the next, and intermittently veering into criticism of the president.

Before they hung up, Kerik imparted one more piece of advice.

"This isn't political, this isn't me defending the president," Kerik said. "I will tell you this, and this is really constructive advice if you want to listen. When I open the Drudge Report, there is a big fucking photo of a rat, and your name is underneath it. Every prisoner, wherever you go, they're going to know everything about you.

"What they are going to know is that you're a rat. They are not going to care whether you ratted out the president, whether you ratted out your mother, the Cali Cartel, the mob. They don't give a damn who you ratted out. What is relevant is that they know they cannot trust you. That's what's relevant, and for you, that's not good. So what I would do if I were you is I would do everything in your power from now to the time you get in to shut the fuck up. Stop talking all that shit. Go in like a man, do your thing, and get out."

Kerik explained the danger of being perceived as someone who couldn't be trusted. Cohen didn't want to wake up one day to find another prisoner beating him with a sock filled with bars of soap or a lock.

It seemed like Cohen had heard him. But he didn't heed Kerik's advice.

The next day, December 13, Cohen sat down for an interview with George Stephanopoulos, his first on camera since the investigation, aside from brief comments he had made on the sidewalk when reporters chased him down. The interview aired the next morning. Cohen exhorted viewers not to trust the president and pledged to continue to cooperate with authorities investigating Trump and his company.

"I am here and I am willing to answer whatever additional questions that they may have for me," he said.

Between his guilty plea, in August, and his sentencing, in December, Cohen had met with Southern District prosecutors twice to discuss the campaign-finance investigation. He sat down with them again in January 2019 and answered their questions about Imaad Zuberi, the Trump inaugural donor for whom he nearly became a consultant. Cohen also volunteered information about insurance claims filed by the Trump Organization over the years. Making himself available to federal prosecutors was a no-brainer, notwithstanding Kerik's warning. Under federal law, prosecutors could ask Judge Pauley to trim Cohen's prison term at any point within a year of his sentencing, if he supplied evidence in an investigation.

The new Democratic majority in the House of Representatives was also eager to put him in the witness chair, but the benefits of testifying in Congress, when weighed against the risks, were harder to calculate. In the second week of January, Cohen accepted an invitation by Representative Elijah Cummings to testify publicly before the House Oversight Committee, but Cohen's advisers were divided over the upcoming appearance. He would be walking into a forum where he'd already admitting to lying. Cohen could invite another criminal charge if he was less than fully honest with lawmakers, especially in a public setting. He would no doubt face Republican questioners who would try to catch him in another lie, and who would come ready to bludgeon Cohen's character and credibility. They didn't lack for material.

Cohen was inclined to tell his side of the story in public, and Lanny Davis, Cohen's lawyer-spokesman, was also in favor. It would be a historic event seen by millions, a chance for Cohen to speak directly to Americans about Trump's perfidy and rehabilitate himself in the process. Guy Petrillo advised against the Oversight Committee appearance, unless Southern District prosecutors gave their blessing. He worried about alienating the office that had the power to influence the length of Cohen's prison sentence. If the threat of a perjury trap wasn't enough, Trump and Giuliani had given Cohen more to think about. They were overtly lobbying investigators and lawmakers to make Cohen's family a topic of questioning. Cohen "should give information maybe on his father-in-law, because that's the one that people want to look at," Trump said in a January 13 Fox News interview. Cohen's father-in-law, Fima Shusterman, had been convicted in 1993 of evading regulations meant to prevent money laundering, receiving a sentence of probation. Giuliani was more blunt in a CNN interview days later, saying that Shusterman "may have ties to something called organized crime." He offered no evidence to support his claim.

Cohen backed out of testifying in the fourth week of January. He still hadn't received any encouragement from the Southern District. Lanny Davis distributed a statement on January 23 saying that Cohen was postponing his appearance indefinitely, on the advice of his lawyer and in response to "ongoing threats against his family from President Trump and Mr. Giuliani."

The next day, the Senate Intelligence Committee subpoenaed Cohen to testify behind closed doors, a demand to which he quickly acceded. The House Intelligence Committee also requested his testimony in a closed hearing. Cohen agreed to that as well.

Petrillo's relationship with Cohen had soured since his sentencing. Cohen wondered what good the defense lawyer's pedigree as a Southern District prosecutor had done for him, now that he was staring at three years in prison. He felt that the Southern District had mistreated him on Petrillo's watch. Why was he the only one they prosecuted? Why wouldn't prosecutors sit down with Petrillo before August? Cohen had fallen behind on his legal bills. Though Cohen seemingly had the means, he refused to catch up. *I can't pay you right now,* he had told Petrillo. Davis was another wedge in their relationship. He and Petrillo repeatedly butted heads. Over the past year, Davis's media leaks had prompted Petrillo to issue ultimatums to Cohen: *Stop talking to the press or I'm out.* Now, in January, Petrillo learned that Davis had contacted the U.S. attorney's office in Manhattan about Cohen's case without telling him. (Davis had called the office on a Saturday and spoken with a senior prosecutor about the process for seeking a sentence reduction.) Petrillo fired off an email to Cohen saying he could no longer work with Davis, who was copied on the note. Davis responded that Cohen had instructed him to make the call. Petrillo left the team soon after.

Cohen retained Michael Monico, a former federal prosecutor in Chicago, and his law partner, Barry Spevack, both veteran criminal defense attorneys. They agreed with Davis that Cohen should testify publicly before the House Oversight Committee. They hoped that he could use the forum to show his usefulness as a witness to crimes by Trump and his family.

Cohen rescheduled his Oversight Committee testimony for February 27 at 10 A.M. He received dispensation from Judge Pauley to postpone the start of his prison sentence from March to May. His lawyers had told Pauley that Cohen was recuperating from shoulder surgery and that time-consuming preparations for his upcoming testimony in Congress made it difficult for Cohen to put his affairs in order before entering Federal Correctional Institution, Otisville, a lockup two hours northwest of New York City with a sizable population of Jewish inmates, a lumpy tennis court, and plenty of open space. It wasn't Club Fed, but Otisville was far from hard time.

IT WAS THE eve of Cohen's public testimony. His new attorneys had spent the previous weeks interrogating him about his time by Trump's side, prying details from Cohen that he didn't know he'd retained or couldn't recognize as significant, because they'd been part of his routine. They coached him to describe key events, like the hush-money deal with Stormy Daniels and his reimbursement, in detailed, narrative form—stories with a beginning and an end that the millions of Americans watching his testimony could comprehend. Cohen, by nature, spoke in fragments, teleporting from one topic to the next, shifting through time without warning. He could be difficult to follow.

As Washington braced for Cohen and Cohen prepared for Washington, a young Florida congressman, who'd distinguished himself among Republicans for his pro-Trump fervor, set a new low standard in the effort to rattle and undermine Trump's former fixer before his testimony.

"Hey @MichaelCohen212 - Do your wife & father-in-law know about your girlfriends? Maybe tonight would be a good time for that chat. I wonder if she'll remain faithful when you're in prison. She's about to learn a lot . . . ," Representative Matt Gaetz tweeted the day before the public hearing.

House Speaker Nancy Pelosi responded with a stern warning: Any effort by House lawmakers to intimidate witnesses, impairing the ability of House committees to obtain information, would be subject to potential investigation by the chamber's ethics watchdog.

Gaetz quickly apologized.

"While it is important 2 create context around the testimony of liars like Michael Cohen, it was NOT my intent to threaten, as some believe I did," the congressman tweeted. "I'm deleting the tweet & I should have chosen words that better showed my intent. I'm sorry."

LIVE CONGRESSIONAL HEARINGS make for poor fact-finding forums. For one thing, each lawmaker generally has only a few minutes to question a witness. It is hard for any one member of Congress to create the type of momentum that defense lawyers and prosecutors use to disarm witnesses in court. But the larger inadequacy has nothing to do with form. Politics dictates that lawmakers score points for their side. Getting to the truth is often a secondary concern, if it is a concern at all.

Cohen sat at the witness table, his hangdog face tilted up to members of the House Oversight and Government Reform Committee, who sat before him in gradually elevated rows. Republicans portrayed him as a pathological liar who turned on Trump after he was denied a place by the president's side in Washington. For Democrats, the goal was to extract from Cohen as many of Trump's sins as they could while creating a foundation for future investigations. They succeeded more in the former than the latter.

Cohen, again in a blue suit and tie, approached the hearing as an opportunity to tell a story about the president of the United States: Trump in his natural state. "He is a racist, he is a con man, and he is a cheat," Cohen told the committee.

He described his and Trump's roles in the Stormy Daniels deal, told of the hundreds of threats he had made on Trump's behalf over the years, and portrayed Trump as obsessed with exaggerating his wealth and popularity.

All of this information was compelling, coming from Trump's one-time fixer. But Cohen seeded his testimony with demonstrable falsehoods that undermined the rest of his remarks. At one point he volunteered, "I have never asked for, nor would I accept, a pardon from Mr. Trump," though Cohen and his representatives had asked. Repeatedly.

Cohen also, bizarrely, refused to admit that he had wanted a White House position, a lie contradicted by so many sources that Republicans were able to identify it as a lie in real time, because some individuals to whom Cohen had expressed his disappointment at getting passed over posted tweets rebutting his testimony.

For all his Trump bashing, Cohen also defended his former boss on at least two occasions against allegations we and others had investigated.

He denied the existence of a video of Trump striking his wife in an elevator, the phantom tape a Los Angeles lawyer briefly offered to *TMZ*. Trump's allies had tried to ascertain whether the tape existed, and to snap it up "for catch-and-kill purposes" if it did, Cohen testified. But they never found the tape, and Cohen didn't think that Trump would ever lay hands on his wife, he said.

"It doesn't exist," Cohen said.

He also addressed the love-child story sold by Dino Sajudin, the former Trump World Tower doorman, to American Media for $30,000.

Pecker had bought the story to "find out whether it was true or not" and suppress it, Cohen testified. It was the first public admission that American Media had bought the story to protect Trump.

"Is there a love child?" asked Representative Jackie Speier, a California Democrat.

"There is not to . . . the best of my knowledge," Cohen said.

"So you would pay off someone to not report—"

"It wasn't me, ma'am. It was AMI. It was David Pecker."

"So he paid off someone about a love child that doesn't exist?"

"Correct."

COHEN HAD RUSHED to his sentencing date, forgoing a full cooperation agreement with the Southern District out of a desire to move on with his life, he had said. But he was in no hurry to serve his three-year sentence. Cohen and his lawyers were doing everything they could to delay and shorten it.

Cohen's testimony in the House Oversight Committee had done him no favors with federal prosecutors in New York. He had publicly contradicted them on a matter of virtually no consequence except, perhaps, for Cohen's ego. He testified that he had never sought a White House job, but Southern District prosecutors had text messages in which Cohen told associates he expected to be given a prominent role in the Trump administration. Prosecutors cited the text messages in court documents. But Cohen insisted in his congressional testimony that the Southern District's claim was "not accurate."

After Cohen's testimony, the U.S. attorney's office seemed to want to be rid of him. Cohen's lawyers tried to schedule a meeting with Southern District prosecutors in March to discuss the possibility of a sentence reduction. They declined.

As his date to report to prison neared, Cohen and his lawyers, realizing they had no support from federal prosecutors, focused their energies on Congress. Maybe lawmakers would support his bid for a lower sentence, or help him forestall it, if Cohen gave them fresh pegs for investigations.

Based on Cohen's testimony, the House Oversight Committee was seeking information about Trump's personal finances from his accounting firm, Mazars USA LLP. The committee's chairman, Elijah Cummings, said in a letter to the firm that his panel was examining Trump's efforts to obtain a loan from Deutsche Bank to buy the Buffalo

Bills. Cohen had testified that Trump submitted false financial statements to the bank.

The House Intelligence Committee, meanwhile, was investigating whether Trump lawyers had helped shape Cohen's false statement to Congress about Trump Tower Moscow, as well as Cohen's claims that members of Trump's camp had dangled a pardon to dissuade him from flipping on the president. In his closed-door testimony, Cohen told the Intelligence Committee that he'd had discussions with Trump's lawyer Jay Sekulow about a possible pardon beginning in 2017, as he prepared his statement to Congress about Trump Tower Moscow, and continuing into 2018, after the FBI searches of his home, hotel room, and office. According to Cohen, Sekulow repeatedly encouraged him to hang tight when he inquired about a pardon.

"He had said, you know, 'It's very difficult right now for political reasons, but . . . he's not going to let anything happen to you. The client loves you and just stay strong. He's really sorry this is happening to you,'" Cohen testified. Sekulow denied encouraging or assisting Cohen in making false statements to Congress, and trashed his credibility.

The Intelligence Committee was also investigating allegations by Cohen that New York lawyers Robert Costello and Jeffrey Citron had reached out to him after the FBI raids, presenting themselves, in essence, as proxies for the White House. The lawyers had claimed to be in close contact with Rudy Giuliani and tempted Cohen with a pardon if he stayed in the president's tent, Cohen told the committee.

Costello, when interviewed by the committee in the spring, disputed Cohen's account. Citron and Costello wanted to represent Cohen because what defense lawyer wouldn't? They had reached out to Cohen and met with him at the Regency before Giuliani was even on Trump's legal team. And Cohen, not Costello, had been the one to raise the issue of a pardon. He leaned on Costello to ask Giuliani if a pardon was on the table, even though Costello had warned Cohen that the conversation was premature. Cohen hadn't even been charged at the time. Southern District prosecutors had also questioned Costello. They told Costello's lawyer he was a witness, not a target, suggesting that they credited Costello's account over Cohen's.

Cohen had also directed Stephen Ryan, his lawyer before Guy

Petrillo, to broach the subject of a pardon with Trump's counsel, our sources told us.

Congressional investigators were left with a messy conflict. Did Trump's lawyers dangle a pardon when Cohen's lawyer raised the subject to keep him on Team Trump? Or did Cohen repeatedly seek a pardon and peel away from Trump after it became clear he wasn't going to get his wish?

Whatever the case, our reporting showed that Cohen had falsely testified in the House Oversight Committee that he "never" sought a pardon from Trump. Lanny Davis told the *Journal* that Cohen's testimony was truthful, because he hadn't sought a pardon since breaking with Trump in July 2018—a statement that defied logic, not to mention the plain definition of "never."

With House committees looking into bits of Cohen's testimony, his new lawyers sought to leverage the congressional investigations. In April, they asked committee chairmen for letters stating that Cohen had "substantially cooperated with Congress"—documents Cohen's team could then use to lobby federal prosecutors and Judge Pauley in the Southern District to lop off part of Cohen's prison term. They also offered congressional committees a hard drive of Cohen's files recently returned by the Justice Department—fourteen million documents and recordings that agents had seized. The catch was that lawmakers had to help Cohen stay out of prison while he guided them through a cache that had already been picked over by federal prosecutors and the FBI.

"Mr. Cohen remains the only member of the Trump Organization who has been prosecuted and who is going to prison for conduct almost all of which was for the benefit of Mr. Trump personally and indeed directed by him," Cohen's lawyers wrote in an April 4 letter to the committee chairmen. "In our opinion, there is something unjust here."

The committees declined to seek a delay of Cohen's prison sentence in exchange for the hard drive. Representative Adam Schiff, a former federal prosecutor who chaired the House Intelligence Committee, said he wouldn't insert himself into sentencing matters by providing Cohen's lawyers with a letter touting Cohen's cooperation. The other chairmen kept their own counsel.

No one was coming to Cohen's aid before he had to surrender to the Bureau of Prisons.

Epilogue

■ ■ ■

THE MEN WHO had pledged loyalty to Donald Trump and made good on their promises to him met ignominious fates. Like Roy Cohn before them, Michael Cohen and David Pecker had been attracted to Trump's aura and his gloss, to the force of the huge personality that had, finally, enabled him to be elected president of the United States.

Trump's gift to these fixers in exchange for their willingness to make unwise, even dangerous, decisions was the same one he offered to all those who had been in his service over the decades: the exposure to his world, the opportunity to play a bit part in Trump's story. When they had fulfilled their missions, even if those missions went bad, Trump didn't feel he owed them anything.

For Cohen and for Pecker, the problems they now faced for their actions on Trump's behalf were their own problems. Trump always seemed to rise above. And wasn't that the point?

After federal prosecutors revealed American Media's non-prosecution agreement, Pecker and his company managed to stay out of the news for approximately a month before another scandal enveloped the publisher. In January 2019, the *National Enquirer* published racy texts and details of an extramarital affair between Amazon.com Inc. founder Jeff Bezos and his girlfriend, Lauren Sanchez, a former television reporter.

The *Enquirer* had approached the Amazon chief for comment on January 7. Two days later, trying to get ahead of the story, Bezos tweeted that he and his wife, MacKenzie Bezos, were splitting up after twenty-five years. The tabloid rushed the Bezos story online that night and into print with a headline: "BEZOS' DIVORCE! THE CHEATING PHOTOS THAT ENDED HIS MARRIAGE."

This was classic *National Enquirer* fare—a huge, sensational scoop about a powerful figure that in its heyday the tabloid would have celebrated and bragged about for years. But the Trump and Weinstein episodes had so shaken America Media and shaded the public perception of its motivations that what should have been a much-needed victory turned into another disaster.

Trump's well-known dislike of Amazon, Bezos, and the Bezos-owned *Washington Post* fueled widespread speculation that American Media's reasons for targeting the billionaire were personal. Had Pecker done Trump's bidding . . . again? It didn't help that Trump gloated about the *Enquirer* story while directing a schoolyard taunt at Bezos.

"So sorry to hear the news about Jeff Bozo being taken down by a competitor whose reporting, I understand, is far more accurate than the reporting in his lobbyist newspaper, the Amazon Washington Post," Trump tweeted.

Bezos enlisted his security consultant, Gavin de Becker, to investigate the source of the leak of his text messages. De Becker was exploring the possibility that Saudi Arabia had hacked Bezos's phone and shared his secrets, in retaliation for the *Post*'s coverage of the macabre murder of Jamal Khashoggi, a Saudi journalist who had fled the kingdom and settled in the United States. Khashoggi had written columns for the *Post* that were critical of Saudi Crown Prince Mohammed bin Salman. In October 2018, Saudi operatives strangled and dismembered Khashoggi inside the Saudi consulate in Istanbul, where he was retrieving documents for his upcoming marriage. According to the *Post*'s reporting, the Central Intelligence Agency concluded that the crown prince had ordered the assassination.

The Trump administration had built a close relationship with the Saudis, and American Media had published a glossy, ad-free hagiography of the crown prince, known by his initials, MBS, when Pecker was seeking Saudi investment in American Media. Pecker had also met with MBS in the kingdom, though the Saudis ultimately declined to invest in American Media. De Becker started connecting the dots, and the media did, too.

The renewed attention so soon after the Karen McDougal hush-money scandal upset the company's 80 percent owners at Chatham Asset Management. Chatham was fed up with Pecker and American

Media over the narrative that was taking hold of collusion between the publisher and the White House and/or the Saudis.

The publisher's fumbling attempt to do so backfired spectacularly. In a pair of emails, chief content officer Dylan Howard and an American Media lawyer, Jon Fine, tried to broker a deal. In exchange for Bezos's publicly stating that he had no evidence that politics had played a role in the *Enquirer* story, the tabloid would withhold other salacious material. Howard had emailed Martin Singer, a lawyer for Bezos and de Becker, with snarky descriptions of racy pictures of the Amazon chief he said the *Enquirer* possessed. One was a photo, Howard wrote, of Bezos in "either tight black cargo pants or shorts—and his semi-erect manhood is penetrating the zipper of said garment." He also told Singer that the *Enquirer* had a "below the belt selfie—otherwise collo-quially known as a 'd*ck pick.'"

The longtime tabloid editor felt safe sending the blunt email because he'd dealt for years with Singer, who was *the* go-to lawyer for celebrities trying to keep their secrets from seeing daylight. In this case, though, Bezos was the client, and he was calling the shots. Rather than cower at the threat of exposure, Bezos published both emails in a February 7 blog post on Medium titled "No Thank You, Mr. Pecker."

"These communications cement AMI's long-earned reputation for weaponizing journalistic privileges, hiding behind important protec-tions, and ignoring the tenets and purpose of true journalism," he wrote.

After Bezos's post, the *Journal* learned that the U.S. Attorney's Office for the Southern District of New York was reviewing its non-prosecution agreement with the publisher. Federal prosecutors also asked the company to produce documents related to its effort to secure financing from Saudi Arabia.

The *Daily Beast* and others had already reported in mid-February that the *Enquirer* had obtained the Bezos material from Lauren San-chez's brother, Michael Sanchez. The revelation didn't end the specula-tion that this had been a politically orchestrated hit. Sanchez, a talent agent who manages television pundits and reality show judges, had long been a source for the *Enquirer*. He was also an outspoken Trump supporter who had a relationship with Trump's former political ad-viser, Roger Stone.

The story behind the leak was less sinister, our sources soon told us. The *Journal* reported on March 18 that the primary motivation appeared to be money. Michael Sanchez, we disclosed, had sold his sister's texts and photos of Bezos to American Media for $200,000, a princely sum in the tabloid world. When we reached Sanchez, he refused to comment on his contract and denied selling "the many penis selfies" referenced in Dylan Howard's email to the tabloid. It was a non-denial denial. Sanchez, we learned, had shown the naked-below-the-waist picture of Bezos to *Enquirer* staff but had declined to relinquish it, unlike the other photos of Bezos in various states of undress that he had peddled to the tabloid.

In our story, "How the National Enquirer Got Bezos' Texts," we detailed for the first time the backstory and internecine drama that preceded the tabloid's scoop. Our reporting showed just how significantly Pecker and others at American Media had been rocked by the McDougal scandal and the ensuing investigation, not to mention their connection to Harvey Weinstein's #MeToo problems. Pecker and his company had been seriously damaged by the alliance he had struck with Trump and Cohen on that day at Trump Tower in August 2015. Currying favor with a powerful and reckless man had put him and American Media in serious legal jeopardy, and Pecker had no interest in further tempting the fates. But what happens when a tabloid isn't sure it can publish tabloid stories anymore?

After Michael Sanchez approached the *Enquirer* in the fall of 2018, Pecker had been reluctant to publish the Bezos story. He feared that the wealthiest man in the world might sue American Media, forcing the debt-laden publisher to expend precious resources to defend itself for a story that executives believed was unlikely to sell well on newsstands, even though it would be a major scoop. Pecker was also trying to refinance $400 million of the company's debt as American Media chased the Bezos story. One underwriter had already backed out because of the hush-money scandal. Pecker couldn't afford to turn off more bankers.

There was another complication. Lauren Sanchez's husband, Patrick Whitesell, was executive chairman of the holding company for talent agency William Morris Endeavor Entertainment. WME's chief executive, super-agent Ari Emanuel, was close to Pecker. Some American Media executives worried that Pecker would catch and kill the Bezos story to save Whitesell, his friend's business partner, from embarrassment.

American Media's October 26, 2018, contract with Michael Sanchez guaranteed him the payment up front. In the wake of the investigation of the McDougal deal, Cameron Stracher, American Media's top media lawyer, inserted an unusual provision into the contract that guarded against the publisher's buying the story to bury it. If American Media didn't publish anything about Bezos within about a month's time, Sanchez could sell the information to another outlet and keep the $200,000. The *Enquirer's* editors executed the contract. But Pecker hadn't fully understood the nuances of the agreement. When he did, he became irate.

Pecker and Stracher met for lunch at Cipriani Wall Street, a restaurant near American Media's offices, about two weeks after the company finalized the contract with Sanchez. They sat down at Pecker's regular table at the front of the restaurant, near the bar. Stracher, a media law specialist who had worked for the company for eleven years, thought he was meeting with his boss to discuss a promotion. Instead, Pecker attacked him.

Raising his voice enough to draw the attention of other patrons, Pecker wanted to know why Stracher had deviated from standard operating procedure by agreeing to pay Sanchez up front. And why hadn't Stracher shown him the contract? Pecker was cursing.

In reality, Stracher responded, American Media did pay up front when the material in question was valuable and a source was threatening to take the information elsewhere. This was the same type of payment Pecker had authorized for Dino Sajudin, the former doorman with the tip about the Trump love child.

The Sanchez contract was different, however. Pecker was boxed in. He couldn't kill the story, because Sanchez could take it elsewhere and American Media would have spent $200,000 for nothing. But if he published it, he'd anger the world's richest man and look like he had returned to shilling for Trump. Pecker was accusing Stracher of going rogue. In a way, the lawyer had, but not by consenting to an upfront payment. He had structured a contract that wouldn't let Pecker catch and kill again. Stracher had tried to protect American Media—and to protect Pecker from himself.

When Stracher took offense at Pecker's tone, the chief executive said the lawyer could quit if he was unhappy. Stracher pushed away from the table and walked out of the restaurant. By the time he returned to American Media's offices, less than a ten-minute walk, his key card had been deactivated.

Ultimately, Pecker decided to move forward with the story, but only after hiring an outside law firm to review the *Enquirer*'s reporting and ensure it was bulletproof. But he didn't predict the firestorm that it would bring.

Chatham, American Media's largest financial backer, could brook no more scandals at the moribund *Enquirer*, whose circulation had continued its steep decline. In April 2019, the publisher announced that American Media was putting its tabloids—the *Enquirer, Globe,* and the *National Examiner*—up for sale. The following week, the company reached a tentative deal with James Cohen, whose family had built Hudson News, known for its stores in airports and train stations. Cohen, a friend and business associate of Pecker, agreed to pay $100 million for American Media's tabloids.

On paper, David Pecker would cede his title. He would no longer be chairman of the tabloids, though American Media would maintain ownership of the lifestyle and celebrity brands, such as *Us Weekly, Men's Journal,* and *Muscle & Fitness.* But the sale to Cohen included a multi-year service agreement: While American Media would no longer own the tabloids, it would continue to provide printing, financial, and distribution services for them. It seemed like a paper transaction, designed to remove the stink of the tabloids from the publisher's more mainstream titles—and to placate Chatham's investors—without actually removing the tabloids themselves from American Media's control. Whether the deal was real, as Pecker asserted, or superficial, the act of distancing himself from the tabloids signified a defeat in the challenge he had taken on twenty years earlier. He had given up his perch atop the mainstream Hachette Filipacchi Media for a job that made his peers in the industry snicker, and he had been determined to prove them wrong.

Pecker had come to American Media and the *Enquirer* with the backing of Evercore Partners in 1999, confident that he could turn a massive profit despite the already building headwinds of the Internet and an aging readership. Pecker thought he could beat the odds by transforming his tabloids into lucrative advertising vehicles and streamlining the business with purchases of more—and more mainstream—publications. But Evercore and other investors lost tens of millions of dollars on his gamble. Like many publishers, Pecker had to shed staff and cut costs to keep turning a profit, while borrowing heavily to expand the empire, hoping to acquire his way out of debt.

Despite its natural stigma as a supermarket tabloid, the *Enquirer's* reporters and editors, both before and after Pecker, had broken major stories with intrepid and aggressive, if sometimes questionable, tactics. From O. J. Simpson to John Edwards, the tabloid reared its head and forced other journalists and readers to take notice. But Pecker's cost cutting had caused editorial quality to plummet. Now it hardly employed any staff. And his prioritizing of business and relationships over the old-school tabloid mission—in which almost any juicy target was fair game—had further devalued the *Enquirer's* brand, making the tabloid a toxic asset.

It was true that Pecker hadn't been the first tabloid publisher to protect his friends. Gene Pope had bought the *Enquirer* in 1952 with an interest-free loan from his godfather, the mobster Frank Costello, and agreed in return to lay off organized crime in its pages. Pecker, however, had made misjudgments that turned his compromises into major news that damaged him personally and harmed the businesses he was running. While at Hachette, he'd killed a *Premiere* magazine column for Ron Perelman and failed to predict how editorial employees would react. At American Media, his paid protection of Arnold Schwarzenegger had become public in the *Los Angeles Times*. If Pecker drew any lessons from these scandals, they seemed to be the wrong ones—because he had eagerly put his company into service for his friend Donald Trump in 2015 and 2016, a fateful decision that had made him and American Media a household name for all the wrong reasons. His reputation had never suffered more.

Still, Pecker had defied expectations throughout his career; after twenty-one years as the chief executive of American Media, he still presided over a celebrity news empire. The company's debt load required constant attention, of course. But the publisher now owned every major star-obsessed publication save for one: *People*. American Media still ran the tabloids, even if it didn't own them. Maybe he'd hang on until the hush-money scandal and the Bezos conflagration receded from memory. He'd survived this long.

Regardless, Pecker's scheming with Donald Trump was certain to trail him into retirement and beyond.

MICHAEL AVENATTI'S FUTURE seemed more precarious.

Demand for his presence on television had dropped off since the fall of 2018, when he inserted himself into Brett Kavanaugh's Supreme Court confirmation hearings with a client whose allegations of sexual misconduct crumbled under scrutiny. Then police arrested him after a fight with his ex-girlfriend in November. Democratic operatives canceled his planned speaking engagements. Though prosecutors declined to bring charges, Avenatti abandoned his presidential aspirations the following month.

In February, federal prosecutors in San Francisco unwound the mystery of how Avenatti had come by the detailed financial information about Michael Cohen that Avenatti posted on Twitter the previous May. John Fry, an investigative analyst for the IRS, was charged with illegally downloading Treasury Department reports about Cohen's banking activity from a federal database and supplying them to Avenatti. Avenatti wasn't accused of wrongdoing, though he had been the beneficiary of a crime.

On March 7, U.S. District Judge S. James Otero dismissed the original legal complaint Avenatti had filed for Stormy Daniels asking the court to invalidate her nondisclosure agreement with Trump. It was in this lawsuit, following the *Journal*'s reporting of her hush-money deal, that Daniels first acknowledged she'd been paid to keep quiet. In its aftermath, the scandal had blossomed exponentially. But Cohen and Trump had abandoned the Daniels NDA soon after Cohen's guilty plea. Since everything had already been disclosed, their lawyers said they'd no longer seek to enforce it. Cohen's lawyer had demanded that Daniels return the $130,000 Cohen had paid her. Avenatti said no reimbursement would be forthcoming unless he could depose Cohen and Trump. But Otero ruled that there was nothing left to litigate. Case closed.

Avenatti might have faded from view but for the U.S. Department of Justice.

On March 25, 2019, he was arrested and charged in separate federal cases in New York and California. Federal prosecutors in the Southern

District of New York accused the attorney of attempting to extort more than $20 million from Nike Inc.

According to prosecutors, he told the company's lawyers that his client, a youth basketball coach named Gary Franklin Sr., had evidence that the apparel giant had funneled secret payments to families of top high school basketball players. Avenatti threatened to go public with the allegations on the eve of Nike's quarterly earnings call unless the company paid his client a $1.5 million settlement and hired him and his friend, celebrity attorney Mark Geragos, to conduct an internal investigation for $15 million to $25 million in fees, prosecutors said.

Nike's lawyers reported him to the U.S. attorney's office in Manhattan and let federal agents electronically monitor their conversations with Avenatti and Geragos.

"If you guys think that, you know, we're going to negotiate a million five, and you're going to hire us to do an internal investigation, but it's gonna be capped at three or five or seven million dollars, like, let's just be done," Avenatti told Nike's lawyers as the FBI listened. "And I'll go take ten billion dollars off your client's market cap. But I'm not fucking around."

A few days later, federal agents surrounded Avenatti as he headed for an escalator in the mall near the offices of Nike's outside counsel at Boies Schiller Flexner LLP, where he had a scheduled meeting. The agents took his phone and briefcase and threw a trench coat over him while they cuffed him, to avoid making a scene.

The day of his arrest, he was separately charged in California with defrauding the Mississippi bank that had loaned him money—the one he allegedly had supplied with false tax returns—and wire fraud in connection with the settlement funds he'd allegedly stolen from Greg Barela, the client he represented in an intellectual property dispute with Brock USA.

Later that evening, Michael Cohen and his sometime friend comedian Tom Arnold discussed Avenatti's legal troubles on a phone call Arnold recorded. Cohen viewed the arrest as cosmic justice. "Look at what's happening to Avenatti—it's called karma boomerang," Cohen said. "The guy lied about me every single day, right? And the world loved it."

Federal prosecutors in Los Angeles would soon charge Avenatti in connection with four other clients who said they had never received money they had coming to them. Federal prosecutors in New York filed additional charges against Avenatti in May for allegedly stealing hundreds of thousands of dollars from Stormy Daniels, identified in court documents as Victim-1.

The indictment alleged that Avenatti embezzled about $300,000 of Daniels's advance for her book *Full Disclosure*. The publisher, St. Martin's Press, had agreed to pay her $800,000 in four tranches. Daniels received the first installment in an account she'd designated. In July 2018, after Daniels submitted her manuscript, Avenatti told her literary agent to wire the second payment to his bank account. When the agent, Luke Janklow, requested authorization from Daniels, Avenatti provided a letter with her forged signature and wiring instructions, according to federal prosecutors. Minus Janklow's fee, Avenatti received $148,750 in his account. According to prosecutors, he used the money to fund payroll at his law firm and coffee company and spent it on airfare, insurance, meals, and other expenses.

For months, according to prosecutors, Avenatti played a shell game with his most famous client. He allegedly used Daniels's third installment for a lease payment on his Ferrari and for hotels, restaurants, dry-cleaning, and other expenses.

Daniels finally connected with a representative of St. Martin's in February and learned that the publisher had made the third payment in September, contrary to what Avenatti had told her, according to prosecutors. She also received the wire instructions he had sent her agent with her forged signature, the indictment said. Then she fired him.

Avenatti denied wrongdoing in his dealings with Daniels ("I was entitled to any monies retained per my agreement with the client," he said on Twitter) and in his dealings with Nike ("The idea that Mark and I would attempt to extort anyone, let alone Nike, is ludicrous and laughable"). He pleaded not guilty to thirty-six charges in the Central District of California. In that case alone, he faced a steep prison sentence, far higher than Michael Cohen's, if convicted.

Taken together, the charges against Avenatti alleged stunning arrogance. At the same time that Avenatti had so publicly taken the fight to Trump and embraced the fame that it brought him, he had already been defrauding clients and the government for years, according to federal prosecutors. Instead of hiding in the shadows, as most criminals would have done, he shouted, *Look at me!* And people did.

Not surprisingly, Avenatti said he would be fully exonerated when all the facts emerged.

On May 28, at a federal courthouse in Manhattan, Avenatti pleaded "100 percent not guilty" to the charges relating to Daniels's book advance. In a tailored navy suit, he then walked to a neighboring federal courthouse and told a judge he was innocent of conspiring to extort Nike. After the hearing, he paused outside to speak into a thicket of cameras, microphones, and smartphones. He'd spent his career fighting for Davids against Goliaths, Avenatti said, with an uncharacteristic quaver in his voice. "I am now facing the fight of my life against the ultimate Goliath, the Trump administration."

Michael Avenatti, the man who spent months on television convicting Michael Cohen and Donald Trump in the press, wanted the benefit of the doubt.

SINCE MARCH 2018, Stormy Daniels, with Avenatti as her attorney, had sued Donald Trump, Essential Consultants, Michael Cohen, and Keith Davidson, her ex-lawyer. Her first lawsuit, seeking to invalidate her nondisclosure deal with Trump and Cohen, could be counted a success: Trump and Cohen let her step away from the agreement. The others did Daniels more harm than good, or were abandoned. Judge Otero dismissed her defamation case against Trump and ordered her to pay his legal fees; fearing a repeat, she and Avenatti withdrew a long-shot defamation suit against Cohen for implying she was a liar when he denied she had sex with Trump. In May 2019, after dumping Avenatti, Daniels halted the lawsuit against Davidson and Cohen that alleged they had colluded to silence her.

Daniels continued to capitalize on her celebrity, packing strip clubs on her tour and drawing crowds at comedy clubs, where she held storytelling events under the cheeky title "An Intimate Evening with Stormy Daniels." She discussed her career, promoted her book, and took audience questions. (Q: Was she offended that Trump denied having sex with her? A: "It doesn't offend me. I mean, he also thinks climate change isn't real.")

Daniels was the most famous porn star in the world, undimmed by Avenatti's spectacular implosion. She stuck by her version of events, portraying herself as the lone truth teller among a vulgar circus of criminals and reprobates. She disdained talk of Michael Cohen as a witness to Trump's depravity who had found the courage to speak up. That was her story, not his.

"While I appreciate Cohen coming clean (eventually), he's NOT the honest one in this story," Daniels wrote on Twitter. "He wouldn't know bravery if it kicked him in the teeth."

IN WILLIAM BARR, the president hoped he'd found an attorney general who would succeed where he believed Jeff Sessions had failed: in protecting Donald Trump. Barr, who was on record opposing the obstruction investigation, described himself as a proponent of broad presidential powers, and he felt that Trump's antagonists had bent the rules to pursue him, weakening the office for future presidents. But the distinction—Barr would insist he was protecting the presidency rather than the president—mattered little to Trump.

Barr had served as attorney general for two years under the first President Bush and had since represented big-name companies as in-house counsel and at the Chicago-based firm Kirkland & Ellis. In June 2018, the sixty-eight-year-old lawyer sent an unsolicited nineteen-page memo to the Justice Department criticizing Mueller's investigation of potential obstructions of justice by Trump. Barr opined that the probe, as he understood it, was based on a "fatally misconceived" legal theory that could diminish executive power. Six months later, Trump tapped him as Sessions's permanent replacement. Barr won confirmation in the Senate on a largely party-line vote, promising, despite his skepticism of Mueller's inquiry, to act independently and not to buckle to pressure from Trump. "I will not be bullied into doing anything I think is wrong," he told the Senate Judiciary Committee in January 2019.

The special counsel's investigation had so far resulted in charges against thirty-four people, most of them Russians allegedly involved in hacking or social media manipulation. Six were Trump associates or campaign aides. Among them, Roger Stone pleaded not guilty to charges of lying to Congress, obstruction of justice, and witness tampering while allegedly trying to cover up his efforts to help Trump's campaign obtain hacked emails from WikiLeaks. Paul Manafort had been charged in two federal jurisdictions, accused of tax and bank fraud, money laundering, conspiracy, and other crimes. A jury convicted him in one case, and he pleaded guilty in another after agreeing to cooperate. (Mueller convinced a judge to revoke his cooperation agreement after telling her that Manafort had lied to investigators.) Former national security adviser Michael Flynn admitted to lying to the FBI about discussing sanctions with the Russian ambassador. And there was Michael Cohen, charged by Mueller with making a false statement to Congress, and by the Southern District with coordinating two hush-money payments, among other things.

But the world was hanging on what Mueller would have to say about the president of the United States.

After receiving the special counsel office's two-volume, 448-page *Report on the Investigation into Russian Interference in the 2016 Presidential Election*, Barr, on March 24, sent a four-page summary to Congress but said he wasn't ready to release the full document, which was laden with grand jury material, private information about witnesses and subjects of the investigation, and details about ongoing inquiries.

Barr wrote that in the special counsel's nearly two-year probe, Mueller had concluded that Russia indeed tried to influence the 2016 election through a social media disinformation campaign and email hacks of Democratic Party operatives and Clinton campaign associates. But Mueller didn't find evidence sufficient to establish that Trump's campaign had coordinated with the Russians. In his investigation of whether Trump obstructed his inquiry, Barr wrote, Mueller laid out arguments on both sides of the issue without reaching a conclusion. Mueller had written that, while the report didn't conclude that the president had committed a crime, "it also does not exonerate him."

Mueller's decision not to say whether he thought Trump had committed a crime of obstruction, Barr wrote, left it to him as attorney general to do so. So the man who had called the inquiry illegitimate in the first place determined that the special counsel's evidence hadn't shown any criminal offense. Barr said he'd made the judgment with Rod Rosenstein, the deputy attorney general, whose memo the White House had attempted to use to justify Jim Comey's firing. Trump declared victory on an airport tarmac in Palm Beach, telling reporters—consistent with Barr's statements but contradicting Mueller's—that he'd been exonerated.

> It was just announced there was no collusion with Russia—the most ridiculous thing I've ever heard. There was no collusion with Russia. There was no obstruction, and none whatsoever, and it was a complete and total exoneration. It's a shame that our country had to go through this. To be honest, it's a shame that your president has had to go through this for—before I even got elected, it began, and it began illegally! And hopefully somebody's going to look at the other side. This was an illegal takedown that failed.

But Barr's letter raised as many questions as it answered. Had Mueller intended that Barr should decide whether Trump obstructed justice? What was the actual evidence? Democrats demanded the report's full release. Two days later, Mueller privately accused Barr in a letter of sowing "public confusion about critical aspects of the results of our investigation."

As the Justice Department undertook to redact the full report for release, Barr created more questions about his independence at a Senate hearing by characterizing the FBI's initial investigation of Trump's campaign as "spying." He said the Justice Department would investigate the agency's surveillance of Trump associates. "I think spying on a political campaign is a big deal," Barr said. Trump had always said the probe was a "witch hunt." Now his attorney general would find out.

Before releasing the redacted report on April 18, Barr held a news conference where he stressed that Mueller had found "no collusion"—a phrase Trump used that had no legal meaning. Barr explained away Trump's efforts to stop the investigation, saying his motives weren't corrupt; he'd simply been "frustrated and angered by a sincere belief that the investigation was undermining his presidency."

As the world absorbed the report, it became clear that Barr's initial summary had failed to capture the weight of Trump's attempts to thwart the probe. Mueller recounted in detail the events leading to Trump's firing of Comey after he failed to control the FBI director, his efforts to stop Sessions from recusing himself, and his reaction upon learning from Sessions about the appointment of a special counsel:

"This is the end of my presidency. I'm fucked." Trump had repeatedly pushed White House counsel Don McGahn to have Mueller fired, but the lawyer didn't obey.

The report also made clear that Mueller hadn't meant for Barr to exonerate Trump. He explained that he didn't think it would be fair to render a decision on obstruction charges when Trump was a sitting president who couldn't be prosecuted based on Justice Department policy. By making that judgment, Mueller said, he'd have hampered Trump's ability to govern. But his report also said that "if we had confidence after a thorough investigation of the facts that the President clearly did not commit obstruction of justice, we would so state." The implication was clear: Mueller thought there was at least a case to be made that Trump had indeed committed obstruction of justice. He had laid out a record that Congress might evaluate for impeachment proceedings, or for prosecutors who might choose to charge Trump once he left office.

Trump again declared victory. "Game Over," he tweeted. At the White House he said, "This should never happen to another president again, this hoax." But a week later, amid ongoing public fascination with his efforts to frustrate the special counsel's investigation, Trump called some of Mueller's findings "total bullshit" and denied that he'd tried to have him fired. "If I wanted to fire Mueller, I didn't need McGahn to do it," Trump tweeted. "I could have done it myself."

One of the ironies of Mueller's report was the revelation that some of Trump's most egregious directives had failed because people surrounding him didn't obey the president's orders. They wanted the professional reputations they had established before Trump's presidency to remain intact when he was gone. In his life as a business mogul, Trump had been able to find people who, attracted to his boundless ego, were willing to cater to his whims. Like the Wizard of Oz—or, as Cohen had suggested in Congress, a Mafia don—he'd make his orders known directly or in code to the fixers who carried them out, without leaving his fingerprints. That wasn't so easy when he became president. If most of those surrounding Trump in the White House had listened to him, the case that he had obstructed justice would certainly have been stronger.

Trump had asked two National Security Agency officials, Admiral Michael Rogers and Deputy Director Rick Ledgett, what they could do to refute news stories he said were falsely linking him to Russia. The men signed a memo documenting the conversation and put it in a safe, but didn't follow through. Ledgett told Mueller's prosecutors that it was the most unusual thing he'd witnessed in forty years of government.

In the spring of 2017, Trump dictated a statement to Corey Lewandowski, his former campaign manager and now a lobbyist, to deliver to Jeff Sessions. The president told Lewandowski he wanted the attorney general to make the statement publicly:

> POTUS . . . is being treated very unfairly. He shouldn't have a Special Prosecutor/Counsel b/c he hasn't done anything wrong. I was on the campaign w/ him for nine months, there were no Russians involved with him. I know it for a fact b/c I was there. He didn't do anything wrong except he ran the greatest campaign in American history.
>
> Now a group of people want to subvert the Constitution of the United States. I am going to meet with the Special Prosecutor to explain this is very unfair and let the Special Prosecutor move forward with investigating election meddling for future elections so that nothing can happen in future elections.

Lewandowski tried to schedule a meeting with Sessions, but the attorney general canceled it. Then Lewandowski asked Rick Dearborn, a White House adviser who was closer to Sessions than he was, to deliver the message. Dearborn thought the message "raised an eyebrow," Mueller wrote, and discarded it without telling Sessions.

Around the same time, Trump repeatedly urged McGahn to have Rosenstein fire Mueller for alleged conflicts of interest that the White House counsel thought were silly. "Mueller has to go . . . Call me back when you do it," Trump told him. McGahn told chief of staff Reince Priebus that Trump had ordered him to "do crazy shit" and that, as a consequence, he planned to resign. But Priebus and White House strategist Steve Bannon convinced McGahn to stay, and the president dropped the matter.

After *The New York Times* later reported that the president asked McGahn to have Mueller fired, Trump told the lawyer that he'd not done so, and asked him to "do a correction." McGahn refused. He also asked McGahn, who had documented the interactions with Trump, why he took notes: "I never had a lawyer who took notes." McGahn responded that he was "a real lawyer," and Trump replied, "I've had a lot of great lawyers, like Roy Cohn. He did not take notes."

Trump's aides told the Mueller team about the president's repeated praise for Cohn, dead now for three decades, when he was frustrated that the people around him didn't get done what he wanted. Trump glamorized his first fixer, whom he had embraced as a young man but then pushed aside when Cohn got sick with AIDS. One man Trump never pined for as he struggled to contain the Russia investigation— one who for years jumped to fulfill the boss's demands, no matter how sketchy—was Michael Cohen.

With a year and a half left until the next presidential election, the darkest clouds over Trump's White House had lifted. Mueller was finished, and the results, while damaging, were muddy enough that Republicans in Congress wouldn't support impeachment. House Speaker Nancy Pelosi signaled that pursuing Trump's removal from office on a partisan basis was politically unpalatable, though she faced pressure from her members and some of her party's presidential candidates. Trump was moving on, and live-streaming his thoughts on Twitter.

Some investigations were continuing, including a federal inquiry in New York of donations to Trump's 2017 inaugural committee, and the New York State probe of his foundation. Democrats in the House were wielding their subpoena power with zeal, still pursuing documents related to his taxes, his business, his family, and his potential obstruction of the special counsel. Trump fought to avoid complying with the document demands from Congress. The Justice Department had already begun digging into the origins of the investigation of the president that William Barr had promised. "I'm so proud of our attorney general," Trump said. Barr told reporters that he wasn't protecting Donald Trump, but the presidency itself.

USING STILL ANOTHER new set of lawyers, Cohen was suing the Trump Organization in New York State Supreme Court for legal fees he said the company had promised to pay. The company and Trump's campaign had already paid $1.7 million to McDermott Will & Emery, between the Russian investigation and the firm's document review after the raids. Now Cohen was asking for $3.8 million more—$1.9 million in legal fees and another $1.9 million for fines, forfeiture, and restitution he'd been ordered to pay, including for his unpaid taxes to the IRS. In response, the company denied that it had promised anything, calling Cohen "a nine-time convicted felon" (he'd pleaded guilty to nine felonies, but only in two cases) who was seeking "a payday as he enters federal prison."

Cohen grew increasingly angry as he prepared for his May 6 report date to the federal prison camp in Otisville in Orange County, New York. He had come to realize that no one—not Mueller's team, not Congress, certainly not the prosecutors who'd disparaged him as dishonest in New York City—was coming to reduce his sentence.

In late March, Cohen had spoken by phone with Tom Arnold, the comedian who'd caused him angst the summer before. Arnold told Cohen he wanted to lend moral support. He was also recording their phone call, and shared the tape with the *Journal* in late April. In the conversation—the same one in which he spoke of Avenatti's karma boomerang—Cohen expressed frustration about his own plight. He had taken a stand against Trump, and, in his mind, no one had come to his aid. We reported their conversation on April 24.

"You would think that you would have folks, you know, stepping up and saying, 'You know what, this guy's lost everything,'" Cohen said. "My family's happiness, and my law license . . . I lost my business . . . my insurance, my bank accounts, all for what? All for what? Because Trump, you know, had an affair with a porn star? That's really what this is about."

Cohen also disavowed his guilty plea to the tax evasion charges his lawyer Guy Petrillo had previously challenged, which angered prosecutors at the time. "There is no tax evasion," Cohen told Arnold. He discounted the omission of his liabilities from an application for a home equity line from First Republic Bank, the basis for one of the charges to which he pleaded guilty: "I have an 18 percent loan-to-value on my home. How could there be a HELOC issue? How? Right? . . . It's a lie." And Cohen said he'd pleaded guilty to protect his wife. "I love this woman, and I am not going to let her get dragged into the mud of this crap. And I never thought the judge was going to throw a three-year fricking sentence. It's terrible what they're doing. What they can do to anybody is just . . . it's obscene."

The recording certainly wouldn't be helpful if Cohen hoped prosecutors might recommend reducing his sentence, though there was little chance of that anyway. His lawyer and spokesman Lanny Davis tried to soften the remarks with a statement that Cohen had taken responsibility for his crimes and meant no offense. But Cohen echoed them in an interview published a few days later in a *New Yorker* article titled "Michael Cohen's Last Days of Freedom," which cast him as "a victim as well as a perpetrator." Cohen told Jeffrey Toobin, "If they would have asked me to plead guilty to the Lufthansa heist, I would have pled guilty to that, too," referencing the infamous robbery by mobsters of a vault at Kennedy airport in 1978. He said he was still receiving requests for evidence from Congress but wasn't going to take any more time away from his family "without knowing what benefit there is now to me."

Cohen expressed similar frustrations the week before he was to leave for prison, during an afternoon spent with Jerry and Becki Falwell. In his call with Tom Arnold, Cohen lamented that friends like the Falwells, whom he said he loved, no longer spoke to him. After learning about what Cohen had said, Falwell called to let him know that he still cared for him. (Before Cohen's sentencing, Falwell had also ignored a request from Cohen to write a letter of support to the judge, hoping to stay clear of the feud between Trump and his former fixer.)

Now, with prison looming, the Falwells made a visit to New York to see Cohen and his family, having lunch and repairing to his apartment. Again, Cohen blamed his accountant for some of his troubles, showing Falwell notebooks he'd supplied the tax preparer with records of his deposits. He also faulted Trump's lawyers for the Southern District investigation; Cohen felt that they could have stopped Mueller from referring his case there. "It's just incredible to me that with all the avenues for information to be disseminated, it took Tom Arnold secretly taping me to get my side of the story out," Cohen said. Despite his complaints, he seemed relaxed and at peace, unlike the agitated state he'd been in when the Falwells had dinner with him after the raid. Laura Cohen was scared about how she'd manage with him in prison, but she was holding up.

Before they left, Cohen went to retrieve a gift from a storage area in his building. In his office at Trump Tower had hung a painting of a woman coincidentally named Becky. Cohen had told Becki Falwell and her husband that he wanted them to have it someday. He made good on the promise in his last days of freedom.

On the Saturday before he had to leave, Cohen walked out of his Park Avenue apartment building with his son, Jake, trailed by reporters, stopping at the Viand coffee shop and then at the Eddie Arthur Salon for haircuts. Afterward they headed for lunch with family and friends, including Davis, at Freds, a café in Barneys department store, on Madison Avenue. Cohen smiled as he walked around, except when asking a photographer to stay away from his family. "Trump has already done enough damage to them," he said.

On Monday morning, Cohen walked out of his home at Trump Park Avenue in a dark sport jacket and jeans and read a statement for the waiting journalists. "I hope that when I rejoin my family and friends that the country will be in a place without xenophobia, injustice, and lies at the helm of our country," he said. "There still remains much to be told, and I look forward to the day that I can share the truth."

He pushed through the media throng and into a black Cadillac Escalade, departing just before 10 A.M. on the eighty-mile trip to Otisville. Less than two hours later, the car was stopped by federal agents on the wooded road leading to the entrance to the facility. Cohen spoke to the officers for a few minutes. He looked somberly out the window at the line of photographers aiming their cameras at him. Then his car kept moving, on to the grounds of the prison and out of view.

WITH COHEN'S DEFECTION and downfall and Pecker's humbling, Trump turned to another associate for help with his problems. With Rudy Giuliani, Trump set out to convince Ukraine, a country dependent on American aid, to investigate former vice president Joe Biden, who was leading Trump by double digits in most early polling for the 2020 election.

Trump and Giuliani had palled around and pushed boundaries over the years. In 2000, while Giuliani was New York City mayor, he dressed up in a gaudy pink dress and a blond wig and sprayed himself with perfume in a video filmed with Trump for a roast. "Oh, you dirty boy,"

Giuliani exclaimed in mock horror, after Trump nuzzled his fake cleavage.

Though Giuliani had been a devoted booster of his campaign, Trump sometimes mistreated him, much as he had Michael Cohen. He mocked Giuliani for sleeping on flights and joked that he was watching cartoons on his iPad. When Giuliani volunteered as one of Trump's only defenders on cable news after the *Access Hollywood* recording's release before the election, the presidential candidate panned his performance. "Man, Rudy, you sucked," Trump told him. "You were weak. Low energy."

Then, after he was president and had passed Giuliani over for secretary of state, Trump humiliated him at the wedding of Treasury Secretary Steven Mnuchin, yelling at him to stand somewhere else because the lawyer was spitting as he talked.

Giuliani remained loyal, however. After becoming the president's personal attorney in 2018, he enjoyed access to the president exceeding that of some cabinet secretaries. When aides at the White House rolled their eyes at Giuliani's sometimes rambling cable news interviews attacking various investigations circling the president, Trump made it clear that he appreciated Giuliani's zeal, silencing the chatter.

Even before the special counsel's report on Russian interference became public, Giuliani had been working in the background to persuade Ukraine's top prosecutor to open investigations that he hoped would portray Trump as a victim of foreign meddling and tarnish Biden, the potential Democratic nominee in the next presidential election. Giuliani wanted to legitimize two theories that had taken root in the far-right corners of the Internet. The first involved Trump's former campaign chief Paul Manafort, who had been pushed out in 2016 after *The New York Times* reported that handwritten ledgers showed Manafort had received $12.7 million in undisclosed cash from a pro-Russian political party in Ukraine. According to the theory Giuliani sought to legitimize, the ledgers were forgeries. Never mind that Manafort had filed disclosures with the federal government, albeit belatedly, that corroborated the ledgers.

The second theory supposed that Joe Biden, as President Obama's vice president, had demanded that Ukraine fire the country's general prosecutor, Viktor Shokin, because he was investigating a company that employed Biden's son Hunter. Burisma Holdings Ltd. was a natural gas extraction company owned by a Ukrainian official. The younger Biden had joined the board of Burisma in May 2014, earning $50,000 a month, while his father was the U.S. government's chief conduit of aid and support to Ukraine. The country was reeling after Russia invaded Ukraine, annexed its peninsula of Crimea, and armed separatist rebels.

It was true that Joe Biden had prevailed on Ukrainian officials to fire the prosecutor, threatening to withhold aid otherwise, but other Western officials and the International Monetary Fund also wanted Shokin gone, as Ukraine's Western lenders viewed Shokin as unwilling to aggressively target the country's rampant corruption. Shokin's office had investigated the owner of Burisma, Mykola Zlochevsky, for various crimes, including abuse of power, but had never made a case. And that was precisely the problem, according to Western diplomats. Shokin was an obstacle to cleaning up the country. He denied dragging his feet on cases and said he was driven out of office by grant-seeking nonprofit groups trying to gain favor with the West.

Giuliani found an ally in Shokin's replacement, Yuriy Lutsenko. They met at least twice in 2019 before Lutsenko announced probes into Burisma and the Manafort ledgers in March. Lutsenko's investigations were a major victory for Giuliani and Trump, who long harbored the belief that Ukraine had attempted to subvert his presidential campaign.

But Lutsenko, like his predecessor, was viewed in Ukraine and beyond as weak on corruption. The U.S. ambassador to Ukraine, Marie Yovanovitch, for one, had criticized his prosecutorial record. Giuliani, seeing her as an obstacle to his machinations, sent Secretary of State Mike Pompeo a nine-page document about the Bidens' supposed activities in Ukraine and allegations of impropriety involving the U.S. ambassador. The document, dated March 28, 2019, described Yovanovitch as "very close" to the former vice president. Trump would soon recall Yovanovitch, a career diplomat.

In April, comedian-turned-politician Volodymyr Zelensky defeated incumbent Ukrainian president Petro Poroshenko, promising on election night to replace the prosecutor general with someone who would lean harder into the country's corruption problem. Lutsenko soon told a Bloomberg reporter that he had found no wrongdoing by the Bidens.

Lutsenko's professional demise put Giuliani's mission in jeopardy, but the lawyer didn't give up. He sought inroads into the new administration in Ukraine, with the goal of ensuring the investigations sought by Trump would resume. The U.S. government's special envoy to Ukraine, Kurt Volker, introduced Giuliani to one of the new Ukrainian president's senior advisers in a text message on July 19. They had a three-way call the following week, with Giuliani again lobbying for the investigations, and Giuliani and the Ukrainian aide would soon meet in Madrid.

About a week after Giuliani's call, Trump had his first substantive phone conversation with the new Ukrainian president. White House staff and Pompeo, the secretary of state, listened in. After congratulating Zelensky, Trump reminded the Ukrainian president that "we do a lot for Ukraine." Then he asked for a favor.

Trump wanted Zelensky to "get to the bottom" of yet another far-right fever dream about an allegedly missing Democratic National Committee server that had been hacked in the 2016 elections. Without the server, the theory went, federal agents couldn't possibly attribute the hack to Russia.

Trump had bought into an extension of this theory that the server was now in Ukraine, falsely claiming that the cybersecurity firm hired by the DNC to investigate the 2016 hack was based in the country.

In fact, Mueller's team had received images of DNC servers and relevant traffic logs, and had substantiated the findings of the intelligence community that Russia was responsible for the hack. There was no missing server. But Trump had embraced theories, no matter how unmoored from reality, that called into doubt Russia's meddling in the 2016 election and thus, in his view, solidified the legitimacy of his presidency.

"Whatever you can do, it's very important that you do it," Trump told Zelensky, who pledged his cooperation.

"In addition to that investigation, I guarantee as the president of Ukraine that all the investigations will be done openly and candidly. That I can assure you," Zelensky said.

Trump was blunt.

"Good, because I heard you had a prosecutor who was very good, and he was shut down, and that's really unfair," Trump said, referring to Lutsenko, the prosecutor who had opened the investigations pushed by Giuliani.

He then told Zelensky that he wanted Giuliani and his attorney general, William Barr, to call the Ukrainian president to discuss the Bidens.

"There's a lot of talk about Biden's son, that Biden stopped the prosecution, and a lot of people want to find out about that, so whatever you can do with the attorney general would be great," Trump said. "Biden went around bragging that he stopped the prosecution, so if you can look into it . . . It sounds horrible to me."

Zelensky assured Trump that the next general prosecutor of Ukraine would be "100% my person, my candidate. . . . He or she will look into the situation," he promised.

Although it was unspoken, Trump had already provided an incentive for Zelensky to work with him. He had personally directed his acting chief of staff to place a hold on $391 million in aid to Ukraine earlier in July. Zelensky also wanted an invitation to the White House, a state visit that would shore up his standing in Ukraine and on the world stage.

On the same day as the July 25 call, Volker, the U.S. special representative to Ukraine, had texted one of Zelensky's top aides: "Heard from White House—assuming President Z convinces Trump he will investigate / 'get to the bottom of what happened' in 2016, we will nail down date for visit to Washington."

For years, Trump had let his fixers do his bidding for him, avoiding email and text messages, dispensing elliptical instructions that kept him insulated. Except for rare slips, such as Cohen secretly recording him talking about Karen McDougal, these tactics had been effective. But the White House posed challenges that Trump hadn't encountered in the private sector. Readouts of his calls with foreign officials were difficult to contain.

Trump hadn't explicitly linked U.S. aid to his requests of Zelensky, and he apparently saw no problem with asking a foreign leader to fight corruption that personally benefited him. But to some of the White House officials who were listening, the Zelensky call seemed far more sinister. A half dozen of them told a CIA officer detailed to the White House that they believed they'd been witnesses to the president of the United States abusing his office for personal political gain. The CIA officer also learned from his sources that senior aides to Trump had restricted access to the rough transcript of Trump's call with the Ukrainian president.

The officer relayed what he'd been told to the inspector general of the intelligence community in a formal whistleblower complaint. He wrote that he was "deeply concerned" that the conduct as described by the White House officials constituted "a serious or flagrant problem, abuse, or violation of law."

"The President's personal lawyer, Mr. Rudolph Giuliani, is a central figure in this effort," the whistleblower noted.

Soon, word of the complaint would make its way to Democrats in Congress.

Trump and his fixer were in trouble again.

MICHAEL COHEN HAD been behind bars for nearly four months when representatives of the Manhattan District Attorney's Office paid him a visit in Otisville on August 20, 2019. Cohen had settled into a routine in the upstate prison. He had been assigned the job of fixing fire hydrants. He had lost weight from exercising regularly. He was hypersocial as always; some of the corrections officers and inmates had already taken to calling him "mayor" of the prison camp. He had befriended rabbis and given a sermon during services. He planned to write a book.

Earlier that month, the Manhattan District Attorney's Office had opened an investigation of the Trump Organization's reimbursement of Cohen for the Stormy Daniels payment. The company had hidden the reimbursement in monthly payments to Cohen and booked them as legal fees. Cyrus Vance Jr., the district attorney, had picked up the case. The office was in a rush: A misdemeanor charge for falsifying business records had to be brought within two years of the crime. Cohen had received his last check for the Daniels payment in late 2017. The office could bring a felony charge if assistant district attorneys had proof that Trump Organization executives intentionally made false entries in the company's books to conceal a crime. Cohen's history of lying made him a problematic witness, but he could still point the district attorney's office in the right direction.

Cohen was also in a rush: He had until December 12, 2019—one year after his sentencing—to convince a judge to reduce his prison term. Without a formal petition from federal prosecutors in New York, Cohen's chances were vanishingly small. But Cohen was an optimist. Maybe the district attorney's office could put in a good word. Maybe members of Congress would come through with letters attesting to Cohen's help in their various investigations. Maybe Cohen would be out of prison soon, and maybe someone else from Trump World would take his place behind bars.

Acknowledgments

■ ■ ■

THIS BOOK IS the culmination of more than two years of our reporting, but it also leans heavily on the excellent work of our colleagues at *The Wall Street Journal,* who propelled the story of two hush-money deals involving the president far beyond what we could have managed by ourselves. We are profoundly grateful for the efforts and friendship of three colleagues in particular: White House reporter Rebecca Ballhaus, and Nicole Hong and Rebecca Davis O'Brien, who covered federal law enforcement agencies in New York. Their contributions are represented in most chapters.

Three *Wall Street Journal* editors—"Boss" Mike Siconolfi, Jennifer Forsyth, and Ashby Jones—guided our core group of five reporters as we uncovered the hush money, bored into the investigation and prosecution of Michael Cohen, and revealed the participation of the president in Cohen's crimes. The three of them share that most desirable trait in an editor: the ability to make a reporter's work better—and often much better. They informed every step of our reporting for the *Journal* and at times contributed their own. Without them, the Pulitzer Prize for national reporting awarded to the newspaper for our hush-money coverage in 2019 certainly wouldn't have been possible. They deserve more than our deep gratitude, but it will have to do.

Many other *Journal* editors and reporters lent their talents to the story, including Lukas I. Alpert, Alexandra Berzon, Mark Maremont, Rob Barry, Peter Nicholas, Shelby Holliday, Carmel Lobello, Jamie Graff, Mike Allen, Matthew Rose, and Joel Eastwood. Their work is also reflected in this book. We are grateful to the two editors in chief who championed our coverage: Matt Murray and Gerard Baker, who forecast "a Stormy night" on the Friday evening we told the world that the president's lawyer had paid off a porn star.

We struck gold again with our editor at Random House, Mark Warren, who had the misfortune of inheriting two first-time authors trained in the spare style of newspaper writing. Without his direction, patience, and gift for storytelling, we might still be writing. If you liked this book, blame him. If you didn't, blame us.

Our agent, Eric Lupfer, also spoiled us. He built the scaffolding for the book and helped us render the world from which Trump came, calling it the "the vulgar circus."

The rest of the Random House team that coalesced around this project has our heartfelt thanks. An incomplete list: Random House editor in chief Andy Ward, deputy publisher Tom Perry, associate general counsel Carolyn Foley, deputy general counsel Matthew Martin, copy editor Will Palmer, production editor Steve Messina, Barbara Fillon and Ayelet Gruenspecht in marketing, publicist Melanie DeNardo, and editorial assistant Chayenne Skeete.

Thank you to Andie Horowitz, who took time between her classes at the University of Michigan to trek to a campus library and dig out a rare transcript of Donald Trump's testimony at Roy Cohn's disbarment hearings.

As reporters, we have no greater appreciation than for our sources, many of whom spent hours with us and continued to answer our calls, texts, and emails until we ran out of space and time for additional reporting. You know who you are. Thank you.

This book also rests in parts on sturdy reporting by New York journalists and authors, especially the earlier chapters on a young Trump, Roy Cohn, and David Pecker. We owe a particular debt to the late Wayne Barrett, Sidney Zion, and Nicholas von Hoffman, and to the *New York Post*'s Keith J. Kelly and Bill Bastone of *The Smoking Gun*.

A tip of the hat to our competitors at other newspapers and networks, who kept us on our toes and added to our understanding of the investigation of Michael Cohen and of Trump's world. Their work also features here.

From Michael: I'm profoundly grateful for family that has always been there for me. My parents, Stuart and Evelyn, worried journalism would be too difficult a field, then became my biggest cheerleaders. Though we lost my dad shortly before the Stormy story, my mom watched it explode with pride enough for both of them. My brother, Eric, checked in whenever he spotted a new headline. I am constantly learning from my daughters, Annabel and Georgia—your curiosity, wisdom, and strength inspire me. Thank you, Tasha Blaine, for years of supporting my career despite the sacrifice, and for raising two amazing girls with me into the incredible women they are becoming. I am so thankful for a group of lifelong friends who are true family to me.

From Joe: I thank my mom and dad, Jackie and Skip, who prop me up and bowl me over with their limitless patience and love; my sister, Andrea, who encourages and inspires me in equal measure; and Tara, my wife, who makes me deliriously happy, even when she's offering constructive criticism. To my friends and family, whom I've neglected over the past year, thanks for your love and support.

On to the next story.

Authors' Note

■ ■ ■

WE SPOKE, EMAILED, or messaged with hundreds of people in the reporting of this book. We also relied on public documents and other media, including substantial reporting by us and our colleagues that previously appeared in *The Wall Street Journal*. We attempted to contact anyone who is mentioned in a substantial way. Many agreed to help us in our efforts to present a narrative that is factually and contextually accurate.

In a great number of cases, we agreed not to reveal the identities of those who spoke with us so that they would feel comfortable discussing events related to the sitting president of the United States and about private encounters involving people with whom they had worked closely. Accordingly, while we cite public documents, media accounts, and other books in the endnotes, we do not reference our own interviews to avoid suggesting who cooperated with us and who did not.

We also caution readers against making inferences about the sources of anecdotes and information, including when the narrative is told from a particular person's point of view. Such passages may be based on interviews with the person whose point of view is presented, with others familiar with someone's thinking, from testimony or statements that have been publicly released, or from private correspondence or other places. The book is written as an omniscient narrative, which required decisions about how to address divergent versions of events spanning several decades. When the sources we asked to reach back into their memories gave us different accounts that we could not reconcile, we presented disparate views within the narrative or used the account we judged to be most credible based on our knowledge of the tellers and the story.

Notes

■ ■ ■

PART I: THE DEALS

1. THE FIRST FIXER

4 **At Cohn's table that day** Donald J. Trump and Tony Schwartz, *Trump: The Art of the Deal* (New York: Ballantine, 1987), 97–99.

4 **he also tended to a colorful roster** Stephen G. Schwarz, "Three Months with Roy Cohn," *American College of Trial Lawyers Journal* 87 (Summer 2018): 79.

8 **David Rosenthal was a twenty-one-year-old** Marie Brenner, "How Donald Trump and Roy Cohn's Ruthless Symbiosis Changed America," *Vanity Fair*, June 28, 2017, https://www.vanityfair.com/news/2017/06/donald-trump-roy-cohn -relationship.

9 **Trump also had to manage another** Wayne Barrett, *Trump: The Deals and the Downfall* (New York: HarperCollins, 1992), 199–200.

9 **Cohn arranged the nearly $2 million purchase** Richard Esposito and T. J. Collins, "Murder Charged in Numbers War," *Newsday*, March 14, 1986.

9 **Trump's role in possible money laundering** Wayne Barrett, "Rudy's Long History of Quashing Trump Probes," *Village Voice*, March 22, 2019, https://www .villagevoice.com/2019/03/22/rudys-long-history-of-quashing-trump-probes/.

11 **At Cohn's request, Reagan sent a note** Letter, Ronald Reagan to Roger Stone, August 20, 1982, file code ME001-02, case file 095888, WHORM: Subject File, Ronald Reagan Library, https://www.reaganlibrary.gov/sites/default/files/digital library/whormsubject/me001-02/40-654-12019891-ME001-02-095888-2018.pdf.

12 **In 1981, Forbes was preparing its** Jonathan Greenberg, "Trump Lied to Me About His Wealth to Get onto the Forbes 400. Here Are the Tapes," *Washington Post*, April 20, 2018, https://www.washingtonpost.com/outlook/trump-lied-to -me-about-his-wealth-to-get-onto-the-forbes-400-here-are-the-tapes/2018/04 /20/ac762b08-4287-11e8-8569-26fda6b404c7_story.html.

14 **In the 1960s, he borrowed** *Matter of Cohn*, 118 A.D.2d, 15 (N.Y. App. Div. 1986), https://casetext.com/case/matter-of-cohn-19.

15 **But before the new league** Robert A. Skitol, "Donald Trump's Major Antitrust Encounters," *The Antitrust Source*, April 2016, A-2, http://app.antitrustsource .com/antitrustsource/april_2016?folio=C-1&pg=16#pg16.

15 **"We have reliable reason to believe"** Michael Janofsky, "Charges Fly from

U.S.F.L.," *New York Times*, October 19, 1984, https://www.nytimes.com/1984/10/19/sports/charges-fly-from-usfl.html.

16 **"Donald Trump is probably one"** Mary Alice Miller, "*Where's My Roy Cohn?* Digs into One of the 20th Century's Most Evil Men," *Vanity Fair*, January 25, 2019, https://www.vanityfair.com/hollywood/2019/01/wheres-my-roy-cohn-digs-into-one-of-the-20th-centurys-most-evil-men.

16 **Cohn received well wishes from Ronald Reagan** Telegram, Ronald Reagan to Roy Cohn, November 22, 1985, file code ME001-03, case file 381952, WHORM: Subject File, Ronald Reagan Library, https://www.reaganlibrary.gov/sites/default/files/digitallibrary/whormsubject/me001-03/40-654-12019891-ME001-03-381952-2018.pdf.

16 **"I can't believe he's doing this"** Barrett, *Trump: The Deals and the Downfall*, 293.

17 **"In the course of being represented by him"** Departmental Disciplinary Committee, First Judicial Department, Supreme Court of the State of New York, *Matter of Cohn, Testimony of Donald John Trump*, 1985, 2395–96.

18 **In early 1986, Trump invited** Nicholas von Hoffman, *Citizen Cohn* (New York: Doubleday, 1988), 378.

18 **Before their marriage** Harry Hurt, *Lost Tycoon: The Many Lives of Donald J. Trump* (Vermont: Echo Point Books & Media, 2016), locations 1798–1815, Kindle.

18 **Trump called Cohn to check** Barrett, *Trump: The Deals and the Downfall*, 293.

19 **Trump and his new lawyer failed** Richard Hoffer, "USFL Awarded Only $3 in Antitrust Decision: Jury Finds NFL Guilty on One of Nine Counts," *Los Angeles Times*, July 30, 1986, https://www.latimes.com/archives/la-xpm-1986-07-30-sp-18643-story.html.

19 **Trump stood in the back** Barrett, *Trump: The Deals and the Downfall*, 293.

19 **Tom Bolan, his law partner** "700 Mourn Roy Cohn at Town Hall Service," *Newsday*, October 23, 1986.

2. GREAT ASSETS

20 **Ivana confronted Maples** Maureen Orth, "The Heart of the Deal: The Love Story of Marla Maples and Donald Trump," *Vanity Fair*, November 1, 1990, https://www.vanityfair.com/news/1990/11/marla-maples-donald-trump-relationship.

20 **Ivana had learned Maples's name** Harry Hurt, *Lost Tycoon: The Many Lives of Donald J. Trump* (Vermont: Echo Point Books & Media, 2016), loc. 4178, Kindle.

22 **Trump could no longer keep up** Peter Grant and Alexandra Berzon, "Trump and His Debts: A Narrow Escape," *Wall Street Journal*, January 4, 2016, https://www.wsj.com/articles/trump-and-his-debts-a-narrow-escape-1451868915.

23 **The Trumps settled** Richard D. Hylton, "Trumps Settle; She Gets $14 Million Plus," *New York Times*, March 21, 1991, https://www.nytimes.com/1991/03/21/nyregion/trumps-settle-she-gets-14-million-plus.html.

23 **After he won** Hurt, *Lost Tycoon,* loc. 6985.

23 **He sued Ivana** Michael Paskevich, "Ivana Trump Offers Advice to Women," *Las Vegas Review-Journal,* May 21, 1993.

24 **Trump, at the time of his divorce** Hylton, "Trumps Settle."

24 **But he convinced his creditors** Grant and Berzon, "Trump and His Debts."

3. PECKER'S PATH

25 **That winter, Pecker rented** Bradley Johnson, "Pecker Pitches Party Line," *Advertising Age,* March 11, 1996.

25 **So did New York governor** Raymond Hernandez, "Pataki Speech in Florida Had New York Ties," *New York Times,* February 8, 1997, https://www.nytimes .com/1997/02/08/nyregion/pataki-speech-in-florida-had-new-york-ties.html.

27 **He swallowed hard** Iain Calder, *The Untold Story: My 20 Years Running the National Enquirer* (New York: Miramax Books, 2004), 268.

29 **Jack Pecker died** Rene Chun, "How David Pecker Built His Tabloid Empire AMI on Fear," *Daily Beast,* March 2, 2019, https://www.thedailybeast.com/how -david-pecker-built-his-tabloid-empire-on-fear.

29 **The best-known of the publisher's** Geraldine Fabrikant, "CBS Inc. to Sell Magazine Unit to Its Executives," *New York Times,* July 14, 1987, https://www.nytimes .com/1987/07/14/business/cbs-inc-to-sell-magazine-unit-to-its-executives .html.

31 **Diamandis and his team expected** Peter Diamandis, "Living Out Every Manager's Dream," *Fortune,* October 9, 1989, https://archive.fortune.com/magazines /fortune/fortune_archive/1989/10/09/72558/index.htm.

31 **In 1952, Generoso "Gene" Pope Jr.** Paul David Pope, *The Deeds of My Fathers: How My Father and Grandfather Built New York and Created the Tabloid World of Today* (Lanham, Md.: Rowman & Littlefield, 2010), loc. 139, 313, 331, 2474, Kindle.

31 **Gene Pope transformed** "Generoso P. Pope Jr. Dead at 61; the National Enquirer's Publisher," *New York Times,* October 3, 1988, https://www.nytimes.com /1988/10/03/obituaries/generoso-p-pope-jr-dead-at-61-the-national-enquirer-s -publisher.html.

31 **By the time of his death** Geraldine Fabrikant, "Accord Reached to Acquire National Enquirer Publisher," *New York Times,* April 14, 1989, https://www.ny times.com/1989/04/14/business/accord-reached-to-acquire-national-enquirer -publisher.html.

32 **Hachette advanced a lowball bid** Keith J. Kelly, "Picking Up the Tabs: American Media's David Pecker Goes on a Rescue Mission," *New York Post,* May 16, 1999.

32 **A rift opened up** Patrick M. Reilly, "Diamandis, Two Top Aides Quit Hachette in Rift over Magazines," *Wall Street Journal,* September 25, 1990.

33 **Within a year of deft infighting** "Hachette Names U.S. Magazine Unit Chief," *Reuters,* September 22, 1991.

4. I'LL BUY IT

34 **Pecker was at his peak** Alan Mirabella, "Hachette's Bets Paying Off in US," *Crain's New York Business,* March 27, 1995.

34 **"David, I've got a '52 Buick"** Rebecca Mead, "Camelot," *New York,* August 7, 1995.

34 **Publishing executives also mocked** "At the AMC, David Pecker-Bashing Was in Fashion," *Media Industry Newsletter,* November 13, 1995.

35 **He wore $300 Brioni shirts** Keith J. Kelly, "Picking Up the Tabs: American Media's David Pecker Goes on a Rescue Mission," *New York Post,* May 16, 1999.

36 **Rao's had four tables** Alex Witchel, "Welcome to Rao's, New York's Most Exclusive Restaurant," *Vanity Fair,* October 10, 2016, https://www.vanityfair.com/culture/2016/10/raos-new-york-exclusive-restaurant.

37 **Perelman had entered into a deal** Patrick M. Reilly, "Two Premiere Editors Quit, Citing Interference," *Wall Street Journal,* May 8, 1996.

5. BUSINESS FIRST

41 **The tabloids' owners had agreed** Patrick M. Reilly, "News Corp. to Sell Star to G.P. Group for $400 Million," *Wall Street Journal,* March 30, 1990.

41 **Three years later, the company** "Enquirer/Star Co. to Change Name to American Media," Dow Jones News Service, August 22, 1994.

42 **Pecker and Beutner told reporters** "Investment Firm to Buy National Enquirer Publisher for $767 Million," *Dow Jones Business News,* February 16, 1999.

42 **When the deal was announced** Noelle Knox, "Publisher of National Enquirer, Star to Be Sold for $300 Million," Associated Press, February 16, 1999.

42 **Pecker, who received an ownership stake** "Investment Firm to Buy National Enquirer Publisher," *Dow Jones Business News.*

43 **He thanked the French executives** Celia McGee, "Picking Up the Tabs: Ex-Clinton Aide Buying Enquirer, Star," New York *Daily News,* February 17, 1999.

43 **The company ran a help-wanted ad** Jonah Goldberg, "Tabloid Turmoil—Inquiring Minds Want to Know: Why Change the Enquirer?," *Wall Street Journal,* November 5, 1999.

44 **Some of the paparazzi** Gayle Fee and Laura Raposa, "Star Dims for Enquiring Photogs," *Boston Herald,* February 22, 1999.

46 **In a slight that stung** Neal Travis, "JFK Jr.'s Will May Spark Furor," *New York Post,* July 26, 1999.

47 **Trump made a few campaign trips** Joel Siegel, "Donald Does Miami as Prez Possibility," New York *Daily News,* November 16, 1999.

47 **After Ventura quit the Reform Party** Ron Fournier, "After Long Flirtation, Trump Decides Not to Run for President," Associated Press, February 13, 2000.

48 **After initially saying** Keith J. Kelly, "Pecker Taking Star to Boca Raton," *New York Post,* January 27, 2000.

48 **He had already saved money** Seth Sutel, "National Enquirer Owner Buys Rival," Associated Press, November 2, 1999.

48 **He launched an investigation** Jose Lambiet, "No Love Lost Between Pecker and His Tabloid Employees," *Sun-Sentinel,* February 4, 2000, https://www.sun-sentinel.com/news/fl-xpm-2000-02-04-0002040237-story.html.

49 **Dietl wrote that he'd pinpointed** George Rush and Joanna Molloy, "Gwen & Guy Are Couch Pet-atoes," New York *Daily News,* October 15, 1999.

6. FIRST CATCH

51 **The *Enquirer* had paid** Laurence Leamer, interviewed by Donna Tetreault, *American Morning,* August 16, 2005, http://transcripts.cnn.com/TRANSCRIPTS/0508/16/ltm.04.html.

52 **In late November, American Media** David Carr, "American Media to Buy Weider for $350 Million," *New York Times,* November 27, 2002.

53 **After Weider brought Schwarzenegger** Robert D. McFadden, "Joe Weider, Creator of Bodybuilding Empire, Dies at 93," *New York Times,* March 25, 2013.

53 **As the eighty-three-year-old** George Rush and Joanna Molloy, "Muscle Mentor Keeps Tabs on Ah-nold," New York *Daily News,* August 20, 2003.

54 **That summer, Pecker met** Ann Louise Bardach, "The Hush-Hush Deal That Made Arnold Schwarzenegger Governor," *Los Angeles Magazine,* September 1, 2004.

54 **Pecker did more than lay off Schwarzenegger** A representative for Arnold Schwarzenegger told the authors: "My client has never entered into any agreement with [American Media Inc.] requesting that AMI buy or kill stories for him."

54 **In the contract, titled "Confidentiality Agreement"** Peter Nicholas and Carla Hall, "Tabloid's Deal with Woman Shielded Schwarzenegger," *Los Angeles Times,* August 12, 2005, https://www.latimes.com/archives/la-xpm-2005-aug-12-me-arnold12-story.html.

55 **The next month, the company agreed** Peter Nicholas, "Tabloid Tried to Suppress Videotape," *Los Angeles Times,* September 12, 2005, https://www.latimes.com/archives/la-xpm-2005-sep-12-me-video12-story.html.

55 **The *Enquirer* had earlier investigated** Bardach, "Hush-Hush Deal."

55 **The next month, two days** Peter Nicholas and Robert Salladay, "Gov. to Be Paid $8 Million by Fitness Magazines," *Los Angeles Times,* July 14, 2005.

55 **After the election, the *Enquirer* published** Bardach, "Hush-Hush Deal."

55 **As governor, Schwarzenegger would** Nicholas and Salladay, "Gov. to Be Paid $8 Million."

56 **The hoped-for transformation** Keith J. Kelly, "Big Layoffs at Pecker's AMI," *New York Post,* September 11, 2003.

56 **The two firms put down** "Evercore Partners and Thomas H. Lee Partners Announce $1.5 Billion Recapitalization of American Media," Business Wire, February 25, 2003.

56 **Pecker chopped more than a hundred** Keith J. Kelly, "An Un-Healthy Staff: Pecker Cans Mag's Edit Team to Face Off with Real Simple," *New York Post,* March 21, 2003.

7. THE CONDO BOARD

58 **Burnett, after watching a BBC documentary** Patrick Radden Keefe, "How Mark Burnett Resurrected Donald Trump as an Icon of American Success," *New Yorker,* January 7, 2019, https://www.newyorker.com/magazine/2019/01/07/how -mark-burnett-resurrected-donald-trump-as-an-icon-of-american-success.

61 **"I'll slap that stupid"** Brian McGrory, "Outrage in the Court," *Boston Globe,* December 7, 1999.

61 **The Massachusetts attorney general's office** David Weber, "Injunction Issued vs. Man Who Hurled Racist Insults," *Boston Herald,* January 7, 2000.

61 **The lawsuit also revealed** *Commonwealth v. Jacobson,* 477 N.E.2d 158, 19 Mass. App. Ct. (1985), https://law.justia.com/cases/massachusetts/court-of-appeals /1985/19-mass-app-ct-666-1.html.

61 **Trump had allies in the building** George Sorial and Damian Bates, *The Real Deal: My Decade Fighting Battles and Winning Wars with Trump* (New York: Broadside Books, 2019), 24–26.

61 **The younger Trump asked if Cohen** *Hearing with Michael Cohen, Former Attorney to President Donald Trump, Before the House Committee on Oversight and Reform,* 116th Cong., 1st sess. (2019), 105. (Hereinafter, "Cohen hearing.")

62 **Outside his school one day** *U.S. v. Cohen,* No. 18-cr-602 (S.D.N.Y. December 7, 2018) (letter from Maurice Cohen, ECF No. 24-1).

63 **After receiving his driver's license** *U.S. v. Cohen,* No. 18-cr-602 (S.D.N.Y. December 7, 2018) (letter from Beth Rosenthal, ECF No. 24-24).

63 **One night, while at a club** *U.S. v. Cohen,* No. 18-cr-602 (S.D.N.Y. December 7, 2018) (letter from Randall D. Satin, ECF No. 24-28).

63 **At American University** *U.S. v. Cohen,* No. 18-cr-602 (S.D.N.Y. December 7, 2018) (letter from Ranya Idliby, ECF No. 24-18).

63 **He went to work** Ilya Marritz and Andrea Bernstein, "The Company Michael Cohen Kept," *Trump, Inc.* podcast, April 18, 2018, https://www.wnycstudios.org /podcasts/trumpinc/episodes/trump-inc-podcast-company-michael-cohen -kept.

64 **Garber would amass a fortune** Tim Novak, Art Golab, and Mary Wisniewski, "Russian Emigre Now Chicago's Cab King," *Chicago Sun-Times,* February 1, 2010.

65 **He had briefly met Donald Trump** Deposition of Michael Cohen, Part 1, Before the House Select Committee on Intelligence, 116th Cong., 1st sess. (2019), 12. (Hereinafter, "Cohen deposition, part 1.")

8. THE CENTERFOLD AND THE PORN STAR

69 **Fellow students pronounced her** Pat Shellenbarger, "The Girl with the Prettiest . . . Eyes," *Grand Rapids Press,* June 23, 1998.

70 **She was cast in a B movie** IMDb, s.v. "Karen McDougal," https://www.imdb .com/name/nm0568210/.

70 **She had spent a lot of time** *The Millionaire Matchmaker,* season 6, episode 3,

"A Tale of Two Jimmys," directed by Greg Matthews, aired January 24, 2013, on Bravo, https://www.bravotv.com/the-millionaire-matchmaker/season-6/ep-3-a-tale-of-two-jimmys.

70 **McDougal had felt** Karen McDougal, interviewed by Anderson Cooper, *Anderson Cooper 360,* March 20, 2018, http://www.cnn.com/TRANSCRIPTS/1803/22/acd.01.html.

71 **On the course, Trump met Stormy** Stormy Daniels, *Full Disclosure* (New York: St. Martin's Press, 2018), 110–11.

72 **Trump found Daniels** Stormy Daniels, interviewed by Jordi Lippe-McGraw, "Stormy Daniels' Full Interview: Inside Her Affair with Donald Trump," *In Touch Weekly,* May 4, 2018, https://www.intouchweekly.com/posts/stormy-daniels-full-interview-151788/.

72 **Daniels found Trump sprawled** Daniels interview by Lippe-McGraw.

72 **"Well it's never going to happen"** Ibid.

74 **"I know my mom knows about"** McDougal interview by Cooper.

9. THE TRUMP ORGANIZATION EMPLOYEE

75 The developer asked for Cohen's help Cohen hearing, 105.

75 "Would you rather work for me?" Cohen hearing, 105.

77 She wasn't charged Teri Buhl and Richard Wilner, "Trump Organization Feels the Heat in Assault Case," *New York Post,* June 15, 2008.

79 The boss reveled in hearing Ibid., 19.

79 Soon, a local legal newspaper Peter Vieth, "Trump Not Paying Legal Bills, Lawyers Say," *Virginia Lawyers Weekly,* December 2, 2011, https://valawyersweekly.com/2011/12/02/trump-not-paying-legal-bills-lawyers-say/.

80 While shopping for clothes *U.S. v. Cohen,* No. 18-cr-602 (S.D.N.Y. December 7, 2018) (letter from Sara Armet, ECF No. 24-3).

80 When Trump University, the mogul's Cohen deposition, part 1, 20.

80 Trump ordered his fixer Ibid., 17.

81 They'd take a Trump building Cohen hearing, 38.

10. WOODS AND EDWARDS

82 Diaz sued the *Enquirer* "Cameron Diaz Sues Enquirer," Associated Press, June 3, 2005, https://www.cbsnews.com/news/cameron-diaz-sues-enquirer/.

82 The parties eventually reached "National Enquirer Settles Diaz Lawsuit," *The Star,* February 16, 2007, https://www.thestar.com/entertainment/2007/02/16/national_enquirer_settles_diaz_lawsuit.html.

83 "Now I happen to know" Jeannette Walls, "Underwood Is an Idol to 'Animals' Too," MSNBC, May 30, 2005, https://www.today.com/popculture/underwood-idol-animals-too-wbna7750944.

83 The famous pianist and songwriter Page Six Team, "We Hear . . . ," *New York Post,* March 23, 2006.

84 **To free up more cash** Stephanie D. Smith, "AMI to Focus on Core Brands," *Mediaweek*, April 10, 2006.

87 **"The story is false"** "Edwards Denies Tabloid Affair Story," *Los Angeles Times*, October 12, 2007, https://www.latimes.com/archives/la-xpm-2007-oct-12-na -briefs12.s5-story.html.

88 **The bailout agreement reduced** Keith J. Kelly, "Pecker Finally Pulls It Out," *New York Post*, February 1, 2009, https://nypost.com/2009/02/01/pecker-finally -pulls-it-out/.

88 **After reading the tabloid's report** Maureen Callahan, "The Night Tiger Woods Was Exposed as a Serial Cheater," *New York Post*, November 24, 2013, https://ny post.com/2013/11/24/the-night-tiger-woods-was-exposed-as-a-serial-cheater/.

89 **The bailout agreement with bondholders** Matthew Flamm, "With Debtors at Bay, Pecker Turns to Writing AMI's Next Chapter," *Crain's New York Business*, March 23, 2009.

90 **If Pecker needed more bucking up** "Pace Honors David Pecker & Gurbaksh Chahal; Maria Bartiromo Hosts; Donald J. Trump Presents," Targeted News Service, April 6, 2010.

90 **American Media was still generating cash** Mara Lemos Stein, "American Media Working to Woo Holder for Debt Exchange," *Daily Bankruptcy Review*, October 28, 2010.

90 **American Media filed for bankruptcy** Keith J. Kelly and Josh Kosman, "AMI Is on the Block—Apollo Eyed Publisher," *New York Post*, June 13, 2011.

11. MOMMY XXX

92 **Her heart sank** Chris Ayres, "Mistress of Their Fortune; Former Porn Star Gina Rodriguez Runs a Talent Agency—for Hollywood Marriage Wreckers," *The Times*, April 14, 2011.

92 **She barely knew her biological father** Michael D. Harris, "Reputed Mexican Mafia Leader Michael Delia, Sentenced Last Month," United Press International, April 14, 1984, https://www.upi.com/Archives/1984/04/14/Reputed-Mexican -Mafia-leader-Michael-Delia-sentenced-last-month/8222450766800/.

92 **But her acting career stalled** Mitchell Sunderland, "Gina Rodriguez: The D-List Diva," *Vice*, November 2, 2013, https://www.vice.com/en_us/article/exmdb4/gina -rodriguez-the-d-list-diva.

93 **Rodriguez had gone to beauty school** Ayres, "Mistress of Their Fortune."

94 **Her April 2010 strip club appearance** Corky Siemaszko, "Tiger's Porn Pal to Turn Pole Master Down in Ga.," New York *Daily News*, March 30, 2010.

95 **Rodriguez saw herself as a maternal figure** Gina Rodriguez, interviewed by Neal Karlinsky, *Nightline*, February 17, 2011.

95 **Another early client, Jessie Lunderby** "Ark. Sheriff: Nude Pics on Web Site Violate Policy," Associated Press, July 11, 2010.

95 **Rodriguez also represented the alleged mistresses** Colin Stewart, "Mistress Makeovers: At This New Talent Agency, a Brush with Notoriety Isn't the End of a Career—It's the Beginning," *Orange County Register*, February 8, 2011.

95   **That summer, she brought** Burt Constable, "Exxxtacy's Girls of Scandal Put the Miss in Mistress," *Chicago Daily Herald,* July 27, 2010.

95   **Then there was Mistresses Makeover Day** Stewart, "Mistress Makeovers."

95   **On Facebook, Rodriguez messaged** Michael Musto, "For the Infamous, More Than 15 Minutes," *New York Times,* March 6, 2014.

96   **Holland claimed Lohan had pushed her** Anthony McCartney, "Deputies Investigating Lindsay Lohan for Battery on Betty Ford Staffer Fired after Interview," Associated Press, December 22, 2010.

97   **He said Holland was withdrawing** Richard Winton, "Worker Now Supportive of Lohan," *Los Angeles Times,* December 28, 2010.

97   **Brockton schools regularly** William Bastone, "Celeb Dirt to Be Sold? You Better Call Keith," *The Smoking Gun,* April 4, 2018, http://www.thesmokinggun .com/documents/investigation/keith-davidson-profile-907453.

97   **At Boston College, he couldn't afford** Ibid.

97   **After his college graduation** "Who's What Where," *Boston Globe,* August 20, 1995.

98   **Though many later struggled** Sonali Kohli, Rosanna Xia, and Teresa Watanabe, "Whittier Law School Is Closing, Due in Part to Low Student Achievement," *Los Angeles Times,* April 20, 2017, https://www.latimes.com/local/education/la-me -edu-whittier-law-school-closing-20170420-story.html.

98   **Davidson helped with legal advice** Winchell Campos, "Manny Inks Deal with New Management," *Manila Bulletin,* February 4, 2005.

98   **Within two years** "Pacquiao to Drop Finkel and Co.," *Manila Times,* August 21, 2006.

99   **The locker had contained Hilton's diaries** Bastone, "Celeb Dirt to Be Sold?"

100   **Davidson signed up musician** Ibid.

100   **Capri Anderson, a twenty-two-year-old** Kerry Wills, Joe Jackson, Larry McShane, and Alison Gendar, "Porn, Again! Adult Film Star (Shocker!) Is Co-Star of Sheen's Wild Nite," *New York Daily News,* October 28, 2010.

100   **But it was Sheen** Nancy Dillon, "Sheen's Capri-Cious Move. Charlie Drops Extortion Lawsuit Against Bx.-Born Porn Star," *New York Daily News,* August 2, 2011.

12. SHOULDTRUMPRUN.COM

102   **Trump said he didn't know** Alexander Mooney, "Trump Says He's Not Behind Mysterious NH Poll," CNN, October 4, 2010, http://politicalticker.blogs.cnn .com/2010/10/04/trump-says-hes-not-behind-mysterious-nh-poll/.

104   **"People change their positions"** Jonathan Chait, "Is Donald Trump Putting Us On?," *New Republic,* February 15, 2011, https://newrepublic.com/article/83550 /donald-trump-putting-us.

104   **"Every one of them expressed"** Ilya Marritz and Andrea Bernstein, "The Company Michael Cohen Kept," *Trump, Inc.* podcast, April 18, 2018, https://www .wnycstudios.org/podcasts/trumpinc/episodes/trump-inc-podcast-company -michael-cohen-kept.

104 **Trump bragged that Cohen** "Billionaire Trump Denies Using Talk of Run for US President as Way to Create Buzz for TV Show," Associated Press, March 9, 2011.

104 **Days later, an aide to libertarian** Maggie Haberman, "Paul Aide Files Trump Jet Complaint," *Politico,* March 14, 2011, https://www.politico.com/story/2011/03 /paul-aide-files-trump-jet-complaint-051262.

105 **"Good afternoon, everybody"** Marritz and Bernstein, "The Company Michael Cohen Kept."

106 **It seemed to work** Juana Summers, "Poll: Trump Tied for 2nd in GOP Field," *Politico,* April 6, 2011, https://www.politico.com/story/2011/04/poll-trump-tied -for-2nd-in-gop-field-052697.

107 *Enquirer* **editor Barry Levine dispatched** Lloyd Grove, "National Enquirer Boss Is Building a Tabloid Death Star to Do Trump's Bidding," *Daily Beast,* June 26, 2018, https://www.thedailybeast.com/national-enquirer-boss-is-build ing-a-gossip-empire-to-do-trumps-bidding.

107 **With Trump stoking the birther movement** Michael D. Shear, "With Document, Obama Seeks to End 'Birther' Issue," *New York Times,* April 27, 2011, https://www.nytimes.com/2011/04/28/us/politics/28obama.html.

108 **"Now, I know that he's taken"** C-SPAN, "President Obama at the 2011 White House Correspondents' Dinner," YouTube, 18:53, posted April 30, 2011, https:// www.youtube.com/watch?v=n9mzJhvC-8E.

108 **Trump sat stone-faced** Roxanne Roberts, "I Sat Next to Donald Trump at the Infamous 2011 White House Correspondents' Dinner," *Washington Post,* April 28, 2016, https://www.washingtonpost.com/lifestyle/style/i-sat-next-to -donald-trump-at-the-infamous-2011-white-house-correspondents-dinner /2016/04/27/5cf46b74-0bea-11e6-8ab8-9ad050f76d7d_story.html.

108 **"Donald Trump has been saying"** C-SPAN, "Seth Meyers Remarks at the 2011 White House Correspondents' Dinner," YouTube, 20:48, posted April 30, 2011, https://www.youtube.com/watch?v=7YGITlxfT6s.

13. STEPHANIE FROM WICKED PICTURES

110 **The girl with the purple Camaro** Stormy Daniels, *Full Disclosure* (New York: St. Martin's Press, 2018), 49–54.

110 **Stephanie's childhood hadn't been easy** Ibid., 9–12, 15.

110 **Stephanie's mother** Ibid., 16–18, 29.

110 **At a friend's house, she overheard** Ibid., 28–30.

111 **She bought a horse** Ibid., 36.

111 **And she focused on school** Ibid., 40.

111 **She also discarded her first name** Ibid., 46.

111 **When she could no longer stand** Ibid., 49.

111 **Eventually she moved to the Gold Club** Ibid., 66, 70–73.

112 **When she was twenty-three** Ibid., 81, 85, 86, 89.

112 **So began a career** IMDb, s.v. "Stormy Daniels," https://www.imdb.com/name /nm1317917/.

112 **"I actually managed to find"** Clay Calvert and Robert D. Richards, "Porn in Their Words: Female Leaders in the Adult Entertainment Industry Address Free Speech, Censorship, Feminism, Culture and the Mainstreaming of Adult Content," *Vanderbilt Journal of Entertainment and Technology Law* 9, no. 2 (2006): 263, http://www.jetlaw.org/wp-content/journal-pdfs/Calvert.pdf.

112 **After their night together** Daniels, *Full Disclosure*, 138.

113 **In January 2007** Ibid., 139.

113 **As they cuddled, Trump sat entranced** Stormy Daniels, interviewed by Jordi Lippe-McGraw, "Stormy Daniels' Full Interview: Inside Her Affair with Donald Trump," *In Touch Weekly*, May 4, 2018, https://www.intouchweekly.com/posts /stormy-daniels-full-interview-151788/.

113 **Trump called a few more times** Daniels, *Full Disclosure*, 146–47.

114 **Daniels joked to reporters** Jonathan Tilove, "Adult Film Actress Contemplates Run to Unseat Vitter; She Asks Flynt to Be Campaign Manager," New Orleans *Times-Picayune*, February 13, 2009.

114 **The campaign slogan, she said** Stormy Daniels, interviewed by Max Blumenthal, *Daily Beast*, February 8, 2009, https://www.thedailybeast.com/blumenthal -interviews-stormy.

114 **First, an Audi convertible** Cain Burdeau, "Porn Actress Considering La. Senate Race Has a Tough Week with Fla. Arrest, Car Explosion," Associated Press, July 29, 2009.

114 **Two days later** Daniels, *Full Disclosure*, 168–69.

115 **Soon, Crain told her that he** Ibid., 176.

115 **Daniels gave birth** *Matter of the Marriage of Crain and Clifford*, No. 100289-86 (86th Tex. Dist. Ct. July 18, 2018) (Petition for Divorce and Temporary Restraining Order).

116 **"He's one of the great hucksters"** Joel Siegel, "Is Donald Trump Running for President or Marketing His Brand?" ABC News, March 10, 2011, https://abc news.go.com/Politics/donald-trump-campaign-president-marketing-ploy /story?id=13097770.

116 **The network planned to announce** Jim Rutenberg, "Trump Bows Out, but Spotlight Barely Dims," *New York Times*, May 17, 2011.

116 **His poll numbers were now** Maggie Haberman, "Trump's Poll Numbers Collapse," *Politico*, May 10, 2011, https://www.politico.com/story/2011/05/trumps -poll-numbers-collapse-054661.

117 **Trump would later pardon Arpaio** Julie Hirschfeld Davis and Maggie Haberman, "Trump Pardons Joe Arpaio, Who Became Face of Crackdown on Illegal Immigration," *New York Times*, August 25, 2017, https://www.nytimes.com /2017/08/25/us/politics/joe-arpaio-trump-pardon-sheriff-arizona.html.

117 **Trump kept his remarks brief** Mark Leibovich, "Over-the-Top Setting, Run-of-the Mill Endorsement," *New York Times*, February 2, 2012, https://www.ny times.com/2012/02/03/us/politics/trump-endorses-romney-in-las-vegas.html.

121 **Daniels said she had viewed** Daniels interview by Lippe-McGraw.

123 **An editor at TMZ** William Bastone, "Celeb Dirt to Be Sold? You Better Call Keith," *The Smoking Gun*, April 4, 2018, http://www.thesmokinggun.com/docu ments/investigation/keith-davidson-profile-907453.

124 **TMZ sprung into action** Ibid.

124 **Quickly, Davidson broached** Ibid.

124 **After the faux negotiations** Ibid.

14. THE CANDIDATE

126 **He arranged for Stewart Rahr** Brendan J. O'Reilly, "East Hampton Artist's Trump Portrait Caught the Donald's Attention," *Dan's Papers,* November 3, 2015, https://www.danspapers.com/2015/11/east-hampton-artists-trump-portrait -caught-the-donalds-attention/.

126 **Rahr pumped up the price** Cohen hearing, 13.

127 **Then Cohen called in** Michael Cohen, interviewed by Harvey Levin, *TMZ Live,* June 6, 2012, https://www.tmz.com/2012/06/06/miss-usa-pennsylvania -sheena-monnin-ultimatum-lawsuit-defamation/.

127 **Sheena Monnin, who had sought** Brandy Zadrozny and Tim Mak, "Trump Lawyer Bragged: I 'Destroyed' a Beauty Queen's Life," *Daily Beast,* July 31, 2015, https://www.thedailybeast.com/trump-lawyer-bragged-i-destroyed-a-beauty -queens-life.

127 **His experience in politics** Michael Falcone, "Donald Trump's Political 'Pit Bull': Meet Michael Cohen," ABC News, April 16, 2011, https://abcnews.go.com/Poli tics/donald-trumps-political-pit-bull-meet-michael-cohen/story?id=13386747.

129 **Around the same time, Turney** Page Six Team, "Husband Called 'Secret' CEO a 'Sweetheart,'" *New York Post,* September 18, 2013, https://pagesix.com/2013/09 /18/hubby-called-victorias-secret-ceo-a-sweetheart-as-she-was-having-affair/.

129 **"How good do you think"** Cohen deposition, part 1, 18.

132 **Nunberg had been hired** Dylan Byers, "Donald Trump Is 'Totally Unfazed,'" *Politico,* February 17, 2014, https://www.politico.com/blogs/media/2014/02 /donald-trump-is-totally-unfazed-183452.

132 **Lewandowski, a forty-one-year-old** Karen Tumulty, "Who Is Corey Lewan-dowski? His Rise—and His Relationship with Donald Trump," *Washington Post,* March 30, 2016, https://www.washingtonpost.com/politics/trump-and -lewandowski-an-unlikely-pair-of-kindred-spirits/2016/03/30/d82a58ca-f511 -11e5-8b23-538270a1ca31_story.html.

132 **After Ney was convicted** Will Rahn, "Donald Trump's Campaign Chief Backed a Crooked Congressman, Called Him 'My Surrogate Father,'" *Daily Beast,* August 3, 2015, https://www.thedailybeast.com/donald-trumps-campaign-chief -backed-a-crooked-congressman-called-him-my-surrogate-father.

133 **After *Forbes* assigned Trump** Matt Viser, "Appeals to Mainstream Come from Positions of Wealth; 2016 Candidates Face Challenge of Connecting with 'Everyday Americans,'" *Boston Globe,* April 24, 2015.

135 **Trump, who had been calling Lewandowski** Corey Lewandowski and David Bossie, *Let Trump Be Trump* (New York: Center Street, 2017), 89–91.

136 **"Wow. Whoa. That is some group"** C-SPAN, "Donald Trump Presidential Campaign Announcement Full Speech," YouTube, 47:08, posted June 16, 2015, https://www.youtube.com/watch?v=apjNfkysjbM.

138 **Cohen waded into perilous territory** Tim Mak, "How Michael Cohen Protects Trump by Making Legal Threats," *All Things Considered,* NPR, May 31, 2018, https://www.npr.org/2018/05/31/615843930/listen-how-michael-cohen-protects -trump-by-making-legal-threats.

138 **Lewandowski and other campaign aides** Jeremy Diamond, "Trump Adviser Michael Cohen: 'You Cannot Rape Your Spouse,'" CNN, July 28, 2015.

139 **He was fired for good** Jeremy Diamond, "Trump Campaign Fires Staffer Over Facebook Posts," CNN Wire, August 2, 2015.

139 **Less than a week later, Trump** Dana Bash and MJ Lee, "Trump Campaign Claims It Fired Top Adviser—Who Says He Quit," CNN, August 8, 2015, https:// www.cnn.com/2015/08/08/politics/donald-trump-campaign-roger-stone/index .html.

139 **News also broke that Trump's** Andrew Kaczynski, Christopher Massie, and Ilan Ben-Meir, "Trump Cuts Ties to Operative over Facebook Racism," *BuzzFeed,* August 5, 2015, https://www.buzzfeednews.com/article/andrewkaczynski/trump -cuts-ties-to-operative-over-facebook-racism.

15. THE DOORMAN

141 **Trump, asked by Pecker to intervene** Omarosa Manigault Newman, *Unhinged: An Insider's Account of the Trump White House* (New York: Gallery Books, 2018), loc. 875–97, Kindle.

143 **The pictures were snapped at an Atlanta club** Martha Woodham, "In Quest for Media Attention, Trump Is the Drawing Card," *Atlanta Journal-Constitution,* January 30, 1991.

147 **Sajudin had hoped to squeeze cash** Amanda Becker, "New York Private Equity Manager, Firm Charged with $9 Million Theft," Reuters, January 30, 2014, https://www.reuters.com/article/usa-sec-theft/new-york-private-equity-man ager-firm-charged-with-9-million-theft-idUSL2N0L502L20140131.

147 **Penn later pleaded guilty** Rebecca Rosenberg and Kathleen Culliton, "Private Equity Firm Founder Gets up to 6 Years for Stealing $9.3M," *New York Post,* April 20, 2015, https://nypost.com/2015/04/20/private-equity-firm-founder-gets -up-to-6-years-for-stealing-9-3m/.

149 **Cohen would later say** Cohen hearing, 128.

16. PUTIN'S CHAIR, OR GOF.RU

151 **By early November, Trump had signed** U.S. Department of Justice, *Report on the Investigation into Russian Interference in the 2016 Presidential Election, Volume 1,* by Robert S. Mueller III (Washington, D.C., 2019), 5, 70. (Hereinafter, "Mueller Report, vol. 1.")

151 **He also consulted with Ivanka Trump** Deposition of Michael Cohen, Part 2, Before the House Select Comm. on Intelligence, 116th Cong., 1st sess. (2019), 36, 207. (Hereinafter, "Cohen deposition, part 2.")

151 **Sater, meanwhile, looked for land** Ibid., 151–152, majority exhibit 16.

152 **Cohen texted Sater a copy of his** Mueller Report, vol. 1, 76.

152 **"Not you or anyone you know"** Azeen Ghorayshi, Jason Leopold, Anthony Cormier, and Emma Loop, "These Secret Files Show How the Trump Moscow Talks Unfolded While Trump Heaped Praise on Putin," *BuzzFeed*, February 5, 2019, https://www.buzzfeednews.com/article/azeenghorayshi/trump-tower -moscow-the-secret-files-cohen-sater-putin.

152 **Cohen took matters into his own hands** Mueller Report, vol. 1, 74.

153 **He'd been told again, firmly** Tom Llamas, "Donald Trump Takes Heat for His First Political Ad," ABC News video, 1:48, posted January 5, 2016, https://abc news.go.com/WNT/video/donald-trump-takes-heat-political-ad-36089281.

153 **Though he walked back the comments** Kyle Cheney, "Pro-Bush Super PAC Broadens Complaint Against Trump," *Politico*, January 13, 2016, https://www .politico.com/story/2016/01/jeb-bush-donald-trump-super-pac-217730.

153 **But Cohen's efforts led to a public dispute** MJ Lee, "Trump to CNN: 'I Never Agreed' to Hispanic Chamber Meeting," CNN, October 2, 2015.

155 **Trump was closing in** Mueller Report, vol. 1, 76–77.

156 **Lewandowski had drawn negative news** Byron Tau, "Florida Prosecutors Won't Charge Trump Campaign Manager with Battery," *Wall Street Journal*, April 14, 2016, https://www.wsj.com/articles/florida-prosecutors-decline-to-charge-trump -campaign-manager-with-battery-1460658488.

157 **"I liked Corey very much"** Patrick O'Connor, Monica Langley, and Janet Hook, "Donald Trump Severs Ties with Campaign Manager Corey Lewandowski," *Wall Street Journal*, June 20, 2016, https://www.wsj.com/articles/trump-severs -ties-with-campaign-manager-corey-lewandowski-1466432338.

157 **Cohen was in the conference room** Corey Lewandowski and David Bossie, *Let Trump Be Trump* (New York: Center Street, 2017), 156–57.

17. RESOLUTION CONSULTANTS LLC

159 **Rafael had been eating lunch** Bud Kennedy, "'Oh, Yes—I Shot J.R.!' Ted Cruz's Dad Tells the Real Story of Seeing JFK in Dallas," *Fort Worth Star-Telegram*, November 24, 2018, https://www.star-telegram.com/opinion/bud-kennedy/article 222137450.html#storylink=cpy.

160 **Since the launch of his campaign** Chris Deaton, "Study: Trump Has Earned $2 Billion of Free Media Coverage," *Washington Examiner*, October 2, 2019, https:// www.washingtonexaminer.com/weekly-standard/study-trump-has-earned-2 -billion-of-free-media-coverage.

162 **"Ted Cruz, I don't know"** CNN, "Donald Trump's Indiana Victory Speech," YouTube, 19:30, posted May 3, 2016, https://www.youtube.com/watch?v=YeEzYS WwiSU.

163 **Crawford encouraged her to sell** Ronan Farrow, "Donald Trump, the Playboy Model Karen McDougal, and a System for Concealing Infidelity," *New Yorker*, February 16, 2018, https://www.newyorker.com/news/news-desk/donald-trump

-a-playboy-model-and-a-system-for-concealing-infidelity-national-enquirer
-karen-mcdougal.

167 **"I am not in the habit"** Theodore Schleifer and Stephen Collinson, "Defiant Ted Cruz Stands by Refusal to Endorse Trump after Being Booed During Convention Speech," CNN, July 22, 2016, https://www.cnn.com/2016/07/20/politics /ted-cruz-republican-convention-moment/index.html.

167 **"All I did is point out"** Chris Cillizza, "Donald Trump Just Gave Another Absolutely Epic Press Conference," *Washington Post,* July 22, 2016, https://www .washingtonpost.com/news/the-fix/wp/2016/07/22/donald-trump-just-gave -another-press-conference-for-the-ages/.

18. DD AND PP

175 **Hicks had heard from another campaign** *Interview of Hope Hicks Before the House Comm. on the Judiciary,* 116th Cong., 1st sess. (2019), 196–97, https:// judiciary.house.gov/sites/democrats.judiciary.house.gov/files/documents /HJU170550%20Hicks%20interview.pdf.

175 **She also impressed on him** Cohen hearing, 33.

180 **Daniels had been communicating** Jacob Weisberg, "Stormy's Story: Did Donald Trump Pay Porn Star Stormy Daniels to Keep Quiet About an Affair?," *Slate,* January 16, 2018, https://slate.com/news-and-politics/2018/01/did-donald-trump -pay-porn-star-stormy-daniels-to-keep-quiet-about-an-affair.html.

181 **"A porn star says a 2011 report"** Ken LaCorte, "First Person: Here's the Stormy Daniels Story I Wouldn't Publish," *LaCorte News,* March 16, 2019, https:// www.lacortenews.com/p/ken-lacorte-stormy-daniels-story-on-donald-trump -23421ad7-3ac7-4824-a79a-a7c964880d29.

181 **At the same time, Daniels** Marlo Stern and Aurora Snow, "Porn Star: Trump and Stormy Daniels Invited Me to Hotel Room," *Daily Beast,* January 12, 2018, https://www.thedailybeast.com/porn-star-donald-trump-and-stormy-daniels -invited-me-to-their-hotel-room.

182 **She grew exasperated when Jessica Drake** Tamara Audi, "Adult Film Star Accuses Trump of Unwanted Advances, *Wall Street Journal,* October 22, 2016, https://www.wsj.com/articles/adult-film-actor-accuses-donald-trump-of -unwanted-sexual-advances-1477186768.

183 **Cohen had a $500,000 home equity** Cohen hearing, 135.

184 **Daniels lied to her husband** Stormy Daniels, *Full Disclosure* (New York: St. Martin's Press, 2018), 214.

PART II: THE UNRAVELING

19. THE SOURCES

194 **Cohen and Hicks cobbled together** *Interview of Hope Hicks Before the House Comm. on the Judiciary,* 116th Cong., 1st sess. (2019), 264–65.

197 **"I pledge to every citizen"** "Transcript: Donald Trump's Victory Speech," *New York Times,* November 9, 2016, https://www.nytimes.com/2016/11/10/us/politics /trump-speech-transcript.html.

20. THE PRESIDENT'S LAWYER

199 **Reporters chronicled the matters** Jonathan Mahler and Matt Flegenheimer, "What Donald Trump Learned from Joseph McCarthy's Right-Hand Man," *New York Times,* June 20, 2016, https://www.nytimes.com/2016/06/21/us/politics /donald-trump-roy-cohn.html.

201 **Two days after that** Stephanie Baker and Helena Bedwell, "Georgian Businessman Offers More Texts with Cohen to Rebut Mueller Footnote," *Bloomberg,* April 24, 2019, https://www.bloomberg.com/news/articles/2019-04-24 /rtskhiladze-cohen-trump-russia-tapes.

204 **Corey Lewandowski and adviser Barry Bennett** Tal Kopan, "Trump White House Could Be Lobbying Bonanza," CNN, December 23, 2016, https://www .cnn.com/2016/12/23/politics/trump-administration-lobbying/index.html.

204 **Over a meal at a restaurant** Karen DeYoung, Josh Dawsey, and Rosalind S. Helderman, "Trump's Attorney Reportedly Solicited \$1 Million from Qatar's Government," *Washington Post,* May 15, 2018, https://www.washingtonpost .com/world/national-security/trumps-personal-attorney-solicited-1-million -from-government-of-qatar/2018/05/16/e787e716-592c-11e8-858f-12becb4d6067 _story.html.

205 **Intrater and Cohen had met less** Ben Protess, William K. Rashbaum, and Mike McIntire, "Cohen's Million-Dollar Investment Tips: Ice Pops and Taxi Medallion Loans," *New York Times,* May 22, 2018, https://www.nytimes.com/2018/05/22/us /politics/michael-cohen-andrew-intrater.html.

206 **AT&T awarded a \$600,000-a-year** Rosalind S. Helderman, Brian Fung, and Tom Hamburger, "Internal Documents Show Scope of Michael Cohen's Contract with AT&T," *Washington Post,* May 10, 2018, https://apps.washington post.com/g/documents/politics/internal-documents-show-scope-of-michael -cohens-contract-with-att/2963/.

208 **In early May, Korea Aerospace** Amanda Macias, "South Korean Defense Company That Paid Michael Cohen Is Poised to Win Part of a \$16 Billion Pentagon Deal," *CNBC,* June 27, 2018, https://www.cnbc.com/2018/06/27/south-korean -defense-company-that-paid-trump-lawyer-cohen-is-poised-to.html.

208 **"I'm crushing it"** Michael Kranish, Rosalind S. Helderman, Carolyn Y. Johnson, and Josh Dawsey, "Mueller Questioned Payment to Trump Lawyer Michael Cohen," *Washington Post,* May 10, 2018, https://www.washingtonpost.com /politics/mueller-questioned-payment-to-trump-lawyer-michael-cohen/2018 /05/09/6ad3a7d6-538d-11e8-a551-5b648abe29ef_story.html.

209 **Cohen explored a real estate consulting gig** Byron Tau, "Trump Donor Faces a Second Federal Probe," *Wall Street Journal,* April 17, 2019, https://www.wsj.com /articles/trump-donor-faces-a-second-federal-probe-11555523022.

21. THOUGHT STARTERS

211 **With the news of his catch-and-kill** Julia Waldow and Brian Stelter, "How the Trump-Friendly National Enquirer Has Been Promoting His Presidency," CNN, April 12, 2019, https://money.cnn.com/2018/04/12/media/national-enquirer -president-trump-coverage/index.html.

213 **With the purchase of *Us Weekly*** Jeffrey A. Trachtenberg and Lukas I. Alpert, "Us Weekly to Be Bought by Publisher of National Enquirer for $100 Million," *Wall Street Journal,* March 15, 2017, https://www.wsj.com/articles/us-weekly-to -be-bought-by-publisher-of-national-enquirer-for-100-million-1489607196.

213 **In July, Pecker and Grine together** Jim Rutenberg, Kate Kelly, Jessica Silver-Greenberg, and Mike McIntire, "Wooing Saudi Business, Tabloid Mogul Had a Powerful Friend: Trump," *New York Times,* March 29, 2018, https://www.ny times.com/2018/03/29/business/media/david-pecker-trump-saudi-arabia.html.

213 **They also dined with Trump** Julie Bykowicz and Lukas I. Alpert, "National Enquirer Publisher Asked Justice Department for Advice on Saudi Connection," *Wall Street Journal,* February 11, 2019, https://www.wsj.com/articles /national-enquirer-publisher-asked-justice-department-for-advice-on-saudi -connection-11549908996.

214 **He called Jared Kushner** Asawin Suebsaeng, Maxwell Tani, and Lloyd Grove, "Jared Kushner Replaced Michael Cohen as Trump's National Enquirer Connection," *Daily Beast,* December 14, 2018, https://www.thedailybeast.com/how -jared-kushner-replaced-michael-cohen-as-trumps-national-enquirer-connec tion.

215 **At the same time, editors** Sally Holmes, "Here Is an Up-Close Look at Sofia Vergara's Humongous Engagement Ring," *Elle,* January 26, 2015, https://www .elle.com/culture/celebrities/news/a26388/sofia-vergara-engagement-ring/.

216 **Vergara and Manganiello took to social media** Tim Kenneally, "Sofia Vergara Shreds 'Idiot' Star Magazine Editor over Cheating Report," *TheWrap,* May 4, 2017, https://www.thewrap.com/sofia-vergara-shreds-idiot-star-magazine-editor -cheating-report/.

217 **Weinstein had collaborated** Denise Petski, "Weinstein Co Partners with American Media & Jupiter to Launch New TV Production Unit," *Deadline,* December 21, 2015, https://deadline.com/2015/12/weinstein-company-american -media-jupiter-tv-production-unit-1201670463/.

218 **Earlier in 2017, the model** Gabrielle Olya, "Former Playboy Models Get Their Breast Implants Removed Believing They Caused Illness," *People,* February 23, 2017, https://people.com/bodies/former-playboy-models-breast-implants -removed-illness/.

22. BOSS, I MISS YOU SO MUCH

219 **Comey had deflected Trump's demands** U.S. Department of Justice, *Report on the Investigation into Russian Interference in the 2016 Presidential Election,*

Volume 2, by Robert S. Mueller III (Washington, D.C., 2019), 34. (Hereinafter, "Mueller Report, vol. 2.")

220 **"Where's my Roy Cohn?"** Michael S. Schmidt, "Obstruction Inquiry Shows Trump's Struggle to Keep Grip on Russia Investigation," *New York Times,* January 4, 2018, https://www.nytimes.com/2018/01/04/us/politics/trump-sessions -russia-mcgahn.html.

220 **Cohen vehemently denied** Anthony Cormier, "This Is the Inside of Trump's Lawyer's Passport," *BuzzFeed,* May 5, 2017, https://www.buzzfeednews.com /article/anthonycormier/trumps-lawyer-showed-you-the-cover-of-his-pass port-heres.

220 **He told another he'd thrown it** Rosalind S. Helderman, Tom Hamburger, and Josh Dawsey, "Special Counsel Has Examined Episodes Involving Michael Cohen, Trump's Longtime Lawyer," *Washington Post,* March 6, 2018, https:// www.washingtonpost.com/politics/special-counsel-has-examined-episodes -involving-michael-cohen-trumps-longtime-lawyer/2018/03/06/4a2bd064 -1b37-11e8-b2d9-08e748f892c0_story.html.

222 **This messaging was consistent** Mueller Report, vol. 2, 19.

223 **Cohen declined the invitation** Cohen deposition, part 1, 178–79.

223 **The Trump Organization employees working** Ibid., 153.

223 **"The president loves you"** Cohen deposition, part 2, 104.

223 *Stay on message* Mueller Report, vol. 2, 153.

224 **As he did so, reporters printed** Emily Jane Fox, "Michael Cohen Would Take a Bullet for Donald Trump," *Vanity Fair,* September 6, 2017, https://www.vanity fair.com/news/2017/09/michael-cohen-interview-donald-trump.

224 **Afterward, Sekulow told him** Mueller Report, vol. 2,144.

226 **Andrew Intrater, from Columbus Nova** Ben Protess, William K. Rashbaum, and Mike McIntire, "In Michael Cohen's Rolodex, an Investor Tied to Russia Saw Pay Dirt," *New York Times,* May 22, 2018, https://www.nytimes.com/2018/05/22 /us/politics/michael-cohen-andrew-intrater.html.

226 **Cohen also put in a call to** Cohen deposition, part 2, 218–19.

226 **The main purpose** Protess, Rashbaum, and McIntire, "In Michael Cohen's Rolodex, an Investor Tied to Russia Saw Pay Dirt."

24. THE PLAINTIFF'S LAWYER

242 **Cohen was in close contact** Mueller Report, vol. 2, 145.

244 **Center Street, an imprint** Cohen hearing, 134.

246 **Cohen had carefully worded** Ibid., 120.

247 **"Michael, did you really pay"** Cohen deposition, part 1, 196.

251 **Trump was pleased with Cohen's public** Mueller Report, vol. 2, 145.

253 **Don McGahn, the White House counsel** Josh Dawsey and Ashley Parker, "'Everyone Signed One': Trump Is Aggressive in His Use of Nondisclosure Agreements, Even in Government," *Washington Post,* August 13, 2018, https://www .washingtonpost.com/politics/everyone-signed-one-trump-is-aggressive-in

-his-use-of-nondisclosure-agreements-even-in-government/2018/08/13/9d0315
ba-9f15-11e8-93e3-24d1703d2a7a_story.html.

25. THE LAWSUITS

258 **His first big settlement** David Reilly, "KPMG Settles Targus Audit Case,"
Wall Street Journal, March 29, 2006, https://www.wsj.com/articles/SB11435986
2516210767.

258 **Avenatti also turned up in** Page Six Team, "Paris Settlement a Real Gem," *New
York Post,* August 23, 2007, https://pagesix.com/2007/08/23/paris-settlement-a
-real-gem/.

258 **In another malpractice case against KPMG** Charles Toutant, "KPMG As-
sessed $41 Million for Failing to Divulge Fraud Revealed in Audit," *New Jersey
Law Journal,* October 20, 2008.

259 **He secured an $81 million** Artemis Moshtaghian, "California Cemetery Agrees
to $80 Million Settlement over Desecrating Remains," CNN, February 27, 2014,
https://www.cnn.com/2014/02/27/us/california-cemetery-settlement/index
.html.

259 **Dempsey soon sued Avenatti** Melissa Allison, "Dempsey Walks Away from
Tully's After Suing Partner," *Seattle Times,* August 23, 2013, https://www.seattle
times.com/business/dempsey-walks-away-from-tullyrsquos-after-suing
-partner/.

259 **Their Ferrari 458 Italia finished** John Dagys, "Avenatti: 'Le Mans Lived up to the
Expectation Level and Then Some,'" *Sportscar 365,* June 16, 2015, https://sports
car365.com/lemans/lemans24/avenatti-le-mans-lived-up-to-the-expectation
-level-and-then-some/.

259 **About a year before he met** "Hospital Gowns Didn't Protect as Promised, Jury
Says in $454-million Fraud Verdict," Associated Press, April 10, 2017, https://
www.latimes.com/business/la-fi-hospital-gowns-20170410-story.html.

260 **As the company collapsed, Avenatti** Kate Taylor, "Former Employees Reveal What It Was Like to Work at the Mysterious Coffee Chain Once Owned
by Stormy Daniels' Lawyer—Including Running out of Coffee and Questions
About Getting Paid," *Business Insider,* June 4, 2018, https://www.businessinsider
.com/michael-avenatti-ex-coffee-shop-employees-speak-out-2018-5/.

264 **Trump settled the cases** Sara Randazzo, "Judge Approves $25 Million Trump
University Fraud Settlement," *Wall Street Journal,* March 31, 2017, https://
www.wsj.com/articles/judge-approves-25-million-trump-university-fraud
-settlement-1490981837.

272 **Haney was a seventy-seven-year-old developer** Jeanne Cummings, "Franklin
Haney Became Rich by Building Government Offices," *Wall Street Journal,* January 2, 1998, https://www.wsj.com/articles/SB883693627768384000.

272 **Haney had agreed to pay Cohen** Michael Rothfeld, Rebecca Ballhaus, and
Joe Palazzolo, "Top Trump Donor Agreed to Pay Michael Cohen $10 Million
for Nuclear Project Push," *Wall Street Journal,* August 2, 2018, https://www.wsj

.com/articles/top-trump-donor-agreed-to-pay-michael-cohen-10-million-for
-nuclear-project-push-sources-say-1533245330. In a statement to *The Wall Street
Journal,* an attorney for Franklin Haney said that neither Mr. Haney nor the
company he was using for the Bellefonte nuclear project "ever entered into a
contract with Michael Cohen or his affiliate for lobbying services" related to the
project. He declined further comment about the project or Mr. Cohen.

26. THE FEDS

276 *You were supposed to protect me* Mueller Report, vol. 2, 78.
277 "I just heard that they broke" Michael D. Shear, "Trump Reacts to Cohen
Raid, Syria and More: An Annotated Transcript," *New York Times,* April 9, 2018,
https://www.nytimes.com/2018/04/09/us/politics/trump-cohen-mueller-full
-transcript.html.
278 The unit had investigated William K. Rashbaum, "No Charges, but Harsh
Criticism for de Blasio's Fund-Raising," *New York Times,* March 16, 2017, https://
www.nytimes.com/2017/03/16/nyregion/mayor-bill-de-blasio-investigation-no
-criminal-charges.html.
286 "It's terrible, for you" Cohen deposition, part 2, 238.
286 Cohen was encouraged Mueller Report, vol. 2, 146.
287 Daniels showed up to the hearing Kevin Sheehan and Lia Eustachewich,
"Stormy Daniels Makes Flashy Entrance at Court," *New York Post,* April 16,
2018, https://nypost.com/2018/04/16/stormy-daniels-makes-flashy-entrance-at
-court/.
292 Trump had arranged to meet Jonathan Mahler, "All the President's Lawyers,"
New York Times Magazine, July 5, 2017, https://www.nytimes.com/2017/07/05
/magazine/all-the-presidents-lawyers.html.

27. A TINY LITTLE FRACTION

304 Earlier, he had added a second Nicole Hong, "Stormy Daniels Sues Trump for
Defamation," *Wall Street Journal,* April 30, 2018, https://www.wsj.com/articles
/stormy-daniels-sues-trump-for-defamation-1525121996.
309 "He's literally fucking there" Brian Hiatt, "Who's Afraid of Tom Arnold?," *Rolling Stone,* August 12, 2018, https://www.rollingstone.com/tv/tv-features/tom
-arnold-trump-tapes-michael-cohen-709843/amp/.
310 By now, Cohen had concluded Cohen deposition, part 2, 117.

28. SO SAD!

312 In reality, though Davis didn't disclose it Cohen hearing, 15.
314 The Southern District also delved Nicole Hong, Rebecca Ballhaus, and Rebecca Davis O'Brien, "Hush-Money Probe Gathered Evidence from Trump's

Inner Circle," *Wall Street Journal,* April 10, 2019, https://www.wsj.com/articles /hush-money-probe-gathered-evidence-from-trumps-inner-circle-11554897911.

318 **Prosecutors found he'd failed** Mark Maremont and Rob Barry, "Michael Cohen Guilty Plea Reveals Link to Qatari Royal Family," *Wall Street Journal,* August 24, 2018, https://www.wsj.com/articles/michael-cohen-guilty-plea-reveals-link-to -qatari-royal-family-1535127732.

321 **Cohen was subpoenaed** Zolan Kanno-Youngs, "N.Y. State Tax Office Subpoenas Michael Cohen over Trump Foundation," *Wall Street Journal,* August 22, 2018, https://www.wsj.com/articles/n-y-state-tax-office-subpoenas-michael-cohen -over-trump-foundation-1534969323.

321 **He drew raves at the Democratic** Erin Murphy, "Avenatti a Hit at Democratic Fundraiser Iowa Wing Ding," *The Gazette* (Cedar Rapids, Iowa), August 10, 2018, https://www.thegazette.com/subject/news/government/michael-avenatti -a-hit-at-democratic-fundraiser-2018-iowa-wing-ding-clear-lake-surf-ball-room -20180811.

321 **"When they go low"** Chris Mills Rodrigo, "Michelle Obama Defends 'When They Go Low, We Go High,'" *The Hill,* October 11, 2018, https://thehill.com /blogs/blog-briefing-room/news/410917-michelle-obama-defends-when-they -go-low-we-go-high-motto-fear.

322 **Cohen said that Trump and Weisselberg** Cohen hearing, 30.

29. THE SENTENCE

325 **But prosecutors and agents** Mueller Report, vol. 1, 69.

326 **Pauley, an appointee of President** Elie Honig, "Why Sentencing Judge May Not Show Cohen 'Mercy,'" CNN, December 10, 2018, https://www.cnn .com/2018/12/10/opinions/michael-cohen-sentencing-honig/index.html.

326 **It began with a recitation of Cohen's assistance** Erica Orden, "New York Tax Investigators to Meet with Cohen's Attorney, at Odds with Federal Prosecutors' Request," CNN, September 11, 2018, https://www.cnn.com/2018/09/11/politics /new-york-tax-investigators-michael-cohen/index.html.

328 **Floyd Mayweather Jr., the boxer** Ray Martin, "Owe Back Taxes? Don't Do What Floyd Mayweather Did," CBS News, July 17, 2017, https://www.cbsnews .com/news/owe-back-taxes-dont-do-what-floyd-mayweather-did/.

328 **Country music legend Willie Nelson** Stephen L. Betts, "Flashback: Willie Nelson Settles IRS Tax Debt," *Rolling Stone,* February 2, 2017, https://www .rollingstone.com/music/music-country/flashback-willie-nelson-settles-irs -tax-debt-196254/.

328 **Cohn called the IRS** John J. Goldman, "U.S. Sues Roy Cohn for $7 Million in Back Taxes," *Los Angeles Times,* April 4, 1986, https://www.latimes.com/archives /la-xpm-1986-04-04-mn-24457-story.html.

338 **She'd recently had hip surgery** Mara Siegler, "Michael Cohen's Daughter Spotted at Starry Ball Days after His Sentencing," *New York Post,* December 18, 2018, https://pagesix.com/2018/12/18/michael-cohens-daughter-spotted-at-starry -ball-days-after-his-sentencing/.

338 **Jake Cohen, a college freshman** Brendan Pierson, Nathan Layne, and Karen Freifeld, "Trump Ex-Lawyer Cohen Given Three Years in Prison as Risks Rise for Trump," Reuters, December 12, 2018, https://www.reuters.com/article/us-usa-trump-russia-cohen/trump-ex-lawyer-cohen-given-three-years-in-prison-as-risks-rise-for-trump-idUSKBN1OB16H.

339 **He offered no reaction** William K. Rashbaum and Benjamin Weiser, "Michael Cohen Sentenced to 3 Years after Implicating Trump in Hush-Money Scandal," *New York Times,* December 12, 2018, https://www.nytimes.com/2018/12/12/nyregion/michael-cohen-sentence-trump.html.

30. A CON MAN AND A CHEAT

343 **He sat down with them again** Ben Protess, William K. Rashbaum, and Maggie Haberman, "Cohen Gave Prosecutors New Information on the Trump Family Business," *New York Times,* February 22, 2019, https://www.nytimes.com/2019/02/22/us/politics/michael-cohen-prosecutors-trump-organization.html.

344 **Cohen backed out of testifying** Rebecca Ballhaus, "Michael Cohen Postpones House Testimony, Citing Trump Comments About His Family," *Wall Street Journal,* January 23, 2019, https://www.wsj.com/articles/michael-cohen-postpones-house-testimony-citing-trump-tweets-about-his-family-11548269247.

345 **His lawyers had told Pauley** Corey Kilgannon, "Michael Cohen's Prison of Choice: Well-Known to Jewish Offenders," *New York Times,* January 22, 2019, https://www.nytimes.com/2019/01/22/nyregion/michael-cohen-otisville-prison.html.

345 **His new attorneys had spent** Emily Jane Fox, " 'Earth-Shattering': In Testimony Against Trump, Michael Cohen Preparing to Shock Lawmakers with Disclosures," *Vanity Fair,* February 26, 2019, https://www.vanityfair.com/news/2019/02/michael-cohen-preparing-to-shock-lawmakers-with-disclosures.

348 **Cohen's lawyers tried to schedule** Jim Mustian and Michael R. Sisak, "Prosecutors Refuse Final Meeting with Cohen as Prison Looms," Associated Press, May 4, 2019, https://www.inquirer.com/politics/nation/prosecutors-refuse-final-meeting-with-cohen-prison-looms-20190504.html.

350 **Representative Adam Schiff, a former federal prosecutor** Manu Raju and Jeremy Herb, "House Intelligence Chair Throws Cold Water on Cohen's Bid for Help Delaying Prison Term," CNN, April 8, 2019, https://www.cnn.com/2019/04/08/politics/adam-schiff-michael-cohen/index.html.

EPILOGUE

352 **The Trump administration had built** Spencer Ackerman, "Trump's Publisher Pal Puts Saudi Propaganda Magazine in U.S. Supermarkets," *Daily Beast,* March 26, 2018, https://www.thedailybeast.com/trumps-publisher-pal-puts-saudi-propaganda-magazine-in-us-supermarkets.

354 **One underwriter had already** Lukas I. Alpert, "National Enquirer to Be Sold

for $100 Million to Ex-Newsstand Mogul," *Wall Street Journal*, April 18, 2019, https://www.wsj.com/articles/james-cohen-agrees-to-buy-national-enquirer-for-100-million-11555609554.

356 **In April 2019, the publisher announced** Lukas I. Alpert, "National Enquirer Put Up for Sale," *Wall Street Journal*, April 10, 2019, https://www.wsj.com/articles/national-enquirer-put-up-for-sale-11554940248.

356 **The following week, the company** Alpert, "National Enquirer to Be Sold for $100 Million."

357 **Gene Pope had bought** Paul David Pope, *The Deeds of My Fathers: How My Father and Grandfather Built New York and Created the Tabloid World of Today* (Lanham, Md.: Rowman & Littlefield, 2010), location 102, Kindle.

359 **A few days later, federal agents** Emily Jane Fox, "'I Flew Too Close to the Sun. No Question. Icarus': Inside the Epic Fall of Michael Avenatti," *Vanity Fair*, May 21, 2019, https://www.vanityfair.com/news/2019/05/inside-the-epic-fall-of-michael-avenatti.

361 **On May 28, at a federal** Corinne Ramey, "Avenatti Pleads Not Guilty to Criminal Charges in Manhattan," *Wall Street Journal*, May 28, 2019, https://www.wsj.com/articles/avenatti-pleads-not-guilty-to-criminal-charges-in-manhattan-11559081511.

361 **In May 2019, after dumping Avenatti** Samantha Vicent, "Stormy Daniels Announces Tulsa Attorney Clark Brewster as Her New Lawyer," *Tulsa World*, March 13, 2019, https://www.tulsaworld.com/news/national/stormy-daniels-announces-tulsa-attorney-clark-brewster-as-her-new/article_3f5cac16-b7f5-5dce-afb1-822db4511be5.html.

361 **She discussed her career** Joanna Walters, "Stormy Daniels Talks About Trump and 'the Worst 90 Seconds of My Life' on Standup Tour," *Guardian*, May 8, 2019, https://www.theguardian.com/us-news/2019/may/08/stormy-daniels-talks-about-trump-and-the-worst-90-seconds-of-my-life-on-stand-up-tour.

362 **Barr, who was on record** Sadie Gurman and Aruna Viswanatha, "Trump's Attorney General Pick Criticized an Aspect of Mueller Probe in Memo to Justice Department," *Wall Street Journal*, December 19, 2018, https://www.wsj.com/articles/trumps-attorney-general-pick-criticized-an-aspect-of-mueller-probe-in-memo-to-justice-department-11545275973.

362 **Barr won confirmation in the Senate** Sadie Gurman, "Senate Confirms William Barr as Attorney General," *Wall Street Journal*, February 14, 2019, https://www.wsj.com/articles/william-barr-secures-enough-votes-in-senate-for-confirmation-as-attorney-general-11550167293.

362 **"I will not be bullied"** Sadie Gurman and Byron Tau, "William Barr Defends Mueller Probe, Promises Not to Cave to Pressure from Trump," *Wall Street Journal*, January 15, 2019, https://www.wsj.com/articles/at-william-barr-hearings-mueller-probe-will-be-a-focus-11547548201.

362 **The special counsel's investigation** Aruna Viswanatha, Sadie Gurman, and Byron Tau, "Robert Mueller's Report on Trump-Russia Probe Delivered to Attorney General Barr," *Wall Street Journal*, March 22, 2019, https://www.wsj.com/articles/house-committee-told-to-expect-word-that-mueller-report-has-been-delivered-to-attorney-general-barr-11553288563.

364 **"It was just announced"** Associated Press, "Trump: 'It Was a Complete and Total Exoneration,'" YouTube, 1:36, posted March 24, 2019, https://www.youtube.com/watch?v=4sEphjA4xlE.

364 **Two days later, Mueller** Devlin Barrett and Matt Zapotosky, "Mueller Complained That Barr's Letter Did Not Capture 'Context' of Trump Probe," *Washington Post,* April 30, 2019, https://www.washingtonpost.com/world/national-security/mueller-complained-that-barrs-letter-did-not-capture-context-of-trump-probe/2019/04/30/d3c8fdb6-6b7b-11e9-a66d-a82d3f3d96d5_story.html.

364 **Before releasing the redacted report** "Read Barr's News Conference Remarks Ahead of the Mueller Report Release," *New York Times,* April 18, 2019, https://www.nytimes.com/2019/04/18/us/politics/barr-conference-transcript.html.

365 **"This is the end of my presidency"** Mueller Report, vol. 2, 78.

365 **Trump had asked two** Ibid., 56.

366 **In the spring of 2017** Ibid., 90–93.

366 **Around the same time** Ibid., 86.

367 **"I never had a lawyer who took notes"** Ibid., 117.

367 **House Speaker Nancy Pelosi** Jennifer Haberkorn and Janet Hook, "Mueller Statement Ramps Up Pressure on Pelosi and House Democrats," *Los Angeles Times,* May 29, 2019, https://www.latimes.com/politics/la-na-pol-congress-mueller-pressure-impeachment-20190529-story.html.

367 **Some investigations were continuing** Rebecca Davis O'Brien and Rebecca Ballhaus, "Trump Inaugural Committee Challenged Vendor Requests and Budgeting, Documents Show," *Wall Street Journal,* February 21, 2019, https://www.wsj.com/articles/trump-inaugural-committee-challenged-vendor-requests-and-budgeting-documents-show-11550758712.

367 **The Justice Department had already** Sadie Gurman and Aruna Viswanatha, "Barr Says Review of Origins of Russia Probe Could Lead to Rule Changes," *Wall Street Journal,* May 17, 2019, https://www.wsj.com/articles/barr-review-of-origins-of-fbis-trump-russia-probe-could-lead-to-rule-changes-11558090803.

370 **On the Saturday before** Georgett Roberts and Laura Italiano, "Michael Cohen Gets Swanky New Hairdo Before Heading to the Slammer," *New York Post,* May 4, 2019, https://nypost.com/2019/05/04/michael-cohen-gets-swanky-new-hairdo-before-heading-to-the-slammer/.

370 **On Monday morning** *Time,* "Michael Cohen Heads to Prison in Hush Money Scheme," YouTube, 0:24, posted May 6, 2019, https://www.youtube.com/watch?v=v8mXp7I9wFI.

370 **He pushed through the media** Maggie Haberman, Ben Protess, and William K. Rashbaum, "Michael Cohen, by Turns Lawyer and Witness, Becomes an Inmate," *New York Times,* May 6, 2019, https://www.nytimes.com/2019/05/06/us/michael-cohen-prison.html.

370 **With Rudy Giuliani, Trump set** "General Election: Trump v. Biden," RealClearPolitics, https://www.realclearpolitics.com/epolls/2020/president/us/general_election_trump_vs_biden-6247.html.

370 **In 2000, while Giuliani was** itsgiulianitime, "Rudy Giuliani in Drag Smooching Donald Trump," YouTube, 0:46, posted April 14, 2006, https://www.youtube.com/watch?v=4IrE6FMpai8.

371 **"Man, Rudy, you sucked"** Corey Lewandowski and David Bossie, *Let Trump Be Trump* (New York: Center Street, 2017), 243.

371 **Then, after he was president** Rebecca Ballhaus, Sadie Gurman, Andrew Restuccia, and Michael C. Bender, "Tense Relationship Between Barr and Giuliani Complicates Trump Impeachment Defense," *Wall Street Journal,* October 1, 2019, https://www.wsj.com/articles/tense-relationship-between-barr-and-giuli ani-complicates-trump-impeachment-defense-11569942261.

371 **Even before the special counsel's report** Kenneth P. Vogel, Andrew E. Kramer, and David E. Sanger, "How a Shadow Foreign Policy in Ukraine Prompted an Impeachment Inquiry," *New York Times,* September 28, 2019, https://www.ny times.com/2019/09/28/us/politics/how-a-shadow-foreign-policy-in-ukraine -prompted-impeachment-inquiry.html.

372 **The younger Biden** Alan Cullison, "Bidens in Ukraine: An Explainer," *Wall Street Journal,* September 22, 2019, https://www.wsj.com/articles/bidens-anti corruption-effort-in-ukraine-overlapped-with-sons-work-in-country-115691 89782.

372 **It was true that Joe Biden** Ibid.

372 **Giuliani found an ally** Vogel, Kramer, and Sanger, "How a Shadow Foreign Policy in Ukraine."

372 **The U.S. ambassador to Ukraine** Rebecca Ballhaus, Michael C. Bender, and Vivian Salama, "Trump Ordered Ukraine Ambassador Removed After Complaints from Giuliani, Others," *Wall Street Journal,* October 3, 2019, https:// www.wsj.com/articles/trump-ordered-ukraine-ambassador-removed-after -complaints-from-giuliani-others-11570137147.

372 **In April, comedian-turned-politician** Daniel Uria, "Comedian Volodymyr Zelensky Elected Ukraine's President," United Press International, April 21, 2019, https://www.upi.com/Top_News/World-News/2019/04/21/Comedian-Volodymyr -Zelensky-elected-Ukraines-president/8821555872333/.

373 **The U.S. government's special envoy** Rebecca Ballhaus, Alan Cullison, Georgi Kantchev, and Brett Forrest, "Giuliani Sits at the Center of the Ukraine Controversy," *Wall Street Journal,* September 26, 2019, https://www.wsj.com/articles /giuliani-sits-at-the-center-of-the-ukraine-controversy-11569546774.

373 **White House staff and Pompeo** Courtney McBride and Sadie Gurman, "Pompeo Took Part in Ukraine Call, Official Says," *Wall Street Journal,* September 30, 2019, https://www.wsj.com/articles/pompeo-took-part-in-ukraine-call-official -says-11569865002.

373 **Trump had bought into** Donald Trump, interviewed by Julie Pace, Associated Press, April 23, 2017, https://apnews.com/c810d7de280a47e88848b0ac74690c83.

373 **In fact, Mueller's team** Mueller Report, vol. 1, 40.

374 **He had personally directed** Rebecca Ballhaus, Andrew Restuccia, and Siobhan Hughes, "Trump Put Hold on Military Aid Ahead of Phone Call with Ukraine's President," *Wall Street Journal,* September 24, 2019, https://www.wsj .com/articles/president-trump-repeats-criticism-of-biden-in-impromptu-u-n -appearance-11569254230.

374 **On the same day as** Rebecca Ballhaus, Siobhan Hughes, and Dustin Volz, "Trump Administration Used Potential Meeting to Pressure Ukraine on Biden,

Texts Indicate," *Wall Street Journal,* October 4, 2019, https://www.wsj.com /articles/trump-urges-ukraine-china-to-investigate-the-bidens-11570114755.

375 **Michael Cohen had been behind bars** Kara Scannell, "Exclusive: Michael Cohen Is Interviewed for Probe into Trump Organization," CNN, September 11, 2019, https://www.cnn.com/2019/09/11/politics/michael-cohen-new-york -district-attorney-trump-organization/index.html.

Index

■ ■ ■

Key to abbreviations: AMI = American Media, Inc.; NDA = nondisclosure agreement; WSJ = *The Wall Street Journal*

About the Authors

■ ■ ■

Joe Palazzolo and Michael Rothfeld led a team at *The Wall Street Journal* that won the 2019 Pulitzer Prize for National Reporting for a series of stories that revealed the hush-money payments to Stormy Daniels and Karen McDougal, and President Trump's direct participation in both.

Palazzolo has been a reporter for the *Journal* since 2010. He has covered federal law enforcement, criminal justice issues, corporate corruption, and state and federal courts. He lives in Brooklyn with his wife, Tara Kelly.

Rothfeld is an investigative reporter on the Metro desk of *The New York Times*. He previously reported for the *Journal*, the *Los Angeles Times*, *Newsday*, and *The Philadelphia Inquirer*. Rothfeld also lives in Brooklyn, with his daughters.